Mometrix

TEST PREPARATION

MTTC

Biology (17) Test Secrets Study Guide

Dear Future Exam Success Story

First of all, **THANK YOU** for purchasing Mometrix study materials!

Second, congratulations! You are one of the few determined test-takers who are committed to doing whatever it takes to excel on your exam. **You have come to the right place.** We developed these study materials with one goal in mind: to deliver you the information you need in a format that's concise and easy to use.

In addition to optimizing your guide for the content of the test, we've outlined our recommended steps for breaking down the preparation process into small, attainable goals so you can make sure you stay on track.

We've also analyzed the entire test-taking process, identifying the most common pitfalls and showing how you can overcome them and be ready for any curveball the test throws you.

Standardized testing is one of the biggest obstacles on your road to success, which only increases the importance of doing well in the high-pressure, high-stakes environment of test day. Your results on this test could have a significant impact on your future, and this guide provides the information and practical advice to help you achieve your full potential on test day.

Your success is our success

We would love to hear from you! If you would like to share the story of your exam success or if you have any questions or comments in regard to our products, please contact us at **800-673-8175** or **support@mometrix.com**.

Thanks again for your business and we wish you continued success!

Sincerely,
The Mometrix Test Preparation Team

Need more help? Check out our flashcards at:
http://MometrixFlashcards.com/MTTC

Written and edited by the Mometrix Exam Secrets Test Prep Team
Printed in the United States of America

TABLE OF CONTENTS

Introduction

Thank you for purchasing this resource! You have made the choice to prepare yourself for a test that could have a huge impact on your future, and this guide is designed to help you be fully ready for test day. Obviously, it's important to have a solid understanding of the test material, but you also need to be prepared for the unique environment and stressors of the test, so that you can perform to the best of your abilities.

For this purpose, the first section that appears in this guide is the **Secret Keys**. We've devoted countless hours to meticulously researching what works and what doesn't, and we've boiled down our findings to the five most impactful steps you can take to improve your performance on the test. We start at the beginning with study planning and move through the preparation process, all the way to the testing strategies that will help you get the most out of what you know when you're finally sitting in front of the test.

We recommend that you start preparing for your test as far in advance as possible. However, if you've bought this guide as a last-minute study resource and only have a few days before your test, we recommend that you skip over the first two Secret Keys since they address a long-term study plan.

If you struggle with **test anxiety**, we strongly encourage you to check out our recommendations for how you can overcome it. Test anxiety is a formidable foe, but it can be beaten, and we want to make sure you have the tools you need to defeat it.

Secret Key #1 – Plan Big, Study Small

There's a lot riding on your performance. If you want to ace this test, you're going to need to keep your skills sharp and the material fresh in your mind. You need a plan that lets you review everything you need to know while still fitting in your schedule. We'll break this strategy down into three categories.

Information Organization

Start with the information you already have: the official test outline. From this, you can make a complete list of all the concepts you need to cover before the test. Organize these concepts into groups that can be studied together, and create a list of any related vocabulary you need to learn so you can brush up on any difficult terms. You'll want to keep this vocabulary list handy once you actually start studying since you may need to add to it along the way.

Time Management

Once you have your set of study concepts, decide how to spread them out over the time you have left before the test. Break your study plan into small, clear goals so you have a manageable task for each day and know exactly what you're doing. Then just focus on one small step at a time. When you manage your time this way, you don't need to spend hours at a time studying. Studying a small block of content for a short period each day helps you retain information better and avoid stressing over how much you have left to do. You can relax knowing that you have a plan to cover everything in time. In order for this strategy to be effective though, you have to start studying early and stick to your schedule. Avoid the exhaustion and futility that comes from last-minute cramming!

Study Environment

The environment you study in has a big impact on your learning. Studying in a coffee shop, while probably more enjoyable, is not likely to be as fruitful as studying in a quiet room. It's important to keep distractions to a minimum. You're only planning to study for a short block of time, so make the most of it. Don't pause to check your phone or get up to find a snack. It's also important to **avoid multitasking**. Research has consistently shown that multitasking will make your studying dramatically less effective. Your study area should also be comfortable and well-lit so you don't have the distraction of straining your eyes or sitting on an uncomfortable chair.

The time of day you study is also important. You want to be rested and alert. Don't wait until just before bedtime. Study when you'll be most likely to comprehend and remember. Even better, if you know what time of day your test will be, set that time aside for study. That way your brain will be used to working on that subject at that specific time and you'll have a better chance of recalling information.

Finally, it can be helpful to team up with others who are studying for the same test. Your actual studying should be done in as isolated an environment as possible, but the work of organizing the information and setting up the study plan can be divided up. In between study sessions, you can discuss with your teammates the concepts that you're all studying and quiz each other on the details. Just be sure that your teammates are as serious about the test as you are. If you find that your study time is being replaced with social time, you might need to find a new team.

Secret Key #2 – Make Your Studying Count

You're devoting a lot of time and effort to preparing for this test, so you want to be absolutely certain it will pay off. This means doing more than just reading the content and hoping you can remember it on test day. It's important to make every minute of study count. There are two main areas you can focus on to make your studying count.

Retention

It doesn't matter how much time you study if you can't remember the material. You need to make sure you are retaining the concepts. To check your retention of the information you're learning, try recalling it at later times with minimal prompting. Try carrying around flashcards and glance at one or two from time to time or ask a friend who's also studying for the test to quiz you.

To enhance your retention, look for ways to put the information into practice so that you can apply it rather than simply recalling it. If you're using the information in practical ways, it will be much easier to remember. Similarly, it helps to solidify a concept in your mind if you're not only reading it to yourself but also explaining it to someone else. Ask a friend to let you teach them about a concept you're a little shaky on (or speak aloud to an imaginary audience if necessary). As you try to summarize, define, give examples, and answer your friend's questions, you'll understand the concepts better and they will stay with you longer. Finally, step back for a big picture view and ask yourself how each piece of information fits with the whole subject. When you link the different concepts together and see them working together as a whole, it's easier to remember the individual components.

Finally, practice showing your work on any multi-step problems, even if you're just studying. Writing out each step you take to solve a problem will help solidify the process in your mind, and you'll be more likely to remember it during the test.

Modality

Modality simply refers to the means or method by which you study. Choosing a study modality that fits your own individual learning style is crucial. No two people learn best in exactly the same way, so it's important to know your strengths and use them to your advantage.

For example, if you learn best by visualization, focus on visualizing a concept in your mind and draw an image or a diagram. Try color-coding your notes, illustrating them, or creating symbols that will trigger your mind to recall a learned concept. If you learn best by hearing or discussing information, find a study partner who learns the same way or read aloud to yourself. Think about how to put the information in your own words. Imagine that you are giving a lecture on the topic and record yourself so you can listen to it later.

For any learning style, flashcards can be helpful. Organize the information so you can take advantage of spare moments to review. Underline key words or phrases. Use different colors for different categories. Mnemonic devices (such as creating a short list in which every item starts with the same letter) can also help with retention. Find what works best for you and use it to store the information in your mind most effectively and easily.

Secret Key #3 – Practice the Right Way

Your success on test day depends not only on how many hours you put into preparing, but also on whether you prepared the right way. It's good to check along the way to see if your studying is paying off. One of the most effective ways to do this is by taking practice tests to evaluate your progress. Practice tests are useful because they show exactly where you need to improve. Every time you take a practice test, pay special attention to these three groups of questions:

- The questions you got wrong
- The questions you had to guess on, even if you guessed right
- The questions you found difficult or slow to work through

This will show you exactly what your weak areas are, and where you need to devote more study time. Ask yourself why each of these questions gave you trouble. Was it because you didn't understand the material? Was it because you didn't remember the vocabulary? Do you need more repetitions on this type of question to build speed and confidence? Dig into those questions and figure out how you can strengthen your weak areas as you go back to review the material.

Additionally, many practice tests have a section explaining the answer choices. It can be tempting to read the explanation and think that you now have a good understanding of the concept. However, an explanation likely only covers part of the question's broader context. Even if the explanation makes perfect sense, **go back and investigate** every concept related to the question until you're positive you have a thorough understanding.

As you go along, keep in mind that the practice test is just that: practice. Memorizing these questions and answers will not be very helpful on the actual test because it is unlikely to have any of the same exact questions. If you only know the right answers to the sample questions, you won't be prepared for the real thing. **Study the concepts** until you understand them fully, and then you'll be able to answer any question that shows up on the test.

It's important to wait on the practice tests until you're ready. If you take a test on your first day of study, you may be overwhelmed by the amount of material covered and how much you need to learn. Work up to it gradually.

On test day, you'll need to be prepared for answering questions, managing your time, and using the test-taking strategies you've learned. It's a lot to balance, like a mental marathon that will have a big impact on your future. Like training for a marathon, you'll need to start slowly and work your way up. When test day arrives, you'll be ready.

Start with the strategies you've read in the first two Secret Keys—plan your course and study in the way that works best for you. If you have time, consider using multiple study resources to get different approaches to the same concepts. It can be helpful to see difficult concepts from more than one angle. Then find a good source for practice tests. Many times, the test website will suggest potential study resources or provide sample tests.

Practice Test Strategy

If you're able to find at least three practice tests, we recommend this strategy:

Untimed and Open-Book Practice

Take the first test with no time constraints and with your notes and study guide handy. Take your time and focus on applying the strategies you've learned.

Timed and Open-Book Practice

Take the second practice test open-book as well, but set a timer and practice pacing yourself to finish in time.

Timed and Closed-Book Practice

Take any other practice tests as if it were test day. Set a timer and put away your study materials. Sit at a table or desk in a quiet room, imagine yourself at the testing center, and answer questions as quickly and accurately as possible.

Keep repeating timed and closed-book tests on a regular basis until you run out of practice tests or it's time for the actual test. Your mind will be ready for the schedule and stress of test day, and you'll be able to focus on recalling the material you've learned.

Secret Key #4 – Pace Yourself

Once you're fully prepared for the material on the test, your biggest challenge on test day will be managing your time. Just knowing that the clock is ticking can make you panic even if you have plenty of time left. Work on pacing yourself so you can build confidence against the time constraints of the exam. Pacing is a difficult skill to master, especially in a high-pressure environment, so **practice is vital**.

Set time expectations for your pace based on how much time is available. For example, if a section has 60 questions and the time limit is 30 minutes, you know you have to average 30 seconds or less per question in order to answer them all. Although 30 seconds is the hard limit, set 25 seconds per question as your goal, so you reserve extra time to spend on harder questions. When you budget extra time for the harder questions, you no longer have any reason to stress when those questions take longer to answer.

Don't let this time expectation distract you from working through the test at a calm, steady pace, but keep it in mind so you don't spend too much time on any one question. Recognize that taking extra time on one question you don't understand may keep you from answering two that you do understand later in the test. If your time limit for a question is up and you're still not sure of the answer, mark it and move on, and come back to it later if the time and the test format allow. If the testing format doesn't allow you to return to earlier questions, just make an educated guess; then put it out of your mind and move on.

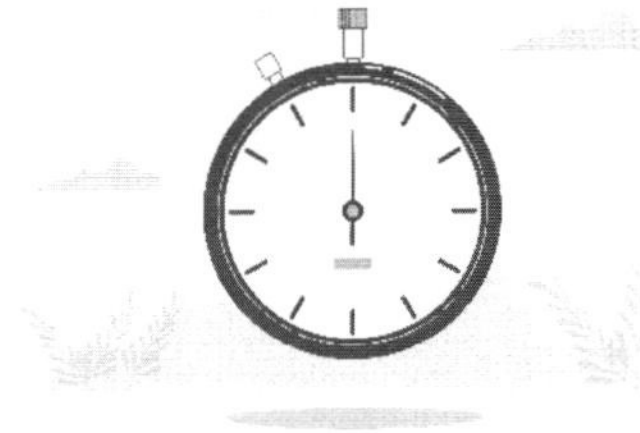

On the easier questions, be careful not to rush. It may seem wise to hurry through them so you have more time for the challenging ones, but it's not worth missing one if you know the concept and just didn't take the time to read the question fully. Work efficiently but make sure you understand the question and have looked at all of the answer choices, since more than one may seem right at first.

Even if you're paying attention to the time, you may find yourself a little behind at some point. You should speed up to get back on track, but do so wisely. Don't panic; just take a few seconds less on each question until you're caught up. Don't guess without thinking, but do look through the answer choices and eliminate any you know are wrong. If you can get down to two choices, it is often worthwhile to guess from those. Once you've chosen an answer, move on and don't dwell on any that you skipped or had to hurry through. If a question was taking too long, chances are it was one of the harder ones, so you weren't as likely to get it right anyway.

On the other hand, if you find yourself getting ahead of schedule, it may be beneficial to slow down a little. The more quickly you work, the more likely you are to make a careless mistake that will affect your score. You've budgeted time for each question, so don't be afraid to spend that time. Practice an efficient but careful pace to get the most out of the time you have.

Secret Key #5 – Have a Plan for Guessing

When you're taking the test, you may find yourself stuck on a question. Some of the answer choices seem better than others, but you don't see the one answer choice that is obviously correct. What do you do?

The scenario described above is very common, yet most test takers have not effectively prepared for it. Developing and practicing a plan for guessing may be one of the single most effective uses of your time as you get ready for the exam.

In developing your plan for guessing, there are three questions to address:

- When should you start the guessing process?
- How should you narrow down the choices?
- Which answer should you choose?

When to Start the Guessing Process

Unless your plan for guessing is to select C every time (which, despite its merits, is not what we recommend), you need to leave yourself enough time to apply your answer elimination strategies. Since you have a limited amount of time for each question, that means that if you're going to give yourself the best shot at guessing correctly, you have to decide quickly whether or not you will guess.

Of course, the best-case scenario is that you don't have to guess at all, so first, see if you can answer the question based on your knowledge of the subject and basic reasoning skills. Focus on the key words in the question and try to jog your memory of related topics. Give yourself a chance to bring the knowledge to mind, but once you realize that you don't have (or you can't access) the knowledge you need to answer the question, it's time to start the guessing process.

It's almost always better to start the guessing process too early than too late. It only takes a few seconds to remember something and answer the question from knowledge. Carefully eliminating wrong answer choices takes longer. Plus, going through the process of eliminating answer choices can actually help jog your memory.

Summary: Start the guessing process as soon as you decide that you can't answer the question based on your knowledge.

How to Narrow Down the Choices

The next chapter in this book (**Test-Taking Strategies**) includes a wide range of strategies for how to approach questions and how to look for answer choices to eliminate. You will definitely want to read those carefully, practice them, and figure out which ones work best for you. Here though, we're going to address a mindset rather than a particular strategy.

Your odds of guessing an answer correctly depend on how many options you are choosing from.

Number of options left	5	4	3	2	1
Odds of guessing correctly	20%	25%	33%	50%	100%

You can see from this chart just how valuable it is to be able to eliminate incorrect answers and make an educated guess, but there are two things that many test takers do that cause them to miss out on the benefits of guessing:

- Accidentally eliminating the correct answer
- Selecting an answer based on an impression

We'll look at the first one here, and the second one in the next section.

To avoid accidentally eliminating the correct answer, we recommend a thought exercise called **the $5 challenge**. In this challenge, you only eliminate an answer choice from contention if you are willing to bet $5 on it being wrong. Why $5? Five dollars is a small but not insignificant amount of money. It's an amount you could afford to lose but wouldn't want to throw away. And while losing $5 once might not hurt too much, doing it twenty times will set you back $100. In the same way, each small decision you make—eliminating a choice here, guessing on a question there—won't by itself impact your score very much, but when you put them all together, they can make a big difference. By holding each answer choice elimination decision to a higher standard, you can reduce the risk of accidentally eliminating the correct answer.

The $5 challenge can also be applied in a positive sense: If you are willing to bet $5 that an answer choice *is* correct, go ahead and mark it as correct.

Summary: Only eliminate an answer choice if you are willing to bet $5 that it is wrong.

Which Answer to Choose

You're taking the test. You've run into a hard question and decided you'll have to guess. You've eliminated all the answer choices you're willing to bet $5 on. Now you have to pick an answer. Why do we even need to talk about this? Why can't you just pick whichever one you feel like when the time comes?

The answer to these questions is that if you don't come into the test with a plan, you'll rely on your impression to select an answer choice, and if you do that, you risk falling into a trap. The test writers know that everyone who takes their test will be guessing on some of the questions, so they intentionally write wrong answer choices to seem plausible. You still have to pick an answer though, and if the wrong answer choices are designed to look right, how can you ever be sure that you're not falling for their trap? The best solution we've found to this dilemma is to take the decision out of your hands entirely. Here is the process we recommend:

Once you've eliminated any choices that you are confident (willing to bet $5) are wrong, select the first remaining choice as your answer.

Whether you choose to select the first remaining choice, the second, or the last, the important thing is that you use some preselected standard. Using this approach guarantees that you will not be enticed into selecting an answer choice that looks right, because you are not basing your decision on how the answer choices look.

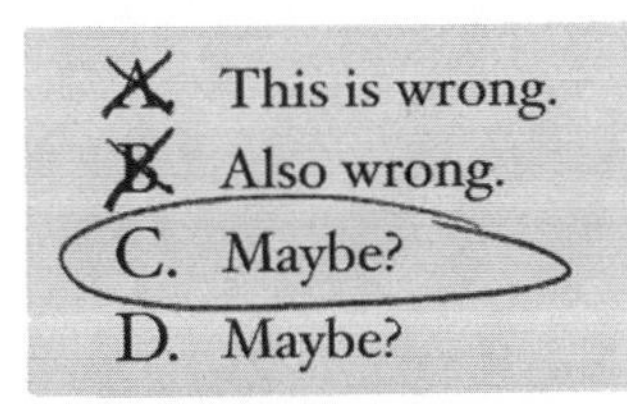

This is not meant to make you question your knowledge. Instead, it is to help you recognize the difference between your knowledge and your impressions. There's a huge difference between thinking an answer is right because of what you know, and thinking an answer is right because it looks or sounds like it should be right.

Summary: To ensure that your selection is appropriately random, make a predetermined selection from among all answer choices you have not eliminated.

Test-Taking Strategies

This section contains a list of test-taking strategies that you may find helpful as you work through the test. By taking what you know and applying logical thought, you can maximize your chances of answering any question correctly!

It is very important to realize that every question is different and every person is different: no single strategy will work on every question, and no single strategy will work for every person. That's why we've included all of them here, so you can try them out and determine which ones work best for different types of questions and which ones work best for you.

Question Strategies

☑ Read Carefully

Read the question and the answer choices carefully. Don't miss the question because you misread the terms. You have plenty of time to read each question thoroughly and make sure you understand what is being asked. Yet a happy medium must be attained, so don't waste too much time. You must read carefully and efficiently.

☑ Contextual Clues

Look for contextual clues. If the question includes a word you are not familiar with, look at the immediate context for some indication of what the word might mean. Contextual clues can often give you all the information you need to decipher the meaning of an unfamiliar word. Even if you can't determine the meaning, you may be able to narrow down the possibilities enough to make a solid guess at the answer to the question.

☑ Prefixes

If you're having trouble with a word in the question or answer choices, try dissecting it. Take advantage of every clue that the word might include. Prefixes can be a huge help. Usually, they allow you to determine a basic meaning. *Pre-* means before, *post-* means after, *pro-* is positive, *de-* is negative. From prefixes, you can get an idea of the general meaning of the word and try to put it into context.

☑ Hedge Words

Watch out for critical hedge words, such as *likely, may, can, often, almost, mostly, usually, generally, rarely,* and *sometimes.* Question writers insert these hedge phrases to cover every possibility. Often an answer choice will be wrong simply because it leaves no room for exception. Be on guard for answer choices that have definitive words such as *exactly* and *always.*

☑ Switchback Words

Stay alert for *switchbacks.* These are the words and phrases frequently used to alert you to shifts in thought. The most common switchback words are *but, although,* and *however.* Others include *nevertheless, on the other hand, even though, while, in spite of, despite,* and *regardless of.* Switchback words are important to catch because they can change the direction of the question or an answer choice.

✓ Face Value

When in doubt, use common sense. Accept the situation in the problem at face value. Don't read too much into it. These problems will not require you to make wild assumptions. If you have to go beyond creativity and warp time or space in order to have an answer choice fit the question, then you should move on and consider the other answer choices. These are normal problems rooted in reality. The applicable relationship or explanation may not be readily apparent, but it is there for you to figure out. Use your common sense to interpret anything that isn't clear.

Answer Choice Strategies

✓ Answer Selection

The most thorough way to pick an answer choice is to identify and eliminate wrong answers until only one is left, then confirm it is the correct answer. Sometimes an answer choice may immediately seem right, but be careful. The test writers will usually put more than one reasonable answer choice on each question, so take a second to read all of them and make sure that the other choices are not equally obvious. As long as you have time left, it is better to read every answer choice than to pick the first one that looks right without checking the others.

✓ Answer Choice Families

An answer choice family consists of two (in rare cases, three) answer choices that are very similar in construction and cannot all be true at the same time. If you see two answer choices that are direct opposites or parallels, one of them is usually the correct answer. For instance, if one answer choice says that quantity x increases and another either says that quantity x decreases (opposite) or says that quantity y increases (parallel), then those answer choices would fall into the same family. An answer choice that doesn't match the construction of the answer choice family is more likely to be incorrect. Most questions will not have answer choice families, but when they do appear, you should be prepared to recognize them.

✓ Eliminate Answers

Eliminate answer choices as soon as you realize they are wrong, but make sure you consider all possibilities. If you are eliminating answer choices and realize that the last one you are left with is also wrong, don't panic. Start over and consider each choice again. There may be something you missed the first time that you will realize on the second pass.

✓ Avoid Fact Traps

Don't be distracted by an answer choice that is factually true but doesn't answer the question. You are looking for the choice that answers the question. Stay focused on what the question is asking for so you don't accidentally pick an answer that is true but incorrect. Always go back to the question and make sure the answer choice you've selected actually answers the question and is not merely a true statement.

✓ Extreme Statements

In general, you should avoid answers that put forth extreme actions as standard practice or proclaim controversial ideas as established fact. An answer choice that states the "process should be used in certain situations, if..." is much more likely to be correct than one that states the "process should be discontinued completely." The first is a calm rational statement and doesn't even make a definitive, uncompromising stance, using a hedge word *if* to provide wiggle room, whereas the second choice is far more extreme.

☑ BENCHMARK

As you read through the answer choices and you come across one that seems to answer the question well, mentally select that answer choice. This is not your final answer, but it's the one that will help you evaluate the other answer choices. The one that you selected is your benchmark or standard for judging each of the other answer choices. Every other answer choice must be compared to your benchmark. That choice is correct until proven otherwise by another answer choice beating it. If you find a better answer, then that one becomes your new benchmark. Once you've decided that no other choice answers the question as well as your benchmark, you have your final answer.

☑ PREDICT THE ANSWER

Before you even start looking at the answer choices, it is often best to try to predict the answer. When you come up with the answer on your own, it is easier to avoid distractions and traps because you will know exactly what to look for. The right answer choice is unlikely to be word-for-word what you came up with, but it should be a close match. Even if you are confident that you have the right answer, you should still take the time to read each option before moving on.

General Strategies

☑ TOUGH QUESTIONS

If you are stumped on a problem or it appears too hard or too difficult, don't waste time. Move on! Remember though, if you can quickly check for obviously incorrect answer choices, your chances of guessing correctly are greatly improved. Before you completely give up, at least try to knock out a couple of possible answers. Eliminate what you can and then guess at the remaining answer choices before moving on.

☑ CHECK YOUR WORK

Since you will probably not know every term listed and the answer to every question, it is important that you get credit for the ones that you do know. Don't miss any questions through careless mistakes. If at all possible, try to take a second to look back over your answer selection and make sure you've selected the correct answer choice and haven't made a costly careless mistake (such as marking an answer choice that you didn't mean to mark). This quick double check should more than pay for itself in caught mistakes for the time it costs.

☑ PACE YOURSELF

It's easy to be overwhelmed when you're looking at a page full of questions; your mind is confused and full of random thoughts, and the clock is ticking down faster than you would like. Calm down and maintain the pace that you have set for yourself. Especially as you get down to the last few minutes of the test, don't let the small numbers on the clock make you panic. As long as you are on track by monitoring your pace, you are guaranteed to have time for each question.

☑ DON'T RUSH

It is very easy to make errors when you are in a hurry. Maintaining a fast pace in answering questions is pointless if it makes you miss questions that you would have gotten right otherwise. Test writers like to include distracting information and wrong answers that seem right. Taking a little extra time to avoid careless mistakes can make all the difference in your test score. Find a pace that allows you to be confident in the answers that you select.

⊘ KEEP MOVING

Panicking will not help you pass the test, so do your best to stay calm and keep moving. Taking deep breaths and going through the answer elimination steps you practiced can help to break through a stress barrier and keep your pace.

Final Notes

The combination of a solid foundation of content knowledge and the confidence that comes from practicing your plan for applying that knowledge is the key to maximizing your performance on test day. As your foundation of content knowledge is built up and strengthened, you'll find that the strategies included in this chapter become more and more effective in helping you quickly sift through the distractions and traps of the test to isolate the correct answer.

Now that you're preparing to move forward into the test content chapters of this book, be sure to keep your goal in mind. As you read, think about how you will be able to apply this information on the test. If you've already seen sample questions for the test and you have an idea of the question format and style, try to come up with questions of your own that you can answer based on what you're reading. This will give you valuable practice applying your knowledge in the same ways you can expect to on test day.

Good luck and good studying!

Foundations of Scientific Inquiry

Safety and Equipment

Laboratory Accidents

Any spills or accidents should be **reported** to the teacher so that the teacher can determine the safest clean-up method. The student should start to wash off a **chemical** spilled on the skin while reporting the incident. Some spills may require removal of contaminated clothing and use of the **safety shower**. Broken glass should be disposed of in a designated container. If someone's clothing catches fire they should walk to the safety shower and use it to extinguish the flames. A fire blanket may be used to smother a **lab fire**. A fire extinguisher, phone, spill neutralizers, and a first aid box are other types of **safety equipment** found in the lab. Students should be familiar with **routes** out of the room and the building in case of fire. Students should use the **eye wash station** if a chemical gets in the eyes.

Safety Procedures

Students should wear a **lab apron** and **safety goggles**. Loose or dangling clothing and jewelry, necklaces, and earrings should not be worn. Those with long hair should tie it back. Care should always be taken not to splash chemicals. Open-toed shoes such as sandals and flip-flops should not be worn, nor should wrist watches. Glasses are preferable to contact lenses since the latter carry a risk of chemicals getting caught between the lens and the eye. Students should always be supervised. The area where the experiment is taking place and the surrounding floor should be free of clutter. Only the lab book and the items necessary for the experiment should be present. Smoking, eating, and chewing gum are not permitted in the lab. Cords should not be allowed to dangle from work stations. There should be no rough-housing in the lab. Hands should be washed after the lab is complete.

Fume Hoods

Because of the potential safety hazards associated with chemistry lab experiments, such as fire from vapors and the inhalation of toxic fumes, a **fume hood** should be used in many instances. A fume hood carries away vapors from reagents or reactions. Equipment or reactions are placed as far back in the hood as practical to help enhance the collection of the fumes. The **glass safety shield** automatically closes to the appropriate height, and it should be low enough to protect the face and body. The safety shield should only be raised to move equipment in and out of the hood. One should not climb inside a hood or stick one's head inside. All spills should be wiped up immediately, and the glass should be cleaned if a splash occurs.

Common Safety Hazards

Some specific safety hazards possible in a chemistry lab include:

- **Fire**: Fire can be caused by volatile solvents such as ether, acetone, or benzene being kept in an open beaker or Erlenmeyer flask. Vapors can creep along the table and ignite if they reach a flame or spark. Solvents should be heated in a hood with a steam bath, not on a hot plate.
- **Explosion**: Heating or creating a reaction in a closed system can cause an explosion, resulting in flying glass and chemical splashes. The system should be vented to prevent this.
- **Chemical and thermal burns**: Many chemicals are corrosive to the skin and eyes.

- **Inhalation of toxic fumes**: Some compounds severely irritate membranes in the eyes, nose, throat, and lungs.
- **Absorption** of toxic chemicals such as dimethyl sulfoxide (DMSO) and nitrobenzene through the skin.
- **Ingestion** of toxic chemicals.

Safety Gloves

There are many types of **gloves** available to help protect the skin from cuts, burns, and chemical splashes. There are many considerations when choosing a glove. For example, gloves that are highly protective may limit dexterity. Some gloves may not offer appropriate protection against a specific chemical. Other considerations include degradation rating, which indicates how effective a glove is when exposed to chemicals; breakthrough time, which indicates how quickly a chemical can break through the surface of the glove; and permeation rate, which indicates how quickly chemicals seep through after the initial breakthrough. Disposable latex, vinyl, or nitrile gloves are usually appropriate for most circumstances, and offer protection from incidental splashes and contact. Other types of gloves include butyl, neoprene, PVC, PVA, Viton, Silver Shield, and natural rubber. Each offers its own type of protection but may have drawbacks as well.

Proper Handling and Storage of Chemicals

Students should take care when **carrying chemicals** from one place to another. Chemicals should never be taken from the room, tasted, or touched with bare hands. **Safety gloves** should be worn when appropriate and glove/chemical interactions and glove deterioration should be considered. Hands should always be **washed** thoroughly after a lab. Potentially hazardous materials intended for use in chemistry, biology, or other science labs should be secured in a safe area where relevant **Safety Data Sheets (SDS)** can be accessed. Chemicals and solutions should be used as directed and labels should be read before handling solutions and chemicals. Extra chemicals should not be returned to their original containers, but should be disposed of as directed by the school district's rules or local ordinances. Local municipalities often have hazardous waste disposal programs. Acids should be stored separately from other chemicals. Flammable liquids should be stored away from acids, bases, and oxidizers.

Bunsen Burners

When using a **Bunsen burner**, loose clothing should be tucked in, long hair should be tied back, and safety goggles and aprons should be worn. Students should know what to do in case of a fire or accident. When lighting the burner, strikers should always be used instead of matches. Do not touch the hot barrel. Tongs (never fingers) should be used to hold the material in the flame. To heat liquid, a flask may be set upon wire gauze on a tripod and secured with an iron ring or clamp on a stand. The flame is extinguished by turning off the gas at the source.

Safety Procedures Related to Animals

Animals to be used for **dissections** should be obtained from a company that provides animals for this purpose. Road kill or decaying animals that a student brings in should not be used. It is possible that such an animal may have a pathogen or a virus, such as rabies, which can be transmitted via the saliva of even a dead animal. Students should use gloves and should not participate if they have open sores or moral objections to dissections. It is generally accepted that biological experiments may be performed on lower-order life forms and invertebrates, but not on mammalian vertebrates and birds. No animals should be harmed physiologically. Experimental animals should be kept, cared for, and handled in a safe manner and with compassion. Pathogenic (anything able to cause a disease) substances should not be used in lab experiments.

Lab Notebooks

A **lab notebook** is a record of all pre-lab work and lab work. It differs from a lab report, which is prepared after lab work is completed. A lab notebook is a formal record of lab preparations and what was done. **Observational recordings** should not be altered, erased, or whited-out to make corrections. Drawing a single line through an entry is sufficient to make changes. Pages should be numbered and should not be torn out. Entries should be made neatly, but don't necessarily have to be complete sentences. **Entries** should provide detailed information and be recorded in such a way that another person could use them to replicate the experiment. **Quantitative data** may be recorded in tabular form, and may include calculations made during an experiment. Lab book entries can also include references and research performed before the experiment. Entries may also consist of information about a lab experiment, including the objective or purpose, the procedures, data collected, and the results.

Lab Reports

A **lab report** is an item developed after an experiment that is intended to present the results of a lab experiment. Generally, it should be prepared using a word processor, not hand-written or recorded in a notebook. A lab report should be formally presented. It is intended to persuade others to accept or reject a hypothesis. It should include a brief but descriptive **title** and an **abstract**. The abstract is a summary of the report. It should include a purpose that states the problem that was explored or the question that was answered. It should also include a **hypothesis** that describes the anticipated results of the experiment. The experiment should include a **control** and one **variable** to ensure that the results can be interpreted correctly. Observations and results can be presented using written narratives, tables, graphs, and illustrations. The report should also include a **summation** or **conclusion** explaining whether the results supported the hypothesis.

Types of Laboratory Glassware

Two types of flasks are Erlenmeyer flasks and volumetric flasks. **Volumetric flasks** are used to accurately prepare a specific volume and concentration of a solution. **Erlenmeyer flasks** can be used for mixing, transporting, and reacting, but are not appropriate for accurate measurements.

A **pipette** can be used to accurately measure small amounts of liquid. Liquid is drawn into the pipette through a bulb. The liquid measurement is read at the **meniscus**. There are also plastic disposable pipettes. A **repipette** is a hand-operated pump that dispenses solutions.

Beakers can be used to measure mass or dissolve a solvent into a solute. They do not measure volume as accurately as a volumetric flask, pipette, graduated cylinder, or burette.

Graduated cylinders are used for precise measurements and are considered more accurate than Erlenmeyer flasks or beakers. To read a graduated cylinder, it should be placed on a flat surface and read at eye level. The surface of a liquid in a graduated cylinder forms a lens-shaped curve. The measurement should be taken from the bottom of the curve. A ring may be placed at the top of tall, narrow cylinders to help avoid breakage if they are tipped over.

A **burette**, or buret, is a piece of lab glassware used to accurately dispense liquid. It looks similar to a narrow graduated cylinder, but it includes a stopcock and tip. It may be filled with a funnel or pipette.

Microscopes

There are different kinds of microscopes, but **optical** or **light microscopes** are the most commonly used in lab settings. Light and lenses are used to magnify and view samples. A specimen or sample is placed on a slide, and the slide is placed on a stage with a hole in it. Light passes through the hole and illuminates the sample. The sample is magnified by lenses and viewed through the eyepiece. A simple microscope has one lens, while a typical compound microscope has three lenses. The light source can be room light redirected by a mirror, or the microscope can have its own independent light source that passes through a condenser. In this case, there are diaphragms and filters to allow light intensity to be controlled. Optical microscopes also have coarse and fine adjustment knobs.

Other types of microscopes include **digital microscopes**, which use a camera and a monitor to allow viewing of the sample. **Scanning electron microscopes (SEMs)** provide greater detail in terms of a sample's surface topography and can produce magnifications much greater than those possible with optical microscopes. The technology of an SEM is quite different from an optical microscope in that it does not rely on lenses to magnify objects, but uses samples placed in a chamber. In one type of SEM, a beam of electrons from an electron gun scans and actually interacts with the sample to produce an image.

Wet mount slides designed for use with a light microscope typically require a thin portion of the specimen to be placed on a standard glass slide. A drop of water is added, and a cover slip or cover glass is placed on top. Air bubbles and fingerprints can make viewing difficult. Placing the cover slip at a 45-degree angle and allowing it to drop into place can help avoid the problem of air bubbles. A **cover slip** should always be used when viewing wet mount slides. The viewer should start with the objective in its lowest position and then fine-focus. The microscope should be carried with two hands and stored with the low-power objective in the down position. **Lenses** should be cleaned with lens paper only. A **graticule slide** is marked with a grid line, and is useful for counting or estimating a quantity.

BALANCES

Balances such as triple-beam balances, spring balances, and electronic balances measure mass and force. An **electronic balance** is the most accurate, followed by a **triple-beam balance** and then a **spring balance**. One part of a **triple-beam balance** is the plate, which is where the item to be weighed is placed. There are also three beams, which have hash marks indicating amounts and which hold the weights that rest in the notches. The front beam measures weights between 0 and 10 grams, the middle beam measures weights in 100-gram increments, and the far beam measures weights in 10-gram increments. The sum of the weight of each beam is the total weight of the object. A triple beam balance also includes a set screw to calibrate the equipment, as well as a mark indicating that the object and counterweights are in balance.

CHROMATOGRAPHY

Chromatography refers to a set of laboratory techniques used to separate or analyze **mixtures**. Mixtures are dissolved in their mobile phases. In the stationary or bonded phase, the desired component is separated from other molecules in the mixture. In chromatography, the analyte is the substance to be separated. **Preparative chromatography** refers to the type of chromatography that involves purifying a substance for further use rather than further analysis. **Analytical chromatography** involves analyzing the isolated substance. Other types of chromatography include column, planar, paper, thin layer, displacement, supercritical fluid, affinity, ion exchange, and size exclusion chromatography. Reversed phase, two-dimensional, simulated moving bed, pyrolysis, fast protein, counter current, and chiral are also types of chromatography. **Gas**

chromatography refers to the separation technique in which the mobile phase of a substance is in gas form.

Review Video: Paper Chromatography
Visit mometrix.com/academy and enter code: 543963

Reagents and Reactants

A **reagent** or **reactant** is a chemical agent for use in chemical reactions. When preparing for a lab, it should be confirmed that glassware and other equipment have been cleaned and/or sterilized. There should be enough materials, reagents, or other solutions needed for the lab for every group of students completing the experiment. Distilled water should be used instead of tap water when performing lab experiments because distilled water has most of its impurities removed. Other needed apparatus such as funnels, filter paper, balances, Bunsen burners, ring stands, and/or microscopes should also be set up. After the lab, it should be confirmed that sinks, workstations, and any equipment used have been cleaned. If chemicals or specimens need to be kept at a certain temperature by refrigerating them or using another storage method, the temperature should be checked periodically to ensure the sample does not spoil.

Diluting Acids

When preparing a solution of **dilute acid**, always add the concentrated acid solution to water, not water to concentrated acid. Start by adding approximately $\frac{2}{3}$ of the total volume of water to the graduated cylinder or volumetric flask. Next, add the concentrated acid to the water. Add additional water to the diluted acid to bring the solution to the final desired volume.

Cleaning After Acid Spills

In the event of an **acid spill**, any clothes that have come into contact with the acid should be removed and any skin contacted with acid must be rinsed with clean water. To the extent a window can be opened or a fume hood can be turned on, do so. Do not try to force air circulation, such as by adding a fan, as acid fumes can be harmful if spread.

Next, pour one of the following over the spill area: sodium bicarbonate, baking soda, soda ash, or cat litter. Start from the outside of the spill and then move towards the center, in order to prevent splashing. When the clumps have thoroughly dried, sweep up the clumps and dispose of them as chemical waste.

Centrifuges

A centrifuge is used to separate the components of a heterogeneous mixture (consisting of two or more compounds) by spinning it. The solid precipitate settles in the bottom of the container, and the liquid component of the solution, called the **centrifugate**, is at the top. A well-known application of this process is using a centrifuge to separate blood cells and plasma. The heavier cells settle on the bottom of the test tube, and the lighter plasma stays on top. Another example is using a salad spinner to help dry lettuce.

ELECTROPHORESIS, CALORIMETRY, AND TITRATION

- **Electrophoresis** is the separation of molecules based on electrical charge. This is possible because particles dispersed in a fluid usually carry electric charges on their surfaces. Molecules are pulled through the fluid toward the positive end if the molecules have a negative charge and are pulled through the fluid toward the negative end if the molecules have a positive charge.
- **Calorimetry** is used to determine the heat released or absorbed in a chemical reaction.
- **Titration** helps determine the precise endpoint of a reaction. With this information, the precise quantity of reactant in the titration flask can be determined. A burette is used to deliver the second reactant to the flask and an indicator or pH meter is used to detect the endpoint of the reaction.

FIELD STUDIES AND RESEARCH PROJECTS

Field studies may facilitate scientific inquiry in a manner similar to indoor lab experiments. Field studies can be interdisciplinary in nature and can help students learn and apply scientific concepts and processes. **Research projects** can be conducted in any number of locations, including school campuses, local parks, national parks, beaches, or mountains. Students can practice the general techniques of observation, data collection, collaborative planning, and analysis of experiments. Field studies give students the chance to learn through hands-on applications of scientific processes, such as map making in geography, observation of stratification in geology, observation of life cycles of plants and animals, and analysis of water quality.

Students should watch out for obvious outdoor **hazards**. These include poisonous flora and fauna such as poison ivy, poison oak, and sumac. Depending on the region of the United States in which the field study is being conducted, hazards may also include rattlesnakes and black widow or brown recluse spiders. Students should also be made aware of potentially hazardous situations specific to **geographic locales** and the possibility of coming into contact with **pathogens**.

Field studies allow for great flexibility in the use of traditional and technological methods for **making observations** and **collecting data**. For example, a nature study could consist of a simple survey of bird species within a given area. Information could be recorded using still photography or a video camera. This type of activity gives students the chance to use technologies other than computers. Computers could still be used to create a slide show of transferred images or a digital lab report. If a quantitative study of birds was being performed, the simple technique of using a pencil and paper to tabulate the number of birds counted in the field could also be used. Other techniques used during field studies could include collecting specimens for lab study, observing coastal ecosystems and tides, and collecting weather data such as temperature, precipitation amounts, and air pressure in a particular locale.

Scientific Concepts Related to Biology

CHEMICAL NATURE OF BIOLOGY

All organisms are made up of matter and display the typical physical and chemical properties of matter. Every cell of an organism is composed of molecules, atoms, and ions. **Chemistry** is needed to explain the structure and function of all cellular processes at the molecular level. **Organic chemistry** involves many large and complex molecules including biochemical compounds like carbohydrates, lipids, proteins, and nucleic acids. Chemical reactions occur in the daily function of organisms even at the cellular level. Chemical reactions that are important for life include oxidation-reduction, dehydration synthesis, hydrolysis, phosphorylation, and acid-base reactions.

Use of Mathematics in Biology

Mathematics is becoming increasingly prevalent in modern biology, especially with the use of computers for statistical programs. Mathematics is used in the **studies of populations**. For example, biologists study human population growth, bacteria growth, and virus growth. Populations of organisms in feeding relationships such as predator and prey are studied. Mathematics is used in classical genetics. For example, biologists use probability theory to predict offspring in **genetic crosses**. Mathematics, with the help of computer science, is used extensively in bioinformatics to analyze large amounts of biological information. For example, biological data are extracted and analyzed using sophisticated computer programing. Mathematics is also used in studies of epidemics. For example, studies concerning the spread of the flu and acquired immune deficiency syndrome (AIDS) have been performed.

Physical Laws and Principles Governing Biological Systems

Biological systems are governed by the same physical laws and principles that govern the rest of the universe. For example, biological systems must obey the laws of thermodynamics. These laws govern energy and the transformations of energy. The first law of thermodynamics is the law of **conservation of energy**, which states that energy is neither created nor destroyed but can change forms. The energy needed for life on Earth comes from the Sun. Sunlight reaches the Earth and is transformed by green plants and cyanobacteria (producers) during photosynthesis into the chemical bonds of ATP molecules, which can be used by these organisms for energy. Consumers eat the producers or other consumers in order to obtain energy. The second law of thermodynamics states that systems tend toward more disorder or randomness, also known as **entropy**. This is evident in the fact that organisms must continually acquire or transfer energy to sustain life and, as such, the energy is dispersed through the whole biosphere. This diffusion of energy isn't perfectly efficient and much of the energy becomes heat and is essentially unusable.

Cell Theory

Cell theory states that all living things are composed of cells, which are the basic unit of structure and function in living things, and that cells come from preexisting cells. Cells were first observed in 1655 by Robert Hooke when he was studying thin slices of a piece of cork under his primitive microscope. Because the cork cells were dead, Hooke actually only observed the cell walls of the cork cells. Hooke was the first to use the word "cell," which comes from the Latin word *cellula*, which means small compartment. Hooke documented his observations with sketches and published his work in his book commonly called *Micrographia.*

Germ Theory of Disease

The **germ theory of disease** states that most infectious diseases are caused by germs or disease-causing microbes or pathogens. The germ theory is the foundation of microbiology and modern medicine. Pasteur studied the fermentation of wine and the spoiling of milk. He discovered that yeast caused the fermentation of wine and bacteria caused the spoiling of milk. He developed the process of pasteurization of milk that killed the harmful microbes without ruining the taste of the milk. Then he studied diseases in silkworms and was able to determine that the causes of those diseases were protozoa and bacteria. Pasteur also thought that microbes in hospitals came from preexisting microbes instead of **spontaneous generation**. He disproved spontaneous generation with his work with bacteria and broth. He discovered that weakened microbes could be used in **vaccines** or **immunizations** to prevent or protect against the diseases caused by those microbes. Pasteur discovered viruses in his work, developing the rabies vaccine and treatments for those already infected with the rabies virus.

Mendel's Contributions to Genetics

Johann Gregor Mendel is known as the **father of genetics**. Mendel was an Austrian monk who performed thousands of experiments involving the breeding of the common pea plant in the monastery garden. Mendel kept detailed records including seed color, pod color, seed type, flower color, and plant height for eight years and published his work in 1865. Unfortunately, his work was largely ignored until the early 1900s. Mendel's work showed that genes come in pairs and that dominant and recessive traits are inherited independently of each other. His work established the law of segregation, the law of independent assortment, and the law of dominance.

Darwin's Contributions to Theory of Evolution

Charles Darwin's **theory of evolution** by natural selection is the unifying concept in biology today. From 1831 to 1836, Darwin traveled as a naturalist on a five-year voyage on the *H.M.S. Beagle* around the tip of South America and to the Galápagos Islands. He studied finches, took copious amounts of meticulous notes, and collected thousands of plant and animal specimens. He collected 13 species of finches, each with a unique bill for a distinct food source These similarities between the finches led him to believe that the finches shared a common ancestor. The similarities and differences of fossils of extinct rodents and modern mammal fossils led him to believe that the mammals had changed over time. Darwin believed that these changes were the result of random genetic changes called **mutations**. He believed that mutations could be beneficial and eventually result in a different organism over time. In 1859, in his first book, *On the Origin of Species*, Darwin coined the term "**natural selection**" and proposed that it was the means by which adaptations would arise over time. He said that it is the mechanism of evolution. Because variety exists among individuals of a species, he stated that those individuals must compete for the same limited resources. Some would die, and others would survive. According to Darwin, evolution is a slow, gradual process. In 1871, Darwin published his second book, *Descent of Man, and Selection in Relation to Sex*, in which he discussed the evolution of man.

Contribution to Genetics by Alfred Hershey and Martha Chase

Alfred Hershey and Martha Chase did a series of experiments in 1952 known as the **Hershey-Chase experiments**. These experiments showed that deoxyribonucleic acid (DNA), not protein, is the genetic material that transfers information for inheritance. The Hershey-Chase experiments used a bacteriophage, a virus that infects bacteria, to infect the bacteria *Escherichia coli.* The bacteriophage T2 is basically a small piece of DNA enclosed in a protein coating. The DNA contains phosphorus, and the protein coating contains sulfur. In the first set of experiments, the T2 was marked with radioactive phosphorus-32. In the second set of experiments, the T2 was marked with radioactive sulfur-35. For both sets of experiments, after the *E. coli* was infected by the T2, the *E. coli* was isolated using a centrifuge. In the first set of experiments, the radioactive isotope (P-32) was found in the *E. coli*, showing that the genetic information was transferred by the DNA. In the second set of experiments, the radioactive isotope (S-35) was not found in the *E. coli*, showing that the genetic information was not transferred by the protein as was previously thought. Hershey and Chase conducted further experiments allowing the bacteria from the first set of experiments to reproduce, and the offspring was also found to contain the radioactive isotope (P-32) further confirming that the DNA transferred the genetic material.

Contributions to the Knowledge of DNA

The three-dimensional double-helix structure of the DNA molecule was formulated by James Watson and Francis Crick in 1953. But the actual discovery of DNA took place in 1869 when Friedrich Miescher discovered DNA, which he called "nuclein" in the nuclei of human white blood cells while attempting to isolate proteins. Years later in 1919, Phoebus Levene identified the components of a nucleotide. Then in 1950, Erwin Chargaff published his discovery that DNA varies among species and states what is now known as **Chargaff's rule**: Adenine always combines with thymine, and cytosine always combines with guanine. In 1951, Rosalind Franklin studied the molecular structure of DNA using x-rays. Her work laid the foundation for the work that Watson and Crick did in 1953, in which they discovered the three-dimensional double-helix structure of DNA. Watson and Crick showed that the complementary bases are joined by hydrogen bonds. Franklin also studied the structure of RNA and discovered that RNA is a single-strand helix structure, not a double strand like DNA.

Population Models

Ecologists use population models to study the populations in an ecosystem and their interactions of populations with the environment. **Population models** are mathematical models that are designed to study population dynamics. Ecologists can model the growth of a population. For example, models can be designed to describe increases, decreases, or fluctuations in the size of populations due to births, deaths, and migrations. Ecologists can model the interactions of populations with other populations. For example, models of the interactions between predator and prey describe the fluctuating cycles associated with these relationships. Models can also include other factors such as diseases and limiting resources.

Ethical Concerns of Embryonic Stem Cells for Research

Research involving the use of embryonic stem cells offers hope for genetics-related health issues. However, ethical issues are seriously debated. New therapies could be developed using embryonic stem cells that would greatly alleviate suffering for many people. However, that benefit comes at the cost of human embryos. Proponents of embryonic stem cell research argue that an early embryo is not yet a person because the embryo cannot survive without being implanted in the uterus. Some believe that the embryo should have no moral status and that fertilized eggs should be treated as the property of the parents who should have the right to donate that property to research. Opponents of embryonic stem cell research argue that the embryo is a human life at fertilization and should have full moral status at fertilization, and that a human embryo is a human being. Opponents argue that judgments determining when an embryo is viable or when an embryo is fully human cannot be made. Some opponents of stem cell research do not believe that the fertilized egg is a human being, but they still argue that by removing the stem cells from the early embryo, the embryo is prevented from becoming a human being. They argue that embryonic stem cell research destroys potential life.

Ethical and Societal Concerns Regarding Genetically Modified Food

Genetically modified (GM) foods are transgenic crops that have had their genes altered by technology. For example, herbicide-tolerant soybeans and insect-resistant corn have been grown for years in the United States. Several issues have been raised concerning GM foods. Some people do not want to go against nature. Even scientists may feel that because the genes in organisms have evolved over millions of years that man should not interfere. Others would argue that man has been selectively breeding plants and animals for hundreds of years, and genetic modification is just an extension of that concept. Scientists are concerned about introducing new allergens into the food supply. For example, if a gene from a peanut plant is introduced into a soybean plant, there may be a potential for allergic reactions. Proteins from microorganisms may have never been tested as allergens. Many are concerned that the genetic modifications will not be contained. Pollen from fields of genetically modified crops may be carried by insects or wind to other fields. In some cases, traits such as herbicide resistance might pass from the cultivated plants to the wild populations of those plants. Insect-resistant plants may harm insects other than those that were being targeted.

For example, studies show that pollinators such as the monarch butterfly may be harmed from GM corn.

Ethical Concerns Regarding Human Cloning and Animal Cloning

Many issues are raised with the topic of human cloning and animal cloning. Disagreements arise over who, if any, should be allowed to produce human clones. Many are concerned about how clones would integrate into families and societies. Some believe that human cloning for procreation purposes should be regulated based on motivation. For example, individuals interested in raising a genetically-related child should be granted approval, but those seeking immortality or viewing cloning as a novelty should be denied. Many believe that mandatory counseling and a waiting period should be enforced. Others argue that individuals do not have a right to a genetically-related child, that cloning is not safe, and that cloning is not medically necessary. Proponents argue that cloning is needed to generate tissues and whole organs that eliminate the need for immunosuppressive drugs. Cloned tissues and organs could be used to counter the effects of aging. Others fear that this will lead to the generation of humans solely for the purpose of harvesting tissues and organs. Animals are being cloned in laboratories and in livestock production. Animal rights activists are opposed to the cloning of animals and argue that many cloned animals suffer from defects before they die. Some believe that animals have moral rights and should be treated with the same ethical consideration given to humans.

Societal Concerns About Genetic Testing

Society has not fully embraced genetic testing. Many people do not consider genetic testing to be a medical test and many feel pressure from family members who do not want the family genes revealed. Some do not want to know of potential health problems they may face later in life. Many are concerned about the psychological impact and stigma associated with carrying gene mutations. Others fear genetic discrimination from employers such as not being hired, losing a job, or being denied promotions. Some people fear being denied services from health insurers, while others fear being denied educational opportunities. However, the Genetic Information Nondiscrimination Act of 2008 protects Americans from discrimination due to differences in their DNA.

Concerns about privacy and confidentiality in regard to genetic testing raise questions that have yet to be answered. For example, who owns an individual's genetic information and who has access to that information? Should courts and schools have access to that information? Genetic testing also raises philosophical issues. Do genes determine behavior? If so, then are people responsible for their behavior?

Genetic Engineering

Genetic engineering is putting DNA from one species into another species. DNA from a species with desirable traits is spliced into the chromosomes in cells of other species. Through mitosis, those transgenic cells produce other similar cells, which are cultured to produce new organisms. Food produced by using these transgenic organisms is called GM (genetically modified) food. There is controversy over the safety of GM foods.

Genetic engineering is much faster than the older process—artificial selection—used to make better agricultural plants and animals. In agriculture, desirable traits include better resistance to pests and disease, quicker growth, and development of more of the edible parts. Genetic engineering may also produce plants that need less investment of water or fertilizer, are more resistant to drought and poor soil conditions, and spoil less when stored or transported.

Scientific Inquiry and Reasoning

Scientific Inquiry

The concept of **scientific inquiry** refers to the idea of how one thinks and asks questions in a logical way to gain trustworthy information. The underlying motivation of science is to try to understand the natural world. Much of human thought is based on assumptions about how things work that may or may not be true. The goal of scientific inquiry is to test those assumptions to gain a greater understanding of the world with good questions and objective tests, and then re-use what was learned to ask better questions. The more we understand about the natural world, the better the questions we can ask, and that is the general idea behind scientific inquiry. The applied practice of scientific inquiry is to ask questions in a systematic method, called the scientific method.

Scientific Knowledge

Scientific knowledge refers to any topic that is studied **empirically**, meaning that it is based on observation of a **phenomenon** in an objective way. The body of **scientific knowledge** is often broken down into several domains including biology, ecology, Earth science, space science, physics, and chemistry. These each have further subdomains and are overlapping in many ways. For instance, ecology is the study of ecosystems, which are made up of biological factors and geological factors, so it contains elements of both biology and Earth science. Each of these domains is subject to the concepts of scientific inquiry, such as the scientific method, scientific facts, hypotheses, and scientific laws.

Important Terminology

- A **phenomenon** is an event or effect that is observed.
- A **scientific fact** is considered an objective and verifiable observation. Usually, a fact can be repeated or demonstrated to others.
- A **scientific theory** is a proposition explaining why or how something happens and is built on scientific facts and laws. Scientific theories can be tested, but are not fully proven. If new evidence is found that disproves the theory, it is no longer considered true.
- A **hypothesis** is an educated guess that is not yet proven. It is used to predict the outcome of an experiment in an attempt to solve a problem or answer a question.
- A **law** is an explanation of events that always leads to the same outcome. It is a fact that an object falls. The law of gravity explains why an object falls. The theory of relativity, although generally accepted, has been neither proven nor disproved.
- A **model** is used to explain something on a smaller scale or in simpler terms to provide an example. It is a representation of an idea that can be used to explain events or applied to new situations to predict outcomes or determine results.

History of Scientific Knowledge

When one examines the history of **scientific knowledge**, it is clear that it is constantly **evolving**. The body of facts, models, theories, and laws grows and changes over time. In other words, one scientific discovery leads to the next. Some advances in science and technology have important and long-lasting effects on science and society. Some discoveries were so alien to the accepted beliefs of the time that not only were they rejected as wrong, but were also considered outright blasphemy. Today, however, many beliefs once considered incorrect have become an ingrained part of scientific knowledge, and have also been the basis of new advances. Examples of advances include: Copernicus's heliocentric view of the universe, Newton's laws of motion and planetary orbits, relativity, geologic time scale, plate tectonics, atomic theory, nuclear physics, biological evolution, germ theory, industrial revolution, molecular biology, information and communication, quantum theory, galactic universe, and medical and health technology.

SCIENTIFIC INQUIRY AND SCIENTIFIC METHOD

Scientists use a number of generally accepted techniques collectively known as the **scientific method**. The scientific method generally involves carrying out the following steps:

- Identifying a problem or posing a question
- Formulating a hypothesis or an educated guess
- Conducting experiments or tests that will provide a basis to solve the problem or answer the question
- Observing the results of the test
- Drawing conclusions

An important part of the scientific method is using acceptable experimental techniques. Objectivity is also important if valid results are to be obtained. Another important part of the scientific method is peer review. It is essential that experiments be performed and data be recorded in such a way that experiments can be reproduced to verify results. Historically, the scientific method has been taught with a more linear approach, but it is important to recognize that the scientific method should be a cyclical or **recursive process**. This means that as hypotheses are tested and more is learned, the questions should continue to change to reflect the changing body of knowledge. One cycle of experimentation is not enough.

Review Video: The Scientific Method
Visit mometrix.com/academy and enter code: 191386

METRIC AND INTERNATIONAL SYSTEM OF UNITS

The **metric system** is the accepted standard of measurement in the scientific community. The **International System of Units (SI)** is a set of measurements (including the metric system) that is almost globally accepted. The United States, Liberia, and Myanmar have not accepted this system. **Standardization** is important because it allows the results of experiments to be compared and reproduced without the need to laboriously convert measurements. The SI is based partially on the **meter-kilogram-second (MKS) system** rather than the **centimeter-gram-second (CGS) system**. The MKS system considers meters, kilograms, and seconds to be the basic units of measurement, while the CGS system considers centimeters, grams, and seconds to be the basic units of measurement. Under the MKS system, the length of an object would be expressed as 1 meter instead of 100 centimeters, which is how it would be described under the CGS system.

Review Video: Metric System Conversions
Visit mometrix.com/academy and enter code: 163709

BASIC UNITS OF MEASUREMENT

Using the **metric system** is generally accepted as the preferred method for taking measurements. Having a **universal standard** allows individuals to interpret measurements more easily, regardless of where they are located. The basic units of measurement are: the **meter**, which measures length; the **liter**, which measures volume; and the **gram**, which measures mass. The metric system starts with a base unit and increases or decreases in units of 10. The prefix and the base unit combined are used to indicate an amount. For example, deka- is 10 times the base unit. A dekameter is 10 meters; a dekaliter is 10 liters; and a dekagram is 10 grams. The prefix hecto- refers to 100 times the base amount; kilo- is 1,000 times the base amount. The prefixes that indicate a fraction of the base unit are deci-, which is $\frac{1}{10}$ of the base unit; centi-, which is $\frac{1}{100}$ of the base unit; and milli-, which is $\frac{1}{1,000}$ of the base unit.

COMMON PREFIXES

The prefixes for multiples are as follows:

Deka	(da)	**10^1** (deka is the American spelling, but deca is also used)
Hecto	(h)	10^2
Kilo	(k)	10^3
Mega	(M)	10^6
Giga	(G)	10^9
Tera	(T)	10^{12}

The prefixes for subdivisions are as follows:

Deci	(d)	**10^{-1}**
Centi	(c)	10^{-2}
Milli	(m)	10^{-3}
Micro	(μ)	10^{-6}
Nano	(n)	10^{-9}
Pico	(p)	10^{-12}

The rule of thumb is that prefixes greater than 10^3 are capitalized when abbreviating. Abbreviations do not need a period after them. A decimeter (dm) is a tenth of a meter, a deciliter (dL) is a tenth of a liter, and a decigram (dg) is a tenth of a gram. Pluralization is understood. For example, when referring to 5 mL of water, no "s" needs to be added to the abbreviation.

BASIC SI UNITS OF MEASUREMENT

SI uses **second(s)** to measure time. Fractions of seconds are usually measured in metric terms using prefixes such as millisecond ($\frac{1}{1,000}$ of a second) or nanosecond ($\frac{1}{1,000,000,000}$ of a second). Increments of time larger than a second are measured in **minutes** and **hours**, which are multiples of 60 and 24. An example of this is a swimmer's time in the 800-meter freestyle being described as 7:32.67, meaning 7 minutes, 32 seconds, and 67 one-hundredths of a second. One second is equal to $\frac{1}{60}$ of a minute, $\frac{1}{3,600}$ of an hour, and $\frac{1}{86,400}$ of a day. Other SI base units are the **ampere** (A) (used to measure electric current), the **kelvin** (K) (used to measure thermodynamic temperature), the **candela** (cd) (used to measure luminous intensity), and the **mole** (mol) (used to measure the amount of a substance at a molecular level). **Meter** (m) is used to measure length and **kilogram** (kg) is used to measure mass.

SIGNIFICANT FIGURES

The mathematical concept of **significant figures** or **significant digits** is often used to determine the accuracy of measurements or the level of confidence one has in a specific measurement. The significant figures of a measurement include all the digits known with certainty plus one estimated or uncertain digit. There are a number of rules for determining which digits are considered "important" or "interesting." They are:

- All non-zero digits are *significant.*
- Zeros between digits are *significant.*
- Leading and trailing zeros are *not significant* unless they appear to the right of the non-zero digits in a decimal.

For example, in 0.01230, the significant digits are 1230, and this number would be said to be accurate to the hundred-thousandths place. The zero indicates that the amount has actually been measured as 0. Other zeros are considered placeholders and are not important. A decimal point may be placed after zeros to indicate their importance (in "100." for example).

Graphs and Charts

Graphs and charts are effective ways to present scientific data such as observations, statistical analyses, and comparisons between dependent variables and independent variables. On a line chart, the **independent variable** (the one that is being manipulated for the experiment) is represented on the horizontal axis (the x-axis). Any **dependent variables** (the ones that may change as the independent variable changes) are represented on the y-axis. An **XY** or **scatter plot** is often used to plot many points. A "best fit" line is drawn, which allows outliers to be identified more easily. Charts and their axes should have titles. The x and y interval units should be evenly spaced and labeled. Other types of charts are **bar charts** and **histograms**, which can be used to compare differences between the data collected for two variables. A **pie chart** can graphically show the relation of parts to a whole.

Review Video: Identifying Variables
Visit mometrix.com/academy and enter code: 627181

Review Video: Data Interpretation of Graphs
Visit mometrix.com/academy and enter code: 200439

Data Presentation

Data collected during a science lab can be organized and **presented** in any number of ways. While **straight narrative** is a suitable method for presenting some lab results, it is not a suitable way to present numbers and quantitative measurements. These types of observations can often be better presented with **tables** and **graphs**. Data that is presented in tables and organized in rows and columns may also be used to make graphs quite easily. Other methods of presenting data include illustrations, photographs, video, and even audio formats. In a **formal report**, tables and figures are labeled and referred to by their labels. For example, a picture of a bubbly solution might be labeled Figure 1, Bubbly Solution. It would be referred to in the text in the following way: "The reaction created bubbles 10 mm in size, as shown in Figure 1, Bubbly Solution." Graphs are also labeled as figures. Tables are labeled in a different way. Examples include: Table 1, Results of Statistical Analysis, or Table 2, Data from Lab 2.

Statistical Precision and Errors

Errors that occur during an experiment can be classified into two categories: random errors and systematic errors. **Random errors** can result in collected data that is wildly different from the rest of the data, or they may result in data that is indistinguishable from the rest. Random errors are not consistent across the data set. In large data sets, random errors may contribute to the variability of data, but they will not affect the average. Random errors are sometimes referred to as noise. They may be caused by a student's inability to take the same measurement in exactly the same way or by outside factors that are not considered variables, but influence the data. A **systematic error** will show up consistently across a sample or data set, and may be the result of a flaw in the experimental design. This type of error affects the average, and is also known as bias.

SCIENTIFIC NOTATION

Scientific notation is used because values in science can be very large or very small, which makes them unwieldy. A number in **decimal notation** is 93,000,000. In **scientific notation**, it is 9.3×10^7. The first number, 9.3, is the **coefficient**. It is always greater than or equal to 1 and less than 10. This number is followed by a multiplication sign. The base is always 10 in scientific notation. If the number is greater than ten, the exponent is positive. If the number is between zero and one, the exponent is negative. The first digit of the number is followed by a decimal point and then the rest of the number. In this case, the number is 9.3, and the decimal point was moved seven places to the right from the end of the number to get 93,000,000. The number of places moved, seven, is the exponent.

STATISTICAL TERMINOLOGY

- **Mean**—The average, found by taking the sum of a set of numbers and dividing by the number of numbers in the set.
- **Median**—The middle number in a set of numbers sorted from least to greatest. If the set has an even number of entries, the median is the average of the two in the middle.
- **Mode**—The value that appears most frequently in a data set. There may be more than one mode. If no value appears more than once, there is no mode.
- **Range**—The difference between the highest and lowest numbers in a data set.
- **Standard deviation**—Measures the dispersion of a data set, or how far from the mean a single data point is likely to be.
- **Regression analysis**—A method of analyzing sets of data and sets of variables. It involves studying how the typical value of the dependent variable changes when any one of the independent variables is varied and the other independent variables remain fixed.

Review Video: Mean, Median, and Mode
Visit mometrix.com/academy and enter code: 286207

Review Video: Standard Deviation
Visit mometrix.com/academy and enter code: 419469

Chapter Quiz

Ready to see how well you retained what you just read? Scan the QR code to go directly to the chapter quiz interface for this study guide. If you're using a computer, simply visit the online resources page at **mometrix.com/resources719/mttcbiology** and click the Chapter Quizzes link.

Cellular Function

Chemical Structures and Properties of Biologically Important Molecules

Chemical Bonding Properties of Carbon

Carbon is considered to be the central atom of organic compounds. Carbon atoms each have four valence electrons and require four more electrons to have a stable outer shell. Due to the repulsion between the valence electrons, the bond sites are all equidistant from each other. This enables carbon to form longs chains and rings. Carbon atoms can form four single covalent bonds with other atoms. For example, methane (CH_4) consists of one carbon atom singly bonded to four separate hydrogen atoms. Carbon atoms can also form double or triple covalent bonds. For example, an oxygen atom can form a double bond with a carbon atom, and a nitrogen atom can form a triple bond with a carbon atom.

Organic and Inorganic Molecules

Organic molecules contain carbon and hydrogen. Because carbon can form four covalent bonds, organic molecules can be very complex structures. Organic molecules can have carbon backbones that form long chains, branched chains, or even rings. Organic compounds tend to be less soluble in water than inorganic compounds. Organic compounds are often classified as either natural (found in plants and animals) or as synthetic (made via laboratory or industrial processes). **Inorganic molecules** generally do not contain carbon-carbon or carbon-hydrogen bonds, but there are some exceptions. Inorganic compounds include salts and metals. Specific examples of inorganic molecules include sodium chloride, oxygen, and carbon dioxide.

Covalent Bonds

Chemical bonds are the attractive forces that bind atoms together to form molecules. Chemical bonds include covalent bonds, ionic bonds, and metallic bonds. **Covalent bonds** are formed from the sharing of electron pairs between two atoms in a molecule. In organic molecules, carbon atoms form single, double, or triple covalent bonds. Organic compounds including proteins, carbohydrates, lipids, and nucleic acids are molecular compounds formed by covalent bonds.

Review Video: Covalent Bonds
Visit mometrix.com/academy and enter code: 482899

Hydrogen Bonds

Intermolecular forces are the attractive forces between molecules. Intermolecular forces include hydrogen bonds, London or dispersion forces, and dipole-dipole forces. **Hydrogen bonds** are the attractive forces between molecules containing hydrogen atoms covalently bonded to oxygen, fluorine, or nitrogen. Hydrogen bonds bind the two strands of a DNA molecule to each other. Two hydrogen bonds join each adenosine and thymine, and three hydrogen bonds join each cytosine and guanine.

ATP

Adenosine triphosphate (ATP) is the energy source for most cellular functions. Each ATP molecule is a nucleotide consisting of a central ribose sugar flanked by a purine base and a chain of three phosphate groups. The purine base is adenine, and when adenine is joined to ribose, an adenosine is formed, explaining the name adenosine triphosphate. If one phosphate is removed from the end of the molecule, adenosine diphosphate (ADP) is formed.

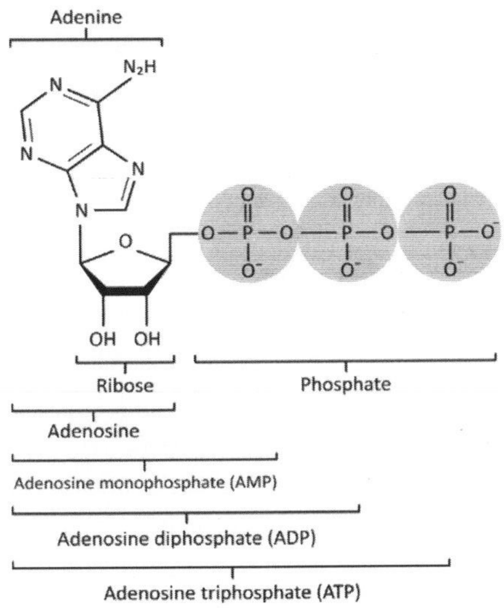

Properties of Water

Water exhibits numerous properties. Water has a high surface tension due to the cohesion between water molecules from the hydrogen bonds between the molecules. The capillary action of water is also due to this cohesion, and the adhesion of water is due to its polarity. Water is an excellent solvent due to its polarity and is considered the universal solvent. Water exists naturally as a solid, liquid, and gas. The density of water decreases as ice freezes and forms crystals in the solid phase. Water is most dense at 4 °C. Water can act as an acid or base in chemical reactions. Pure water is an insulator because it has virtually no ions. Water has a high specific heat capacity due to its low molecular mass and bent molecular shape.

Review Video: Properties of Water
Visit mometrix.com/academy and enter code: 279526

Biological Macromolecules

Macromolecules are large molecules made up of smaller organic molecules. Four classes of macromolecules include carbohydrates, nucleic acids, proteins, and lipids. Carbohydrates, proteins, and nucleic acids are polymers that are formed when the monomers are joined together in a dehydration process. In this dehydration process, the monomers are joined by a covalent bond and a water molecule is released. The monomers in carbohydrates are simple sugars such as glucose, while polysaccharides are polymers of carbohydrates. The monomers in proteins are amino acids. The amino acids form polypeptide chains, which are folded into proteins. The monomers in nucleic acids are nucleotides. Lipids are not actually considered to be polymers. Lipids typically are classified as fats, phospholipids, or steroids.

Review Video: Macromolecules
Visit mometrix.com/academy and enter code: 220156

Biological Processes Dependent on Chemical Principles

Biochemical Pathways

Autotrophs that use light to produce energy use **photosynthesis** as a biochemical pathway. In eukaryotic autotrophs photosynthesis takes place in chloroplasts. Prokaryotic autotrophs that use inorganic chemical reactions to produce energy use **chemosynthesis** as a biochemical pathway. Heterotrophs require food and use **cellular respiration** to release energy from chemical bonds in the food. All organisms use cellular respiration to release energy from stored food. Cellular respiration can be aerobic or anaerobic. Most eukaryotes use cellular respiration that takes place in the mitochondria.

Photosynthesis

Photosynthesis is a food-making process that occurs in three processes: light-capturing events, light-dependent reactions, and light-independent reactions. In light-capturing events, the thylakoids of the chloroplasts, which contain chlorophyll and accessory pigments, absorb light energy and produce excited electrons. Thylakoids also contain enzymes and electron-transport molecules. Molecules involved in this process are arranged in groups called photosystems. In light-dependent reactions, the excited electrons from the light-capturing events are moved by electron transport in a series of steps in which they are used to split water into hydrogen and oxygen ions. The oxygen is released, and the $NADP^+$ bonds with the hydrogen atoms and forms NADPH. ATP is produced from the excited elections. The light-independent reactions use this ATP, NADPH, and carbon dioxide to produce sugars.

Review Video: Photosynthesis
Visit mometrix.com/academy and enter code: 227035

C_3 and C_4 Photosynthesis

Plants undergo an additional process during photosynthesis that is known as photorespiration. Photorespiration is a wasteful process that uses energy and decreases sugar synthesis. This process occurs when the enzyme rubisco binds to oxygen rather than atmospheric carbon dioxide. There are three different processes that plants use to fix carbon during photosynthesis and these include C_3, C_4, and crassulacean acid metabolism (CAM). Some plants, such as C_4 and CAM plants, can decrease photorespiration and therefore minimize energy lost while C_3 plants, which make up more than 85% of plants, have no special adaptations to stop photorespiration from occuring. C_3 and C_4 plants are named for the type of carbon molecule (three-carbon or four-carbon) that is made during the first step of the reaction. The first step of the C_3 process involves the formation of two three-carbon molecules (3-phosphoglycerate; 3-PGA) from carbon dioxide being fixed by the enzyme. The first step of C_4 photosynthesis is carbon dioxide beign fixed by the enzyme PEP carboxylase, which unlike rubisco does not have the ability to bind to oxygen. This fixation forms a four-carbon molecule (oxaloaceate) and these initial steps occur in the mesophyll cell. Next, oxaloacetate is converted into a malate, a molecule that can enter the bundle sheath cells, and then is broken down to release carbon dioxide. From there, the carbon dioxide is fixed by rubisco as it undergoes the Calvin cycle seen in C_3 photosynthesis. Because C_4 plants undergo an initial step that allows carbon dioxide to be more readily available, with the use of malate, photorespiration is minimized.

Crassulacean Acid Metabolism

Crassulacean acid metabolism (CAM) is a form of photosynthesis adapted to dry environments. While C_4 plants separate the Calvin cycle via space, or by having different cells for different functions and processes, CAM plants separate the processes by time of day. During the night, pores of the plant leaves, called stomata, open to receive carbon dioxide, which combines with PEP carboxylase to form oxaloacetate. Oxaloacetate is eventually converted into malate, which is stored in vacuoles until the next day. During the following day, the stomata are closed and the malate is transported to chloroplasts, where malate is broken down into pyruvate (three-carbon molecule) and carbon dioxide. The carbon dioxide released from malate is used in photosynthesis during the daytime. One advantage of the CAM cycle is that it minimizes loss of water through the stomata during the daytime. A second advantage is that concentrating carbon dioxide in the chloroplasts in this manner increases the efficiency of the enzyme rubisco to fix carbon dioxide and complete the Calvin cycle.

AEROBIC RESPIRATION

Aerobic cellular respiration is a series of enzyme-controlled chemical reactions in which oxygen reacts with glucose to produce carbon dioxide and water, releasing energy in the form of adenosine triphosphate (ATP). Cellular respiration occurs in a series of three processes: glycolysis, the Krebs cycle, and the electron-transport system.

Review Video: Aerobic Respiration
Visit mometrix.com/academy and enter code: 770290

GLYCOLYSIS

Glycolysis is a series of enzyme-controlled chemical reactions that occur in the cell's cytoplasm. Each glucose molecule is split in half to produce two pyruvic acid molecules, four ATP molecules, and two NADH molecules. Because two ATP molecules are used to split the glucose molecule, the net ATP yield for glycolysis is two ATP molecules.

Review Video: Glycolysis
Visit mometrix.com/academy and enter code: 466815

KREBS CYCLE

The **Krebs cycle** is also called the citric acid cycle or the tricarboxylic acid cycle (TCA). It is a **catabolic pathway** in which the bonds of glucose and occasionally fats or lipids are broken down and reformed into ATP. It is a respiration process that uses oxygen and produces carbon dioxide, water, and ATP. Cells require energy from ATP to synthesize proteins from amino acids and replicate DNA. The cycle is acetyl CoA, citric acid, isocitric acid, ketoglutaric acid (products are amino acids and CO_2), succinyl CoA, succinic acid, fumaric acid, malic acid, and oxaloacetic acid. One of the products of the Krebs cycle is NADH, which is then used in the electron chain transport system to manufacture ATP. From glycolysis, pyruvate is oxidized in a step linking to the Krebs cycle. After the Krebs cycle, NADH and succinate are oxidized in the electron transport chain.

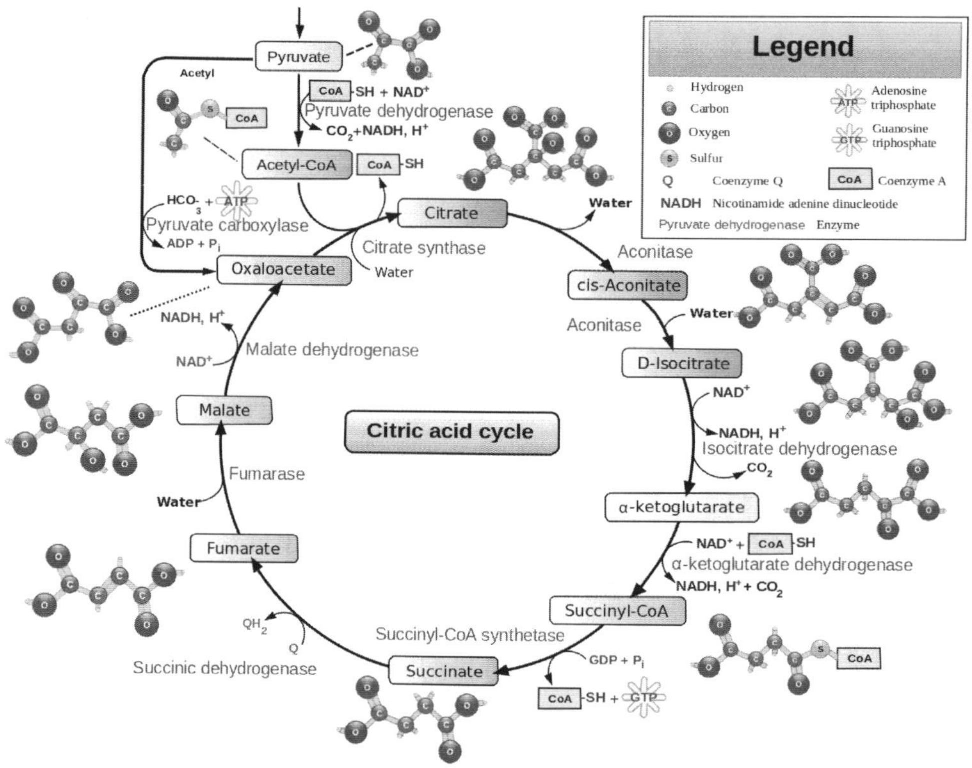

Electron Transport Chain

The **electron transport chain** is part of phosphorylation, whereby electrons are transported from enzyme to enzyme until they reach a final acceptor. The electron transport chain includes a series of oxidizing and reducing molecules involved in the release of energy. In **redox reactions**, electrons are removed from a substrate (oxidative) and H^+ (protons) can also be simultaneously removed. A substrate gains electrons during reduction. For example, when glucose is oxidized, electrons are lost and energy is released. There are enzymes in the membranes of mitochondria. The electrons are carried from one enzyme to another by a co-enzyme. Protons are also released to the other side of the membrane. For example, FAD and $FADH_2$ are used in oxidative phosphorylation. FAD is reduced to $FADH_2$. Electrons are stored there and then sent onward, and the $FADH_2$ becomes FAD again. In aerobic respiration, the final electron acceptor is O_2. In anaerobic respiration, it is something other than O_2.

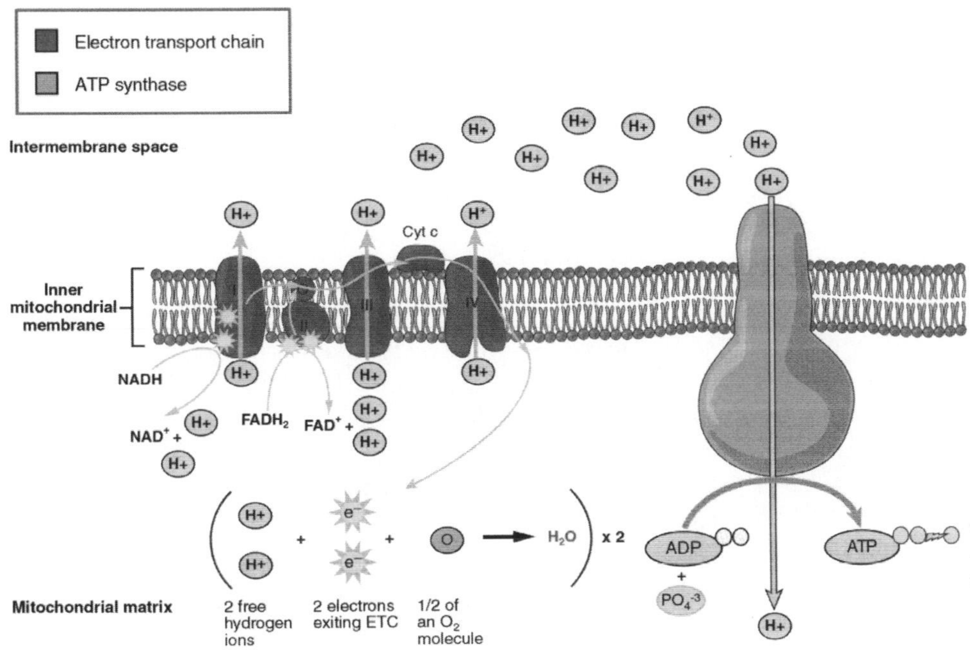

FERMENTATION

Fermentation is an anaerobic reaction in which glucose is only partially broken down. It releases energy through the oxidation of sugars or other types of organic molecules. Oxygen is sometimes involved, but not always. It is different from respiration in that it uses neither the Krebs cycle nor the electron transport chain and the final electron acceptor is an organic molecule. It uses **substrate-level phosphorylation** to form ATP. NAD^+ is reduced to NADH and NADH further reduces pyruvic acid to various end products. Fermentation can lead to excess waste products and is less efficient than aerobic respiration. **Homolactic fermentation** refers to lactic acid fermentation in which the sugars are converted to lactic acid only (there is one end product). In **heterolactic fermentation**, the sugars are converted to a range of products.

EXAMPLES OF FERMENTATION

Lactic acid fermentation is the breakdown of glucose and six-carbon sugars into lactic acid to release energy. It is an anaerobic process, meaning that it does not require oxygen. It can occur in muscle cells and is also performed by streptococcus and lactobacillus bacteria. It can also be used to making yogurt and other food products.

Alcohol fermentation is the breakdown of glucose and six-carbon sugars into ethanol and carbon dioxide to release energy. It is an anaerobic process. It is performed by yeast and used in the production of alcoholic beverages.

CHEMOSYNTHESIS

Chemosynthesis is the food-making process of chemoautotrophs in extreme environments such as deep-sea-vents, or hydrothermal vents. Unlike photosynthesis, chemosynthesis does not require light. In general, chemosynthesis involves the oxidation of inorganic substances to make a sugar, but there are several species that use different pathways or processses. For example, sulfur bacteria live near or in deep-sea vents and oxidize hydrogen sulfide released from those vents to make a sugar. Instead of sunlight, chemosynthesis uses the energy stored in the chemical bonds of chemicals such as hydrogen sulfide to produce food. During chemosynthesis, the electrons that are removed from the inorganic molecules are combined with carbon dioxide and oxygen to produce sugar, sulfur, and water. Some bacteria use metal ions such as iron and magnesium to obtain the needed electrons. For example, methanobacteria such as those found in human intestines combine carbon dioxide and hydrogen gas and release methane as a waste product. Nitrogen bacteria such as nitrogen-fixing bacteria in the nodules of legumes convert atmospheric nitrogen into nitrates.

Structure and Function of Enzymes

Active Site Structure and Substrate Binding

Each enzyme has a complex three-dimensional shape that is specifically designed to fit to a particular reactant, which is called the **substrate**. The enzyme and the substrate join temporarily forming the enzyme-substrate complex. This complex is unstable, and the chemical bonds are likely to be altered to produce a new molecule or molecules. Each enzyme can only combine with specific substrates because of this "lock-and-key" fit. Each enzyme has a designated binding site on the surface that binds to the substrate. Often, the binding site and the active site are at the same location. The enzyme and the substrate are specifically designed for each other, and as the substrate binds to the active site of the enzyme, that active site can bend and fold to form around the substrate. This concept of the active site slightly altering its shape is the **induced fit hypothesis**. The active site of the enzyme with return to its original shape after the products are released.

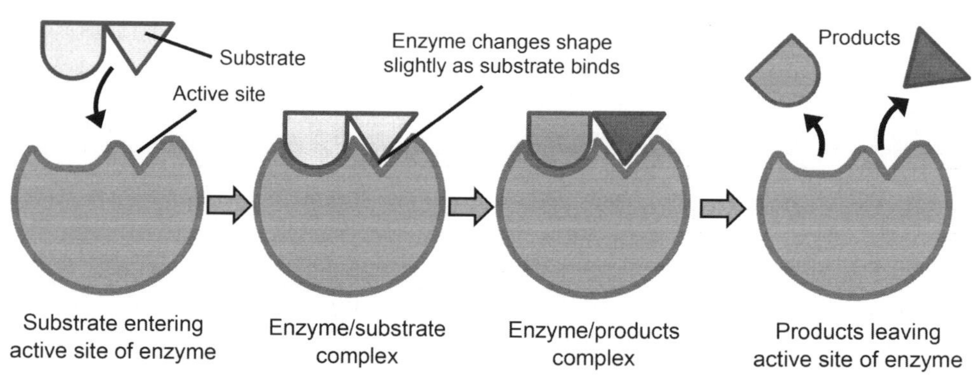

Effects of Temperature, pH, and Inhibitors on Enzyme Activity

The rate of an enzyme-controlled reaction is affected by factors such as temperature, pH, and inhibitors. According to kinetic-molecular theory, increasing the temperature increases the rate of molecular motion. Typically, increasing the temperature increases the rate of these reactions. The optimum temperature is the temperature at which the rate is the fastest and the most product is formed. Increasing the temperature above the optimum temperature actually decreases the reaction rate due to changes on the enzyme's structure that affect substrate binding. The pH also affects enzyme activity due to hydrogen ions binding to the enzyme's surface and changing the enzyme's surface shape. Because enzymes must have a specific shape for their specific substrate, enzymes have a certain pH range in which they can function. Inhibitors are molecules that attach to the enzymes and interfere with substrate binding, thus decreasing or even halting enzyme-controlled reactions.

Regulation of Enzymes by Feedback Inhibition

Enzyme-controlled reactions can be regulated by feedback inhibition, or negative feedback. **Feedback inhibition** can be illustrated by a furnace and thermostat. The inhibitor in this system is the heat. When the furnace runs, the temperature increases. When the temperature reaches a specific level, the thermostat switches the furnace off. When the temperature decreases below a specific level, the thermostat switches the furnace back on, and the cycle begins again. In enzyme-controlled reactions, the end products of a metabolic pathway bind to the enzymes that initiate the metabolic pathway. This causes the reaction rate to decrease. The more product there is, the less product is produced. The less product there is, the more product is produced. This process of feedback inhibition enables a stable range of concentrations that are necessary for homeostasis.

Biochemical Processes Within an Organism

Concentration Gradients

Concentration gradients, also called diffusion gradients, are differences in the concentration (i.e., the number of molecules of solutes in a solution) between two regions. A gradient can also result from an unequal distribution of ions across a cell membrane. Solutes move along a concentration gradient by random motion from the region of high concentration toward the region of low concentration in a process called diffusion. In other words, **diffusion** is the movement of molecules or ions down a concentration gradient. Diffusion is the method by which oxygen, carbon dioxide, and other nonpolar molecules cross a cell membrane. The steepness of the concentration gradient affects the rate of diffusion. **Passive transport** makes use of concentration gradients as well as electric gradients to move substances across the cell membrane, while **active transport** can move a substance against its concentration gradient.

Laws of Thermodynamics and Gibbs Free Energy

The **first law of thermodynamics** states that energy can neither be created nor destroyed. Energy may change forms, but the energy in a closed system is constant. The **second law of thermodynamics** states that systems tend toward a state of lower energy and greater disorder. This disorder is called **entropy**. According to the second law of thermodynamics, entropy is increasing. **Gibbs free energy** is the energy a system that is available or "free" to be released to perform work at a constant temperature. Organisms must be able to use energy to survive, and biological processes such as the chemical reactions involved in metabolism are governed by these laws.

Anabolic and Catabolic Reactions

Anabolism and catabolism are metabolic processes. **Anabolism** is essentially the synthesis of large molecules from monomers, whereas **catabolism** is the decomposition of large molecules into their component monomers. Anabolism uses energy, whereas catabolism produces energy. Anabolism typically builds and repair tissues, and catabolism typically burns stored food to produce energy. Protein synthesis, which is the polymerization of amino acids to form proteins, is an anabolic reaction. Another anabolic process is the mineralization of bones. An example of a catabolic reaction is hydrolysis, which is the decomposition of polymers into monomers that releases a water molecule and energy. Cellular respiration is a catabolic process in which typically glucose combines with oxygen to release energy in the form of adenosine triphosphate (ATP).

Oxidation-Reduction Reactions

Oxidation-reduction reactions, or redox reactions, involve the transfer of electrons from one substance to another. Reduction occurs in the substance that gains the electrons. Oxidation occurs in the substance that loses the electrons. Cellular respiration and photosynthesis are examples of redox reactions. During cellular respiration, glucose molecules are oxidized and oxygen molecules are reduced. Because electrons lose energy when being transferred to oxygen, the electrons are usually first transferred to the coenzyme NAD^+, which is reduced to NADH. The NADH then releases the energy to oxygen. During photosynthesis, water molecules are split and oxidized and carbon dioxide molecules are reduced. When the water molecules are split, electrons are transferred with the hydrogen ions to the carbon dioxide molecules.

Differences Between Prokaryotic and Eukaryotic Cells

Prokaryotes and Eukaryotes

Sizes and Metabolism

Cells of the domains of Bacteria and Archaea are **prokaryotes**. Bacteria cells and Archaea cells are much smaller than cells of eukaryotes. Prokaryote cells are usually only 1 to 2 micrometers in diameter, but eukaryotic cells are usually at least 10 times and possibly 100 times larger than prokaryotic cells. Eukaryotic cells are usually 10 to 100 micrometers in diameter. Most prokaryotes are unicellular organisms, although some prokaryotes live in colonies. Because of their large surface-area-to-volume ratios, prokaryotes have a very high metabolic rate. **Eukaryotic cells** are much larger than prokaryotic cells. Due to their larger sizes, they have a much smaller surface-area-to-volume ratio and consequently have much lower metabolic rates.

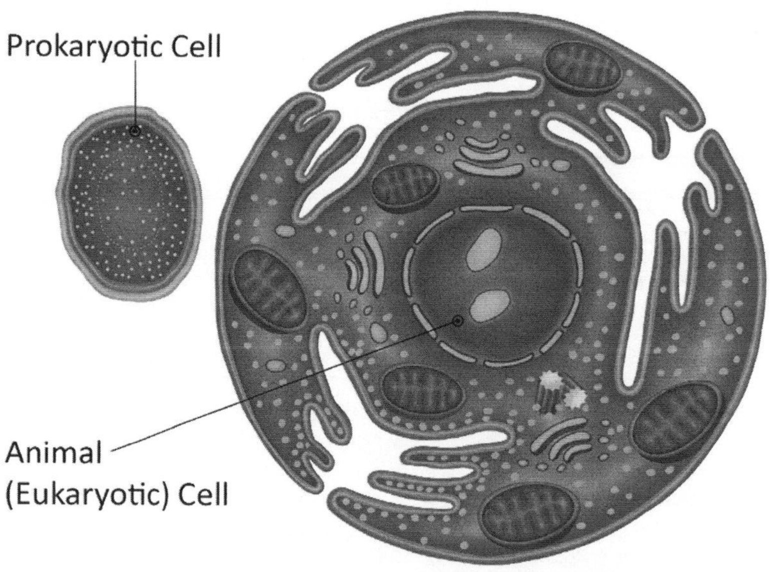

Review Video: Eukaryotic and Prokaryotic Cells
Visit mometrix.com/academy and enter code: 231438

Review Video: Cell Structure
Visit mometrix.com/academy and enter code: 591293

Membrane-Bound Organelles

Prokaryotic cells are much simpler than eukaryotic cells. Prokaryote cells do not have a nucleus due to their small size and their DNA is located in the center of the cell in a region referred to as a **nucleoid**. Eukaryote cells have a **nucleus** bound by a double membrane. Eukaryotic cells typically have hundreds or thousands of additional **membrane-bound organelles** that are independent of the cell membrane. Prokaryotic cells do not have any membrane-bound organelles that are independent of the cell membrane. Once again, this is probably due to the much larger size of the eukaryotic cells. The organelles of eukaryotes give them much higher levels of intracellular division than is possible in prokaryotic cells.

CELL WALLS

Not all cells have cell walls, but most prokaryotes have cell walls. The cell walls of organisms from the domain Bacteria differ from the cell walls of the organisms from the domain Archaea. Some eukaryotes, such as some fungi, some algae, and plants, have cell walls that differ from the cell walls of the Bacteria and Archaea domains. The main difference between the cell walls of different domains or kingdoms is the composition of the cell walls. For example, most bacteria have cell walls outside of the plasma membrane that contains the molecule peptidoglycan. **Peptidoglycan** is a large polymer of amino acids and sugars. The peptidoglycan helps maintain the strength of the cell wall. Some of the Archaea cells have cell walls containing the molecule pseudopeptidoglycan, which differs in chemical structure from the peptidoglycan but basically provides the same strength to the cell wall. Some fungi cell walls contain **chitin**. The cell walls of diatoms, a type of yellow algae, contain silica. Plant cell walls contain cellulose, and woody plants are further strengthened by lignin. Some algae also contain lignin. Animal cells do not have cell walls.

CHROMOSOME STRUCTURE

Prokaryote cells have DNA arranged in a **circular structure** that should not be referred to as a chromosome. Due to the small size of a prokaryote cell, the DNA material is simply located near the center of the cell in a region called the nucleoid. A prokaryotic cell may also contain tiny rings of DNA called plasmids. Prokaryote cells lack histone proteins, and therefore the DNA is not actually packaged into chromosomes. Prokaryotes reproduce by binary fission, while eukaryotes reproduce by mitosis with the help of **linear chromosomes** and histone proteins. During mitosis, the chromatin is tightly wound on the histone proteins and packaged as a chromosome. The DNA in a eukaryotic cell is located in the membrane-bound nucleus.

Review Video: Chromosomes
Visit mometrix.com/academy and enter code: 132083

Structure and Function of Cells and Organelles

CELLS AND ORGANELLES OF PLANT CELLS AND ANIMAL CELLS

Plant cells and animal cells both have a nucleus, cytoplasm, cell membrane, ribosomes, mitochondria, endoplasmic reticulum, Golgi apparatus, and vacuoles. Plant cells have only one or two extremely large vacuoles. Animal cells typically have several small vacuoles. Plant cells have chloroplasts for photosynthesis and use this process to produce their own food, distinguishing plants as **autotrophs**. Animal cells do not have chloroplasts and therefore cannot use photosynthesis to produce their own food. Instead animal cells rely on other sources for food, which classifies them as **heterotrophs**. Animal cells have centrioles, which are used to help organize microtubules and in in cell division, but only some plant cells have centrioles. Additionally, plant cells have a rectangular and more rigid shape due to the cell wall, while animal cells have more of a circular shape because they lack a cell wall.

Review Video: Difference Between Plant and Animal Cells
Visit mometrix.com/academy and enter code: 115568

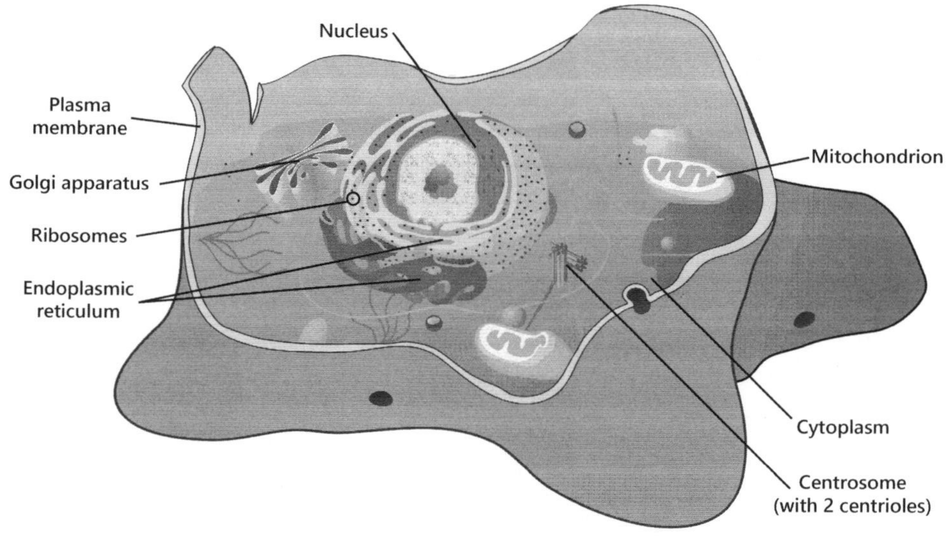

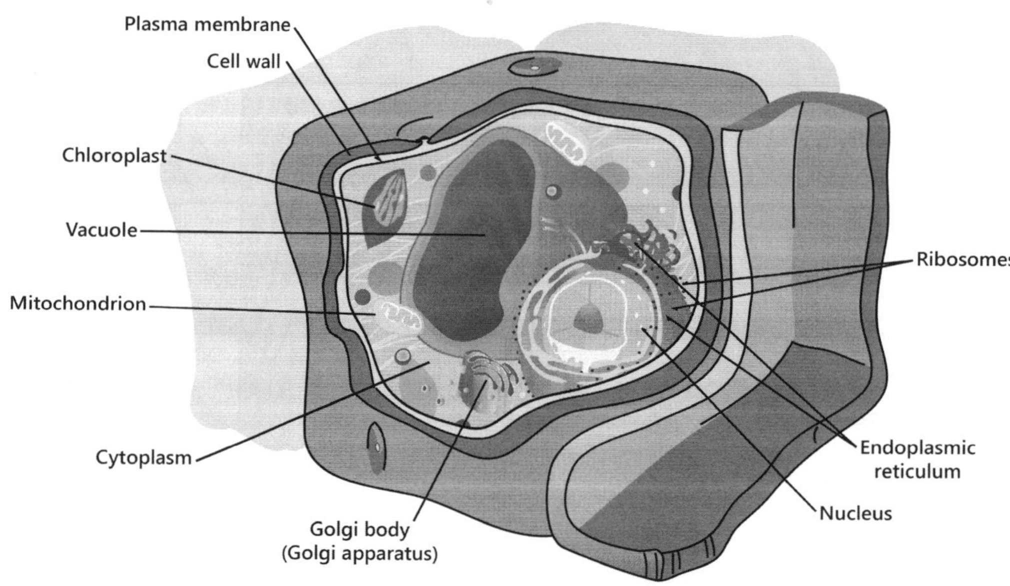

CELL MEMBRANES

The **cell membrane**, also referred to as the plasma membrane, is a thin semipermeable membrane of lipids and proteins. The cell membrane isolates the cell from its external environment while still enabling the cell to communicate with that outside environment. It consists of a phospholipid bilayer, or double layer, with the hydrophilic ("water-loving") ends of the outer layer facing the external environment, the inner layer facing the inside of the cell, and the hydrophobic ("water-fearing") ends facing each other. Cholesterol in the cell membrane adds stiffness and flexibility. Glycolipids help the cell to recognize other cells of the organisms. The proteins in the cell membrane help give the cells shape. Special proteins help the cell communicate with its external environment, while other proteins transport molecules across the cell membrane.

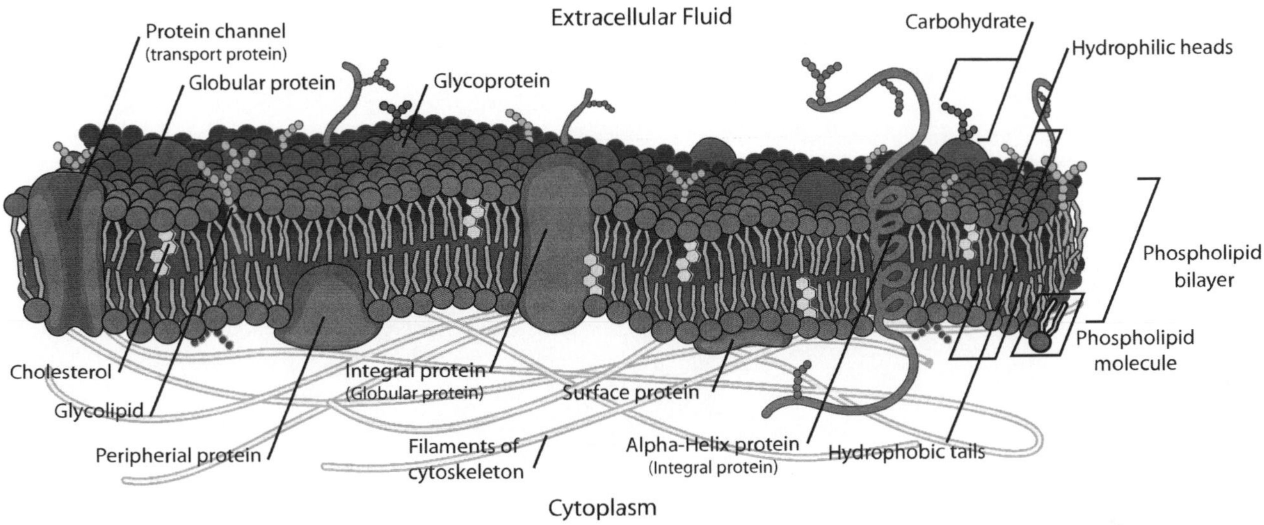

Review Video: Function of the Plasma Membrane
Visit mometrix.com/academy and enter code: 943095

NUCLEUS

Typically, a eukaryote has a single nucleus that takes up approximately 10% of the volume of the cell. Components of the nucleus include the nuclear envelope, nucleoplasm, chromatin, and nucleolus. The **nuclear envelope** is a double-layered membrane with the outer layer connected to the endoplasmic reticulum. The nucleus can communicate with the rest of the cell through several nuclear pores. The chromatin consists of deoxyribonucleic acid (DNA) and histones that are packaged into chromosomes during mitosis. The **nucleolus**, which is the dense central portion of the nucleus, produced and assembles ribosomes with the help of ribosomal RNA and proteins.

Functions of the nucleus include the storage of genetic material, production of ribosomes, and transcription of ribonucleic acid (RNA).

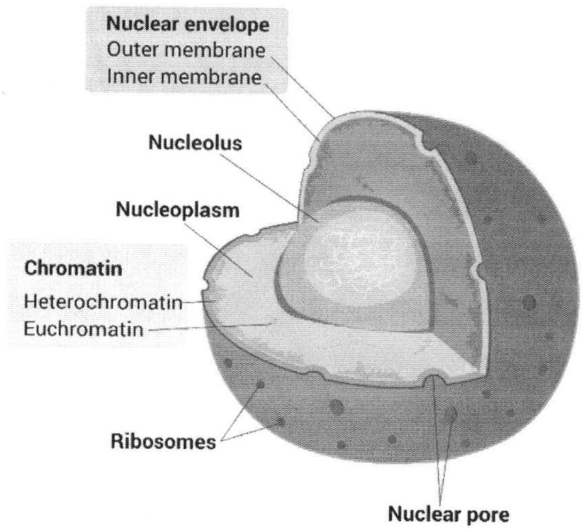

Review Video: Nucleic Acids
Visit mometrix.com/academy and enter code: 503931

Chloroplasts

Chloroplasts are large organelles that are enclosed in a double membrane. Just as cells contain a fluid called cytoplasm, chloroplasts contain a fluid called the **stroma**. Within the stroma, there are discs called **thylakoids**, which are arranged in stacks called **grana** (singular: granum). The thylakoids have chlorophyll molecules on their surfaces. **Stromal lamellae** separate the thylakoid stacks. Chloroplasts perform photosynthesis and make food (in the form of sugars) for the plant. The light reaction stage of photosynthesis occurs in the grana, and the dark reaction stage of photosynthesis occurs in the stroma. Sugars are formed in the stroma. Chloroplasts have their own DNA and can reproduce by fission independently.

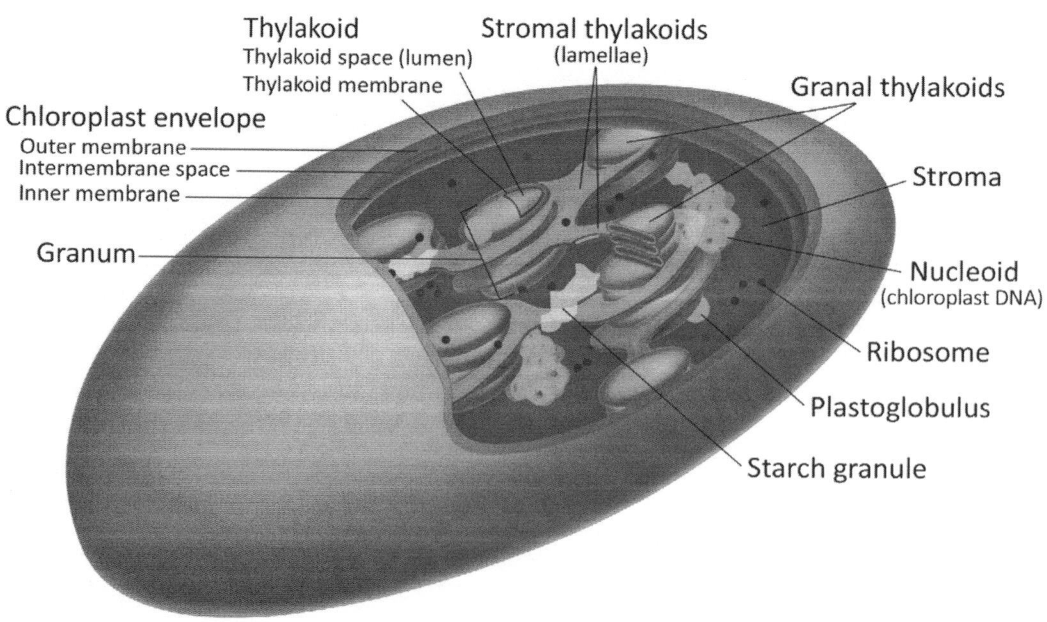

PLASTIDS

Plastids are major organelles found in plants and algae that are used to synthesize and store food. Because plastids can differentiate, there are many forms of plastids. Specialized plastids can store pigments, starches, fats, or proteins. Two examples of plastids are amyloplasts and chloroplasts. **Amyloplasts** are the plastids that store the starch formed from long chains of glucose produced during photosynthesis. Amyloplasts synthesize and store the starch granules through the polymerization of glucose. When needed, amyloplasts also convert these starch granules back into sugar. Fruits and potato tubers have large numbers of amyloplasts. **Chloroplasts** can synthesize and store starch. Interestingly, amyloplasts can redifferentiate and transform into chloroplasts.

MITOCHONDRIA

Mitochondria break down sugar molecules and produce energy in the form of molecules of adenosine triphosphate (ATP). Both plant and animal cells contain mitochondria. Mitochondria are enclosed in a bilayer semi-membrane of phospholipids and proteins. The intermembrane space is the space between the two layers. The outer membrane has proteins called porins, which allow small molecules through. The inner membrane contains proteins that aid in the synthesis of ATP. The matrix consists of enzymes that help synthesize ATP. Mitochondria have their own DNA and can reproduce by fission independently. Mitochondria also help to maintain calcium concentrations, form blood components and hormones, and are involved in activating cell death pathways.

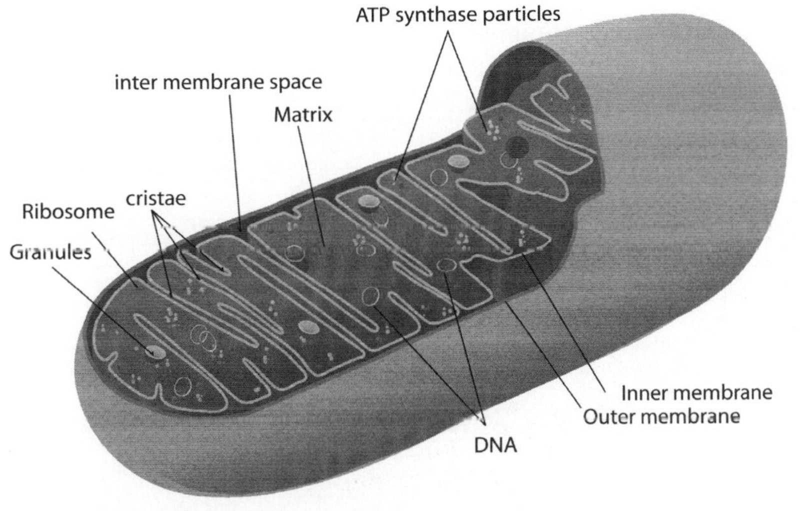

Review Video: Mitochondria
Visit mometrix.com/academy and enter code: 444287

RIBOSOMES

A **ribosome** consists of RNA and proteins. The RNA component of the ribosome is known as ribosomal RNA (rRNA). Ribosomes consist of two subunits, a large subunit and a small subunit. Few ribosomes are free in the cell. Most of the ribosomes in the cell are embedded in the rough endoplasmic reticulum located near the nucleus. Ribosomes are protein factories and translate the code of DNA into proteins by assembling long chains of amino acids. **Messenger RNA** (mRNA) is used by the ribosome to generate a specific protein sequence, while **transfer RNA** (tRNA) collects the needed amino acids and delivers them to the ribosome.

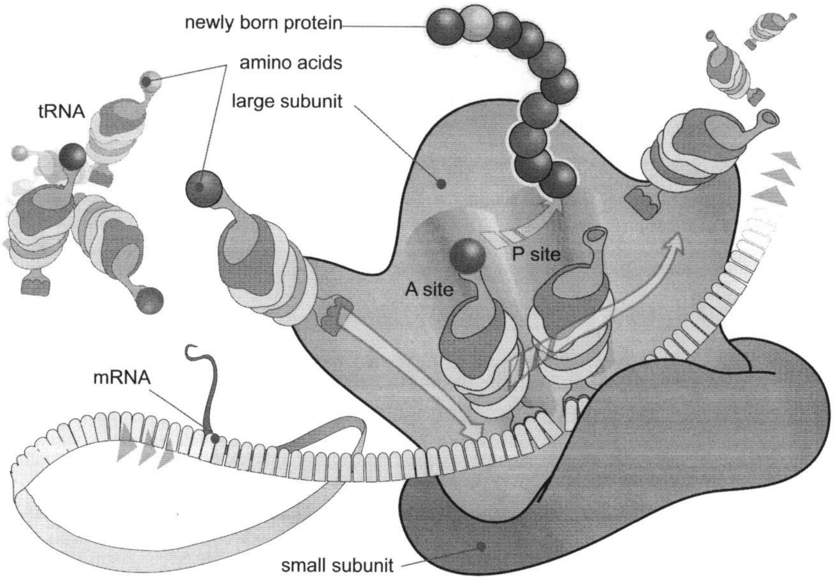

Golgi Apparatus

The **Golgi apparatus**, also called the Golgi body or Golgi complex, is a stack of flattened membranes called **cisternae** that package, ship, and distribute macromolecules such as carbohydrates, proteins, and lipids in shipping containers called **vesicles**. It also helps modify proteins and lipids before they are shipped. Most Golgi apparatuses have six to eight cisternae. Each Golgi apparatus has four regions: the cis region, the endo region, the medial region, and the trans region. Transfer vesicles from the rough endoplasmic reticulum (ER) enter at the cis region, and secretory vesicles leave the Golgi apparatus from the trans region.

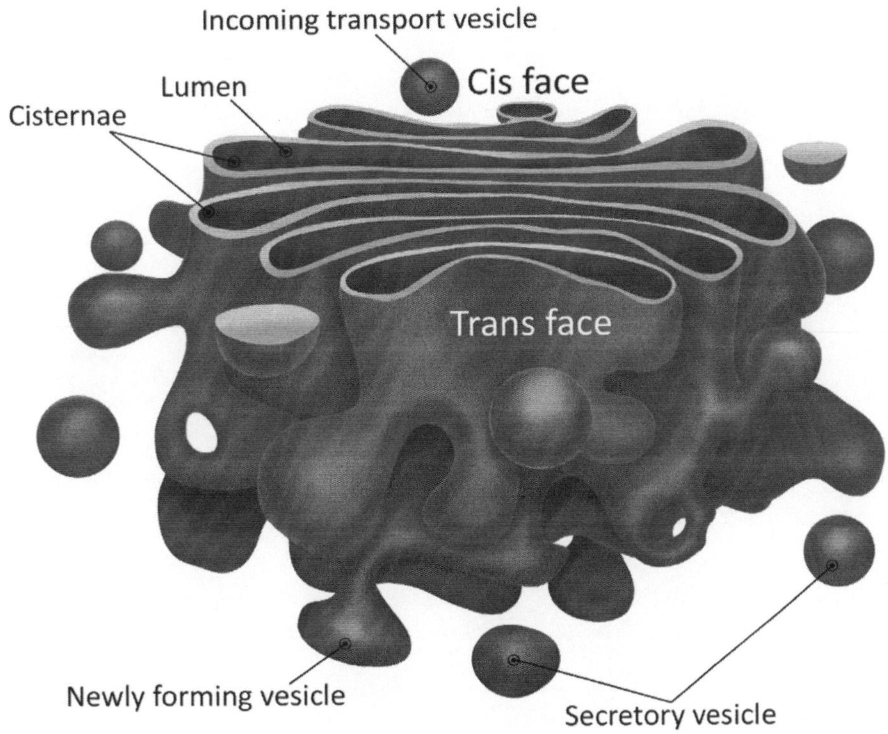

CYTOSKELETON

The **cytoskeleton** is a scaffolding system located in the cytoplasm. The cytoskeleton consists of elongated organelles made of proteins called microtubules, microfilaments, and intermediate filaments. These organelles provide shape, support, and the ability to move. These structures also assist in moving the chromosomes during mitosis. Microtubules and microfilaments help transport materials throughout the cell and are the major components in cilia and flagella.

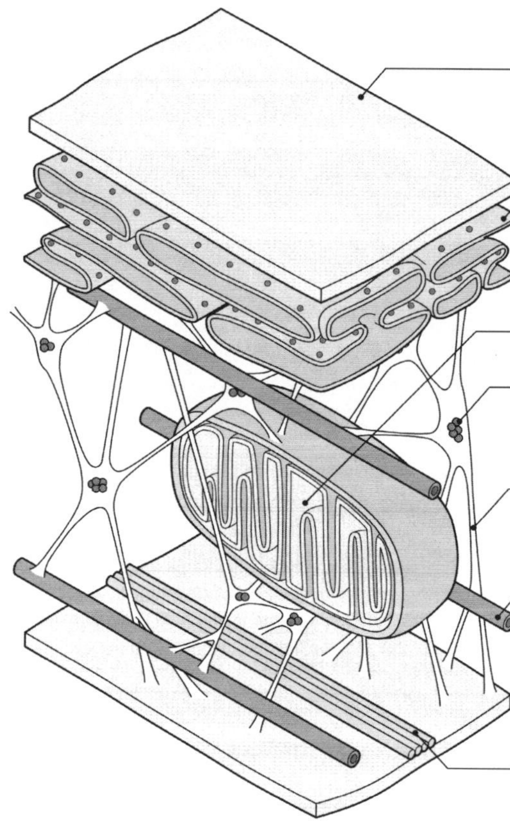

Cellular Homeostasis

Selective Permeability

The cell membrane, or plasma membrane, has selective permeability with regard to size, charge, and solubility. With regard to molecule size, the cell membrane allows only small molecules to diffuse through it. Oxygen and water molecules are small and typically can pass through the cell membrane. The charge of the ions on the cell's surface also either attracts or repels ions. Ions with like charges are repelled, and ions with opposite charges are attracted to the cell's surface. Molecules that are soluble in phospholipids can usually pass through the cell membrane. Many molecules are not able to diffuse the cell membrane, but, if needed, those molecules must be moved through by active transport and vesicles.

Active and Passive Transport

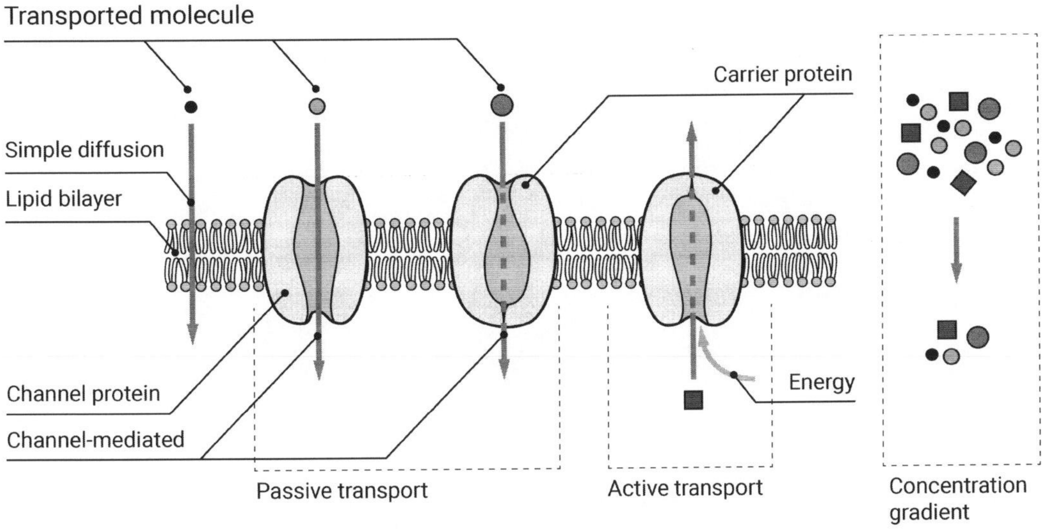

Cells can move materials in and out through the cell membrane by active and passive transport. In **passive transport**, the molecules diffuse across the cell membrane by osmosis. These molecules are moving from a region where they have a high concentration to a region where the concentration is lower. In passive transport, the molecules move across the cell membrane without the cell expending any extra energy. Diffusion and facilitated diffusion are considered passive transport. **Facilitated diffusion** occurs when molecules are helped across the membrane by certain proteins called channel proteins or carrier proteins. Because facilitated diffusion is still from a region of high to low concentration, it does not require additional energy and is therefore a type of passive transport. In active transport, molecules are forcibly moved from regions where the concentration is low into a region where the concentration is higher. Carrier proteins must carry these ions and molecules, and this requires an expenditure of energy. Some ions are actively pumped across the cell membrane by proteins. Sodium ions are pumped out of the cell and potassium ions are pumped into the cell in this manner.

Review Video: Passive Transport: Diffusion and Osmosis
Visit mometrix.com/academy and enter code: 642038

Water Movement to Maintain Internal Environments of Cells

Cells must maintain their water balance for **homeostasis**. If cells have too little water, wastes and poisons can build up in the cells. If cells have too much water, the chemicals in the cells may be diluted. Water is moved in and out of cells by **osmosis**. Because osmosis is a type of passive transport, the cell cannot actually control this diffusion of water in and out of the cells. The amount of water that diffuses into or out of cells depends on the cell's environment. When the cell's concentration of water and dissolved solids equals that of its environment, the cells are **isotonic** with their environment. Cells with a lower concentration of water than their environment tend to rapidly gain water by osmosis. These cells are **hypotonic** with their environment. Cells with a higher concentration of water than their environment tend to rapidly lose water by osmosis. The cells are **hypertonic** with their environment. If cells are hypotonic or hypertonic, they must expend energy to maintain the proper water balance.

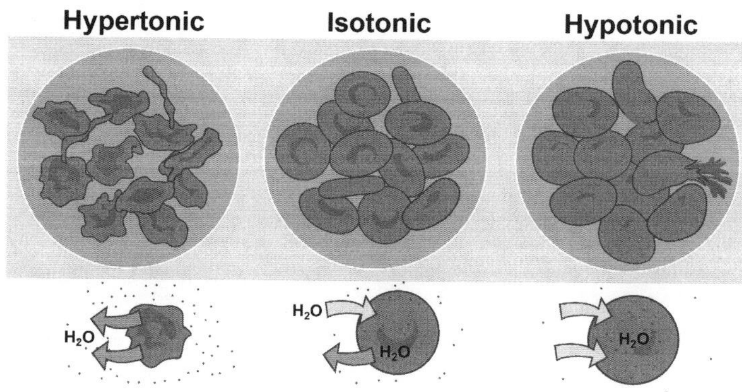

Use of Cell Surface Proteins and Cell Communication

In order to maintain a stable internal environment, cells need to send and receive signals from the external environment. Cells have specialized surface proteins called **receptors** embedded in the cell membrane that allow them to communicate with this external environment. Surface proteins are exposed to the external side of the membrane. Some surface proteins allow entry to specific materials, and others trigger chemical signals inside the cell. Because these proteins have attached carbohydrates, they are called **glycoproteins**. Due to the cholesterol in the cell membrane, fat-soluble materials can pass straight through the membrane, but water-soluble materials cannot diffuse. Sodium, calcium, and potassium must use these specialized surface proteins to gain entry to the cell. These surface proteins bind to specific chemicals in the materials seeking access to the cell. This triggers a chemical signal to the interior of the cell.

Exocytosis and Endocytosis

Larger particles or groups of particles can be transported whole across the cell membrane by being packaged in a piece of cell membrane. **Endocytosis** is the process by which large particles are moved into the cell, and **exocytosis** is the process by which large molecules are moved out of the cell. The three main types of endocytosis are phagocytosis, pinocytosis, and receptor-mediated endocytosis. **Phagocytosis**, or "cell eating," is the process by which large solid particles are engulfed. **Pinocytosis**, or "cell drinking," is the process by which liquids and dissolved substances are surrounded by small sacs of cell membrane. **Receptor-mediated endocytosis** is the process by which molecules enter cells through receptor molecules on the cell membrane.

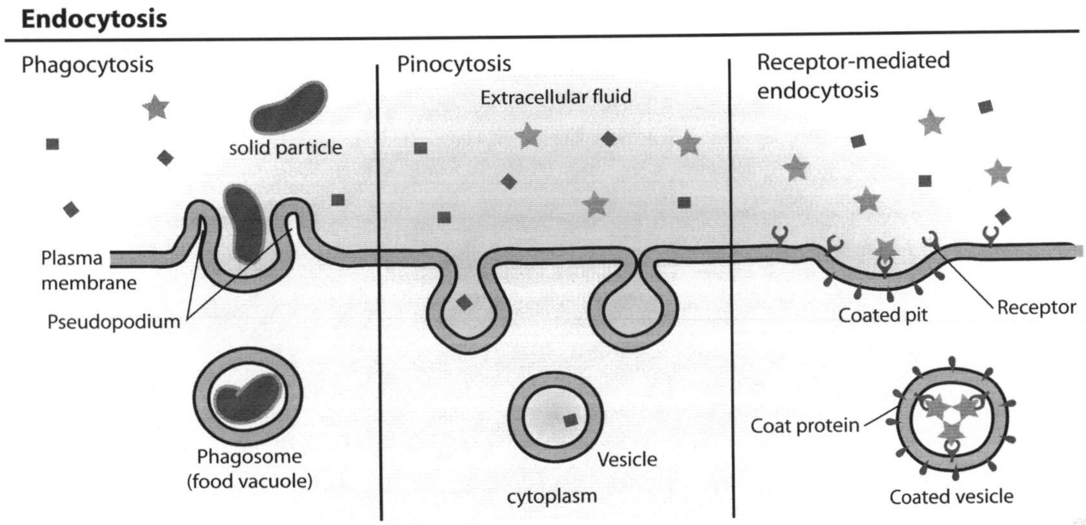

Hormone Action and Feedback

In order to maintain homeostasis, the endocrine system often employs negative-feedback inhibition or positive-feedback regulation. In **negative-feedback inhibition**, an increase in an output of a reaction to a stimulus triggers a decrease in the stimulus, which in turn causes a decrease in the original output. In **positive-feedback regulation**, an increase in an output leads to further increase of the stimulus. An example of negative-feedback inhibition is the release of the hormones insulin and glucagon to maintain the level of glucose in the blood.

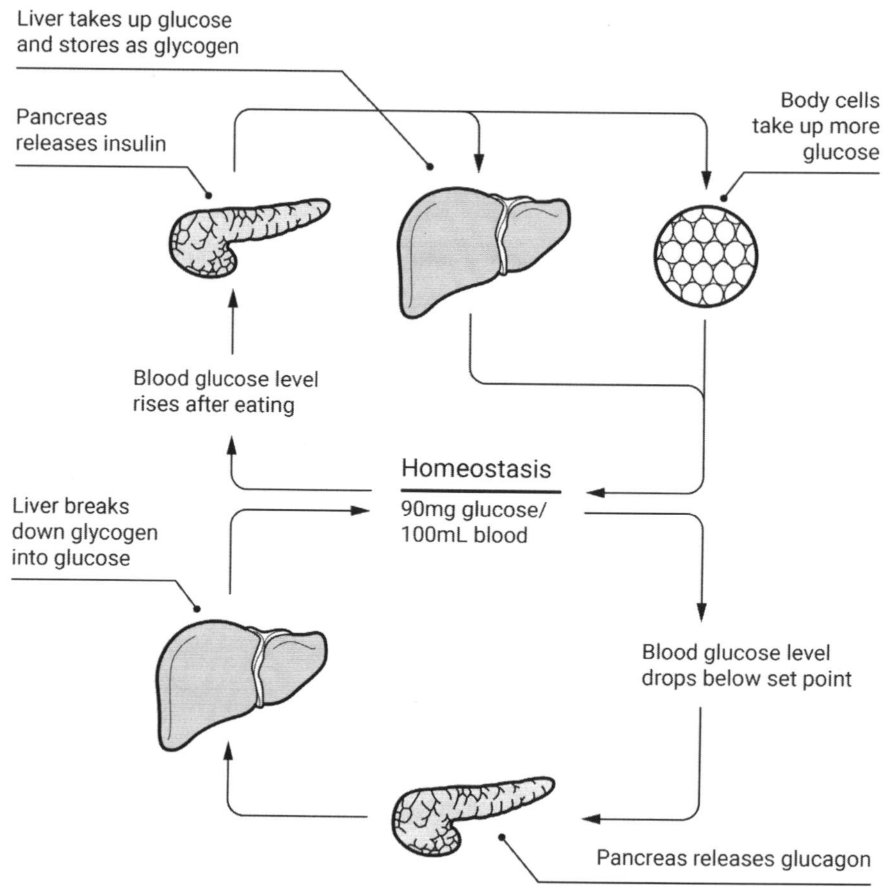

Cell Cycle and Cellular Division

Cell Cycle Stages

The cell cycle consists of three stages: interphase, mitosis, and cytokinesis. **Interphase** is the longest stage of the cell cycle and involves the cell growing and making a copy of its DNA. Cells typically spend more than 90% of the cell cycle in interphase. Interphase includes two growth phases called G_1 and G_2. The order of interphase is the first growth cycle, **GAP 1** (G_1 phase), followed by the **synthesis phase** (S), and ending with the second growth phase, **GAP 2** (G_2 phase). During the G_1 phase of interphase, the cell increases the number of organelles by forming diploid cells. During the S phase of interphase, the DNA is replicated, and the chromosomes are doubled.

During the G_2 phase of interphase, the cell synthesizes needed proteins and organelles, continues to increase in size, and prepares for mitosis. Once the G_2 phase ends, mitosis can begin.

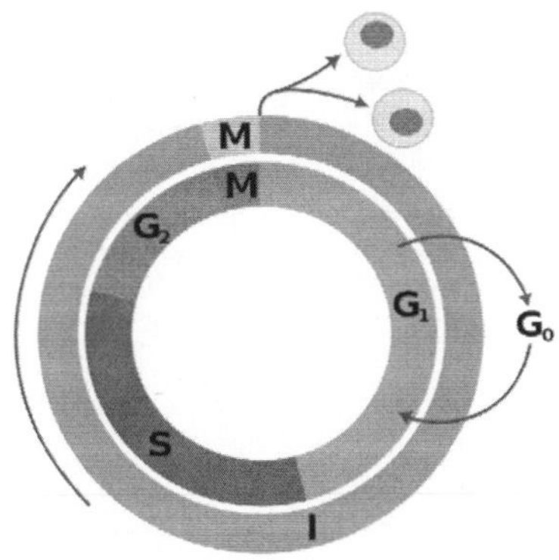

MITOSIS

Mitosis is the asexual process of cell division. During mitosis, one parent cell divides into two identical daughter cells. Mitosis is used for growth, repair, and replacement of cells. Some unicellular organisms reproduce asexually by mitosis. Some multicellular organisms can reproduce by fragmentation or budding, which involves mitosis. Mitosis consists of four phases: prophase, metaphase, anaphase, and telophase. During **prophase**, the spindle fibers appear and the DNA is condensed and packaged as chromosomes that become visible. The nuclear membrane also breaks down, and the nucleolus disappears. During **metaphase**, the spindle apparatus is formed and the centromeres of the chromosomes line up on the equatorial plane. During **anaphase**, the centromeres divide and the two chromatids separate and are pulled toward the opposite poles of the cell. During **telophase**, the spindle fibers disappear, the nuclear membrane reforms, and the DNA in the chromatids is decondensed.

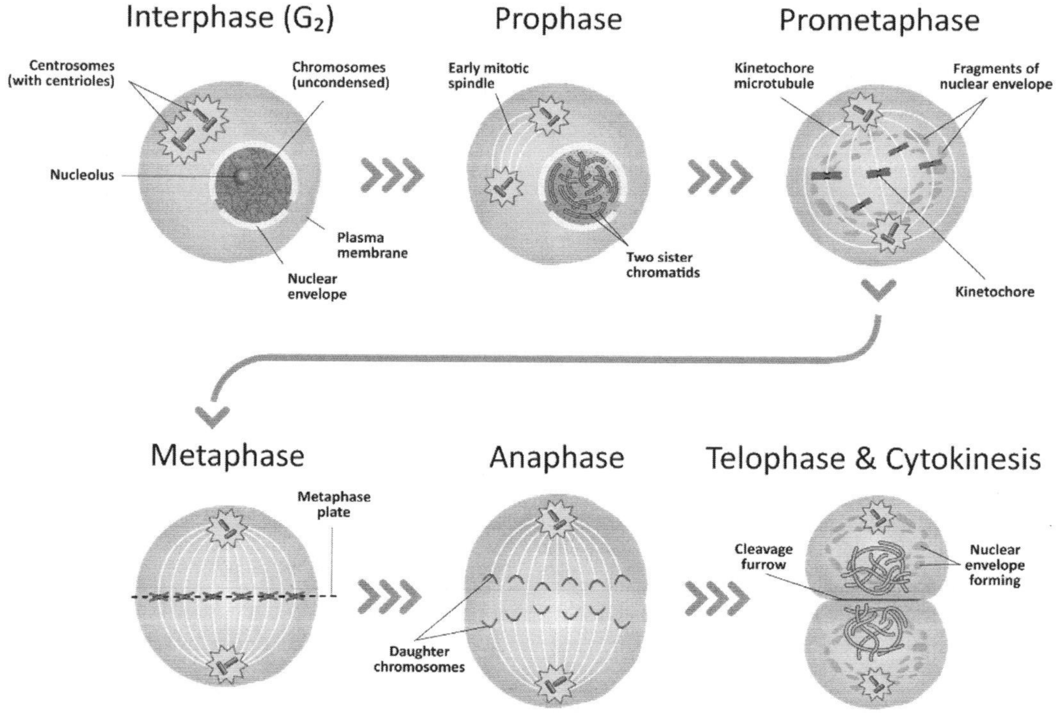

Review Video: Mitosis
Visit mometrix.com/academy and enter code: 849894

CYTOKINESIS

Cytokinesis is the dividing of the cytoplasm and cell membrane by the pinching of a cell into two new daughter cells at the end of mitosis. This occurs at the end of telophase when the actin filaments in the cytoskeleton form a contractile ring that narrows and divides the cell. In plant cells, a cell plate forms across the phragmoplast, which is the center of the spindle apparatus. In animal cells, as the contractile ring narrows, the cleavage furrow forms. Eventually, the contractile ring narrows down to the spindle apparatus joining the two cells and the cells eventually divide. Diagrams of the cleavage furrow of an animal cell and cell plate of a plant are shown below.

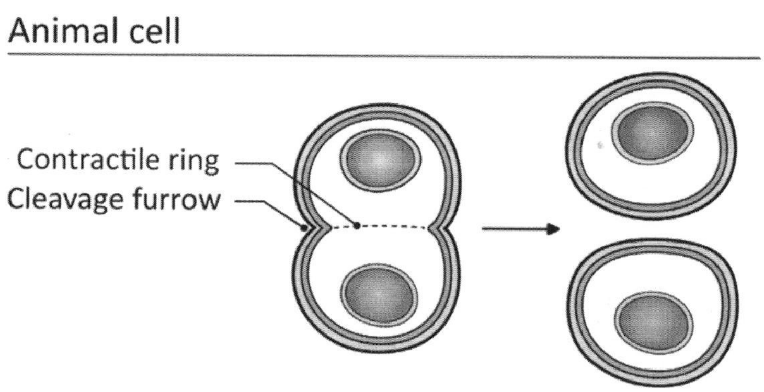

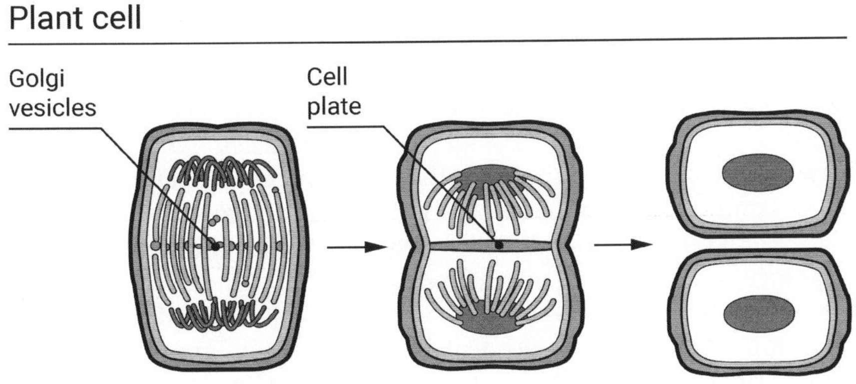

MEIOSIS

Meiosis is a type of cell division in which the number of chromosomes is reduced by half. Meiosis produces gametes, or egg and sperm cells. Meiosis occurs in two successive stages, which consist of a first mitotic division followed by a second mitotic division. During **meiosis I**, or the first meiotic division, the cell replicates its DNA in interphase and then continues through prophase I, metaphase I, anaphase I, and telophase I. At the end of meiosis I, there are two haploid daughter cells, each with half the number of chromosomes as the original diploid parent cell. Each chromosome consists of two sister chromatids, but these are considered a single chromosome. During **meiosis II**, the cell enters a brief interphase but does not replicate its DNA. Then, the cell continues through prophase II, metaphase II, anaphase II, and telophase II. During prophase II, the unduplicated chromosomes split. At the end of telophase II, there are four daughter cells that have half the number of chromosomes as the parent cell.

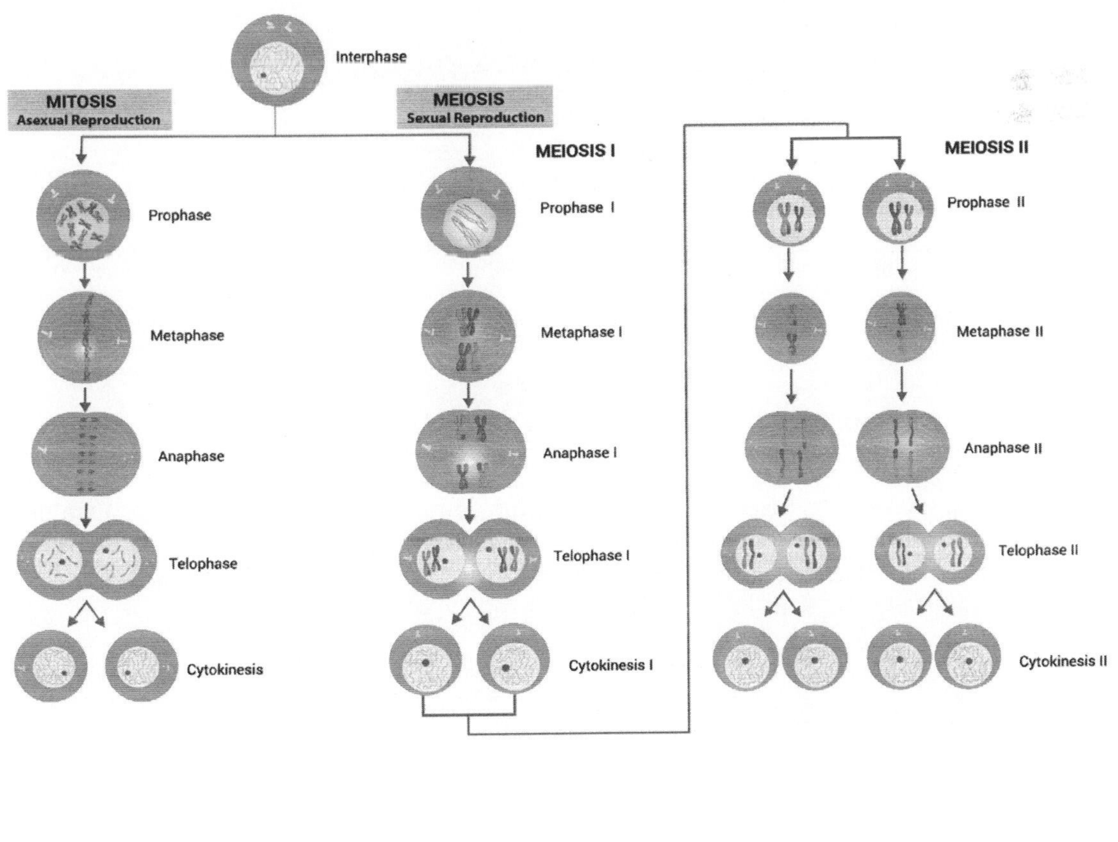

Cell Cycle Checkpoints

During the cell cycle, the cell goes through three checkpoints to ensure that the cell is dividing properly at each phase, that it is the appropriate time for division, and that the cell has not been damaged. The **first checkpoint** is at the end of the G_1 phase just before the cell undergoes the S phase, or synthesis. At this checkpoint, a cell may continue with cell division, delay the division, or rest. This **resting phase** is called G_0. In animal cells, the G_1 checkpoint is called **restriction.** Proteins called cyclin D and cyclin E, which are dependent on enzymes cyclin-dependent kinase 4 and cyclin-dependent kinase 2 (CDK4 and CDK2), respectively, largely control this first checkpoint. The **second checkpoint** is at the end of the G_2 phase just before the cell begins prophase during mitosis. The protein cyclin A, which is dependent on the enzyme CDK2, largely controls this checkpoint. During mitosis, the **third checkpoint** occurs at metaphase to check that the chromosomes are lined up along the equatorial plane. This checkpoint is largely controlled by cyclin B, which is dependent upon the enzyme CDK1.

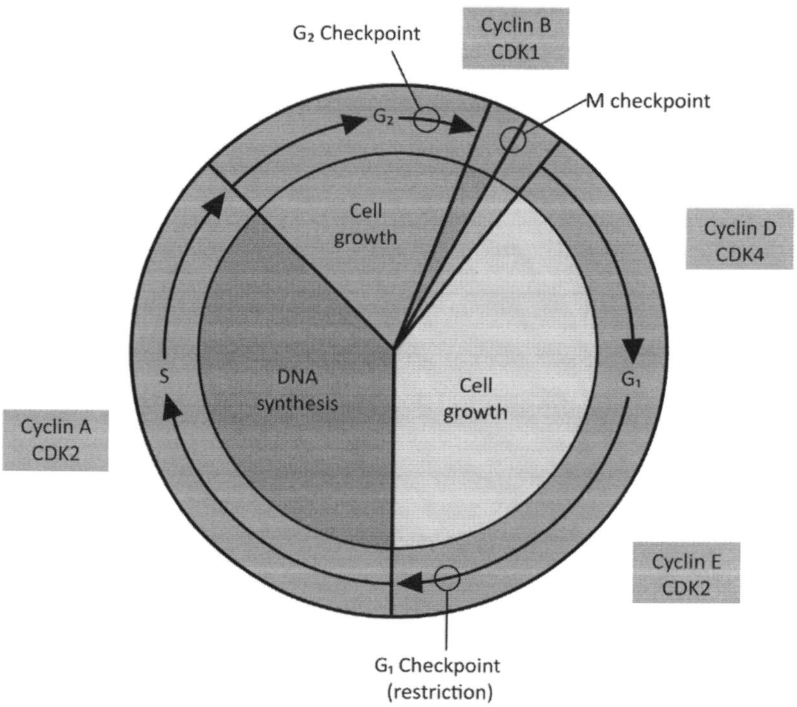

Nucleic Acids

Nucleotide Structure

A **nucleotide**, whether DNA or RNA, contains three components: a phosphate group, a ringed, five-carbon sugar (deoxyribose in DNA, ribose in RNA), and a nitrogen-containing base. The **phosphate group** binds to one side of the **ringed, five-carbon sugar**. The **nitrogen-containing base** binds to the opposite side of the ringed, five-carbon sugar. A nucleotide strand is formed by covalently linking the phosphate groups of the nucleotides into a linear sequence.

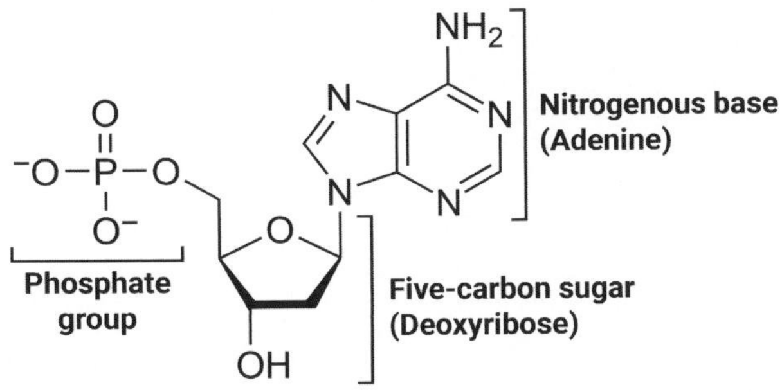

DNA AND RNA

STRUCTURAL SIMILARITIES

Structural similarities between DNA and RNA:

- DNA and RNA are both **nucleic acids** composed of nucleotides made up of a sugar, a base, and a phosphate molecule.
- DNA and RNA have three of their four bases in common: guanine, cytosine, and adenine.

Review Video: DNA Vs. RNA
Visit mometrix.com/academy and enter code: 184871

STRUCTURAL, LOCATIONAL, AND FUNCTIONAL DIFFERENCES

Structural differences between DNA and RNA:

- DNA contains the base thymine, but RNA replaces thymine with uracil.
- DNA contains the sugar deoxyribose, but RNA contains the sugar ribose.
- DNA is double stranded, but RNA is single stranded.

Locational: DNA is located in the nucleus and mitochondria. RNA is found in the nucleus, ribosomes, and cytoplasm.

Functional: DNA contains the genetic blueprint and instructions for the cell. RNA carries out those instructions and synthesizes proteins.

TYPES AND FUNCTIONS OF RNA

Types of RNA include ribosomal RNA (rRNA), transfer RNA (tRNA), and messenger RNA (mRNA).

- **rRNA** forms the RNA component of the ribosome. It is evolutionarily conserved, which means it can be used to study relationships in organisms.
- **mRNA** is used by the ribosome to generate proteins (translation). The mRNA contains three-nucleotide "codons" that code for specific amino acids in a protein sequence.
- **tRNA** functions in translation by transferring an amino acid to the corresponding codon on the mRNA strand.

Review Video: DNA
Visit mometrix.com/academy and enter code: 639552

COMPLEMENTARY BASE PAIRING

According to **Chargaff's rule**, a DNA molecule always has a 1:1 ratio of purine to pyrimidine within it. The amount of adenine always equals the amount of thymine, and the amount of guanine always equals the amount of cytosine. (Note that the same rule holds for RNA, but the thymine is replaced with uracil.) In DNA, adenine always pairs with thymine, and guanine always pairs with cytosine. In RNA, adenine always pairs with uracil, and guanine always pairs with cytosine. The pairs are bonded together with hydrogen bonds.

DOUBLE HELIX STRUCTURE OF DNA

Double-stranded DNA consists of two complementary strands that adopt the shape of a double helix, which resembles a twisted ladder. The "sides" of the ladder are the sugar-phosphate backbones of the complementary strands. The "rungs" of the ladder are the nitrogenous bases, which are held together (base paired) by hydrogen bonds between the complementary nitrogenous bases in the opposite strand. In DNA, **adenine** (A) base pairs with **thymine** (T) and **guanine** (G) base pairs with **cytosine** (C). DNA also has an antiparallel structure, consisting of a 5' end and a 3' end, where the two strands of the DNA run in opposite directions for one another. The two ends of the DNA strand are coined 5' or 3' based on the specific carbon atom within the purine or pyrimidine ring that makes up the deoxyribose sugar. The 5' end of a DNA strand has a free phosphate group attached to the 5'-carbon atom of the deoxyribose sugar, while the 3' end of DNA has a free hydroxyl group at the 3'-carbon.

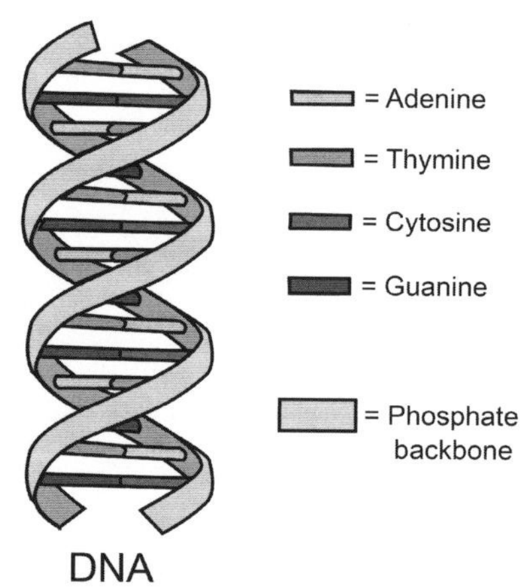

ORGANIZATION OF PROKARYOTIC DNA

Prokaryotes lack a nucleus and therefore prokaryotic DNA is organized primarily into a central loop contained in the cytoplasm. Prokaryotes may also contain smaller loops of DNA known as **plasmids** that contain other genes. Most prokaryotes lack histones, but Archaea are an example of prokaryotes that do contain histones.

ORGANIZATION OF EUKARYOTIC DNA

Eukaryotes have a nucleus with multiple chromosomes, each containing a tightly-compacted, double-helix DNA molecule. The structural sub-components of chromosomes include histones, nucleosomes, and chromatin.

- **Histones** are positively-charged, DNA-binding proteins.
- A **nucleosome** is composed of eight histone proteins around which approximately 146 base pairs of DNA are wrapped. The nucleosome is often called a "beads on a string" structure.

- **Chromatin** is made up of compacted nucleosomes.
- **Chromosomes** are made up of compacted chromatin.

RNA is also thought to play a role in chromatin structure.

Telomeres

Eukaryotic chromosomes have **telomeres** located at their tips. Telomeres are repetitive sequences of DNA that maintain the ends of the linear chromosomes and keep those ends from deteriorating.

DNA Replication

DNA replication begins when the double strands of the parent DNA molecule are unwound and unzipped. The enzyme **helicase** separates the two strands by breaking the hydrogen bonds between the base pairs that make up the rungs of the twisted ladder. These two single strands of DNA are called the **replication fork**. Each separate DNA strand provides a template for the complementary DNA bases, G with C and A with T. The opposite ends of DNA are called the 5' and 3' ends. After the DNA is separated, the enzyme **RNA primase** lays down an RNA primer that the enzyme **DNA polymerase** binds to initiate replication. DNA polymerase only synthesizes DNA from the 5' end towards the 3' end. Of the two strands open during replication, the strand with the 3' end will be replicated as a single, continuous strand, also known as the **leading strand**. The strand with the 5' end, which runs away from the fork, is known as the **lagging strand**, and will be replicated into shorter, unlinked segments known as Okazaki fragments. After bases are joined to the complementary base, the enzyme **exonuclease** removes the RNA primers used to initiate replication of the two strands. A separate DNA polymerase fills in gaps after the RNA primer is removed. The Okazaki fragments are joined by the enzyme DNA ligase.

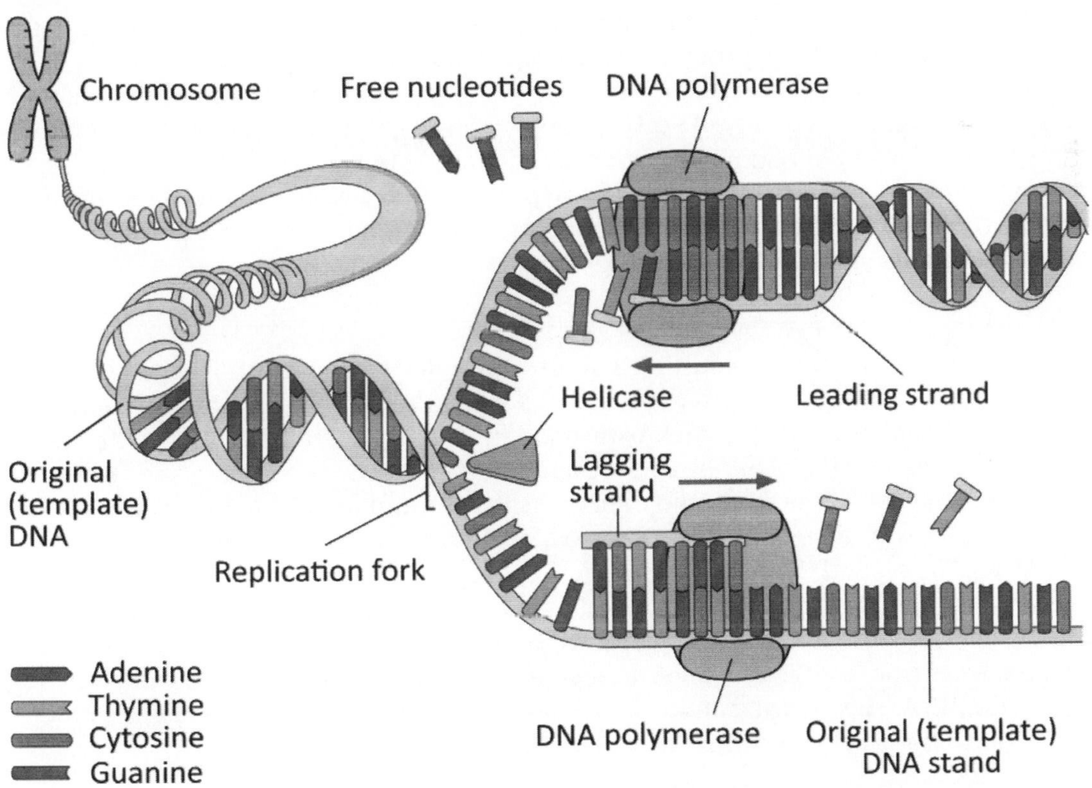

Protein Synthesis

Transcription

Transcription is the process by which a segment of DNA is copied onto a working blueprint called RNA. Each gene has a special region called a **promoter** that guides the beginning of the transcription process. **RNA polymerase** unwinds the DNA at the promoter region and makes an RNA copy of the DNA gene by adding the **complementary nucleotides**, G with C, C with G, T with A, and A with U. This forms a single strand of messenger RNA or mRNA.

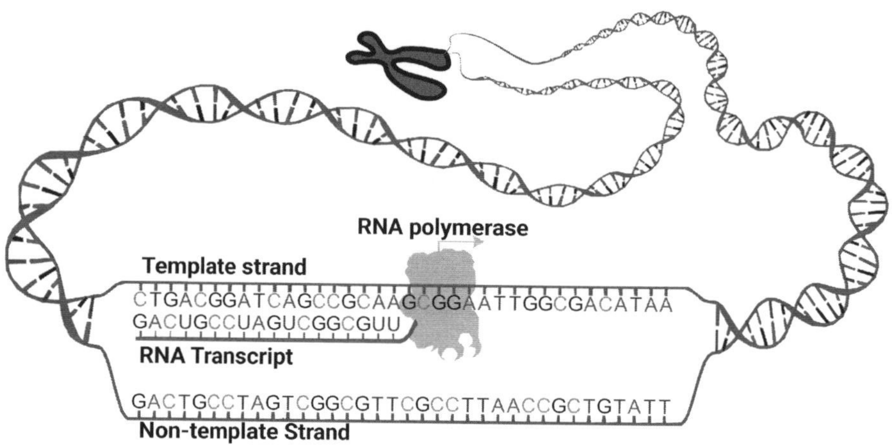

Processing mRNA

In addition to being transcribed, the mRNA must also be processed. First, a 5' cap (modified guanine nucleotide) is added, which helps promote ribosome recognition and preventing mRNA degradation. Second, a string of adenosine ribonucleotides are added to the 3' end of the mRNA, forming a structure known as a **poly(A) tail**. The poly(A) tail helps prevent mRNA degradation. The mRNA transcript may contain regions that do not code for protein, called **introns**. The regions that do code for protein are called **exons**. If introns are present, they will be removed in a process called splicing by a structure known as the **spliceosome**. After addition of the 5' cap, addition of the poly(A) tail, and splicing, the mRNA is ready for translation.

Translation

Ribosomes synthesize proteins from mRNA in a process called **translation**. The ribosome has three tRNA binding sites—A, P, and E. Translation initiates when the "**A site**" becomes occupied by the tRNA molecule corresponding to the mRNA start codon. The ribosome then moves the first tRNA from the "A site" to the "**P site**." The "A site" is then occupied by the tRNA molecule corresponding to the second mRNA codon. The ribosome then transfers the amino acid on the "P site" tRNA to the amino acid on the "A site" tRNA. The first tRNA, which now has no amino acid, is moved from the "P site" the "**E site**." The second tRNA, complexed to a chain of two amino acids, is moved from the "A site" to the "P site." The "A site" is then occupied by the tRNA corresponding to the third mRNA codon. The "P site" amino acid chain is transferred to the amino acid bound to the "A site" tRNA. The first tRNA then exits from the "E site" and the second and third tRNA molecules shift, opening the "A site" for the next tRNA. The growing amino acid chain continues to be transferred from the "P site" to the "A site" until translation is complete.

Review Video: Amino Acids
Visit mometrix.com/academy and enter code: 190385

Regulation of Gene Expression

Regulation of Gene Expression

Role of Promoters

Promoters are DNA sequences located upstream of the gene needed for transcription. Promoters signal the beginning of transcription. Special proteins called **transcription factors**, which bind to promoters, subsequently provide binding sites for the **RNA polymerase**, which is the enzyme that transcribes the RNA. Promoters in the Archaea and Eukaryota domains often contain a nucleotide sequence TATA, which is called a **TATA box**. The TATA box is usually 25 nucleotides upstream of the transcription start site, and it is the location at which the DNA is unwound.

Role of Enhancers

Enhancers are DNA sequences that regulate gene expression by providing a binding site for proteins that regulate RNA polymerase in transcribing proteins. Enhancers can greatly increase the expression of genes in their range. Enhancers are functional over large distances. Some enhancers are located within the gene they control while others can be hundreds or thousands of base pairs upstream or downstream from the genes they control. Most genes are controlled by two or three enhancers, but some may be controlled by more. Enhancers provide binding sites for regulatory proteins that either promote or inhibit RNA polymerase activity. Enhancers are more common in eukaryotes than prokaryotes.

Review Video: Regulation of Gene Expression
Visit mometrix.com/academy and enter code: 651793

Role of Transcription Factors

Transcription factors are DNA-binding proteins that help regulate gene expression in eukaryotes and prokaryotes. In eukaryotes that have promoter or enhancer regions, transcription factors bind near these regions and increase the ability of the RNA polymerase to start transcription. In eukaryotes, because genes are typically turned "off," transcription factors typically work to turn genes "on." The opposite is often true in bacteria, and transcription factors often work to turn genes off.

Role of Operons

Operons are segments of DNA or groups of genes that are controlled by one promoter. Operons consist of an operator, a promoter, and one or more structural genes. The **operator** provides a binding side for a repressor that inhibits the binding of RNA polymerase. The **promoter** provides the binding site for the RNA polymerase. The **structural genes** provide the sequence that codes for a protein. Operons are transcribed as single units and code for a single mRNA molecule, which produces proteins with related functions. Operons have been found in prokaryotes, eukaryotes, and viruses. For example, the lac (lactose) operon in certain bacteria controls the production of the enzymes needed to digest lactose. If lactose is already available in the cell, the lactose binds to the repressor protein to prevent the repressor protein from binding to the operator. The gene is transcribed, and the enzymes necessary for the digestion of the lactose are produced. If there is no lactose that needs to be digested, the repressor protein binds to the operator. The gene is not transcribed, and the enzyme is not produced. This allows the cell to only code for proteins as needed by the cell.

Role of Epigenetics

Epigenetics studies factors or mechanisms that determine if genes are active (switched on) or dormant (switched off). These mechanisms can alter gene function or gene expression without altering the sequences of the DNA itself. An example is the addition of a methyl group (**methylation**) to the histones. **Acetylation**, the addition of an acetyl group, and **phosphorylation**, the addition of a phosphoryl group, are also modifications to the proteins associated with DNA that can switch genes on or off or affect their activity level.

Differentiation and Specialization of Cells

Differential Gene Expression

Differential gene expression is the expression of different sets of gene by cells with identical DNA molecules. The unused genes in a differentiated cell remain in the cell but are not expressed. Actually, only a few genes are expressed in each cell. For example, during mammalian embryonic development, the undifferentiated zygote undergoes cell division through mitosis. As the number of cells increases, selected cells undergo differentiation to become specialized components in the developing tissues of the embryo.

Stem Cells

Stem cells are undifferentiated cells that can divide without limit and that can differentiate to produce the specialized cells that each organism needs. **Embryonic stem cells** are harvested from the embryo at the blastocyst stage or from the developing gonads of the embryo. Stem cells can be pluripotent or multipotent depending on their source. Early embryonic stem cells are **pluripotent**, which means they have not undergone any differentiation and have the ability to become any special type of cell. After embryonic stem cells begin to differentiate, they may be limited to specializing into a specific tissue type. These stem cells are considered to be **multipotent** because they can only develop into a few different types of cells. Adult stem cells, also called **somatic stem cells**, are harvested from organs and tissues and can differentiate into those types of cells in that particular organ or tissue. Umbilical cord blood stem cells can be harvested from the umbilical cord of a newborn baby. Adult stem cells and umbilical cord blood stem cells are multipotent. **Induced pluripotent cells** (iPS) are somatic cells that have been manipulated to act like pluripotent cells. Experiments have shown that iPS may be useful in treating diseases.

Mutations

Missense Mutations, Silent Mutations, and Nonsense Mutations

Mutations are changes in DNA sequences. **Point mutations** are changes in a single nucleotide in a DNA sequence. Three types of point mutations are missense, silent, and nonsense.

- **Missense mutations** result in a codon for a different amino acid. An example is mutating TGT (Cysteine codon) to TGG (Tryptophan codon).
- **Silent mutations** result in a codon for the same amino acid as the original sequence. An example is mutating TGT (Cysteine codon) to TGC (a different Cysteine codon).
- **Nonsense mutations** insert a premature stop codon, typically resulting in a non-functional protein. An example is mutating TGT (Cysteine codon) to TGA (STOP codon).

Review Video: Codons
Visit mometrix.com/academy and enter code: 978172

FRAMESHIFT MUTATIONS AND INVERSION MUTATIONS

Deletions and insertions can result in the addition of amino acids, the removal of amino acids, or cause a frameshift mutation. A **frameshift mutation** changes the reading frame of the mRNA (a new group of codons will be read), resulting in the formation of a new protein product. Mutations can also occur on the chromosomal level. For example, an **inversion** is when a piece of the chromosome inverts or flips its orientation.

GERMLINE MUTATIONS AND SOMATIC MUTATIONS

Mutations can occur in somatic (body) cells and germ cells (egg and sperm). **Somatic mutations** develop after conception and occur in an organism's body cells such as bone cells, liver cells, or brain cells. Somatic mutations cannot be passed on from parent to offspring. The mutation is limited to the specific descendent of the cell in which the mutation occurred. The mutation is not in the other body cells unless they are descendants of the originally mutated cell. Somatic mutations may cause cancer or diseases. Some somatic mutations are silent. **Germline mutations** are present at conception and occur in an organism's germ cells, which are only egg and sperms cells. Germline mutations may be passed on from parent to offspring. Germline mutations will be present in every cell of an offspring that inherits a germline mutation. Germline mutations may cause diseases. Some germline mutations are silent.

MUTAGENS

Mutagens are physical and chemical agents that cause changes or errors in DNA replication. Mutagens are external factors to an organism. Examples include ionizing radiation such as ultraviolet radiation, x-rays, and gamma radiation. Viruses and microorganisms that integrate their DNA into host chromosomes are also mutagens. Mutagens include environmental poisons such as asbestos, coal tars, tobacco, and benzene. Alcohol and diets high in fat have been shown to be mutagenic. Not all mutations are caused by mutagens. **Spontaneous mutations** can occur in DNA due to molecular decay.

Lab Techniques for Studying Biological Processes

GEL ELECTROPHORESIS

Gel electrophoresis is a technique used to separate macromolecules such as nucleic acids and proteins with regard to size. Fragments of DNA and RNA, as well as proteins, are separated according to length. Using different types of gel electrophoresis, proteins can also be separated according to electrical charge. The technique for gel electrophoresis is relatively simple. For example, to separate DNA strands, a solution containing the DNA strand is placed in a gel. When an electric current is passed through the gel, the DNA strands migrate from the negative end of the container to the positive end due to their negative charge because of their phosphate ions. Shorter DNA strands migrate faster than the longer DNA strands. This results in a series of bands. Each band contains DNA strands of a specific length. A DNA standard, commonly called a DNA ladder, is placed in the gel to provide a reference to determine the strand length. Lengths are measured in base pairs (bps).

MICROSCOPY

Microscopy is used in many fields of biology, including microbiology. Bacteria, viruses, cell components, and molecules are too small to be seen by the naked eye. Several types of microscopes are available to examine these samples. There are **light microscopes**, which use visible light to study samples, and electron microscopes, which use beams of electrons. The light microscope (also called the compound microscope) uses two types of lenses (ocular and objective) to magnify objects. These are typically used when studying samples at the cellular level. Basic compound light microscopes are typically used in high school biology classes. Other compound light microscopes such as the dark-field microscope, phase-contrast microscope, and the fluorescent microscope are available for more specific uses. For tiny samples, such as viruses, cell components, or individual molecules, electron microscopes can be used. **Electron microscopes** use beams of electrons instead of light. Because beams of electrons have shorter wavelengths, electron microscopes have greater resolution than light microscopes. Resolution is the ability of a lens to reveal two points as being distinct. The two types of electron microscopy are transmission electron microscopy (TEM) and scanning electron microscopy (SEM). SEM is a newer technology than TEM and produces three-dimensional images.

Spectrophotometry

Spectrophotometry involves measuring the amount of visible light absorbed by a colored solution. There are **analog** and **digital spectrometers** that measure absorbance and transmittance. A **single beam spectrometer** measures relative light intensity. A **double beam spectrometer** compares light intensity between a reference sample and a test sample. Spectrometers measure the wavelength of light. Spectrometry not only involves working with visible light, but also near-ultraviolet and near-infrared light. A **spectrophotometer** includes an illumination source. An output wavelength is selected and beamed at the sample, the sample absorbs light, and the detector responds to the light and outputs an analog electronic current in a usable form. A spectrophotometer may require calibration. Some types can be used to identify unknown chemicals.

Review Video: Spectrophotometer
Visit mometrix.com/academy and enter code: 104413

DNA Technologies and Genetic Engineering

PCR

The **polymerase chain reaction (PCR)** is a laboratory technique used to rapidly copy selected segments of DNA. PCR can be performed on the DNA from a single cell. PCR is a hot-and-cold cycled reaction that uses a special heat-tolerant polymerase. The DNA sample is combined with this special DNA polymerase, primers, and free nucleotides. Primers are synthetic strands of DNA containing just a few bases. The first step is a high-temperature **denaturation step** (90–95°C) that causes the DNA strands to unwind. The second step is a low-temperature **annealing step** (~60°C) in which the primers anneal to the single-stranded DNA. The final step is an **activation step** that matches the activation temperature for the heat-resistant DNA polymerase (~70°C, depending on the enzyme). This final step results in the formation of newly-synthesized, double-stranded DNA. These steps will be repeated on the same sample for multiple cycles, typically about 30. The number of DNA copies generated is 2^N, where N is the number of cycles.

DNA Sequencing

DNA sequencing is a laboratory technique used to determine the order or linear sequence of nucleotides of DNA fragments. A PCR is used to isolate the needed DNA segment or DNA template. During PCR, some of each of the nucleotides containing the four bases (G, C, A, and T) are chemically altered and fluorescently tagged with different colors of dye. Also, the chemically altered nucleotides have the dideoxyribose sugar, which contains one less oxygen atom than the usual deoxyribose. When synthesis begins, the polymerase randomly adds either a regular nucleotide or an altered nucleotide. If the polymerase adds an altered nucleotide, synthesis stops. This way, each

DNA fragment of the same length is tagged with the same color. Then, electrophoresis is used to separate DNA fragments according to length. The DNA sequence can be read by reading the tags of the shortest fragments to the tags of the longest fragments.

Human Genome Project

In 1990, the **Human Genome Project (HGP)** was launched to map the human genome. The project involved scientists from 16 laboratories located in at least 6 different countries, and it was completed in 2003. The human genome consists of approximately 3.12 billion paired nucleotides. The genomes of several plants, animal, fungi, protists, bacteria, viruses, and even cell organelles have also been studied and mapped. Interesting comparisons can be made between these genomes. For example, the number of genes in an organism's genome does not indicate the complexity of that organism. Humans have approximately 21,000 genes, but the simpler roundworms have approximately 26,000 genes.

Gene Therapy

Gene therapy is an experimental but promising technique that introduces new genes into an organism to correct a specific disease caused by a defective gene. In gene therapy, the defective gene is replaced by a properly functioning gene. Gene therapy is most promising for diseases that are caused by a single defective gene. For example, gene therapy was first successfully used to treat severe combined immunodeficiency (SCID). One type of SCID is caused by a single defective gene on the X chromosome. Doctors removed some bone marrow from the test subjects, injected a retrovirus that was carrying the gene, and then re-implanted the bone marrow. The bone marrow cells then have the correct DNA sequence for the production of proteins for much-needed enzymes. Unfortunately, some of the first recipients developed leukemia, and the trials were halted. Later, researchers discovered that the leukemia was related to the location of the insertion of the retroviral vectors.

Cloning

Clones are exact biological copies of genes, cells, or multicellular organisms. There are natural clones and artificial clones. Many clones are produced in nature. For example, animals that can reproduce asexually by fragmentation or budding produce natural clones. Some plants such as strawberries can reproduce by stolons. Typically, in biology, cloning refers to gene cloning or the cloning of organisms. Gene cloning is the process of splicing genes that are needed to code for a specific protein and introducing them into a new cell with a DNA vector. Gene cloning has been used with bacteria in the production of human insulin and a human growth hormone replacement.

Cloning can also occur with an entire organism. This type of cloning is called a **somatic cell nuclear transfer**. The first mammal clone was Dolly the sheep. In this procedure, a nucleus of a somatic cell from the sheep to be cloned was transferred or injected into a denucleated egg cell of the surrogate mother sheep. The egg was stimulated to divide by electric shock, and then the embryo was implanted into the uterus of the surrogate mother. Dolly was born identical to the egg nucleus donor, not the surrogate mother. Dolly and other cloned mammals typically have serious health problems. Dolly aged prematurely possibly due to the shortened telomeres from the adult somatic cell nucleus.

Review Video: Genetic Cloning
Visit mometrix.com/academy and enter code: 289634

Genetic Engineering and Genetically Engineered Cells

Genetic engineering is the manipulation of DNA outside of normal reproduction. This modified DNA is called **recombinant DNA**. Genetic engineering is prevalent in gene cloning, which is used in the production of genetically modified (GM) organisms and the production of GM food. **Gene cloning** involves cloning a specific gene that is needed for a specific purpose. Genes can be inserted into cells of an entirely different species. Genetically engineered cells are also called transgenic cells. GM organisms such as plants or crops contain recombinant DNA. Many types of organisms such as plants, animals, fungi, and bacteria have been genetically modified. GM crops such as corn and soybeans can be engineered to be herbicide resistant to ensure that herbicides kill the weeds but not the crop plants. Crops can also be modified to be pest resistant in order to kill the insects that might damage the crops. In addition, several foods can be genetically modified to increase nutritional value.

Review Video: Genetic Engineering and Genetically Engineered Cells
Visit mometrix.com/academy and enter code: 548687

Chapter Quiz

Ready to see how well you retained what you just read? Scan the QR code to go directly to the chapter quiz interface for this study guide. If you're using a computer, simply visit the online resources page at **mometrix.com/resources719/mttcbiology** and click the Chapter Quizzes link.

Heredity and Evolutionary Changes

Mendel's Laws

Law of Segregation

The **law of segregation** states that the alleles for a trait separate when gametes are formed, which means that only one of the pair of alleles for a given trait is passed to the gamete. This can be shown in monohybrid crosses, which can be used to show which allele is **dominant** for a single trait. A **monohybrid cross** is a genetic cross between two organisms with a different variation for a single trait. The first monohybrid cross typically occurs between two **homozygous** parents. Each parent is homozygous for a separate allele (gg or GG) for a particular trait. For example, in pea plants, green seeds (G) are dominant over yellow seeds (g). Therefore, in a genetic cross of two pea plants that are homozygous for seed color, the F_1 generation will be 100% **heterozygous** green seeds.

	g	**g**
G	Gg	Gg
G	Gg	Gg

Review Video: Punnett Square
Visit mometrix.com/academy and enter code: 853855

Monohybrid Cross for a Cross Between Two Gg Parents

If the plants with the heterozygous green seeds are crossed, the F_1 generation should be 50% heterozygous green (Gg), 25% homozygous green (GG), and 25% homozygous yellow (gg).

	G	**g**
G	GG	Gg
g	Gg	gg

Law of Independent Assortment

Mendel's law of independent assortment states that alleles of one characteristic or trait separate independently of the alleles of another characteristic. Therefore, the allele a gamete receives for one gene does not influence the allele received for another gene due to the allele pairs separating independently during gamete formation. This means that traits are transmitted independently of each other. This can be shown in dihybrid crosses.

Gene, Genotype, Phenotype, and Allele

A **gene** is a portion of DNA that identifies how traits are expressed and passed on in an organism. A gene is part of the genetic code. Collectively, all genes form the **genotype** of an individual. The genotype includes genes that may not be expressed, such as recessive genes. The **phenotype** is the physical, visual manifestation of genes. It is determined by the basic genetic information and how genes have been affected by their environment.

An **allele** is a variation of a gene. Also known as a trait, it determines the manifestation of a gene. This manifestation results in a specific physical appearance of some facet of an organism, such as eye color or height. The genetic information for eye color is a gene. The gene variations responsible for blue, green, brown, or black eyes are called alleles. **Locus** (plural, *loci*) refers to the location of a gene or alleles.

Review Video: Genotype vs Phenotype
Visit mometrix.com/academy and enter code: 922853

Dominant and Recessive Genes

Gene traits are represented in pairs with an uppercase letter for the **dominant trait** (A) and a lowercase letter for the **recessive trait** (a). Genes occur in pairs (AA, Aa, or aa). There is one gene on each chromosome half supplied by each parent organism. Since half the genetic material is from each parent, the offspring's traits are represented as a combination of these. A dominant trait only requires one gene of a gene pair for it to be expressed in a phenotype, whereas a recessive requires both genes in order to be manifested. For example, if the mother's genotype is Dd and the father's is dd, the possible combinations are Dd and dd. The dominant trait will be manifested if the genotype is DD or Dd. The recessive trait will be manifested if the genotype is dd. Both DD and dd are **homozygous** pairs. Dd is **heterozygous**.

Dihybrid Cross for the F_2 Generation of a Cross between GGRR and ggrr Parents

A **dihybrid cross** is a genetic cross for two traits that each have two alleles. For example, in pea plants, green seeds (G) are dominant over yellow seeds (g), and round seeds (R) are dominant over wrinkled seeds (r). In a genetic cross of two pea plants that are homozygous for seed color and seed shape (GGRR or ggRR), the F_1 generation will be 100% heterozygous green and round seeds (GgRr). If these F_1 plants (GgRr) are crossed, the resulting F_2 generation is shown below. Out of the 16 total genotypes for the cross of green, round seeds, there are only four possible phenotypes, or physical traits of the seed: green and round seed (GGRR, GGRr, GgRR, or GgRr), green and wrinkled seed (GGrr or Ggrr), yellow and round seed (ggRR or ggRr) , or yellow and wrinkled seed (ggrr). There are nine green and round seed plants, three green and wrinkled seed plants, three yellow and round seed plants, and only one yellow and wrinkled seed plant. This cross has a **9:3:3:1 ratio**.

	GR	**gR**	**Gr**	**gr**
GR	GGRR	GgRR	GGRr	GgRr
gR	GgRR	ggRR	GgRr	ggRr
Gr	GGRr	GgRr	GGrr	Ggrr
gr	GgRr	ggRr	Ggrr	ggrr

Pedigree

Pedigree analysis is a type of genetic analysis in which an inherited trait is studied and traced through several generations of a family to determine how that trait is inherited. A **pedigree** is a chart arranged as a type of family tree using symbols for people and lines to represent the relationships between those people. Squares usually represent males, and circles represent females. Horizontal lines represent a male and female mating, and the vertical lines beneath them represent their children. Usually, family members who possess the trait are fully shaded and those who only carry the trait are half-shaded. Genotypes and phenotypes are determined for each individual if possible. The pedigree below shows the family tree of a family in which the first male who was red-green color blind mated with the first female who was unaffected. They had five children. The three sons were unaffected, and the two daughters were carriers.

Inheritance of Red-Green Color Blindness:
an X-linked Recessive Trait

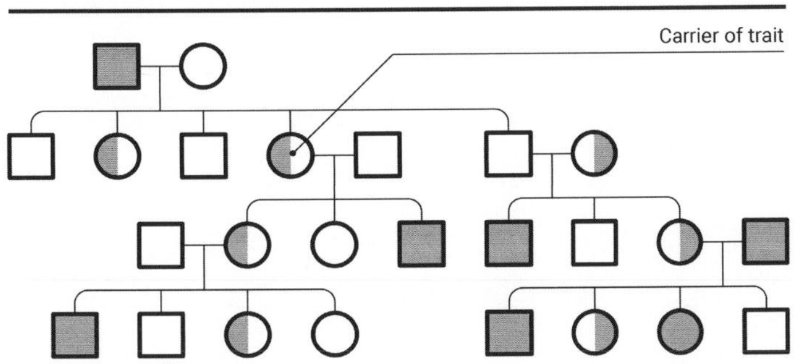

Non-Mendelian Inheritance

NON-MENDELIAN INHERITANCE CONCEPTS

LINKAGE

Linkage is an exception to Mendel's law of independent assortment. Linkage can occur when two genes are located on the same chromosome. Each chromosome has several genes, and those genes tend to be inherited together. Genes that are located on the same chromosome and tend to be inherited together are called **linkage groups**. Because the genes are on the same chromosome, they do not separate during meiosis. During meiosis, the genes in a linkage group always go into the same gamete together. Due to linkage, genes with different characteristics are inherited together more frequently than is predicted using the laws of probability. An example of a linkage group is found on chromosome number 4. This linkage group includes genes for Parkinson's disease, narcolepsy, and Huntington's disease.

Review Video: Mendelian and Non-Mendelian Genetics
Visit mometrix.com/academy and enter code: 113159

SEX-LINKED INHERITANCE

Sex-linked inheritance is an exception to Mendel's law of independent assortment. In human genetics, females have two X chromosomes, and males have one X and one Y chromosome. **Sex-linked traits** are carried on the X chromosome. Because females have two X chromosomes, they have two copies of genes found on the X chromosome. Females may possess a recessive allele for various disorders on one X chromosome, but as long as they possess the dominant allele for normal functioning on the other X chromosome, they will not have the disorder. Females who are heterozygous for a trait such as color blindness or hemophilia are only carriers. Because males have only one X chromosome, if they possess the recessive allele for a disorder, it will be expressed. Examples of traits that are a result of sex linkage are color blindness, hemophilia, a form of muscular dystrophy, and some forms of anemia.

MULTIPLE ALLELES

Multiple alleles result in a type of non-Mendelian inheritance. In Mendelian inheritance, only two alleles for each gene exist. For example, Mendel's pea plants were either tall or short, and the plants had either yellow or green pods. Often, there are more than two possibilities for a particular trait.

For example, in human genetics, blood type has many variations. Multiple allele inheritance occurs where there are more than two different alleles of a gene for a particular trait. Even though there may be several alleles for a particular trait, each individual can still only possess two of those possible alleles. For example, the three human blood alleles are I^A (blood contains type A antigens), I^B (blood contains type B antigens), and *i* (blood contains neither type A nor type B antigens).

Blood types and their possible genotypes are shown below.

Blood Type (Phenotype)	Genotype
A	I^AI^A, I^AI^O
B	I^BI^B, I^BI^O
AB	I^AI^B
O	*ii*

INCOMPLETE DOMINANCE

Incomplete dominance is an exception to Mendel's law of dominance. In these situations, there is no dominant or recessive allele. Instead, both alleles of a heterozygote are expressed, and when they are, they blend or mix. For example, there are two alleles for petal color for snapdragons: red (C^R) and white (C^W). Crossing a red snapdragon with a white snapdragon yields an F_1 generation that is 100% heterozygous pink. Crossing two pink snapdragons yields an F_2 generation that is 50% heterozygous pink (C^RC^W), 25% homozygous white (C^WC^W), and 25% homozygous red (C^RC^R).

LAWS OF DOMINANCE AND CODOMINANCE

The **law of dominance** states that a dominant trait is always expressed. **Codominance** is an exception to the law of dominance. In codominance, a heterozygote simultaneously expresses both genes for a trait without blending. For example, in certain horses, the hair colors red (D^R) and white (D^W) are codominant. Horses with the genotype D^RD^W have coats composed of both red hairs and white hairs, which—when mixed together—causes their coats to have a golden color.

POLYGENIC INHERITANCE

Polygenic inheritance occurs when a trait is determined by the interaction of many different genes. In Mendelian genetics, traits are determined by just one pair of genes with two alleles. For example, Mendel's pea plants had either red or white flowers, and his plants were either tall or short. An example of polygenic genetic inheritance in human genetics is skin color and height. Each is controlled by at least four pairs of genes. Skin color has many variations between very light and very dark. Height has many variations between very short and very tall. Eye color and intelligence are also polygenic.

EPISTASIS

Epistasis occurs when a gene at one locus inhibits the expression of a gene at another locus. For example, in mice, black hair (B) is dominant over brown hair (b). But a different gene at a different locus determines whether or not pigment is deposited (C for deposited and c for not deposited) on the mouse hair. A black mouse with genotypes BB or Bb will only have that color deposited if the pigment genotype is CC or Cc. A black mouse with genotype BBcc will be white. A brown mouse can have genotypes bbCC or bbCc, but a mouse with genotype bbcc will also be white.

PLEIOTROPY

In Mendelian inheritance, each gene can influence only one trait. Most genes can affect many traits or have multiple phenotypes. **Pleiotropy** is the situation in which one gene influences several seemingly unrelated traits. A gene that affects multiple traits is **pleiotropic**. Pleiotropy can be due to normal or mutated genes. Genes code for proteins. Because proteins are often used in more than one tissue or more than one area of the body, a missing protein can cause many complications. For example, the hormone insulin is a protein. If the insulin receptors are faulty, then the cells cannot recognize and use the insulin. Other examples of pleiotropy include inherited diseases such as cystic fibrosis, sickle-cell anemia, phenylketonuria (PKU), and albinism.

MITOCHONDRIAL INHERITANCE

Mitochondria are cellular organelles that produce energy for the cell. Mitochondria contain their own DNA consisting of 37 genes arranged in a circular structure. Mitochondrial DNA is transmitted maternally, which means that these mitochondrial genes are only inherited from the mother. The offspring's mitochondria only come from the oocyte (egg cell), not from the sperm. Sperm cells only contain mitochondria in their tails, which does not enter the egg during fertilization. Mitochondrial inheritance is not consistent with Mendelian inheritance in which the zygote derives half of the genetic material from the mother and half from the father. Most of these genes code for proteins related to muscular disorders.

Common Human Genetic Disorders

Chromosomal Changes that Lead to Down Syndrome

Down syndrome is a type of **aneuploidy** (abnormal number of chromosomes) in which an individual has three copies of chromosome 21, as shown in the karyotype below. When a gamete with an extra 21st chromosome unites with a normal gamete, the result is a group of three chromosomes instead of a diploid set. A **trisomy** can occur as a result of nondisjunction, which occurs when a pair of chromosomes fails to separate during meiosis in the formation of an egg or sperm cell.

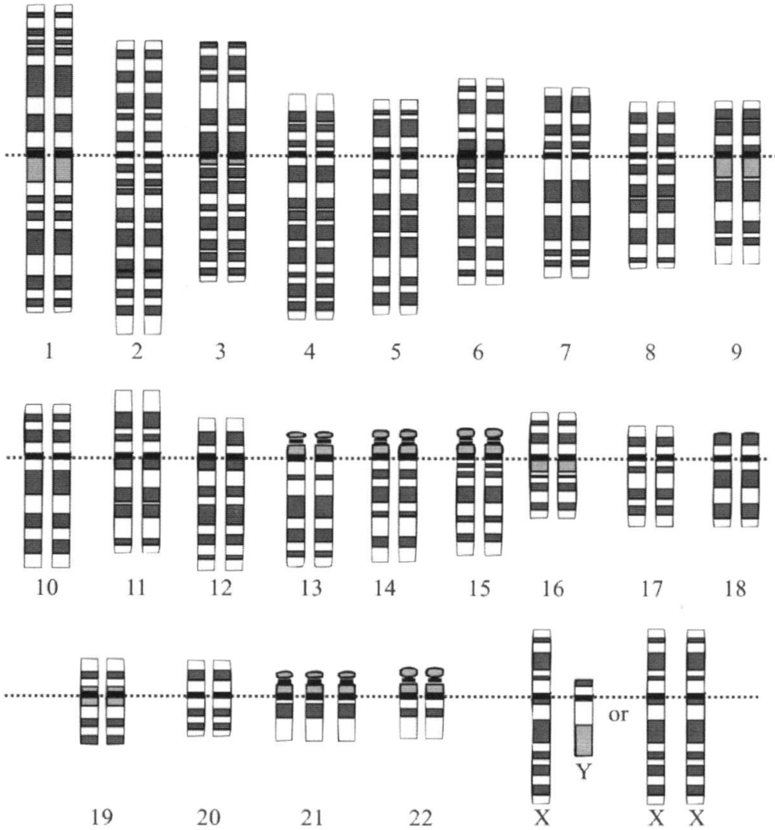

Genetics of Sickle-Cell Anemia

Sickle cell anemia is a genetic disorder that is the result of a gene mutation. Specifically, sickle cell anemia is the result of the point mutation in which adenine is substituted for thymine. This results in a defective form of hemoglobin. Sickle-cell anemia occurs when a person is homozygous for the defective gene. Sickle-cell trait occurs when a person is heterozygous for the defective gene, and this person is a carrier but usually suffers no ill effects. Sickle cell anemia is an example of **pleiotropy**, in which a change in one gene affects multiple aspects of a person's health. These health problems are due to the abnormally sickle-shaped red blood cells that block the flow of blood, damaging tissues and organs. The sickle-shaped cells tend to rupture, leading to anemia.

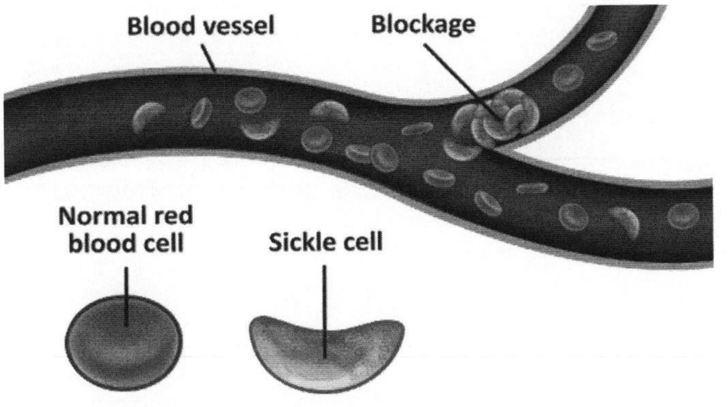

Sources of Genetic Variation

Genetic Variation

Mutations

Mutations are changes in DNA. Mutations are one of the main sources of genetic variation and can introduce new genetic information into the genome. The changes can be gene mutations such as the **point mutations** of substitution, addition, or deletion, or the changes can be on the chromosomal level such as the chromosomal aberrations of translocations, deletions, inversions, and duplications. Mutations are random and can benefit, harm, or have no effect on the individual. **Somatic mutations** do not affect inheritance and therefore do not affect genetic variation with regard to evolution. **Germline mutations** that occur in gametes (eggs and sperm) can be passed to offspring and therefore are very important to genetic variation and evolution.

Crossing Over

Crossing over is a major source of genetic variation. **Crossing over** is the exchange of equivalent segments of DNA between homologous chromosomes. Crossing over occurs during meiosis in prophase I. During synapsis, a **tetrad** is formed when homologous chromosomes pair up. Also during synapsis, the chromatids are extremely close together and sometimes the chromatids swap genes. Because genes have more than one allele, this allows for an exchange of genetic information. Crossing over is that exchange of genes. Crossing over can occur several times along the length of the chromosomes. Although crossing over does not introduce new information, it does introduce new combinations of the information that is available. Without crossing over during meiosis, only two genetically different gametes can be formed. With just one instance of crossing over, four genetically different gametes can be formed. With crossing over, each gamete contains genes from both the father and the mother. Crossing over leads to variation in traits among gametes, which leads to variation in traits among offspring.

Independent Assortment During Sexual Reproduction

Independent assortment during sexual reproduction is a source of genetic variation. Mutations originally brought about changes in DNA leading to alleles or different forms of the same gene. During sexual reproduction, these alleles are "shuffled" or "independently sorted," producing individuals with unique combinations of traits. Gametes are produced during meiosis, which consists of two cell divisions: meiosis I and meiosis II. Meiosis I is a reduction division in which the diploid parent cell divides into two haploid daughter cells. During the metaphase of meiosis I, the homologous pairs (one from the mother and one from the father) align on the equatorial plane. The orientation of the homologous pairs is random, and each placement is independent of another's placement. The number of possible arrangements increases exponentially as the number of chromosomes increases. The independent assortment of chromosomes during metaphase in meiosis I provides a variety of gametes with tremendous differences in their combinations of chromosomes.

Review Video: Gene Mutation
Visit mometrix.com/academy and enter code: 955485

Chromosomal Aberrations

Chromosomal aberrations are changes in DNA sequences on the chromosomal level. These mutations typically involve many genes and often result in miscarriages. Chromosomal aberrations include translocations, deletions, inversions, and duplications. **Translocations** occur when a piece of DNA breaks off of one chromosome and is joined to another chromosome. **Deletions** occur when a piece of DNA breaks off on a chromosome and is lost without reattaching. **Inversions** occur when a piece of DNA breaks off of one chromosome and becomes reattached to that same chromosome but with an inverted or flipped orientation. **Duplications** occur when a piece of DNA is replicated and attached to the original piece of DNA in sequence.

Sources of Genetic Exchange

Genetic exchange, or the transfer of DNA from one organism to another, is a source of genetic variation. Three general types of genetic exchange are transduction, transformation, and conjugation. **Transduction** occurs when genetic material is transferred from one bacterium to another by a bacteriophage. A bacteriophage is a virus that infects a bacterium. As the new bacteriophages are replicated, some of the host bacteria DNA can be added to the virus particles. **Transformation** occurs when a cell obtains new genetic information from its environment or surroundings. Many bacteria take up DNA fragments such as plasmids from their surroundings to obtain new genes. **Conjugation** occurs when bacteria or single-celled organisms are in direct contact with each other. Genes can be transferred from one into the other while the two cells are joined.

Processes Affecting the Gene Pool

Genetic Drift

Genetic drift is a microevolutionary process that causes random changes in allele frequencies that are not the result of natural selection. Genetic drift can result in a loss of genetic diversity. Genetic drift greatly impacts small populations. Two special forms of genetic drift are the genetic bottleneck and the founder effect. A **genetic bottleneck** occurs when there is a drastic reduction in population due to some change such as overhunting, disease, or habitat loss. When a population is greatly reduced in size, many alleles can be lost. Even if the population size greatly increases again, the lost alleles represent lost genetic diversity. The **founder effect** occurs when one individual or a few individuals populate a new area such as an island. This new population is limited to the alleles of the founder(s) unless mutations occur or new individuals immigrate to the region.

Gene Flow

Gene flow is a microevolutionary process in which alleles enter a population by immigration and leave a population by emigration. Gene flow helps counter genetic drift. When individuals from one genetically distinct population immigrate to a different genetically distinct population, alleles and their genetic information are added to the new population. The added alleles will change the gene frequencies within the population. This increases genetic diversity. If individuals with rare alleles emigrate from a population, the genetic diversity is decreased. Gene flow reduces the genetic differences between populations.

Hardy-Weinberg Equilibrium

HW Equilibrium

Hardy–Weinberg (HW) equilibrium is a theoretical concept that uses a mathematical relationship to study gene frequencies. According to HW, if specific conditions are met, the proportions of genotypes in a population can be described by the equation: $p^2 + 2pq + q^2 = 1$, in which p is the frequency of the dominant allele and q is the frequency of the recessive allele. Also, p^2 is the frequency of the homozygous dominant genotype, $2pq$ is the frequency of the heterozygous genotype, and q^2 is the frequency of the homozygous recessive genotype. In addition, the sum of p and q must be equal to one. If the frequencies on the left side of the equation have a sum of one, then the population is in equilibrium, and evolution is not taking place. If the frequencies on the left side of the equation do not have a sum of one, then evolution is taking place. Therefore, the HW equation is only true for populations that are in equilibrium.

The HW equilibrium requires the following five conditions to be met:

1. The population must be very large.
2. Mating is random.
3. There are no mutations.
4. No immigration or emigration can occur.
5. All individuals of the population have an equal chance to survive and reproduce.

According to this concept, if all five conditions are met, the gene frequencies will remain constant. In reality, these five conditions are rarely met except in a laboratory situation.

Calculation of Allele Frequency

> Explain how to calculate allele frequencies of a simple genetic locus at which there are two alleles (A and a) in a population of 1,000 individuals given that the population consists of 120 individuals homozygous for the dominant allele (AA), 480 heterozygous individuals (Aa), and 400 individuals homozygous for the recessive allele (aa).

To calculate the frequency of an allele, divide the total number of those alleles in the population by the total number of alleles in the population for that locus as shown in the following equation:

$$\text{allele frequency} = \frac{\text{total \# of allelles in population}}{\text{total \# of alleles in the population for that locus}}$$

First, find the total number of each type of allele. The 120 AA individuals produce 240 A alleles. The 480 heterozygous individuals produce 480 A alleles and 480 a alleles. The 400 aa individuals produce 800 a alleles. Therefore, there is a total of 720 A alleles and 1,280 a alleles. Adding the 720 and 1,280 yields a total of 2,000 alleles in the population for that locus. The allele frequency for $A = \frac{720}{2,000}$ or 0.36. The allele frequency for $a = \frac{1,280}{2,000}$ or 0.64.

Mechanics of Evolution

Mechanisms of Evolution

Natural and Artificial Selection

Natural selection and artificial selection are both mechanisms of evolution. **Natural selection** is a process of nature in which a population can change over generations. Every population has variations in individual heritable traits and organisms best suited for survival typically reproduce and pass on those genetic traits to offspring to increase the likelihood of them surviving. Typically, the more advantageous a trait is, the more common that trait becomes in a population. Natural selection brings about evolutionary **adaptations** and is responsible for biological diversity. Artificial selection is another mechanism of evolution. **Artificial selection** is a process brought about by humans. Artificial selection is the selective breeding of domesticated animals and plants such as when farmers choose animals or plants with desirable traits to reproduce. Artificial selection has led to the evolution of farm stock and crops. For example, cauliflower, broccoli, and cabbage all evolved due to artificial selection of the wild mustard plant.

Sexual Selection

Sexual selection is a special case of natural selection in animal populations. **Sexual selection** occurs because some animals are more likely to find mates than other animals. The two main contributors to sexual selection are **competition** of males and **mate selection** by females. An example of male competition is in the mating practices of the redwing blackbird. Some males have huge territories and numerous mates that they defend. Other males have small territories, and some even have no mates. An example of mate selection by females is the mating practices of peacocks. Male peacocks display large, colorful tail feathers to attract females. Females are more likely to choose males with the larger, more colorful displays.

Coevolution

Coevolution describes a rare phenomenon in which two populations with a close ecological relationship undergo reciprocal adaptations simultaneously and evolve together, affecting each other's evolution. General examples of coevolution include predator and prey, or plant and pollinator, and parasites and their hosts. A specific example of coevolution is the yucca moths and the yucca plants. Yucca plants can only be pollinated by the yucca moths. The yucca moths lay their eggs in the yucca flowers, and their larvae grow inside the ovary.

Adaptive Radiation

Adaptive radiation is an evolutionary process in which a species branches out and adapts and fills numerous unoccupied ecological niches. The adaptations occur relatively quickly, driven by natural selection and resulting in new phenotypes and possibly new species eventually. An example of adaptive radiation is the finches that Darwin studied on the Galápagos Islands. Darwin recorded 13 different varieties of finches, which differed in the size and shape of their beaks. Through the process of natural selection, each type of finch adapted to the specific environment and specifically the food sources of the island to which it belonged. On newly formed islands with many unoccupied ecological niches, the adaptive radiation process occurred quickly due to the lack of competing species and predators.

Evidence Supporting Evolution

Molecular Evidence

Because all organisms are made up of cells, all organisms are alike on a fundamental level. Cells share similar components, which are made up of molecules. Specifically, all cells contain DNA and RNA. This should indicate that all species descended from a **common ancestor**. Humans and chimpanzees share approximately 98% of their genes in common, while humans and bacteria share approximately 7% of their genes in common suggesting that bacteria and humans are not closely related. Biologists have been able to use DNA sequence comparisons of modern organisms to reconstruct the "root" of the tree of life. The fact that RNA can store information, replicate itself, and code for proteins suggests that RNA could have could have evolved first, followed by DNA.

Homology

Homology is the similarity of structures of different species based on a similar anatomy in a common evolutionary ancestor. For instance, the forelimbs of humans, dogs, birds, and whales all have the same basic pattern of the bones. Specifically, all of these organisms have a humerus, radius, and ulna. They are all modifications of the same basic evolutionary structure from a common ancestor. Tetrapods resemble the fossils of extinct transitional animal called the *Eusthenopteron*. This would seem to indicate that evolution primarily modifies preexisting structures.

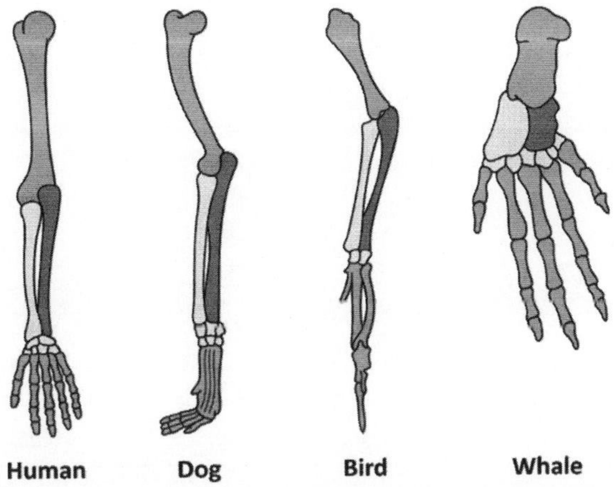

Review Video: Homologous vs Analogous Structures
Visit mometrix.com/academy and enter code: 355157

Embryology

The stages of **embryonic development** reveal homologies between species. These homologies are evidence of a **common ancestor**. For example, in chicken embryos and mammalian embryos, both include a stage in which slits and arches appear in the embryo's neck region that are strikingly similar to gill slits and gill arches in fish embryos. Adult chickens and adult mammals do not have gills, but this embryonic homology indicates that birds and mammals share a common ancestor with fish. As another example, some species of toothless whales have embryos that initially develop teeth that are later absorbed, which indicates that these whales have an ancestor with teeth in the adult form. Finally, most tetrapods have five-digit limbs, but birds have three-digit limbs in their wings. However, embryonic birds initially have five-digit limbs in their wings, which develop into a three-digit wing. Tetrapods such as reptiles, mammals, and birds all share a common ancestor with five-digit limbs.

ENDOSYMBIOSIS THEORY

The endosymbiosis theory is foundational to evolution. Endosymbiosis provides the path for prokaryotes to give rise to eukaryotes. Specifically, **endosymbiosis** explains the development of the organelles of mitochondria in animals and chloroplasts in plants. This theory states that some eukaryotic organelles such as mitochondria and chloroplasts originated as free living cells. According to this theory, primitive, heterotrophic eukaryotes engulfed smaller, autotrophic bacteria prokaryotes, but the bacteria were not digested. Instead, the eukaryotes and the bacteria formed a symbiotic relationship. Eventually, the bacteria transformed into mitochondrion or chloroplasts.

SUPPORTING EVIDENCE

Several facts support the endosymbiosis theory. Mitochondria and chloroplasts contain their own DNA and can both only arise from other preexisting mitochondria and chloroplasts. The genomes of mitochondria and chloroplasts consist of single, circular DNA molecules with no histones. This is similar to bacteria genomes, not eukaryote genomes. Also, the RNA, ribosomes, and protein synthesis of mitochondria and chloroplasts are remarkably similar to those of bacteria, and both use oxygen to produce ATP. These organelles have a double phospholipid layer that is typical of engulfed bacteria. This theory also involves a secondary endosymbiosis in which the original eukaryotic cells that have engulfed the bacteria are then engulfed themselves by another free-living eukaryote.

CONVERGENT EVOLUTION

Convergent evolution is the evolutionary process in which two or more unrelated species become increasingly similar in appearance. In convergent evolution, similar adaptations in these unrelated species occur due to these species inhabiting the same kind of environment. For example, the mammals shown below, although found in different parts of the world, developed similar appearances due to their similar environments.

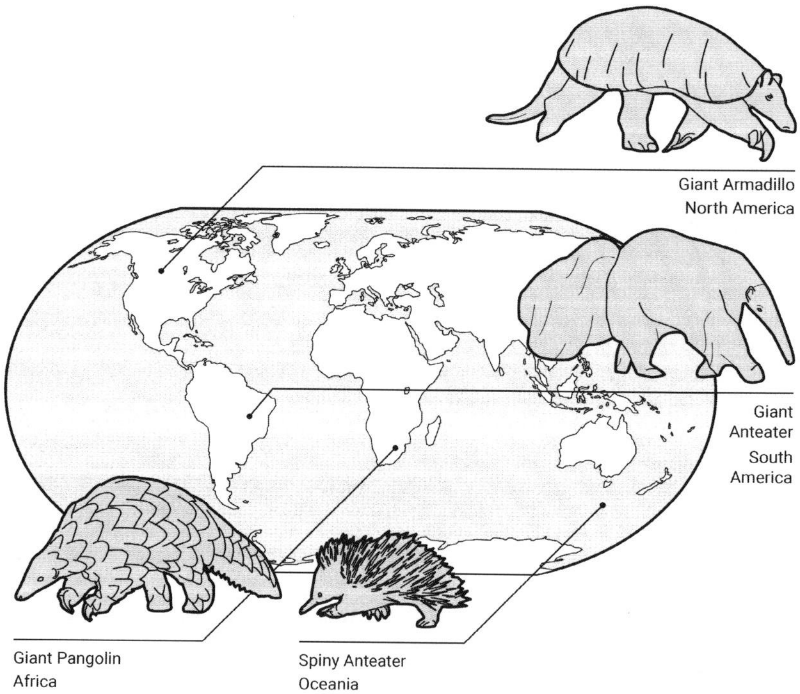

Divergent Evolution

Divergent evolution is the evolutionary process in which organisms of one species become increasingly dissimilar in appearance. As several small adaptations occur due to natural selection, the organisms will finally reach a point at which two new species are formed, also known as **speciation**. Then, these two species will further diverge from each other as they continue to evolve. Adaptive radiation is an example of divergent evolution. Another example is the divergent evolution of the wooly mammoth and the modern elephant from a common ancestor.

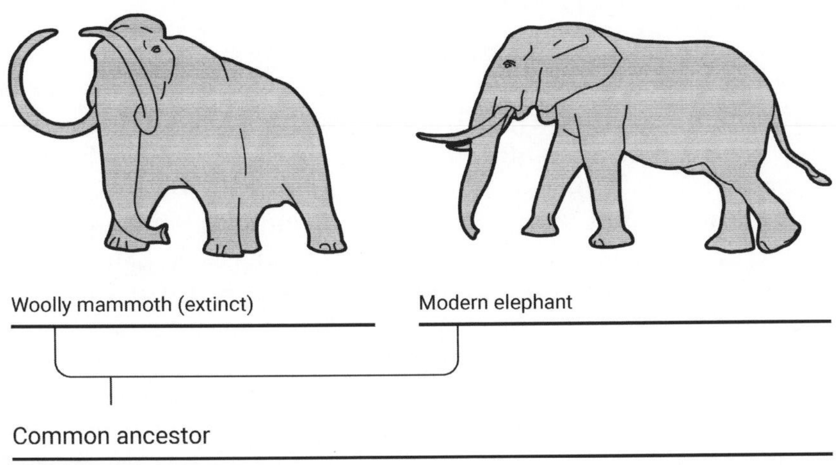

Fossil Record

The **fossil record** provides many types of support for evolution including comparisons from rock layers, transition fossils, and homologies with modern organisms. First, fossils from rock layers from all over the world have been compared, enabling scientists to develop a sequence of life from simple to complex. Based on the fossil record, the **geologic timeline** chronicles the history of all living things. For example, the fossil record clearly indicates that invertebrates developed before vertebrates and that fish developed before amphibians. Second, numerous transitional fossils have been found. **Transitional fossils** show an intermediate state between an ancestral form of an organism and the form of its descendants. These fossils show the path of evolutionary change. For example, many transition fossils documenting the evolutionary change from fish to amphibians have been discovered. In 2004, scientists discovered *Tiktaalik roseae*, or the "fishapod," which is a 375-million-year-old fossil that exhibits both fish and amphibian characteristics. Another example would be *Pakicetus*, an extinct land mammal, that scientists determined is an early ancestor of modern whales and dolphins based on the specialized structures of the inner ear. Most fossils exhibit homologies with modern organisms. For example, extinct horses are similar to modern horses, indicating a common ancestor.

Cephalization and Multicellularity

Cephalization is the evolutionary trend that can be summarized as "the evolution of the head." In most animals, nerve tissue has been concentrated into a brain at one end of an organism over many generations. Eventually, a head enclosing a brain and housing sensory organs was produced at one end of the organism. Many invertebrates, such as arthropods and annelids and all vertebrates, have undergone cephalization. However, some invertebrates, such as echinoderms and sponges, have not undergone cephalization, and these organisms literally do not have a head.

Another evolutionary trend is **multicellularity**. Life has evolved from simple, single-celled organisms to complex, multicellular organisms. Over millions of years, single-celled organisms gave rise to biofilms, which gave rise to multicellular organisms, which gave rise to all of the major phyla of multicellular organisms present today.

Genetic Basis of Speciation

Speciation

Significance of Reproductive Isolation

A biological species is a group of similar organisms that can breed and produce viable offspring. If gene flow between two groups of a species is hindered or stopped completely through **reproductive isolation**, more significant genetic differences between the two groups can accumulate and a new species may originate. This process is known as **speciation**. For the two incipient species to completely split, one of two things must occur: either successful mating between the incipient species cannot occur or the offspring must be nonviable or sterile. **Prezygotic barriers** occur before fertilization and stop or hinder species from mating. These barriers include, but are not limited to, habitat isolation, behavioral isolation, or temporal isolation. For instance, a change in the mating location or a change in the mating rituals can keep mating from occurring. **Postzygotic barriers** occur after fertilization but prevent the offspring or hybrid from living or being fertile. Some examples of postzygotic barriers include differences in chromosome numbers or the arrangement of genes on certain chromosomes. Various modes of geographic and population isolation may occur, but the key to speciation in each type is still the reduced gene flow.

Modes

Speciation has various modes that bring about the reduced gene flow needed for incipient species to fully separate. **Allopatric speciation** occurs between two incipient species that become geographically isolated populations. This would include if, for some geographic reason, two or more groups within a species cannot mate with each other due to a barrier like a desert or river. Some may still mate, but the gene flow is greatly reduced. Peripatric speciation is a more specific type of allopatric speciation. **Peripatric speciation** occurs when an extremely small group is geographically isolated at the edge of the rest of the population. This small population size brings about genetic drift relatively quickly, with unique characteristics of the smaller group getting passed on to future generations of that group and further diffientiating them from their original population. **Parapatric speciation** occurs within a population that is distributed over a large geographic area, thus creating "barrier" of space to distance. Individuals in the population simply choose to mate with close neighbors in their specific region, leading to a reduced gene flow. Natural selection in the range of those individuals brings about further differentiation among members of the species spread out across the population. **Sympatric speciation** occurs when a new species develops in a population, even though there is no geographic isolation or physical barrier separating or preventing this species from mating. Sympatric speciation is uncommon but may occur when a species inhabits a new niche.

Models of Evolutionary Rates

Gradualism

Gradualism is a model of evolutionary rates that states that evolutionary changes occurred slowly or gradually by a divergence of lineages due largely to natural selection. These accumulated changes occurred over millions of years at a slow and consistent rate. Many transitional forms occurred between ancestors and modern descendants. Although not all of these transitional forms were preserved in the fossil record, the fossil record clearly supports gradualism. Many transition fossils show adaptations as organisms evolve. The geologic time scale describes this gradual change from simple to complex organisms over millions of years.

Punctuated Equilibrium

Punctuated equilibrium is a model of evolutionary rates that states that in some instances, evolutionary changes occurred in relatively short bursts that "punctuate" long periods of equilibrium of little or no change. These "short" periods would still consist of hundreds of thousands of years, but include one or more substantial changes. Most scientists believe that punctuated equilibrium occurred along with gradualism. The fossil record supports punctuated equilibrium for many organisms. Punctuated equilibrium provides an explanation for the supposed numerous "missing links" in the fossil record. If punctuated equilibrium is validated, then there actually are no missing links.

Scientific Explanations for the Origin of Life on Earth

Explanations for the Origin of Life on Earth

Panspermia

The word *panspermia* is a Greek work that means "seeds everywhere." **Panspermia** is one possible explanation for the origin of life on Earth that states that "seeds" of life exist throughout the universe and can be transferred from one location to another. Three types of panspermia based on the seed-dispersal method have been proposed. **Lithopanspermia** is described as rocks or dust transferring microorganisms between solar systems. **Ballistic panspermia** is described as rocks or dust transferring microorganisms between planets within the same solar system. **Directed panspermia** is described as intelligent extraterrestrials purposely spreading the seeds to other planets and solar systems. The panspermia hypothesis only proposes the origin of life on Earth. It does not offer an explanation for the origin of life in the universe or explain the origin of the seeds themselves.

Abiotic Synthesis of Organic Compounds

Scientists have performed sophisticated experiments to determine how the first organic compounds appeared on Earth. First, scientists performed controlled experiments that closely resembled the conditions similar to an early Earth. In the classic **Miller–Urey experiment** (1953), the Earth's early atmosphere was simulated with water, methane, ammonia, and hydrogen that were stimulated by an electric discharge. The Miller–Urey experiment produced complex organic compounds including several amino acids, sugars, and hydrocarbons. Later experiments by other scientists produced nucleic acids. Recently, Jeffrey Bada, a former student of Miller, was able to produce amino acids in a simulation using the Earth's current atmospheric conditions with the addition of iron and carbonate to the simulation. This is significant because in previous studies using Earth's current atmosphere, the amino acids were destroyed by the nitrites produced by the nitrogen.

Atmospheric Composition

The early atmosphere of Earth had little or possibly no oxygen. Early rocks had high levels of iron at their surfaces. Without oxygen, the iron just entered into the early oceans as ions. In the same time frame, early photosynthetic algae were beginning to grow abundantly in the early ocean. During photosynthesis, the algae would produce oxygen gas, which oxidized the iron at the rocks' surfaces, forming an iron oxide. This process basically kept the algae in an oxygen-free environment. As the algae population grew much larger, it eventually produced such a large amount of oxygen that it could not be removed by the iron in the rocks. Because the algae at this time were intolerant to oxygen, the algae became extinct. Over time, a new iron-rich layer of sediments formed, and algae populations reformed, and the cycle began again. This cycle repeated itself for millions of years. Iron-rich layers of sediment alternated with iron-poor layers. Gradually, algae and other life forms evolved that were tolerant to oxygen, stabilizing the oxygen concentration in the atmosphere at levels similar to those of today.

Development of Self-Replication

Several hypotheses for the origin of life involve the self-replication of molecules. In order for life to have originated on Earth, proteins and RNA must have been replicated. Hypotheses that combine the replication of proteins and RNA seem promising. One such hypothesis is called **RNA world**. RNA world explains how the pathway of DNA to RNA to protein may have originated by proposing the reverse process. RNA world proposes that self-replicating RNA was the precursor to DNA. Scientists have shown that RNA can actually function both as a gene and as an enzyme and could therefore have carried genetic information in earlier life stages. Also, RNA can be transcribed into DNA using reverse transcription. In RNA world, RNA molecules self-replicated and evolved through recombination and mutations. RNA molecules developed the ability to act as enzymes. Eventually, RNA began to synthesize proteins. Finally, DNA molecules were copied from the RNA in a process of reverse transcription.

Extinction of Species

Causes of Extinction of Species

Lack of Genetic Diversity

Genetic diversity provides a mechanism for populations to adapt to changing environments or even human impacts. With a diverse genome, individuals possessing genes making them better suited for the environment are more likely to exist. Without genetic diversity, populations cannot develop adaptations. Populations cannot resist diseases or adapt to changes in the habitat. As the populations of endangered species decrease, genetic diversity decreases even further. Normally, specific genes that resist disease or help the organism to adapt to changes in the habitat and therefore increase survivability are passed on to future generations. However, if those genes have drifted out of the population, the population cannot evolve with their changing environment and may become extinct. A small gene pool does not provide much variety for selection. For example, tigers in India are now in danger of extinction. Studies show that more than 90% of the genome has been lost largely due to a period when tigers were heavily killed by British officials and Indian royalty. With fewer than 2,000 tigers in the world and these in small populations, the genetic diversity can continue to decrease, possibly leading to extinction if much effort is not made to preserve the remaining genetic diversity.

Environmental Pressures

A changing environment may lead to the extinction of a species. If an animal has a small tolerance range to food sources and habitat needs or if a population is small, it is less likely to adapt to changes in the environment. For example, the giant panda feeds almost exclusively on bamboo. Bamboo is being threatened by global warming. Due to the dwindling of their food source, giant pandas are less able to adapt to a changing environment. **Climate change** and global warming can affect an ecosystem and some species may not be able to adapt to even seemingly minor temperature changes especially if their populations are small. If possible, animals needing cooler climates may need to move to cooler habitats. Melting ice caps and glaciers and rising sea levels can seriously disrupt many ecosystems and affect numerous species. For example, the polar bear may become extinct due to global warming as the polar bears' habitat is destroyed. Sea turtles may become extinct as the rising sea levels destroy the beaches needed for laying eggs. Even if the beaches are not destroyed, increasing temperatures affect the incubation process and the number of offspring being produced.

Human Impacts

Humans are responsible for impacting the environment in ways that endanger or harm species, which may even lead to those species' extinction. Humans destroy habitats directly through deforestation and clearing land for agriculture, logging, mining, and urbanization. Humans also threaten or endanger species through overfishing and overhunting. Pollution can destroy a habitat, and if a species is unable to relocate, this can eventually cause extinction if the effects cause drastic impacts. The intentional or unintentional introduction of an invasive species allows a new predator or competitor into the ecosystem, and it can threaten native species in that specific ecosystem if they cannot outcompete the invasive species. An example of human impacts leading to the extinction of a species is the case of the passenger pigeon. Millions of passenger pigeons were killed for meat from around 1850 to 1880. Because passenger pigeons only laid one egg at a time, huge flocks were destroyed. The last passenger pigeon died in 1914.

Interspecific Competition

Interspecific competition is competition between individuals of different species for the same limited resources such as food, water, sunlight, and living space. This is especially threatening if the two species share a limiting resource and that resource is not in abundant supply. Interspecific competition can limit the population size of a species. With reduced population size, there is less genetic variation. The species may not be able to adapt to environmental changes. For example, firs and spruces compete for resources in coniferous forests. Cheetahs and lions compete for prey in savannas.

Chapter Quiz

Ready to see how well you retained what you just read? Scan the QR code to go directly to the chapter quiz interface for this study guide. If you're using a computer, simply visit the online resources page at **mometrix.com/resources719/mttcbiology** and click the Chapter Quizzes link.

Organization of Living Things

Characteristics of Living Versus Nonliving Things

Importance and Structural Organization of Cells

Cells are the basic structural units of all organisms. All organisms have a highly organized cellular structure. In single-celled organisms, that single cell contains all of the components necessary for life. In multicellular organisms, cells can become specialized. Different types of cells can have different functions. Life begins as a single cell whether by asexual or sexual reproduction. All cells contain DNA and RNA and can synthesize proteins. Each cell consists of nucleic acids, cytoplasm, and a cell membrane. Specialized organelles such as mitochondria and chloroplasts have specific functions within the cell.

Energy

All cells must obtain and use energy in order to grow, make repairs, and reproduce. Cells obtain the energy they need by the breaking of bonds of molecules. Cellular respiration is the process of converting nutrient molecules into energy. Cells also use energy to take in food, process that food, and eliminate waste. Organisms differ in how they obtain food. Plants and other autotrophs can produce their own energy through processes such as photosynthesis or chemosynthesis. Animals and other heterotrophs obtain their energy from consuming autotrophs or other heterotrophs.

Growth and Reproduction

All organisms must be capable of growth and reproduction. Growth is necessary for multicellular organisms to develop and mature. While all cells eventually die, growth allows cells to be replaced or repaired. Without growth from cell division, tissues could not be maintained or repaired. Through mitosis, most cells routinely replace themselves with identical daughter cells. Reproduction is necessary to increase the number of individuals in a population, since all organisms eventually die. Reproduction is either sexual by the joining of gametes or asexual by binary fission or some other related method.

Adaptation to Environment

Organisms must be able to adapt to their environment in order to thrive or survive. Individuals must be able to recognize stimuli in their surroundings and adapt quickly. For example, an individual euglena can sense light and respond by moving toward the light. Individual organisms must also be able to adapt to changes in the environment on a larger scale. For example, plants must be able to respond to the change in the length of the day to flower at the correct time. Populations must also be able to adapt to a changing environment. Evolution by **natural selection** is the process by which populations change over many generations to become better adapted to their environment, thus surviving longer and reproducing more successfully. For example, wooly mammoths were unable to adapt to a warming climate and are now extinct, but many species of deer did adapt and are abundant today.

Historical and Current Biological Classifications of Organisms

Historical and Current Kingdom Systems

In 1735 Carolus Linnaeus devised a two-kingdom classification system. He placed all living things into either the *Animalia* kingdom or the *Plantae* kingdom. Fungi and algae were classified as plants. Also, Linnaeus developed the binomial nomenclature system that is still used today. In 1866, Ernst Haeckel introduced a three-kingdom classification system, adding the *Protista* kingdom to Linnaeus's animal and plant kingdoms. Bacteria were classified as protists and cyanobacteria were still classified as plants. In 1938, Herbert Copeland introduced a four-kingdom classification system in which bacteria and cyanobacteria were moved to the *Monera* kingdom. In 1969, Robert Whittaker introduced a five-kingdom system that moved fungi from the plant kingdom to the *Fungi* kingdom. Some algae were still classified as plants. In 1977, Carl Woese introduced a six-kingdom system in which in the *Monera* kingdom was replaced with the *Eubacteria* kingdom and the *Archaebacteria* kingdom.

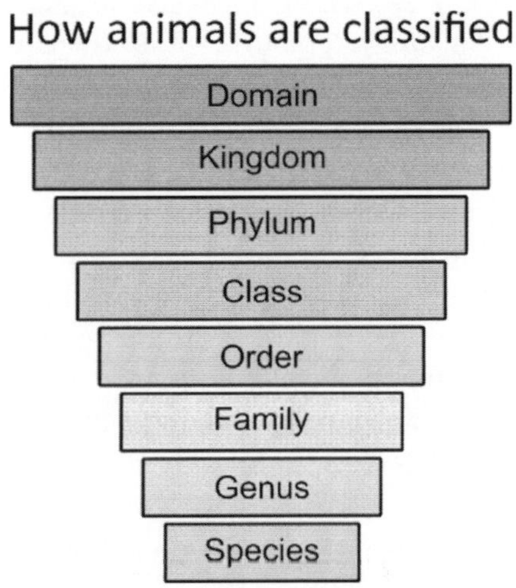

Domain Classification System

In 1990, Carl Woese introduced his domain classification system. **Domains** are broader groupings above the kingdom level. This system consists of three domains—*Archaea*, *Bacteria*, and *Eukarya*. All eukaryotes such as plants, animals, fungi, and protists are classified in the *Eukarya* domain. The *Bacteria* and *Archaea* domains consist of prokaryotes. Organisms previously classified in the *Monera* kingdom are now classified into either the *Bacteria* or *Archaea* domain based on their ribosomal RNA structure. Members of the *Archaea* domain often live in extremely harsh environments.

Review Video: Biological Classification Systems
Visit mometrix.com/academy and enter code: 736052

Viruses, Bacteria, Protists, Fungi, Plants, and Animals

Viruses

Viruses are nonliving, infectious particles that act as parasites in living organisms. Viruses are acellular, which means that they lack cell structure. Viruses cannot reproduce outside of living cells. The structure of a virus is a nucleic acid genome, which may be either DNA or RNA, surrounded by a protective protein coat or **capsid**. In some viruses, the capsid may be surrounded by a lipid membrane or envelope. Viruses can contain up to 500 genes and have various shapes. They usually are too small to be seen without the aid of an electron microscope. Viruses can infect plants, animals, fungi, protists, and bacteria. Viruses can attack only specific types of cells that have specific receptors on their surfaces. Viruses do not divide or reproduce like living cells. Instead, they use the host cell they infect by "reprogramming" it, using the nucleic acid genome, to make more copies of the virus. The host cell usually bursts to release these copies.

Review Video: Viruses and Antiviral Drugs
Visit mometrix.com/academy and enter code: 984455

Bacteria

Bacteria are small, prokaryotic, single-celled organisms. Bacteria have a circular loop of DNA (plasmid) that is not contained within a nuclear membrane. Bacterial ribosomes are not bound to the endoplasmic reticulum, as in eukaryotes. A cell wall containing peptidoglycan surrounds the bacterial plasma membrane. Some bacteria such as pathogens are further encased in a gel-like, sticky layer called the **capsule**, which enhances their ability to cause disease. Bacteria can be autotrophs or heterotrophs. Some bacterial heterotrophs are saprophytes that function as decomposers in ecosystems. Many types of bacteria share commensal or mutualistic relationships with other organisms. Most bacteria reproduce asexually by binary fission. Two identical daughter cells are produced from one parent cell. Some bacteria can transfer genetic material to other bacteria through a process called conjugation, while some bacteria can incorporate DNA from the environment in a process called transformation.

Protists

Protists are small, eukaryotic, single-celled organisms. Although protists are small, they are much larger than prokaryotic bacteria. Protists have three general forms, which include plantlike protists, animal-like protists, and fungus-like protists. **Plantlike protists** are algae that contain chlorophyll and perform photosynthesis. Animal-like protists are **protozoa** with no cell walls that typically lack chlorophyll and are grouped by their method of locomotion, which may use flagella, cilia, or a different structure. **Fungus-like protists**, which do not have chitin in their cell walls, are generally grouped as either slime molds or water molds. Protists may be autotrophic or heterotrophic. Autotrophic protists include many species of algae, while heterotrophic protists include parasitic, commensal, and mutualistic protozoa. Slime molds are heterotrophic fungus-like protists, which consume microorganisms. Some protists reproduce sexually, but most reproduce asexually by binary fission. Some reproduce asexually by spores while others reproduce by alternation of generations and require two hosts in their life cycle.

Fungi

Fungi are nonmotile organisms with eukaryotic cells and contain chitin in their cell walls. Most fungi are multicellular, but a few including yeast are unicellular. Fungi have multicellular filaments called **hyphae** that are grouped together into the mycelium. Fungi do not perform photosynthesis and are considered heterotrophs. Fungi can be parasitic, mutualistic or free living. Free-living fungi include mushrooms and toadstools. Parasitic fungi include fungi responsible for ringworm and athlete's foot. Mycorrhizae are mutualistic fungi that live in or near plant roots increasing the roots' surface area of absorption. Almost all fungi reproduce asexually by spores, but most fungi also have a sexual phase in the production of spores. Some fungi reproduce by budding or fragmentation.

> **Review Video: Feeding Among Heterotrophs**
> Visit mometrix.com/academy and enter code: 836017

PLANTS

Plants are multicellular organisms with eukaryotic cells containing cellulose in their cell walls. Plant cells have chlorophyll and perform photosynthesis. Plants can be vascular or nonvascular. **Vascular plants** have true leaves, stems, and roots that contain xylem and phloem. **Nonvascular plants** lack true leaves, stems and roots and do not have any true vascular tissue but instead rely on diffusion and osmosis to transport most of materials or resources needed to survive. Almost all plants are autotrophic, relying on photosynthesis for food. A small number do not have chlorophyll and are parasitic, but these are extremely rare. Plants can reproduce sexually or asexually. Many plants reproduce by seeds produced in the fruits of the plants, while some plants reproduce by seeds on cones. One type of plant, ferns, reproduce by a different system that utilizes spores. Some plants can even reproduce asexually by vegetative reproduction.

> **Review Video: Kingdom Plantae**
> Visit mometrix.com/academy and enter code: 710084

STRUCTURE, ORGANIZATION, MODES OF NUTRITION, AND REPRODUCTION OF ANIMALS

Animals are multicellular organism with eukaryotic cells that do not have cell walls surrounding their plasma membranes. Animals have several possible structural body forms. Animals can be relatively simple in structure such as sponges, which do not have a nervous system. Other animals are more complex with cells organized into tissues, and tissues organized into organs, and organs even further organized into systems. Invertebrates such as arthropods, nematodes, and annelids have complex body systems. Vertebrates including fish, amphibians, reptiles, birds, and mammals are the most complex with detailed systems such as those with gills, air sacs, or lungs designed to exchange respiratory gases. All animals are heterotrophs and obtain their nutrition by consuming autotrophs or other heterotrophs. Most animals are motile, but some animals move their environment to bring food to them. All animals reproduce sexually at some point in their life cycle. Typically, this involves the union of a sperm and egg to produce a zygote.

Characteristics of the Major Animal Phyla

CHARACTERISTICS OF THE MAJOR ANIMAL PHYLA

BODY PLANES

Animals can exhibit bilateral symmetry, radial symmetry, or asymmetry. With **bilateral symmetry**, the organism can be cut in half along only one plane to produce two identical halves. Most animals, including all vertebrates such as mammals, birds, reptiles, amphibians, and fish, exhibit bilateral symmetry. Many invertebrates including arthropods and crustaceans also exhibit bilateral symmetry. With **radial symmetry**, the organism can be cut in half along several planes to produce two identical halves. Starfish, sea urchins, and jellyfish exhibit radial symmetry. With **asymmetry**, the organism exhibits no symmetry. Very few organisms in the animal phyla exhibit asymmetry, but a few species of sponges are asymmetrical.

Body Cavities

Animals can be grouped based on their types of body cavities. A **coelom** is a fluid-filled body cavity between the alimentary canal and the body wall. The three body plans based on the formation of the coelom are coelomates, pseudocoelomates, and acoelomates. **Coelomates** have a true coelom located within the mesoderm. Most animals including arthropods, mollusks, annelids, echinoderms, and chordates are coelomates. **Pseudocoelomates** have a body cavity called a pseudocoelom. **Pseudocoeloms** are not considered true coeloms. Pseudocoeloms are located between mesoderm and endoderm instead of actually in the mesoderm as in a true coelom. Pseudocoelomates include roundworms and rotifers. **Acoelomates** do not have body cavities. Simple or primitive animals such as sponges, jellyfish, sea anemones, hydras, flatworms, and ribbon worms are acoelomates.

Modes of Reproduction

Animals can reproduce sexually or asexually. Most animals reproduce sexually. In **sexual reproduction**, males and females have different reproductive organs that produce **gametes**. Males have testes that produce sperm, and females have ovaries that produce eggs. During fertilization, a sperm cell unites with an egg cell, forming a **zygote**. Fertilization can occur internally such as in most mammals and birds or externally such as aquatic animals such as fish and frogs. The zygote undergoes cell division, which develops into an embryo and eventually develops into an adult organism. Some embryos develop in eggs such as in fish, amphibians, reptiles, and birds. Some mammals are **oviparous** meaning that they lay eggs, but most are **viviparous** meaning they have a uterus in which the embryo develops. One particular type of mammal called **marsupials** give birth to an immature fetus that finishes development in a pouch. However, there are some animals reproduce **asexually**. For example, hydras reproduce by budding, and starfish and planarians can reproduce by fragmentation and regeneration. Some fish, frogs, and insects can even reproduce by parthenogenesis, which is a type of self-reproduction without fertilization.

Modes of Temperature Regulation

Animals can be classified as either homeotherms or poikilotherms. **Homeotherms**, also called warm-blooded animals or **endotherms**, maintain a constant body temperature regardless of the temperature of the environment. Homeotherms such as mammals and birds have a high metabolic rate because a lot of energy is needed to maintain the constant temperature. **Poikilotherms**, also called cold-blooded animals or **ectotherms**, do not maintain a constant body temperature. Their body temperature fluctuates with the temperature of the environment. Poikilotherms such as arthropods, fish, amphibians, and reptiles have metabolic rates that fluctuate with their body temperature.

Hierarchy of Multicellular Organisms

Organizational Hierarchy within Multicellular Organisms

Cells are the smallest living units of organisms. Tissues are groups of cells that work together to perform a specific function. Organs are groups of tissues that work together to perform a specific function. Organ systems are groups of organs that work together to perform a specific function. An organism is an individual that contains several body systems.

Cells

Cells are the basic structural units of all living things. Cells are composed of various molecules including proteins, carbohydrates, lipids, and nucleic acids. All animal cells are eukaryotic and have a nucleus, cytoplasm, and a cell membrane. Organelles include mitochondria, ribosomes, endoplasmic reticulum, Golgi apparatuses, and vacuoles. Specialized cells are numerous, including but not limited to, muscle cells, nerve cells, epithelial cells, bone cells, blood cells, and cartilage cells. Cells can be grouped together in tissues to perform specific functions.

TISSUES

Tissues are groups of cells that work together to perform a specific function. Tissues can be grouped into four broad categories: muscle tissue, connective tissue, nerve tissue, and epithelial tissue. Muscle tissue is involved in body movement. **Muscle tissues** can be composed of skeletal muscle cells, cardiac muscle cells, or smooth muscle cells. Skeletal muscles include the muscles commonly called biceps, triceps, hamstrings, and quadriceps. Cardiac muscle tissue is found only in the heart. Smooth muscle tissue provides tension in the blood vessels, controls pupil dilation, and aids in peristalsis. **Connective tissues** include bone tissue, cartilage, tendons, ligaments, fat, blood, and lymph. **Nerve tissue** is located in the brain, spinal cord, and nerves. **Epithelial tissue** makes up the layers of the skin and various membranes. Tissues are grouped together as organs to perform specific functions.

ORGANS AND ORGAN SYSTEMS

Organs are groups of tissues that work together to perform specific functions. **Organ systems** are groups of organs that work together to perform specific functions. Complex animals have several organs that are grouped together in multiple systems. In mammals, there are 11 major organ systems: integumentary system, respiratory system, cardiovascular system, endocrine system, nervous system, immune system, digestive system, excretory system, muscular system, skeletal system, and reproductive system.

Human Anatomy and Physiology

BODY SYSTEMS

Functions of the human body can be divided into the following body systems.

- **Cardiovascular**: Pumps blood throughout the body via the heart and blood vessels
- **Respiratory**: Regulates gas exchange (oxygen intake and carbon dioxide expulsion)
- **Digestive**: Transforms food into energy and eliminates solid waste
- **Urinary**: Removes waste and toxins from the blood and expels them from the body through urine
- **Endocrine**: Releases hormones into the bloodstream to control metabolism, growth, and reproduction
- **Immune and Lymphatic Systems**: Defends against all foreign substances
- **Integumentary**: Skin prevents moisture loss, regulates temperature, protects from sunburn, and senses pain, pressure, touch, hot and cold
- **Musculoskeletal**: Skeletal muscles move the body, smooth muscles control the physical functioning of internal organs, and cardiac muscle pumps blood. The skeleton supports and shapes, protects internal organs, stores minerals, and produces blood cells
- **Nervous**: Controls movement, memory, and senses and communicates with the outside world
- **Reproductive**: Allows continuation of the human species through reproduction and childbearing and differentiates the sexes

Note that different models may have overlapping approaches to the body systems. For instance, the excretory system is not listed above, but the functions of the excretory systems overlap and are covered by the urinary and digestive systems.

The Three Primary Body Planes

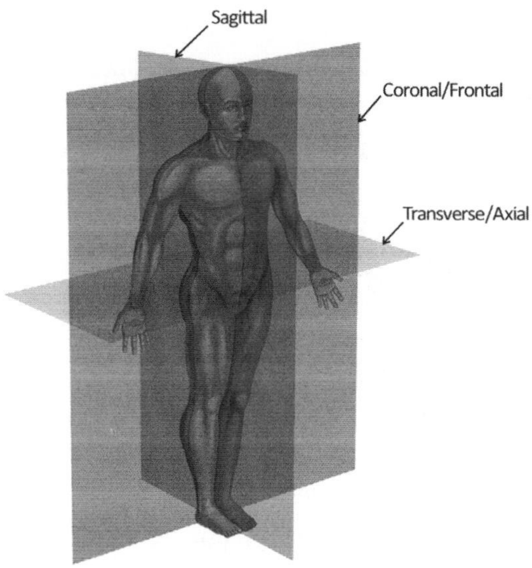

- The **transverse (or horizontal) plane** divides the patient's body into imaginary upper (*superior*) and lower (*inferior or caudal*) halves.
- The **sagittal plane** divides the body, or any body part, vertically into right and left sections. The sagittal plane runs parallel to the midline of the body.
- The **coronal (or frontal) plane** divides the body, or any body structure, vertically into front and back (*anterior* and *posterior*) sections. The coronal plane runs vertically through the body at right angles to the midline.

Terms of Direction

- **Medial** means *nearer to the midline* of the body. In anatomical position, the little finger is medial to the thumb.
- **Lateral** is the opposite of medial. It refers to structures *further away from the body's midline*, at the sides. In anatomical position, the thumb is lateral to the little finger.
- **Proximal** refers to structures *closer to the center* of the body. The hip is proximal to the knee.
- **Distal** refers to structures *further away from the center* of the body. The knee is distal to the hip.
- **Anterior** refers to structures in *front.*
- **Posterior** refers to structures *behind.*
- **Cephalad** and **cephalic** are adverbs meaning towards the *head.* **Cranial** is the adjective, meaning of the *skull.*
- **Caudad** is an adverb meaning towards the *tail* or posterior. **Caudal** is the adjective, meaning of the *hindquarters.*
- **Superior** means *above,* or closer to the head.
- **Inferior** means *below,* or closer to the feet.

Cardiovascular System

The main functions of the **cardiovascular system** are gas exchange, the delivery of nutrients and hormones, and waste removal. The cardiovascular system consists primarily of the heart, blood, and blood vessels. The **heart** is a pump that pushes blood through the arteries. **Arteries** are blood vessels that carry blood away from the heart, and **veins** are blood vessels that carry blood back to the heart. The exchange of materials between blood and cells occur in the **capillaries**, which are the smallest of the blood vessels.

Review Video: Functions of the Circulatory System
Visit mometrix.com/academy and enter code: 376581

Review Video: Mnemonics for Heart Anatomy and Physiology
Visit mometrix.com/academy and enter code: 849489

Review Video: Electrical Conduction System of the Heart
Visit mometrix.com/academy and enter code: 624557

Review Video: How the Heart Functions
Visit mometrix.com/academy and enter code: 569724

Heart Chambers and Valves

There are four chambers of the heart that have valves separating them and regulating a one-way flow of blood between the chambers.

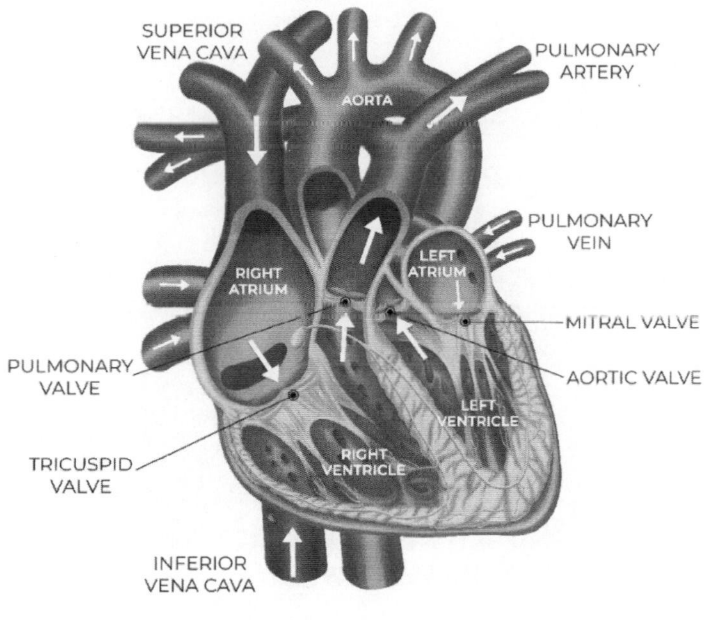

RESPIRATORY SYSTEM

The primary function of the **respiratory system** is to move air in and out of the body in order to facilitate the exchange of oxygen and carbon dioxide. The respiratory system consists of the nasal passages, pharynx, larynx, trachea, bronchial tubes, lungs, and diaphragm. **Bronchial tubes** branch into **bronchioles**, which end in clusters of alveoli. The **alveoli** are tiny sacs inside the lungs where gas exchange takes place. When the **diaphragm** contracts, the volume of the chest increases, which reduces the pressure in the **lungs**. Then, air is inhaled through the nose or mouth and passes through the pharynx, larynx, trachea, and bronchial tubes into the lungs. When the diaphragm relaxes, the volume in the chest cavity decreases, forcing the air out of the lungs. The respiratory system works jointly with the **cardiovascular system** by taking **oxygenated blood** (red blood cells) and distributing them through arteries and capillaries. **Deoxygenated blood** (carbon dioxide) is transported via the venous system back to the lungs to exhaled. The respiratory system also functions to enhance speech and smell.

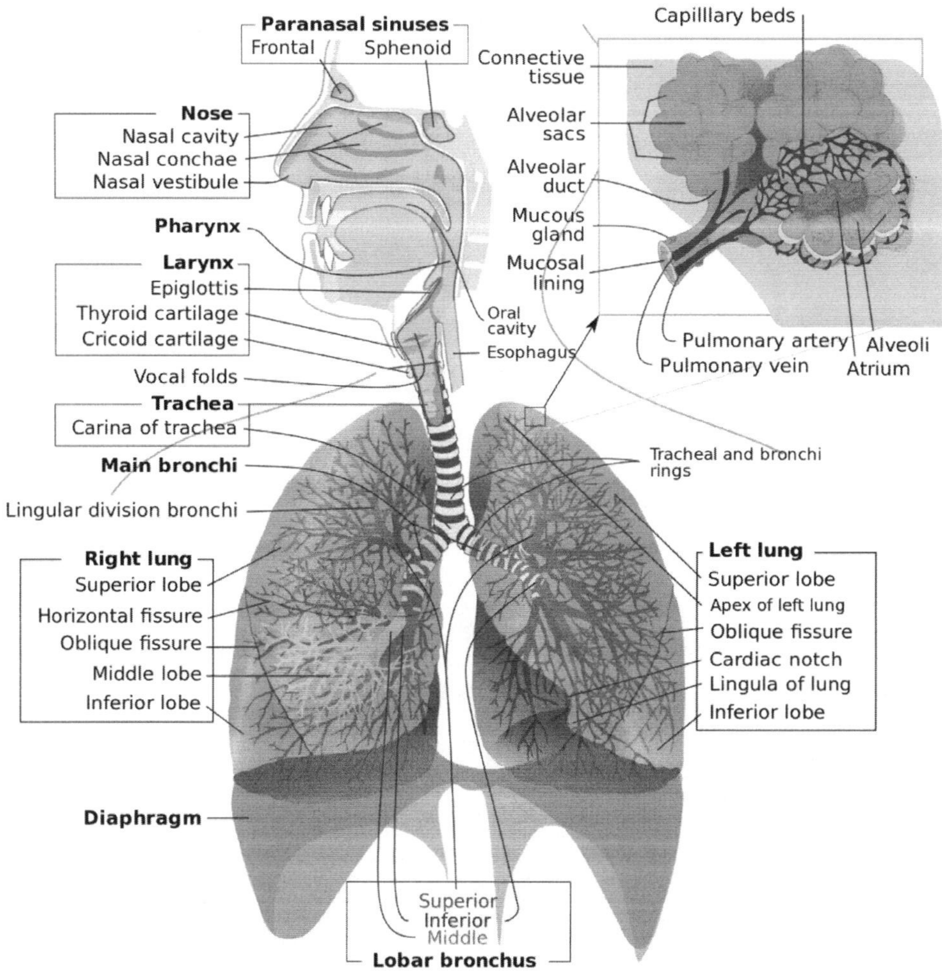

Review Video: Respiratory System
Visit mometrix.com/academy and enter code: 783075

Review Video: Pulmonary Circuit
Visit mometrix.com/academy and enter code: 955608

Digestive System

The main function of the **digestive system** is to process the food that is consumed by an organism. This includes mechanical and chemical processing. Depending on the organism, **mechanical processes**, or the physical process of breaking food into smaller pieces, can happen in various ways. Mammals have teeth to chew their food, while many animals such as birds, earthworms, crocodilians, and crustaceans have a gizzard or gizzard-like organ that grinds their food. **Chemical digestion** includes breaking food into simpler nutrients that the body can use for specific processes. While chewing, saliva (which contains special enzymes) is secreted to begin the breakdown of starches. Many animals such as mammals, birds, reptiles, amphibians, and fish have a stomach that stores and absorbs food. Gastric juice containing enzymes and hydrochloric acid is mixed with the food. The intestine or intestines absorb nutrients and reabsorb water from the undigested material. Additionally, many animals have a liver, gallbladder, and pancreas, which aid in digestion of proteins and fats. Undigested wasted are eliminated from the body through an anus or cloaca.

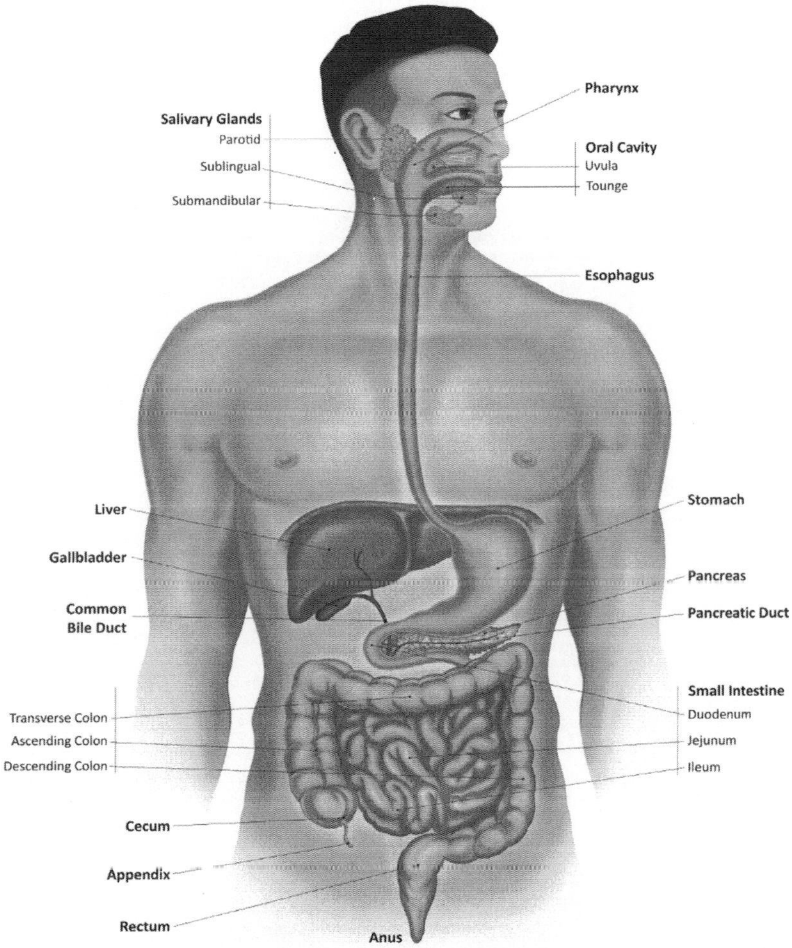

Review Video: Gastrointestinal System
Visit mometrix.com/academy and enter code: 378740

Urinary System

The **urinary system** consists of the bladder, kidneys, ureter, and urethra. Their main function is to eliminate waste products by expelling urine. This system also maintains homeostatic balance of water by excreting excess urine, maintaining electrolytes in the blood stream, and regulating blood Ph levels. This balance of water is crucial to body functioning as dehydration can lead to low blood pressure, which in turn can result in metabolic shock. **Metabolic shock** is characterized by low blood pressure that affects the kidneys, liver, and brain. **Dehydration** can also affect the muscular, system resulting in cramps from poor thermal regulation and altered fluid movement across tissue membranes.

Kidneys

The **kidneys** are involved in blood filtration, pH balance, and the reabsorption of nutrients to maintain proper blood volume and ion balance. The **nephron** is the working unit of the kidney. The parts of the nephron include the glomerulus, Bowman's capsule, and loop of Henle. Filtration takes place in the nephron's **glomerulus.** Water and dissolved materials such as glucose and amino acids pass on into the Bowman's capsule. Depending on concentration gradients, water and dissolved materials can pass back into the blood primarily through the proximal convoluted tubule. Reabsorption and water removal occurs in the **loop of Henle** and the conducting duct. Urine and other nitrogenous wastes pass from the kidneys to the bladders and are expelled.

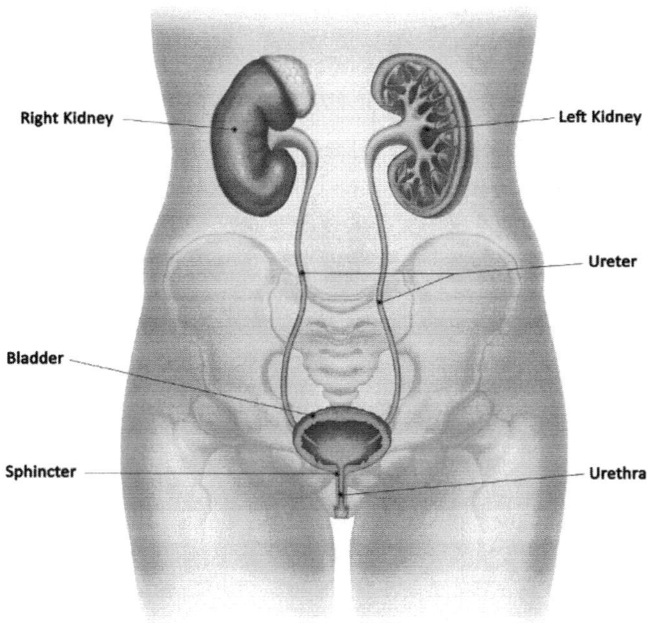

Review Video: Urinary System
Visit mometrix.com/academy and enter code: 601053

Endocrine System

The **endocrine system** consists of several ductless glands, which secrete hormones directly into the bloodstream. The **pituitary gland** controls the functions of the other glands in the system, regulates skeletal growth, and initiates the development of reproductive organs. The **pineal gland** regulates sleep cycles. The **thyroid gland** regulates metabolism and work with the **parathyroid glands** to help regulate the calcium level in the blood. The **adrenal glands** secrete the emergency hormone epinephrine, stimulate body repairs, and regulate sodium and potassium levels in the blood. The **islets of Langerhans**, located in the pancreas, secrete insulin and glucagon to regulate the level of blood sugar. In females, **ovaries** produce estrogen, which stimulates sexual development, and progesterone, which functions during pregnancy. In males, the **testes** secrete testosterone, which stimulates sexual development and sperm production.

Gland	Hormones	Disease
Adrenal Cortex	Aldosterone Cortisol Androgens	Addison's Disease Cushing's Disease
Adrenal Medulla	Epinephrine Norepinephrine	Anxiety Attacks Depression
Anterior Pituitary	Adrenocorticotropic hormone (ACTH) Follicle-stimulating hormone (FSH) Gonadotropic hormones Growth hormone (GH) Luteinizing hormone (LH) Prolactin Thyroid Stimulating Hormone (TSH)	Dwarfism Gigantism
Hypothalamus/ Posterior Pituitary	Inhibiting hormones (stop the release of other hormones) Antidiuretic hormone (ADH) Oxytocin Releasing hormones (trigger the release of other hormones)	Diabetes Insipidus
Kidneys	Calcitriol Erythropoietin	Hypertension
Ovaries	Estrogen Progesterone	Endometriosis Menometrorrhagia
Pancreas	Insulin Glucagon	Diabetes Mellitus
Parathyroid	Parathyroid hormone	Tetany Renal calculi
Pineal	Melatonin	Alzheimer's Disease
Testes	Testosterone	Gynecomastia Klinefelter Syndrome
Thymus	Thymic factor (TF) Thymosin Thymic humoral factor (THF) Thymopoietin	DiGeorge Syndrome

Gland	Hormones	Disease
Thyroid	Calcitonin Thyroxine (T4) Triiodothyronine (T3)	Cretinism Hypo/Hyperthyroidism Goiter Myxedema
Digestive tract	Gastrin Cholecystokinin Secretin Ghrelin Motilin	Gastritis Gastroesophageal reflux

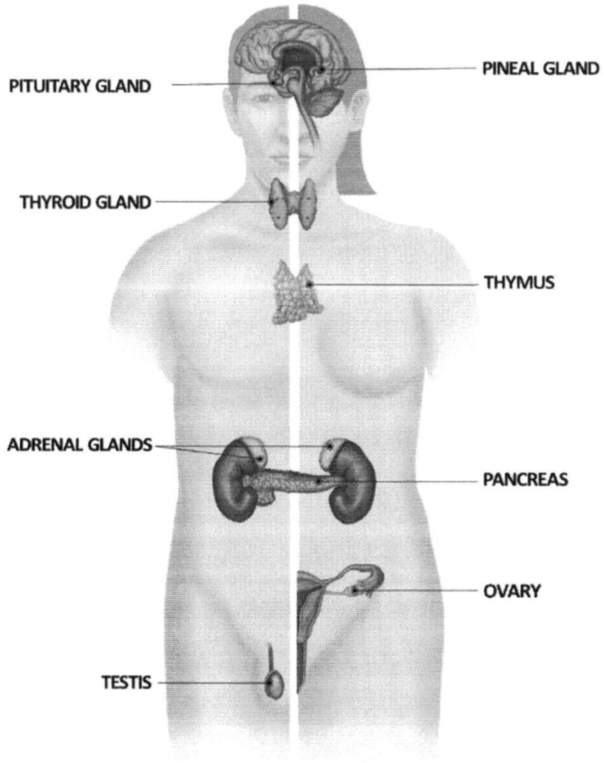

Review Video: Endocrine System
Visit mometrix.com/academy and enter code: 678939

Immune and Lymphatic Systems

Immune System

The **immune system** in animals defends the body against infection and disease. The immune system can be divided into two broad categories: innate immunity and adaptive immunity. **Innate immunity** includes the skin and mucous membranes, which provide a physical barrier to prevent pathogens from entering the body. Special chemicals including enzymes and proteins in mucus, tears, sweat, and stomach juices destroy pathogens. Numerous white blood cells such as neutrophils and macrophages protect the body from invading pathogens. **Adaptive immunity** involves the body responding to a specific antigen. Typically, B-lymphocytes or B cells produce antibodies against a specific antigen, and T-lymphocytes or T-cells take special roles as helpers, regulators, or killers. Some T-cells function as memory cells.

Review Video: Immune System
Visit mometrix.com/academy and enter code: 622899

Lymphatic System

The **lymphatic system** is connected to the cardiovascular system through a network of capillaries. The lymphatic system filters out organisms that cause disease, controls the production of disease-fighting antibodies, and produces white blood cells. The lymphatic system also prevents body tissues from swelling by draining fluids from them. Two of the most important areas in this system are the right lymphatic duct and the thoracic duct. The **right lymphatic duct** moves the immunity-bolstering lymph fluid through the top half of the body, while the **thoracic duct** moves lymph throughout the lower half. The spleen, thymus, and lymph nodes all generate and store the chemicals which form lymph and which are essential to protecting the body from disease.

The **lymphatic system** consists of the **thymus**, **lymph nodes**, **bone marrow**, and **spleen**. They primarily serve to distribute filtered fluids throughout the body and to remove excess fluid and debris. **White blood cells** are a key element of the lymphatic system which serve to prevent disease and repair the body after infection to prevent further illness.

Integumentary System

The integumentary system includes skin, hair, nails, sense receptors, sweat glands, and oil glands. The **skin** acts as a sensory organ, provides an exterior barrier against disease, regulates body temperature through perspiration, manufactures chemicals and hormones, and provides a place for nerves from the nervous system and parts of the circulation system to travel through. Skin has three layers: epidermis, dermis, and subcutaneous. The **epidermis** is the thin, outermost, waterproof layer. The **dermis** has the sweat glands, oil glands, and hair follicles. The **subcutaneous layer** has connective tissue. Also, this layer has **adipose** (i.e., fat) tissue, nerves, arteries, and veins.

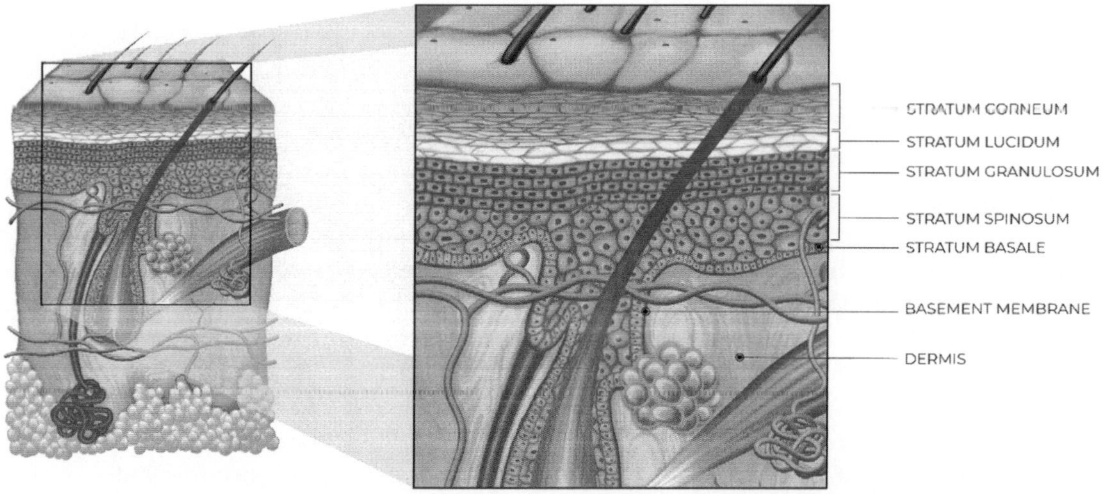

Review Video: Integumentary System
Visit mometrix.com/academy and enter code: 655980

Muscular System

The **muscular system** works in concert with the **skeletal system** to move the body and perform such core functions as cardiac activity. Key elements include:

- **Smooth muscle tissues** are involuntary muscles that are found in the walls of internal organs such as the stomach, intestines, and blood vessels. Smooth muscle tissues, or **visceral tissue,** is nonstriated. Smooth muscle cells are shorter and wider than skeletal muscle fibers. Smooth muscle tissue is also found in sphincters or valves that control the movement of material through openings throughout the body.
- **Cardiac muscle** tissue is involuntary muscle that is found only in the heart. Like skeletal muscle cells, cardiac muscle cells are also striated.
- **Skeletal muscles** are voluntary muscles that work in pairs to move parts of the skeleton. Skeletal muscles are composed of **muscle fibers** (cells) that are bound together in parallel bundles. Skeletal muscles are also known as **striated muscle** due to their striped histological appearance under a microscope.

Only skeletal muscle interacts with the skeleton to move the body. When they contract, the muscles transmit force to the attached bones. Working together, the muscles and bones act as a system of levers that move around the joints.

Review Video: Muscular System
Visit mometrix.com/academy and enter code: 967216

Major Muscles

The human body has more than 650 skeletal muscles than account for approximately half of a person's weight. Starting with the head and face, the temporalis and masseter move the mandible (lower jaw bone). The orbicularis oculi closes the eye. The orbicularis oris draws the lips together. The sternocleidomastoids move the head. The trapezius moves the shoulder, and the pectoralis major, deltoid, and latissimus dorsi move the upper arm. The biceps brachii and the triceps brachii move the lower arm. The rectus abdominis, external oblique, and erector spine move the trunk. The external and internal obliques elevate and depress the ribs. The gluteus maximus moves the upper leg. The quadriceps femoris, hamstrings, and sartorius move the lower leg. The gastrocnemius and the soleus extend the foot.

Skeletal Muscle Contraction

Skeletal muscles consist of numerous muscle fibers. Each muscle fiber contains a bundle of myofibrils, which are composed of multiple repeating contractile units called sarcomeres. **Myofibrils** contain two protein microfilaments: a thick filament and a thin filament. The **thick filament** is composed of the protein myosin. The **thin filament** is composed of the protein actin. The dark bands (striations) in skeletal muscles are formed when thick and thin filaments overlap. Light bands occur where the thin filament is overlapped. Skeletal muscle attraction occurs when the thin filaments slide over the thick filaments shortening the sarcomere. When an action potential (electrical signal) reaches a muscle fiber, calcium ions are released. According to the sliding filament model of muscle contraction, these calcium ions bind to the myosin and actin, which assists in the binding of the myosin heads of the thick filaments to the actin molecules of the thin filaments. Adenosine triphosphate released from glucose provides the energy necessary for the contraction.

Skeletal System

The skeletal system serves many functions including providing structural support, movement, and protection; producing blood cells; and storing substances such as fat and minerals. The **axial skeleton** transfers the weight from the upper body to the lower appendages. Bones provide attachment points for muscles. The cranium protects the brain. The vertebrae protect the spinal cord. The rib cage protects the heart and lungs. The pelvis protects the reproductive organs. **Joints** including hinge joints, ball-and-socket joints, pivot joints, ellipsoid joints, gliding joints, and saddle joints. The **red marrow** manufactures red and white blood cells. All bone marrow is red at birth, but adults have approximately one-half red bone marrow and one-half yellow bone marrow. Yellow bone marrow stores fat.

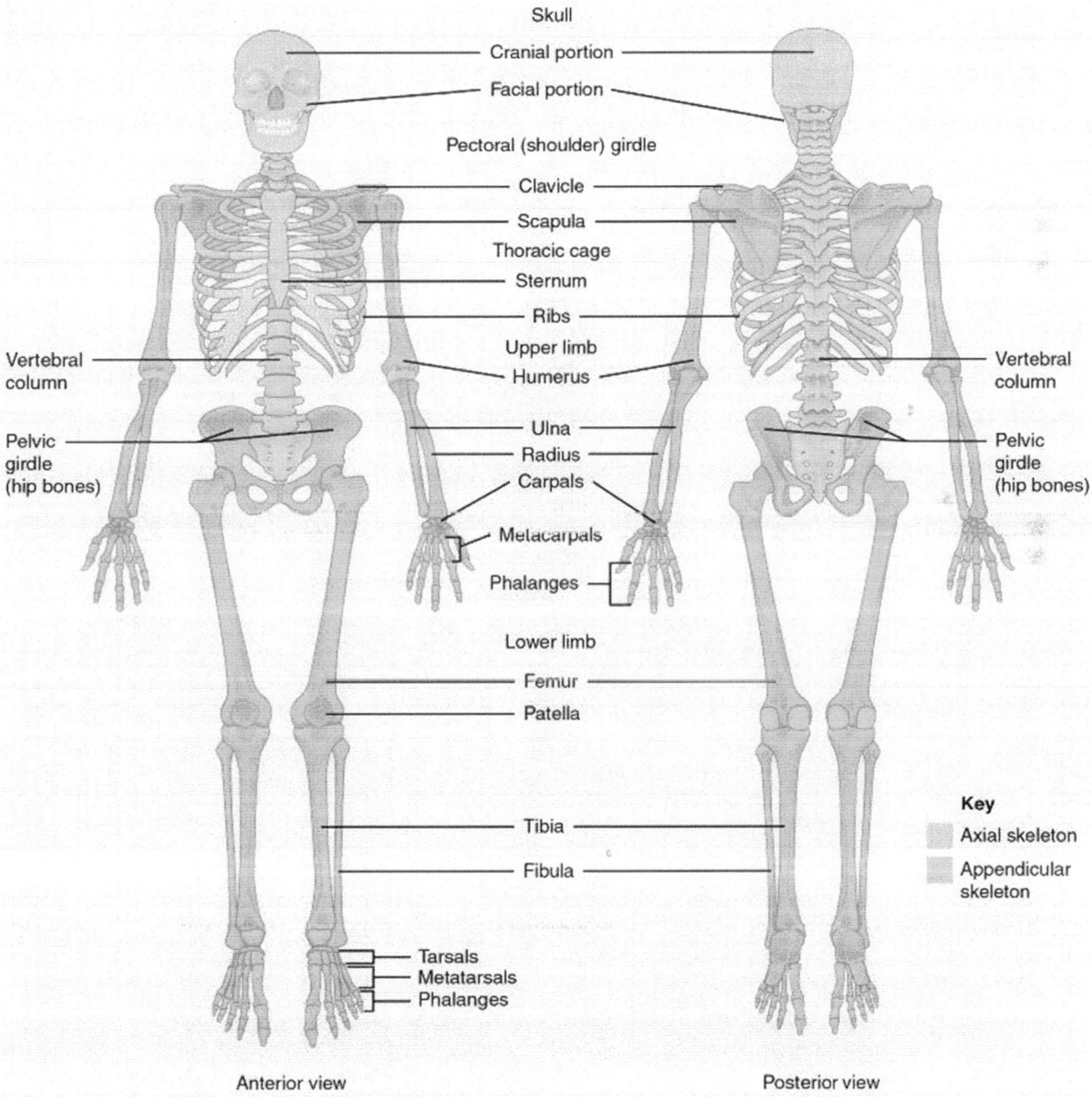

STRUCTURE OF AXIAL SKELETON AND APPENDICULAR SKELETON

The **human skeletal system**, which consists of 206 bones along with numerous tendons, ligaments, and cartilage, is divided into the axial skeleton and the appendicular skeleton.

The **axial skeleton** consists of 80 bones and includes the vertebral column, rib cage, sternum, skull, and hyoid bone. The **vertebral column** consists of 33 vertebrae classified as cervical vertebrae, thoracic vertebrae, lumbar vertebrae, and sacral vertebrae. The **rib cage** includes 12 paired ribs, 10 pairs of true ribs and two pairs of floating ribs, and the **sternum**, which consists of the manubrium, corpus sterni, and xiphoid process. The **skull** includes the cranium and facial bones. The **ossicles** are bones in the middle ear. The **hyoid bone** provides an attachment point for the tongue muscles. The axial skeleton protects vital organs including the brain, heart, and lungs.

The **appendicular skeleton** consists of 126 bones including the pectoral girdle, pelvic girdle, and appendages. The **pectoral girdle** consists of the scapulae (shoulder blades) and clavicles (collarbones). The **pelvic girdle** attaches to the sacrum at the sacroiliac joint. The upper appendages (arms) include the humerus, radius, ulna, carpals, metacarpals, and phalanges. The lower appendages (legs) include the femur, patella, fibula, tibia, tarsals, metatarsals, and phalanges.

The axial skeleton and the appendicular skeleton:

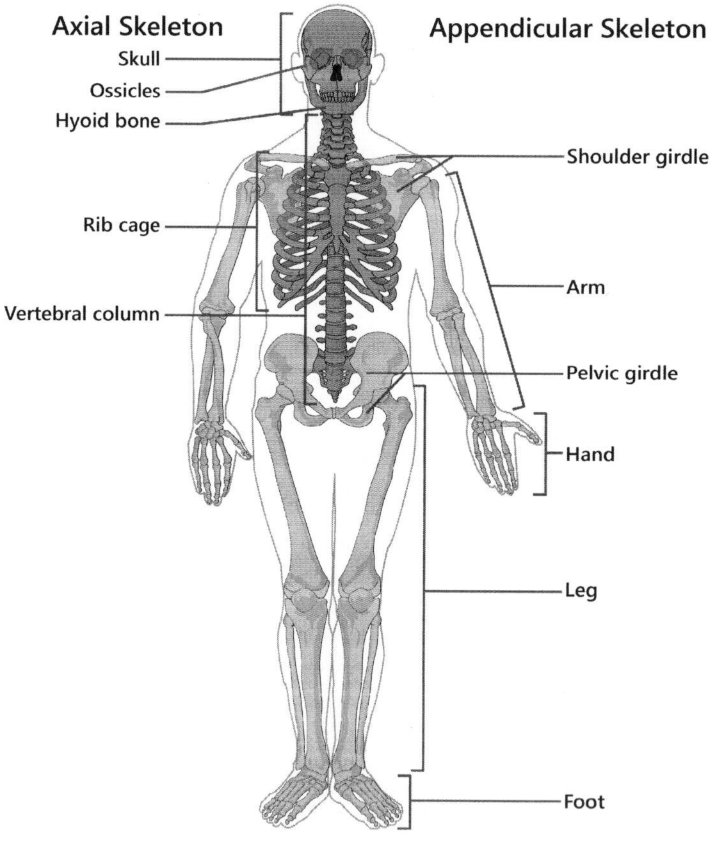

Review Video: Skeletal System
Visit mometrix.com/academy and enter code: 256447

Nervous System

The human **nervous system** consists of the **central nervous system** (i.e., brain and spinal cord) and the **peripheral nervous system** (i.e., nerves). They deliver voluntary and involuntary messages throughout the body. Core functions, such as digestion and respiration, are controlled by the brain via messages sent through the peripheral nervous system. The brain also receives external cues to regulate temperature and activate certain muscle groups.

Review Video: Function of the Nervous System
Visit mometrix.com/academy and enter code: 708428

The human nervous system senses, interprets, and issues commands as a response to conditions in the body's environment. This process is made possible by a complex communication system of cells called **neurons**.

Messages are sent across the plasma membrane of neurons through a process called **action potential**. These messages occur when a neuron is stimulated past a necessary threshold. These stimulations occur in a sequence from the stimulation point of one neuron to its contact with another neuron. At the point of contact, called a **chemical synapse**, a substance is released that stimulates or inhibits the action of the adjoining cell. A network of nerves composed of neurons fans out across the body and forms the framework for the nervous system. The direction the information flows depends on the specific organizations of nerve circuits and pathways.

Review Video: What is the Function of the Nervous System
Visit mometrix.com/academy and enter code: 708428

The Somatic Nervous system and the Reflex Arc

The somatic nervous system (**SNS**) controls the five senses and the voluntary movement of skeletal muscle. So, this system has all of the neurons that are connected to sense organs. Efferent (motor) and afferent (sensory) nerves help the somatic nervous system operate the senses and the movement of skeletal muscle. **Efferent nerves** bring signals from the central nervous system to the sensory organs and the muscles. **Afferent nerves** bring signals from the sensory organs and the muscles to the central nervous system. The somatic nervous system also performs involuntary movements which are known as reflex arcs.

A **reflex**, the simplest act of the nervous system, is an automatic response without any conscious thought to a stimulus via the reflex arc. The **reflex arc** is the simplest nerve pathway, which bypasses the brain and is controlled by the spinal cord. For example, in the classic knee-jerk response (patellar tendon reflex), the stimulus is the reflex hammer hitting the tendon, and the response is the muscle contracting, which jerks the foot upward. The stimulus is detected by sensory receptors, and a message is sent along a **sensory** (afferent) neuron to one or more

interneurons in the spinal cord. The interneuron(s) transmit this message to a **motor** (efferent) neuron, which carries the message to the correct **effector** (muscle).

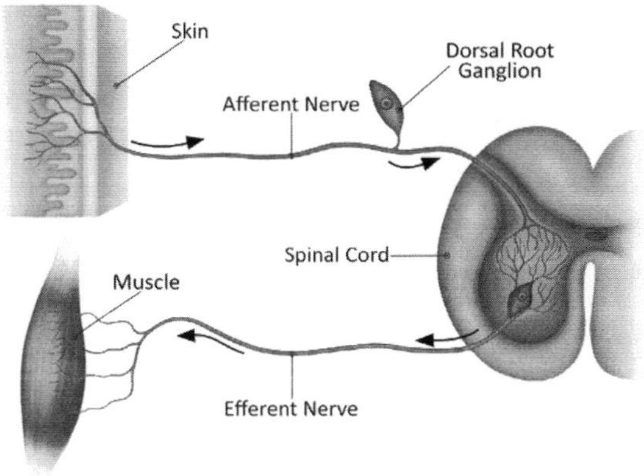

The Eyes

The eyes are a sensory organ, and therefore, belong to the nervous system. The main **parts of the eye** and their functions are as follows:

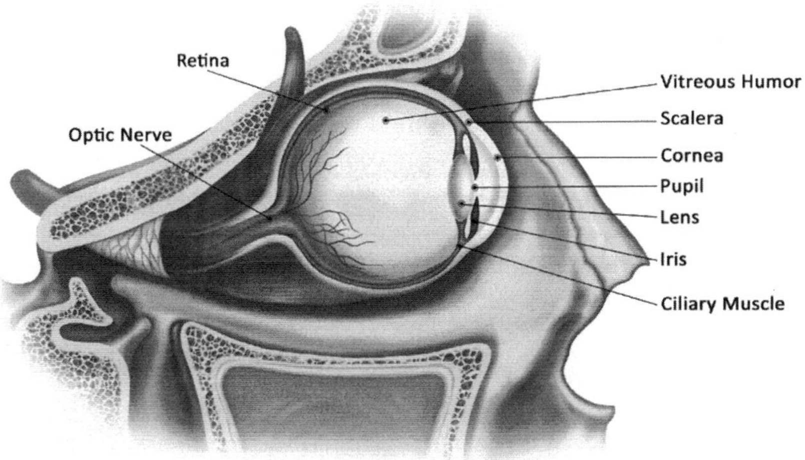

- **Aqueous humor** is watery fluid that maintains eye pressure.
- The **bony orbit** is the socket protecting the eye.
- **Cranial nerves** that help with the function of the eye such as movement or vision include:
    - the optic nerve (cranial nerve II)
    - oculomotor (III)
    - trochlear (IV)
    - trigeminal (V)
    - abducens (VI)
    - vagus (X) nerves
- **Eyelashes and lids** protect the eye and sweep out particles.
- **Extrinsic muscles** focus the eye.
- The **lacrimal glands** are tear ducts to moisten the eye.
- The **lens** refracts light.
- The **optic disc** is the blind spot.
- The **pupil** regulates light entry.
- The **retina** has rods for black and white imaging and cones for color imaging, and helps trigger the optic nerve to send impulses to the brain.
- The **macula** is at the retinal center that is very sensitive to light. The black spot in the center is called the fovea which provides the sharpest vision.
- The **choroid** is a black layer behind the retina that absorbs light and nourishes the retina.
- The **cornea** is the window at the front of the eye that helps with focus.
- The **iris** regulates light entry.
- The **sclera** is tough, white fibrous connective tissue holding nerves and vessels that acts as protection for the eye.
- The **suspensory ligament** connects the lens to the ciliary muscles of the iris.
- The **vitreous humor** is jelly that maintains the eye's shape and refracts images.

REPRODUCTIVE SYSTEM

The **reproductive system** consists of the prostate, testicle, penis, and scrotum in males and ovaries, uterus, vagina, fallopian tubes, and mammary glands in females. The primary function is the creation of human life. **Sperm** is produced by the testes and is delivered to the ovary-produced **eggs** in the fallopian tubes for fertilization. The uterus then serves as the home for the developing fetus. **Mammary glands** secrete nutrients for the newborn child.

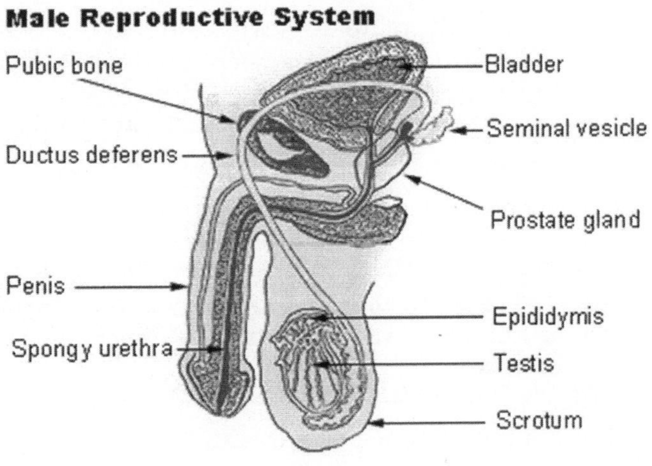

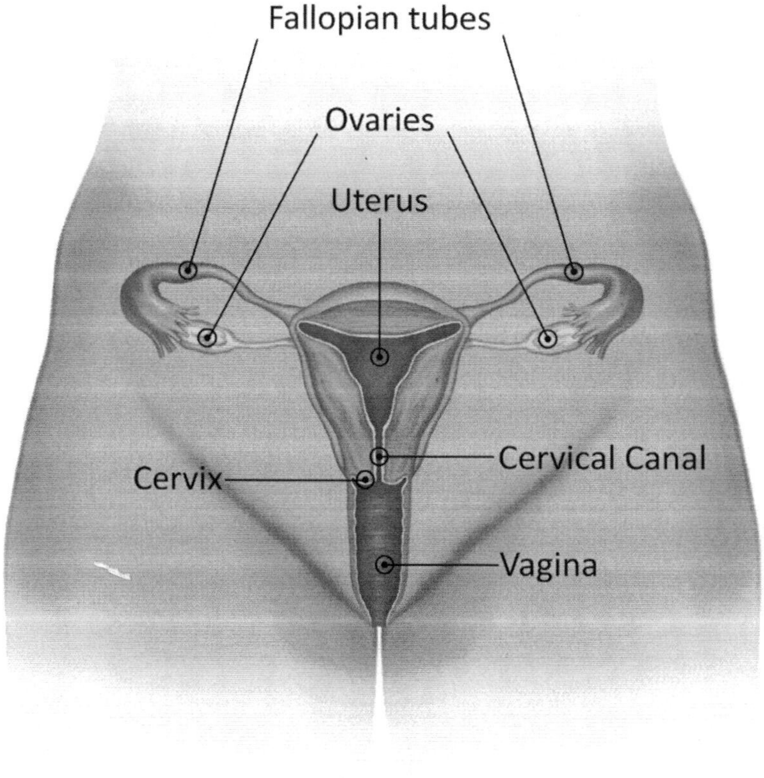

Review Video: Reproductive Systems
Visit mometrix.com/academy and enter code: 505450

INTERCONNECTEDNESS OF BODY SYSTEMS

RESPIRATORY AND CIRCULATORY SYSTEMS WORKING TOGETHER

Body systems work in concert with each other to respond to increasing and decreasing demands on the body and regulate **homeostasis**, the manner in which the human body regulates itself based on internal and external conditions in order to maintain a physiological balance. For example, the heart pumps blood through the **circulatory system** to distribute oxygenated blood throughout the body to meet physiological demands at any given time. Blood becomes oxygenated in the lungs (**respiratory system**) after excess **carbon dioxide** is released from the body through respiration. Inspiration of **oxygen** into the lungs allows the blood to become oxygen-rich so as to be distributed throughout the body. When physiological demands of the body increase (i.e., quickly climbing stairs), inspiration of oxygen increases and the heart pumps faster in order to more efficiently increase the delivery of oxygenated blood throughout the body. When the intense physical activity subsides, breathing slows and the heart returns to a normal resting heart rate.

IMPACT OF DIET AND EXERCISE ON THE CIRCULATORY SYSTEM

The delivery of **oxygenated blood** throughout the body can be accomplished more efficiently with a pattern of consistent exercise and good dietary habits. **Aerobic** activity strengthens the heart by increasing the oxygen carrying capacity of the red blood cells (**hemoglobin**) while also lowering resting blood pressure. In addition, aerobic exercise helps increase high density lipoproteins (HDL) (i.e., "good cholesterol") and decreasing low density lipoproteins (i.e., "bad cholesterol") which helps keep the arteries (**circulatory system**) clear. Consistent and adequate physical activity also helps regulate blood sugars, which can reduce the likelihood of developing Type II diabetes. A high fiber, low fat diet also directly contributes to lower blood sugar levels, cholesterol management, and helps maintain healthy bowels (**digestive system**). Combining regular aerobic physical activity with a high fiber, low fat diet is one of the most effective methods to improve one's cardiovascular health, maintain a healthy weight, and increase personal longevity.

Homeostasis

Maintenance of Homeostasis in Organisms

Role of Feedback Mechanisms

Homeostasis is the regulation of internal chemistry to maintain a constant internal environment. This state is controlled through various feedback mechanisms that consist of receptors, an integrator, and effectors. **Receptors** such as mechanoreceptors or thermoreceptors in the skin detect the stimuli. Then, an **integrator**, such as the brain or spinal cord, receives the information concerning the stimuli and sends out signals to other parts of the body. Finally, **effectors**, such as muscles or glands, respond to the stimulus. Basically, the receptors receive the stimuli and notify an integrator, which signals the effectors to respond.

Feedback mechanisms can be negative or positive. **Negative-feedback** mechanisms are mechanisms that provide a decrease in response with an increase in stimulus that inhibits the stimulus, which in turn decreases the response. **Positive-feedback** mechanisms are mechanisms that provide an increase in response with an increase in stimulus, which actually increases the stimulus, which in turn increases the response.

Role of Hypothalamus

The hypothalamus plays a major role in the homoeostasis of vertebrates. The **hypothalamus** is the central portion of the brain just above the brainstem and is linked to the endocrine system through the pituitary gland. The hypothalamus releases special hormones that influence the secretion of pituitary hormones. The hypothalamus regulates the fundamental physiological state by controlling body temperature, hunger, thirst, sleep, behaviors related to attachment, sexual development, fight-or-flight stress response, and circadian rhythms.

Role of Endocrine System and Hormones

All vertebrates have an **endocrine system** that consists of numerous ductless glands that produce hormones to help coordinate many functions of the body. **Hormones** are signaling molecules that are received by receptors. Many hormones are secreted in response to signals from the pituitary gland and hypothalamus gland. Other hormones are secreted in response to signals from inside the body. Hormones can consist of amino acids, proteins, or lipid molecules such as steroid hormones. Hormones can affect target cells, which have the correct receptor that is able to bind to that particular hormone. Most cells have receptors for more than one type of hormone. Hormones are distributed to the target cells in the blood by the cardiovascular system. Hormones incorporate feedback mechanisms to help the body maintain homeostasis.

Role of Antidiuretic Hormone

Antidiuretic hormone (ADH) helps maintain homeostasis in vertebrates. ADH is produced by the posterior pituitary gland, and it regulates the reabsorption of water in the kidneys and concentrates the urine. The stimulus in this feedback mechanism is a drop in blood volume due to water loss. This signal is picked up by the hypothalamus, which signals the pituitary gland to secrete ADH. ADH is carried by the cardiovascular system to the nephrons in the kidneys signaling them to reabsorb more water and send less out as waste. As more water is reabsorbed, the blood volume increases, which is monitored by the hypothalamus. As the blood volume reaches the set point, the hypothalamus signals for a decrease in the secretion of ADH, and the cycle continues.

Role of Insulin and Glucagon

Insulin and glucagon are hormones that help maintain the glucose concentration in the blood. Insulin and glucagon are secreted by the clumps of endocrine cells called the **pancreatic islets** that are located in the pancreas. Insulin and glucagon work together to maintain the blood glucose level. **Insulin** stimulates cells to remove glucose from the blood. **Glucagon** stimulates the liver to convert glycogen to glucose. After eating, glucose levels increase in the blood. This stimulus signals the pancreas to stop the secretion of glucagon and to start secreting insulin. Cells respond to the insulin and remove glucose from the blood, lowering the level of glucose in the blood. Later, after eating, the level of glucose in the blood decreases further. This stimulus signals the pancreas to secrete glucagon and decrease the secretion of insulin. In response to the stimulus, the liver converts glycogen to glucose, and the level of glucose in the blood rises. When the individual eats, the cycle begins again.

Thermoregulation

Animals exhibit many adaptations that help them achieve homeostasis, or a stable internal environment. Some of these adaptions are behavioral. Most organisms exhibit some type of behavioral thermoregulation. **Thermoregulation** is the ability to keep the body temperature within certain boundaries. The type of behavioral thermoregulation depends on whether the animal is an ectotherm or an endotherm. **Ectotherms** are "cold-blooded," and their body temperature changes with their external environment. **Endotherms** are "warm-blooded" and maintain a stable body temperature by internal means.

To regulate their temperature, ectotherms often move to an appropriate location. For example, fish move to warmer waters while animals will climb to higher grounds. **Diurnal ectotherms** such as reptiles often bask in the sun to increase their body temperatures. Butterflies are special ectotherms classified as **heliotherms** since they get nearly all of their heat from basking in the sun.

While they have internal systems that regulate temperature, many endotherms that live in hot environments have adapted to the nocturnal lifestyle. Desert animals are often nocturnal to escape high daytime temperatures. Other nocturnal animals sleep during the day in underground burrows or dens.

Reproduction, Development, and Growth in Animals

Gamete Formation

Gametogenesis is the formation of gametes, or reproductive cells. Gametes are produced by meiosis. **Meiosis** is a special type of cell division that consists of two consecutive mitotic divisions referred to as meiosis I and meiosis II. **Meiosis I** is a reduction division in which a diploid cell is reduced to two haploid daughter cells that contain only one of each pair of homologous chromosomes. During **meiosis II**, those haploid cells are further divided to form four haploid cells. **Spermatogenesis** in males produces four viable sperm cells from each complete cycle of meiosis. **Oogenesis** produces four daughter cells, but only one is a viable egg and the other three are polar bodies.

Fertilization

Fertilization is the union of a sperm cell and an egg cell to produce a zygote. Many sperm may bind to an egg, but only one joins with the egg and injects its nuclei into the egg. Fertilization can be external or internal. **External fertilization** takes place outside of the female's body. For example, many fish, amphibians, crustaceans, mollusks, and corals reproduce externally by **spawning** or releasing gametes into the water simultaneously or right after each other. Reptiles and birds reproduce by **internal fertilization**. All mammals except monotremes (e.g. platypus) reproduce by internal fertilization.

Embryonic Development

Embryonic development in animals is typically divided into four stages: cleavage, patterning, differentiation, and growth. **Cleavage** occurs immediately after fertilization when the large single-celled zygote immediately begins to divide into smaller and smaller cells without an increase in mass. A hollow ball of cells forms a blastula. Next, during patterning, gastrulation occurs. During gastrulation, the cells are organized into three primary germ layers: ectoderm, mesoderm, and endoderm. Then, the cells in these layers differentiate into special tissues and organs. For example, the nervous system develops from the ectoderm. The muscular system develops from the mesoderm. Much of the digestive system develops from the endoderm. The final stage of embryonic development is growth and further tissue specialization. The embryo continues to grow until ready for hatching or birth.

Postnatal Growth

Postnatal growth occurs from hatching or birth until death. The length of the postnatal growth depends on the species. Elephants can live 70 years, but mice only about 4 years. Right after animals are hatched or born, they go through a period of rapid growth and development. In vertebrates, bones lengthen, muscles grow in bulk, and fat is deposited. At maturity, bones stop growing in length, but bones can grow in width and repair themselves throughout the animal's lifetime, and muscle deposition slows down. Fat cells continue to increase and decrease in size throughout the animal's life. Growth is controlled by genetics but is also influenced by nutrition and disease. Most animals are sexually mature in less than two years and can produce offspring.

Characteristics of Major Plant Divisions

Vascular and Nonvascular Plants

Vascular plants, also referred to as **tracheophytes**, have dermal tissue, meristematic tissue, ground tissues, and vascular tissues. Nonvascular plants, also referred to as **bryophytes**, do not have the vascular tissue xylem and phloem. Vascular plants can grow very tall, whereas nonvascular plants are short and close to the ground. Vascular plants can be found in dry regions, but nonvascular plants typically grow near or in moist areas. Vascular plants have leaves, roots, and stems, but nonvascular plants have leaf-like, root-like, and stem-like structures that do not have true vascular tissue. Nonvascular plants have hair-like **rhizoids**, that act like roots by anchoring them to the ground and absorbing water. Vascular plants include angiosperms, gymnosperms, and ferns. Nonvascular plants include mosses and liverworts.

Flowering Versus Nonflowering Plants

Angiosperms and gymnosperms are both vascular plants. **Angiosperms** are flowering plants, and **gymnosperms** are non-flowering plants. Angiosperms reproduce by seeds that are enclosed in an ovary, usually in a fruit, while gymnosperms reproduce by unenclosed or "naked" seeds on scales, leaves, or cones. Angiosperms can be further classified as either monocots or dicots, depending on if they have one or two cotyledons, respectively. Angiosperms include grasses, garden flowers, vegetables, and broadleaf trees such as maples, birches, elms, and oaks. Gymnosperms include conifers such as pines, spruces, cedars, and redwoods.

Review Video: Kingdom Plantae Characteristics
Visit mometrix.com/academy and enter code: 710084

Monocots and Dicots

Angiosperms can be classified as either monocots or dicots. The seeds of **monocots** have one cotyledon, and the seeds of **dicots** have two cotyledons. The flowers of monocots have petals in multiples of three, and the flowers of dicots have petals in multiples of four or five. The leaves of monocots are slender with parallel veins, while the leaves of dicots are broad and flat with branching veins. The vascular bundles in monocots are distributed throughout the stem, whereas the vascular bundles in dicots are arranged in rings. Monocots have a **fibrous root system**, and dicots have a **taproot system**.

Major Plant Tissues and Organs

Plant Dermal Tissue

Plant dermal tissue is called the epidermis, and is usually a single layer of closely-packed cells that covers leaves and young stems. The epidermis protects the plant by secreting the cuticle, which is a waxy substance that helps prevent water loss and infections. The epidermis in leaves has tiny pores called **stomata**. Guard cells in the epidermis control the opening and closing of the stomata. The epidermis usually does not have chloroplasts. The epidermis may be replaced by periderm in older plants. The **periderm** is also referred to as bark. The layers of the periderm are cork cells or phellem, phelloderm, and cork cambium or phellogen. Cork is the outer layer of the periderm and consists of nonliving cells. The periderm protects the plant and provides insulation.

Plant Vascular Tissue

The two major types of plant vascular tissue are xylem and phloem. Xylem and phloem are bound together in vascular bundles. A meristem called vascular cambium is located between the xylem and phloem and produces new xylem and phloem. **Xylem** is made up of tracheids and vessel elements. All vascular plants contain tracheids, but only angiosperms contain vessel elements. Xylem provides support and transports water and dissolved minerals unidirectionally from the roots upward using processes like transpiration pull and root pressure. Phloem is made up of companion cells and sieve-tube cells. **Phloem** transports dissolved sugars produced during photosynthesis and other nutrients bidirectionally to non-photosynthetic areas of the plant. By active transport, the companion vessels move glucose in and out of the sieve-tube cells.

Plant Ground Tissue

The three major types of ground tissue are parenchyma tissue, collenchyma tissue, and sclerenchyma tissue. Most ground tissue is made up of parenchyma. **Parenchyma** is formed by parenchyma cells, and it function in photosynthesis, food storage, and tissue repair. The inner tissue of a leaf, mesophyll, is an example of parenchyma tissue. **Collenchyma** is made of collenchyma cells and provides support in roots, stems, and petioles. **Sclerenchyma** tissue is made of sclereid cells, which are more rigid than the collenchyma cells, and provides rigid support and protection. Plant sclerenchyma tissue may contain cellulose or lignin. Fabrics such as jute, hemp, and flax are made of sclerenchyma tissue.

PLANT MERISTEMATIC TISSUE

Meristems or meristematic tissues are regions of plant growth. The cells in meristems are undifferentiated and always remain **totipotent**, which means they can always develop into any type of special tissue. Meristem cells can divide and produce new cells, which can aid in the process of regenerating damaged parts. Cells of meristems reproduce asexually through mitosis or cell division that is regulated by hormones. The two types of meristems are lateral meristems and apical meristems. **Primary growth** occurs at **apical meristems**, located at the tip of roots and shoots, and increases the length of the plant. Primary meristems include the protoderm, which produces epidermis; the procambium, which produces cambium, or lateral meristems; xylem and phloem; and the ground meristem, which produces ground tissue including parenchyma. **Secondary growth** occurs at the lateral or secondary meristems and causes an increase in diameter or thickness.

FLOWERS

The primary function of flowers is to produce seeds for reproduction of the plant. Flowers have a **pedicel**, a stalk with a receptacle or enlarged upper portion, which holds the developing seeds. Flowers also can have sepals and petals. **Sepals** are leaflike structures that protect the bud. **Petals**, which are collectively called the corolla, help to attract pollinators. Plants can have stamens, pistils, or both depending on the type of plant. The **stamen** consists of the anther and filament. The end of the stamen is called the **anther** and is where pollen is produced. Pollen also contains sperm, which is needed in order for a proper plant zygot to form. The **pistil** consists of the stigma, style, and ovary. The ovary contains the ovules, which house the egg cells.

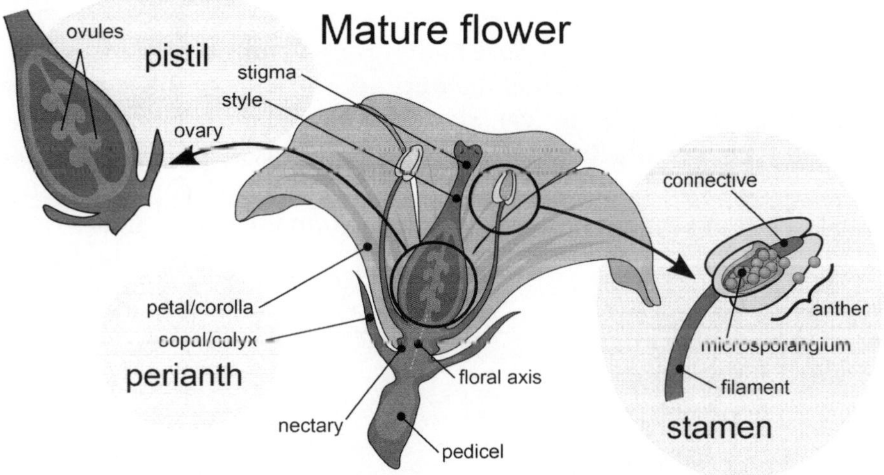

STEMS

Plants can have either woody or nonwoody (herbaceous) stems. **Woody** stems consist of wood, or bark, as a structural tissue, while **herbaceous** stems are very flexible. The stem is divided into nodes and internodes. Buds are located at the nodes and may develop into leaves, roots, flowers, cones, or more stems. Stems consist of dermal tissue, ground tissue, and vascular tissue. **Monocot stems have vascular bundles distributed through the stem. Dicots have rings of vascular bundles**. Stems have four main functions: (1) they provide support to leaves, flowers, and fruits;

(2) they transport materials in the xylem and phloem; (3) they store food; and (4) they have meristems, which provide all of the new cells for the plant.

MONOCOT		DICOT	
Single Cotyledon		Two Cotyledon	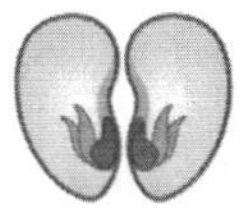
Long Narrow Leaf Parallel Veins		Broad Leaf Network of Veins	
Vascular Bundles Scattered	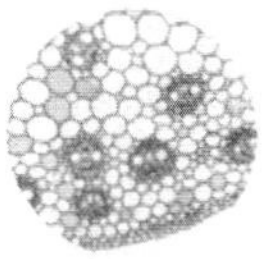	Vascular Bundles in a Ring	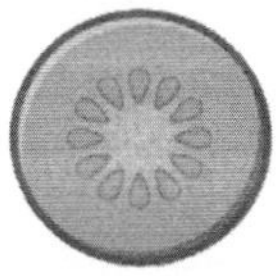
Floral Parts in Multiples of 3		Floral Parts in Multiples of 4 or 5	

Leaves

The primary function of a **leaf** is to manufacture food through photosynthesis. The leaf consists of a flat portion called the **blade** and a stalk called the **petiole**. The edge of the leaf is called the margin and can be entire, toothed, or lobed. Veins transport food and water and make up the skeleton of the leaf. The large central vein is called the **midrib**. The blade has an upper and lower epidermis. The epidermis is covered by a protective cuticle. The lower epidermis contains many stomata, which are pores that allow air to enter and leave the leaf. Stomata also regulate transpiration. The middle portion of the leaf is called the **mesophyll**. The mesophyll consists of the palisade mesophyll and the spongy mesophyll. Most photosynthesis occurs in chloroplasts located in the palisade mesophyll.

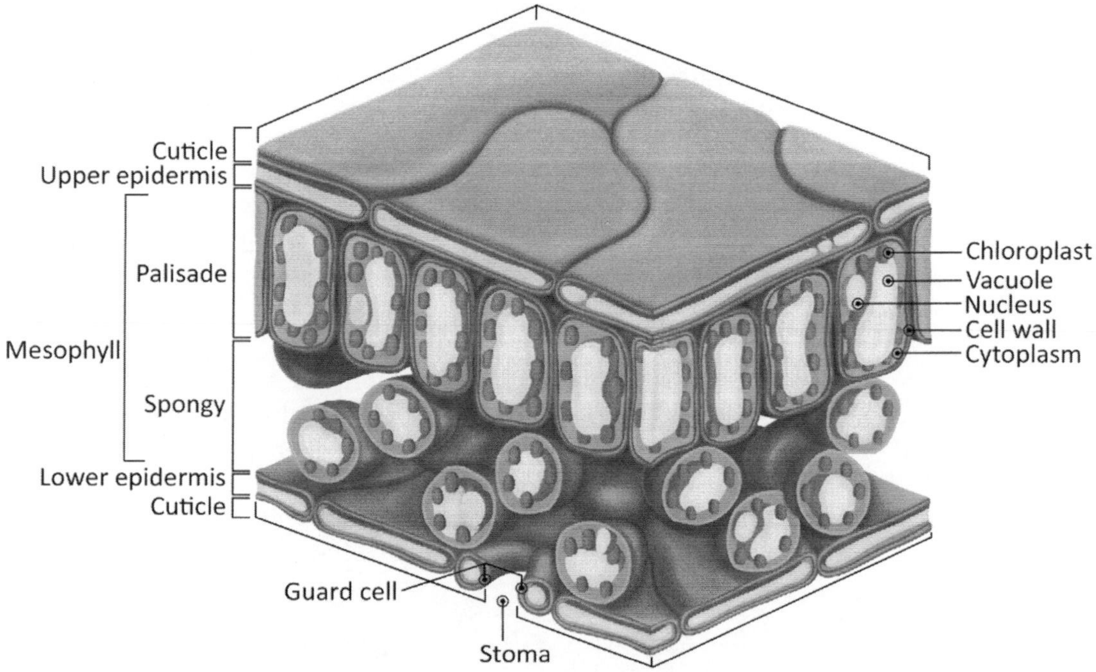

Roots

The primary functions of roots are to anchor the plant, absorb materials, and store food. The two basic types of root systems are taproot systems and fibrous root systems. **Taproot systems** have a primary root with many smaller secondary roots. **Fibrous root systems**, which lack a primary root, consist of a mass of many small secondary roots. The root has three main regions: the area of maturation, the area of elongation, and the area of cell division or the meristematic region. The root is covered by an epidermal cell, some of which develops into root hairs. **Root hairs** absorb water and minerals by osmosis, and capillary action helps move the water upward through the roots to the rest of the plant. The center of the root is the **vascular cylinder**, which contains the xylem and phloem. The vascular cylinder is surrounded by the cortex where the food is stored. Primary growth occurs at the root tip. Secondary growth occurs at the vascular cambium located between the xylem and phloem.

Plant Life Cycles and Reproductive Strategies

Pollination Strategies

Pollination is the transfer of pollen from the anther of the stamen to the stigma of the pistil on the same plant or on a different plant. Pollinators can be either **abiotic** (not derived from a living organism) or **biotic** (derived from a living organism). Abiotic pollinators include wind and water. Approximately 20% of pollination occurs by abiotic pollinators. For example, grasses are typically pollinated by wind, and aquatic plants are typically pollinated by water. Biotic pollinators include insects, birds, mammals, and occasionally reptiles. Most biotic pollinators are insects. Many plants have colored petals and strong scents, which attract insects. Pollen rubs off on the insects and is transferred as they move from plant to plant.

Seed Dispersal Methods

Methods of **seed dispersal** can be abiotic or biotic. Methods of seed dispersal include gravity, wind, water, and animals. Some plants produce seeds in fruits that get eaten by animals and then are distributed to new locations in the animals' waste. Some seeds (e.g. dandelions) have structures to aid in dispersal by wind. Some seeds have barbs that get caught in animal hair or bird feathers and are then carried to new locations by the animals. Interestingly, some animals bury seeds for food storage but do not return for the seeds. The seeds of aquatic plants can be dispersed by water, while the seeds of plants near rivers, streams, lakes, and beaches (e.g. coconuts) are also often dispersed by water. Some plants, in a method called **mechanical dispersal**, can propel or shoot their seeds away from them even up to several feet. For example, touch-me-nots and violets utilize mechanical dispersal.

Alternation of Generations

Alternation of generations, also referred to as **metagenesis**, contains both a sexual phase and an asexual phase in the life cycle of the plant. Mosses and ferns reproduce by alternation of generations: the sexual phase is called the **gametophyte**, and the asexual phase is called the **sporophyte**. During the sexual phase, a sperm fertilizes an egg to form a zygote. By mitosis, the zygote develops into the sporophyte. The sporangia in the sori of the sporophyte produce the spores through meiosis. The spores germinate and by mitosis produce the gametophyte.

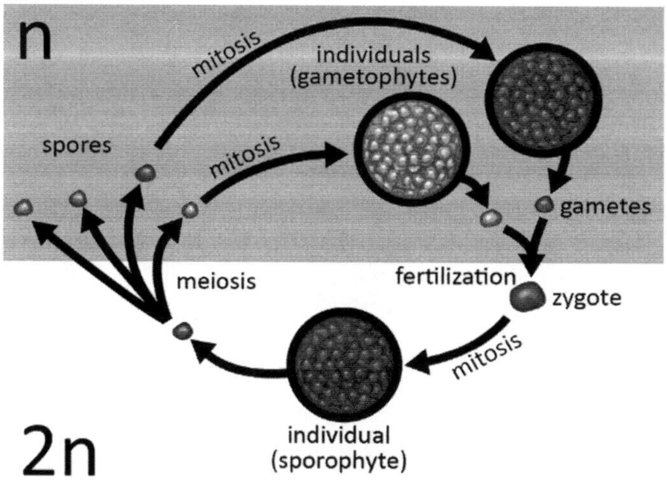

Plant Transportation of Water and Nutrients

Obtaining and Transporting Water and Inorganic Nutrients

Inorganic nutrients and water enter plants through the root hair and travel to the xylem. Once the water, minerals, and salts have crossed the endodermis, they must be moved upward through the xylem by water uptake. Most of a plant's water is lost through the stomata by transpiration. This loss is necessary to provide the tension needed to pull the water and nutrients up through the xylem. In order to maintain the remaining water that is necessary for the functioning of the plant, guard cells control the stomata. Whether an individual stoma is closed or open is controlled by two guard cells. When the guard cells lose water and become flaccid, they collapse together, closing the stoma. When the guard cells swell with water and become turgid, they move apart, opening the stoma.

Use of Roots

Plant roots have numerous root hairs that absorb water and inorganic nutrients such as minerals and salts. Root hairs are thin, hair-like outgrowths of the root's epidermal cells that exponentially increase the root's surface area. Water molecules cross the cell membranes of the root hairs by **osmosis** and then travel on to the vascular cylinder. Inorganic nutrients are transported across the cell membranes of the root endodermis by **active transport**. The endodermis is a single layer of cells that the water and nutrients must pass through by osmosis or active transport. To control mineral uptake by the roots, Casparian strips act as an extracellular diffusion barrier, and forces nutrients to be pulled into the plant. While water passes through by osmosis, mineral uptake is controlled by transport proteins.

Use of Xylem

The xylem contains dead, water-conducting cells called tracheids and vessels. The movement of water upward through the tracheids and vessels is explained by the **cohesion-tension theory**. First, water is lost through evaporation of the plant's surface through transpiration. This can occur at any surface exposed to air but is mainly through the stomata in the epidermis. This transpiration puts the water inside the xylem in a state of tension. Because water is cohesive due to the strong hydrogen bonds between molecules, the water is pulled up the xylem as long as the water is transpiring.

Products of Photosynthesis

Glucose Produced During Photosynthesis

Plants produce glucose, a simple carbohydrate or monosaccharide, during photosynthesis. Plants do not transport glucose molecules directly, but instead glucose undergoes reactions to form sucrose, starch, and cellulose which are then used in different ways. Glucose is joined to a fructose molecule to form **sucrose**, a disaccharide, which is transported in sap. Like glucose, sucrose is also considered a simple carbohydrate. Starches and cellulose are complex carbohydrates consisting of long chains of glucose molecules called polysaccharides. Plants use **starch** to store glucose, and **cellulose** for rigidity in cell walls.

Use of Phloem to Transport Products of Photosynthesis

The movement of sugars and other materials from the leaves to other tissues throughout the plants is called **translocation**. Nutrients are translocated from **sources**, or areas with excess sugars such as mature leaves, to **sinks**, areas where sugars are needed (i.e. roots or developing seeds). Phloem vessels are found in the vascular bundles along with the xylem. Phloem contains conducting cells called sieve elements, which are connected end to end in sieve tubes. **Sieve tubes** carry sap from sugar sources to sugar sinks. Phloem sap contains mostly sucrose dissolved in water. The sap can also contain proteins, amino acids, and hormones. Some plants transport sugar alcohols. Loading the sugar into the sieve tubes causes water to enter the tubes by osmosis, creating a higher hydrostatic pressure at the source end of the tube. This pressure is what causes nutrients to move upward towards the sink areas. Sugar is removed from the sieve tube at the sink end and the solute potential is increased, thus causing water to leave the phloem. This process is referred to as the **pressure-flow mechanism**.

Chapter Quiz

Ready to see how well you retained what you just read? Scan the QR code to go directly to the chapter quiz interface for this study guide. If you're using a computer, simply visit the online resources page at **mometrix.com/resources719/mttcbiology** and click the Chapter Quizzes link.

Ecological Systems

Hierarchical Structure of the Biosphere

Biosphere

Components

The **biosphere** is the region of the earth inhabited by living things. The components of the biosphere from smallest to largest are organisms, populations, communities, ecosystems, and biomes. Organisms of the same species make up a **population**. All of the populations in an area make up the **community**. The community combined with the physical environment for a region forms an **ecosystem**. Several ecosystems are grouped together to form large geographic regions called **biomes**.

Population

A **population** is a group of all the individuals of one species in a specific area or region at a certain time. A **species** is a group of organisms that can breed and produce fertile offspring. There may be many populations of a specific species in a large geographic region. **Ecologists** study the size, density, and growth rate of populations to determine their stability. Population size continuously changes with births, deaths, and migrations. The population density is the number of individuals per unit of area. Growth rates for a population may be exponential or logistic. Ecologists also study how the individuals are dispersed within a population. Some species form clusters, while others are evenly or randomly spaced. However, every population has limiting factors. Changes in the environment or geography can reduce or limit population size. The individuals of a population interact with each other and with other organisms in the community in various ways, including competition and predation, which have direct impacts population size.

Community Interactions

A **community** is all of the populations of different species that live in an area and interact with each other. Community interaction can be intraspecific or interspecific. **Intraspecific interactions** occur between members of the same species. **Interspecific interactions** occur between members of different species. Different types of interactions include competition, predation, and symbiosis. Communities with high diversity are more complex and more stable than communities with low diversity. The level of diversity can be seen in a food web of the community, which shows all the feeding relationships within the community.

Ecosystems

An **ecosystem** is the basic unit of ecology. An ecosystem is the sum of all the biotic and abiotic factors in an area. **Biotic factors** are all living things such as plants, animals, fungi, and microorganisms. **Abiotic factors** include the light, water, air, temperature, and soil in an area. Ecosystems obtain the energy they need from sunlight. Ecosystems also contain biogeochemical cycles such as the hydrologic cycle and the nitrogen cycle. Ecosystems are generally classified as either terrestrial or aquatic. All of the living things within an ecosystem are called its community. The number and variety of living things within a community describes the ecosystem's **biodiversity**. However, each ecosystem can only support a limited number of organisms known as the **carrying capacity**.

Influences on Population Size

Biotic and Abiotic Factors in an Ecosystem

Every ecosystem consists of multiple abiotic and biotic factors. **Abiotic factors** are the nonbiological physical and chemical factors that affect the ecosystem. Abiotic factors include soil type, atmospheric conditions, sunlight, water, wind, chemical elements, and natural disturbances. In aquatic ecosystems, abiotic factors include salinity, turbidity, water depth, current, temperature, and light. **Biotic factors** are all of the living organisms in the ecosystem. Biotic factors include plants, algae, fungi, bacteria, archaea, animals, and protozoa.

Influence of Resource Availability and Abiotic Factors on Population Size

Population size is affected by resource availability and abiotic factors. As the population density increases, intraspecific competition for available resources intensifies. If the availability of resources decreases, death rates may increase and birth rates may decrease. For example, territoriality for mating or nesting may limit available resources for individuals in a population and limit the population size. Abiotic factors such as temperature, rainfall, wind, and light intensity all influence the population size. For example, temperatures near a species' tolerance limit may decrease the population. Natural disasters such as fire or flood can destroy resources and greatly decrease a population's size. In general, any abiotic factor that reduces or limits resources will also reduce or limit population size.

Significance of Habitat and Niche to Populations

The **habitat** of an organism is the type of place where that organism usually lives. A habitat is a piece of an environmental area, which may be a geographic area or even the body of another organism. The habitat describes an organism's natural living environment. A habitat includes biotic and abiotic factors such as temperature, light, food resources, and predators. Whereas a habitat describes an organism's "home," a niche can be thought of as an organism's "occupation." A **niche** describes an organism's functional role in the community and how the organism uses its habitat. A niche can be quite complex because it should include the impacts that the organism has on the biotic and abiotic surroundings. Niches can be broad or narrow.

Influence of Competition and Predation on Population Size

Feeding relationships between organisms can affect population size. Competition and predation both tend to limit population size. **Competition** occurs when two individuals need the same resource. This competition can be **intraspecific**, which is between members of the same species, or **interspecific**, which is between members of different species. Intraspecific competition reduces resources as that species' own population increases, which limits population growth. Interspecific competition reduces resources as a different species uses those same resources. **Predation** occurs when one individual is a food resource for another individual. Predator and prey populations can cycle over a range of years. If prey resources increase, predator numbers increase. An example of the predator-prey population cycle is the Canadian lynx and snowshoe hare.

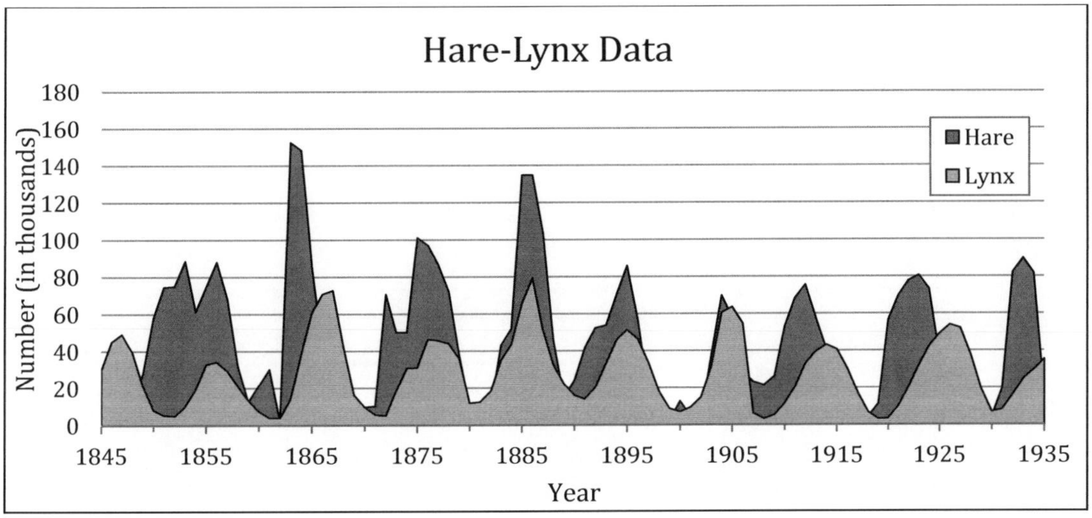

Models of Population Growth

Logistic Population Growth Model

Populations vary over time due to deaths, births, immigration, and emigration. In most situations, resources such as food, water, and shelter are limited. Each environment or habitat can only support a limited number of individuals, which is known as the **carrying capacity**. Population growth models that factor in the carrying capacity are called **logistic growth models**. With logistic population growth models, the rate of population growth decreases as the population size increases. Logistic growth graphs as an S-shaped curve. Comparing logistic growth and exponential growth shows that the graph for exponential growth continues to become steeper, but the graph for logistics growth levels off once the population reaches the carrying capacity. As the population increases, fewer resources are available per individual. This limits the number of individuals that can occupy that environment or habitat.

Exponential Population Growth Model

While populations change over time due to births, deaths, and migrations, sometimes conditions are near ideal and populations can increase at their maximum rate, exhibiting exponential growth. **Exponential growth** is growth in which the rate of change is proportional to the increasing size in an exponential progression. Exponential growth graphs as a J-shaped curve. Exponential growth is often observed in single-celled organisms such as bacteria or protozoa in which the population or number of cells increases by a factor of two per unit of time. One cell divides into two cells, which divide into four cells, and so forth. The exponential growth model describes population growth under ideal conditions and does not take limiting factors or carrying capacity into account. Realistically, exponential growth cannot occur indefinitely, but it may occur for a period of time. It does show a species' capacity for increase and may be helpful when studying a particular species or ecosystem. For example, if a species with no natural predator is introduced into a new habitat, that species may experience exponential growth. If this growth is allowed to go unchecked, the population may overshoot the carrying capacity and then starve. Efforts may need to be taken to reduce the population before this occurs.

Reproduction and Mortality in Populations

Advantages and Disadvantages of Asexual Reproduction in Animals

Very few species of animals reproduce by asexual reproduction, and nearly all of those species also have the ability to reproduce sexually. While not common, asexual reproduction is useful for animals that tend to stay in one place and may not find mates. Asexual reproduction takes considerably less effort and energy than sexual reproduction. In asexual reproduction, all of the offspring are genetically identical to the parent. This can be a disadvantage because of the lack of genetic variation. Although asexual reproduction is advantageous in a stable environment, if the environment changes, the organisms may lack the genetic variability to survive or selectively adapt.

> **Review Video: Asexual Reproduction**
> Visit mometrix.com/academy and enter code: 565616

Life Histories

The **life history** of a species describes the typical organism's life cycle from birth through reproduction to death. Life histories can typically be classified as opportunistic life histories or equilibrial life histories. Species exhibiting **opportunistic life histories** are typically small, short-lived organisms that have a high reproductive capacity but invest little time and care into their offspring. Their population sizes tend to oscillate significantly over periods of several years. Species exhibiting **equilibrial life histories** are typically large, long-lived organisms that have a low reproductive capacity but invest much time and care into their offspring. Their populations tend to fluctuate within a smaller range. A general observation is that species that tend to produce numerous offspring typically tend to invest little care into that offspring, resulting in a high mortality rate of that offspring. Organisms of species that tend to produce few offspring typically invest much more care into that offspring, resulting in a lower mortality rate.

Relationships between Species

Symbiosis

Many species share a special nutritional relationship with another species, called **symbiosis**. The term symbiosis means "living together." In symbiosis, two organisms share a close physical relationship that can be helpful, harmful, or neutral for each organism. Three forms of symbiotic relationships are parasitism, commensalism, and mutualism. **Parasitism** is a relationship between two organisms in which one organism is the parasite, and the other organism is the host. The parasite benefits from the relationship because the parasite obtains its nutrition from the host. The host is harmed from the relationship because the parasite is using the host's energy and giving nothing in return. For example, a tick and a dog share a parasitic relationship in which the tick is the parasite, and the dog is the host. **Commensalism** is a relationship between two organisms in which one benefits, and the other is not affected. For example, a small fish called a remora can attach to the belly of a shark and ride along. The remora is safe under the shark, and the shark is not affected. **Mutualism** is a relationship between two organisms in which both organisms benefit. For example, a rhinoceros usually can be seen with a few tick birds perched on its back. The tick birds are helped by the easy food source of ticks, and the rhino benefits from the tick removal.

Predation

Predation is a special nutritional relationship in which one organism is the predator, and the other organism is the prey. The predator benefits from the relationship, but the prey is harmed. The predator hunts and kills the prey for food. The predator is specially adapted to hunt its prey, and the prey is specially adapted to escape its predator. While predators harm (kill) their individual prey, predation usually helps the prey species. Predation keeps the population of the prey species under control and prevents them from overshooting the carrying capacity, which often leads to starvation. Also, predation usually helps to remove weak or slow members of the prey species leaving the healthier, stronger, and better adapted individuals to reproduce. Examples of predator-prey relationships include lions and zebras, snakes and rats, and hawks and rabbits.

Competition and Territoriality

Competition is a relationship between two organisms in which the organisms compete for the same vital resource that is in short supply. Typically, both organisms are harmed, but one is usually harmed more than the other, which provides an avenue for natural selection. Organisms compete for resources such as food, water, mates, and space. **Interspecific competition** is between members of different species, while **intraspecific competition** is between members of the same species. **Territoriality** can be considered to be a type of interspecific competition for space. Many animals including mammals, birds, reptiles, fish, spiders, and insects have exhibited territorial behavior. Once territories are established, there are fewer conflicts between organisms. For example, a male redwing blackbird can establish a large territory. By singing and flashing his red patches, he is able to warn other males to avoid his territory, and they can avoid fighting.

Altruistic Behaviors Between Animals

Altruism is a self-sacrificing behavior in which an individual animal may serve or protect another animal. For example, in a honey bee colony there is one queen with many workers (females). There are also drones (males), but only during the mating seasons. Adult workers do all the work of the hive and will die defending it. Another example of altruism is seen in a naked mole rat colony. Each colony has one queen that mates with a few males, and the rest of the colony is nonbreeding and lives to service the queen, her mates, and her offspring.

Review Video: Mutualism, Commensalism, and Parasitism
Visit mometrix.com/academy and enter code: 757249

Ecological Succession

Changes During Primary and Secondary Succession

Ecological succession is the process by which a community changes over time. The final stage of this succession is a climax community, which remains relatively unchanged unless a major event causes it to change or become destroyed. The two types of ecological succession are primary succession and secondary succession. **Primary succession** occurs in a region where there is no soil and also has never been populated, such as a new volcanic island or a region where a glacier has retreated. During the pioneer stage, the progression of species is typically lichen and algae, followed by small annual plants, then perennial herbs and grasses. During the intermediate stage, shrubs, grasses, and shade-intolerant trees are dominant. Finally, after hundreds of years, a climax community is reached with shade-tolerant trees. **Secondary succession** occurs when a climax community is destroyed or nearly destroyed, such as after a forest fire or in an abandoned field. With secondary succession, the area starts with soil and seeds from the original climax community. Typically, weeds and annuals are dominant in the first two years. This is followed by grasses and biennials. In a few years, shrubs and perennials are dominant, followed by pine trees, which are eventually replaced by deciduous trees. Secondary succession takes place in less than 100 years.

Review Video: Ecological Succession
Visit mometrix.com/academy and enter code: 466994

Types of Biomes

Biomes

The biosphere consists of numerous biomes. A **biome** is a large region that supports a specific community. Each biome has a characteristic climate and geography. Differences in latitude, altitude, and worldwide patterns affect temperature, precipitation, and humidity. Biomes can be classified as terrestrial or aquatic biomes. **Terrestrial biomes** include ecosystems with land environments, such as tundra, coniferous forest, temperate broadleaf forest, temperate grassland, chaparral, desert, savannas, and tropical forests. Terrestrial biomes tend to grade into each other in regions called ecotones. **Aquatic biomes** are water-dwelling ecosystems. Aquatic biomes include areas such as lakes, rivers, estuaries, coral reefs, oceanic pelagic zone, intertidal zone, and the abyssal zone.

Aquatic Biomes

Aquatic biomes are characterized by multiple factors including the temperature of the water, the amount of dissolved solids in the water, the availability of light, the depth of the water, and the material at the bottom of the biome. Aquatic biomes are classified as marine or freshwater biomes based on the amount of dissolved salt in the water. **Marine biomes** include the intertidal zone, the pelagic zone, the benthic zone, the abyssal zone, coral reefs, and estuaries. Marine biomes have a salinity of at least 35 parts per thousand. **Freshwater biomes** include lakes, ponds, rivers, and streams. Freshwater biomes have a salinity that is less than 0.5 parts per thousand. Lakes and ponds, which are relatively stationary, consist of two zones: the littoral zone and the limnetic zone. The **littoral zone** is closest to the shore and is home to many plants (floating and rooted), invertebrates, crustaceans, amphibians, and fish. The **limnetic zone** is further from the shore and has no rooted plants. Rivers and streams typically originate in the mountains and make their way to the oceans. Because this water is running and colder, it contains different plants and animals than lakes and ponds. For example, salmon, trout, crayfish, plants, and algae are found in rivers and streams.

Marine Regions

Marine regions are located in three broad areas: the ocean, estuaries, and coral reefs. The ocean consists of two general regions: the pelagic zone and the benthic zone. The **pelagic zone** is in the open ocean. Organisms in the pelagic zone include phytoplankton such as algae and bacteria; zooplankton such as protozoa and crustaceans; and larger animals such as squid, sharks, and whales. The **benthic zone** consists of the ocean floor. Organisms in the benthic zone can include sponges, clams, oysters, starfish, sea anemones, sea urchins, worms, and fish. The deepest part of the benthic zone is called the **abyssal plain** and is usually very cold and dark. This is the deep ocean floor, which is home to numerous scavengers, many of which have light-generating capability. **Estuaries** are somewhat-enclosed coastal regions where water from rivers and streams is mixed with seawater. **Coral reefs** are located in warm, shallow water. Corals are small colonial animals that share a mutualistic relationship with algae.

Terrestrial Biomes

Terrestrial biomes are classified predominantly by their vegetation, which is primarily determined by precipitation and temperature. **Tropical rainforests** experience the highest annual precipitation and relatively high temperatures. The dominant vegetation in tropical forests is tall evergreen trees. **Temperate deciduous forests** experience moderate precipitation and temperatures. The dominant vegetation is deciduous trees. **Boreal forests** experience moderate precipitation and lower temperatures. The dominant vegetation is coniferous trees. The **tundra** experiences lower precipitation and cold temperatures. The dominant vegetation is shrubs. The **savanna** experiences lower precipitation and high temperatures. The dominant vegetation is grasses. **Deserts** experience the lowest precipitation and the hottest temperatures. The dominant vegetation is scattered thorny plants.

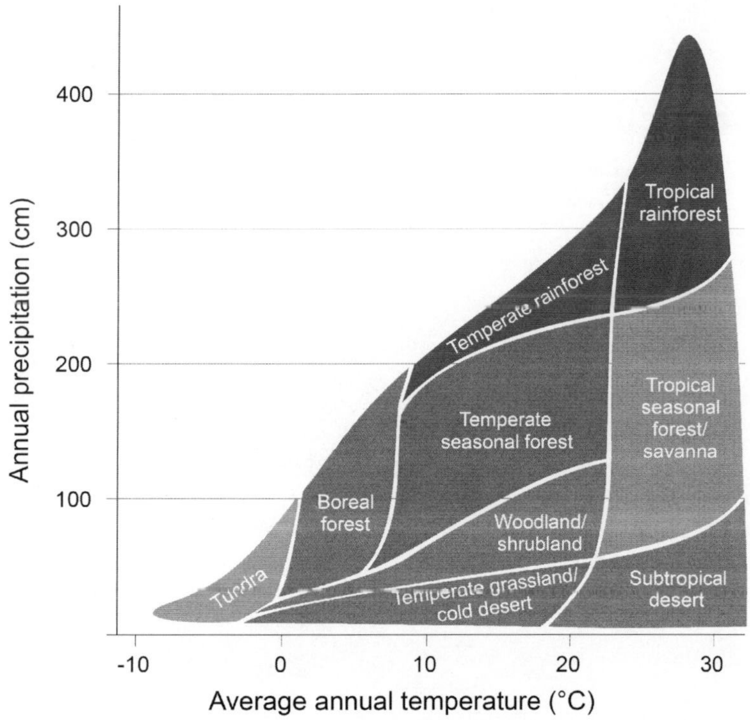

Energy Flow in the Environment

Using Trophic Levels with an Energy Pyramid

Energy flow through an ecosystem can be tracked through an energy pyramid. An **energy pyramid** shows how energy is transferred from one trophic level to another. **Producers** always form the base of an energy pyramid, and the consumers form successive levels above the producers. Producers only store about 1% of the solar energy they receive. Then, each successive level only uses about 10% of the energy of the previous level. That means that **primary consumers** use about 10% of the energy used by primary producers, such as grasses and trees. Next, **secondary consumers** use 10% of primary consumers' 10%, or 1% overall. This continues up for as many trophic levels as exist in a particular ecosystem.

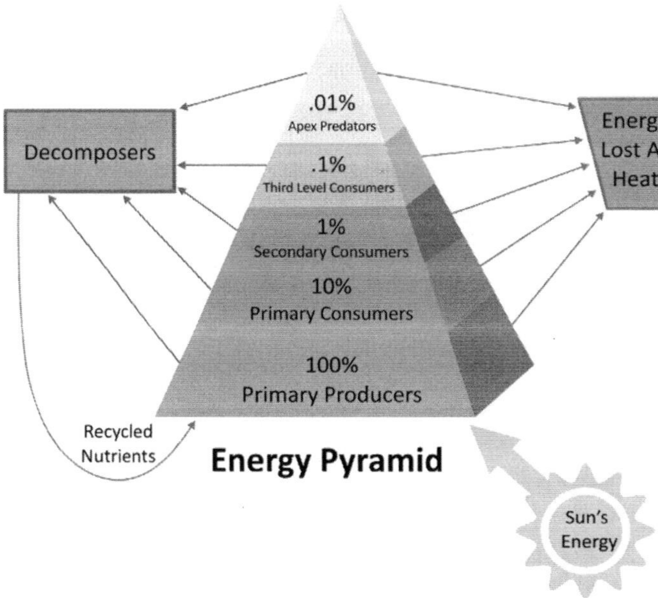

FOOD WEB

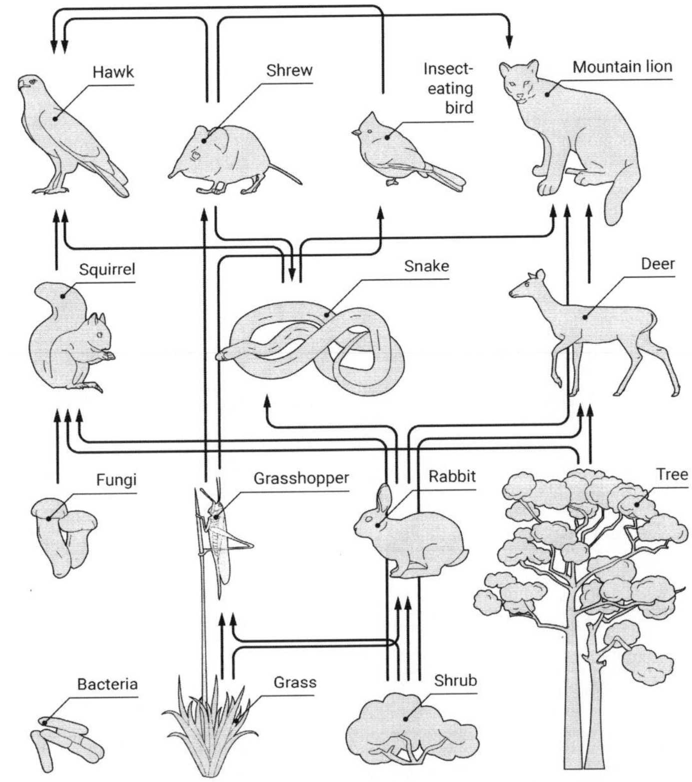

Energy flow through an ecosystem can be illustrated by a **food web**. Energy moves through the food web in the direction of the arrows. In the food web, producers such as grass, trees, and shrubs use energy from the sun to produce food through photosynthesis. Herbivores or primary consumers such as squirrels, grasshoppers, and rabbits obtain energy by eating the producers. Secondary consumers, which are carnivores such as snakes and shrews, obtain energy by eating the primary consumers. Tertiary consumers, which are carnivores such as hawks and mountain lions, obtain energy by eating the secondary consumers. Note that the hawk and the mountain lion can also be considered quaternary consumers in this food web if a different food chain within the web is followed.

Review Video: Food Webs
Visit mometrix.com/academy and enter code: 853254

Biogeochemical Cycles

WATER CYCLE

The water cycle, also referred to as the **hydrologic cycle**, is a biogeochemical cycle that describes the continuous movement of the Earth's water. Water in the form of **precipitation** such as rain or snow moves from the atmosphere to the ground. The water is collected in oceans, lakes, rivers, and other bodies of water. Heat from the sun then causes water to **evaporate** from those oceans, lakes, rivers, and other bodies of water. As plants transpire, this water also undergoes evaporation. This water vapor collects in the sky and forms clouds. As the water vapor in the clouds cools, the water vapor **condenses** or sublimes depending on the conditions. Then, water moves back to the ground in the form of precipitation.

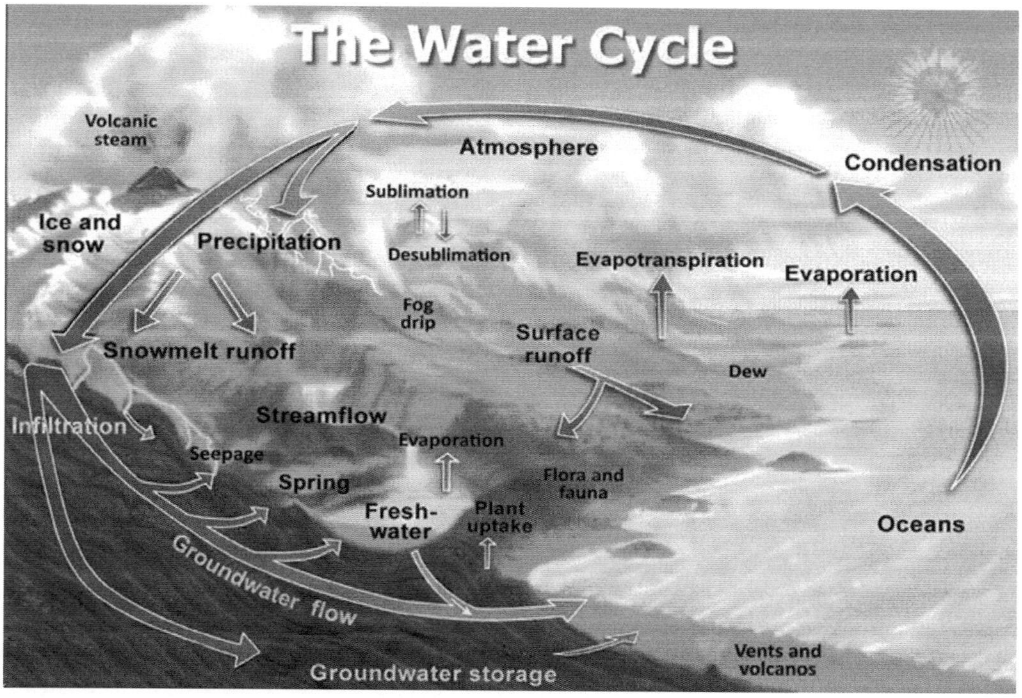

CARBON CYCLE

The **carbon cycle** is a biogeochemical cycle that describes the continuous movement of the Earth's carbon. Carbon is in the atmosphere, the soil, living organisms, fossil fuels, oceans, and freshwater systems. These areas are referred to as **carbon reservoirs**. Carbon flows between these reservoirs in an exchange called the carbon cycle. In the atmosphere, carbon is in the form of carbon dioxide. Carbon moves from the atmosphere to plants through the process of photosynthesis. Carbon moves from plants to animals through food chains, and then moves from living organisms to the soil when these organisms die. Carbon moves from living organisms to the atmosphere through cellular respiration. Carbon moves from fossil fuels to the atmosphere when fossil fuels are burned. Carbon moves from the atmosphere to the oceans and freshwater systems through absorption.

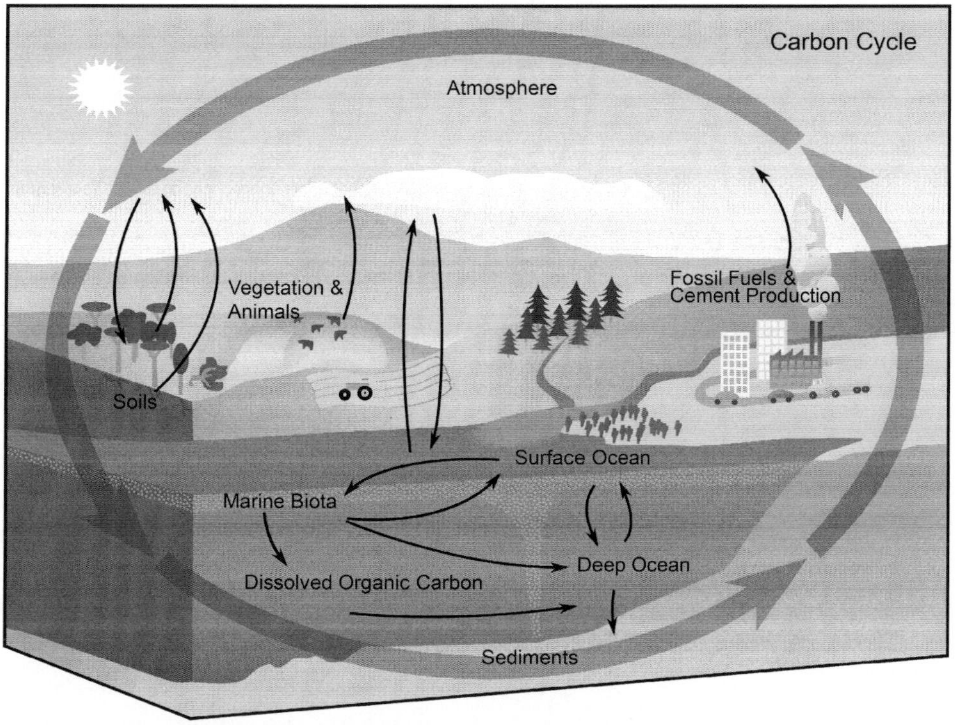

Nitrogen Cycle

The **nitrogen cycle** is a biogeochemical cycle that describes the continuous movement of the Earth's nitrogen. Approximately 78% of the Earth's atmosphere consists of nitrogen in its elemental form N_2. Nitrogen is essential to the formation of proteins, but most organisms cannot use nitrogen in this form and require the nitrogen to be converted into some form of **nitrates**. Lightning can cause nitrates to form in the atmosphere, which can be carried to the soil by rain to be used by plants. Legumes have nitrogen-fixing bacteria in their roots, which can convert the N_2 to ammonia (NH_3). Nitrifying bacteria in the soil can also convert ammonia into nitrates. Plants absorb nitrates from the soil, and animals can consume the plants and other animals for protein. Denitrifying bacteria can convert unused nitrates back to nitrogen to be returned to the atmosphere.

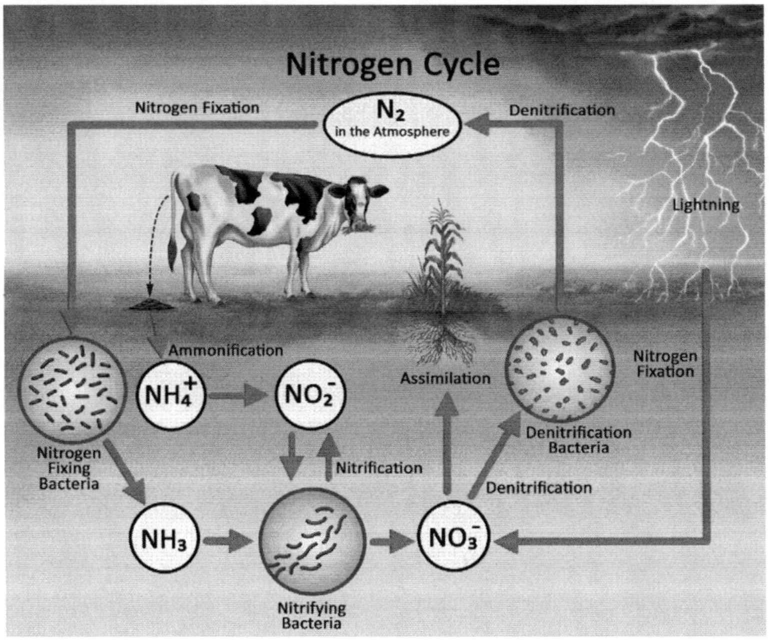

Phosphorus Cycle

The **phosphorus cycle** is a biogeochemical cycle that describes the continuous movement of the Earth's phosphorus. Phosphorus is found in rocks. When these rocks weather and erode, the phosphorus moves into the soil. The phosphorus found in the soil and rocks is in the form of phosphates or compounds with the PO_4^{3-} ion. When it rains, phosphates can be dissolved into the water. Plants are able to use phosphates from the soil. Plants need phosphorus for growth and development. Phosphorus is also a component of DNA, RNA, ATP, cell membranes, and bones. Plants and algae can absorb phosphate ions from the water and convert them into many organic compounds. Animals can get phosphorus by eating food or drinking water. When organisms die, the phosphorus is returned to the soil. This is the slowest of all biogeochemical cycles.

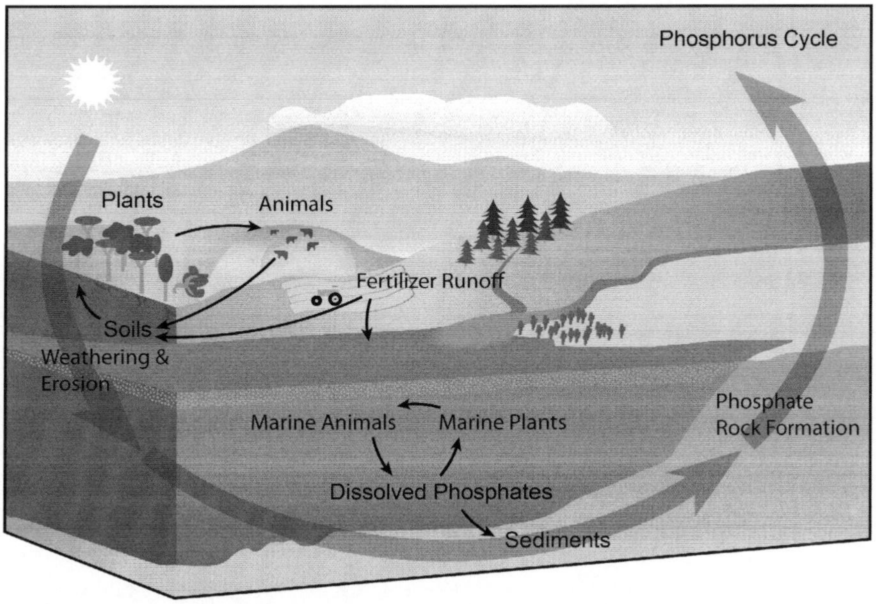

Effects of Natural Disturbances

Natural Disturbances That Affect Ecosystems

A **natural disturbance** is an event caused by nature, not human activity. Natural disturbances can be brought on by weather such as droughts, storms, wind, freezing, and fires from lightning. Other natural disturbances include earthquakes, volcanic eruptions, and diseases. Natural disturbances can disrupt or disturb the ecosystem in many ways, such as altering resources or removing individuals from the community. Natural disturbances can cover small regions, or they can affect an entire ecosystem. The effect may be long lasting and take several years to recover, or the effect may be minor and take only a few months to recover.

Effect of Fragmentation of Ecosystems on Biodiversity

Habitats can become fragmented due to natural disturbances such as fire, volcanic activity, and climate change. Some of the original habitat is destroyed during **fragmentation**, reducing the total area of the habitat. As a result, there may be insufficient food or other resources to support a species. The resulting habitats may also be reproductively isolated from each other, thus limiting genetic variation and biodiversity. Small fluctuations in resources or climate can be catastrophic in small populations. Larger populations may be able to overcome these fluctuations in variation.

Human Effect on Ecological Systems

Effects of Human Population on Ecological Systems and Biodiversity

Human population has been increasing at a near-exponential rate for the past 50 years. As the human population increases, the demand for resources such as food, water, land, and energy also increases. As the human population increases, the number of other species decreases due to habitat destruction, introduced species, and overhunting. The increased greenhouse gases and resulting climate changes have also significantly affected many ecosystems as temperatures rise and habitats are slowly changed or even destroyed. Increasing human population means increasing pollution, which harms habitats. Many animals have become extinct due to the effects of an exponentially increasing human population. High rates of extinction greatly reduce biodiversity.

Habitat Destruction by Humans on Ecological Systems and Biodiversity

Many habitats have been altered or destroyed by humans. In fact, habitat destruction brought about by human endeavors has been the most significant cause of species extinctions, which has resulted in the decrease in biodiversity throughout the world. As the human population has increased exponentially, the extinction rate has also increased exponentially. This is largely due to habitat destruction by humans. Humans use many resources in their agriculture, industry, mining, logging, and recreation. For example, humans have cleared much land for agriculture and urban development. As habitats are destroyed, species are either destroyed or displaced. Often, habitats are fragmented into smaller areas, which only allow for small populations that are under threat by predators, diseases, weather, and limited resources. Areas near the coastline are especially affected, including estuaries, coral reefs, wetlands, and mangrove forests. Nearly half of all mangrove ecosystems have been destroyed by human activity. Coral reefs have nearly been decimated from pollution such as oil spills and exploitation from the aquarium fish market and coral market.

Effects of Introduced Species on Ecological Systems and Biodiversity

Introduced species are species that are moved into new geographic regions by humans. They are also called invasive or nonnative species. Introduction can be intentional, such as the introduction of livestock, or unintentional, such as the introduction of Dutch elm disease. Introduced species can disrupt their new communities by using the limited resources and preying on other members of the community. Introduced species are often free from predators and can reproduce exponentially. This typically causes a decrease in biodiversity. Introduced species are contributors or even responsible for numerous extinctions. For example, zebra mussels, which are native to the Black Sea and the Caspian Sea, were accidentally introduced to the Great Lakes. The zebra mussels greatly reduced the amount of plankton available for the native mussel species, many of which are now endangered.

Impact of Nonpoint Sources of Pollution on the Environment

Nonpoint-source pollution is the leading cause of water pollution in the United States. Nonpoint-source pollution is pollution that does not flow through a pipe, channel, or container. Most nonpoint-source pollution is due to agricultural runoff. Urban runoff from lawns, streets, and parking lots is also treated as nonpoint-source pollution because much of that storm water does not go into a storm drain before entering streams, rivers, lakes, or other bodies of water. Urban runoff contains chemicals such as lawn fertilizers, motor oils, grease, pesticides, soaps, and detergents, each of which is harmful to the environment.

Effects of Remediation on Ecological Systems and Biodiversity

In **remediation**, or land rehabilitation, environmental damages are reversed or stopped by attempting to restore land to its prior condition. Examples of remediation are reforestation and mine reclamation. Mining reclamation includes the backfilling of open-pit mines and covering ores containing sulfides to prevent rain from mixing with them to produce sulfuric acid. **Reforestation** is the restocking of forests and wetlands. This can at least partially offset the damaging effects brought about by the deforestation. Reforestation can help reduce global warming due to an increase in the absorption of light by the trees. Restoration can also help to restore the carbon cycle and counter erosion. Reforestation can help maintain or preserve the biodiversity of the region and possibly increase biodiversity if new organisms immigrate into the region.

Pollution Mitigation and the Clean Air Act

Pollution mitigation has greatly reduced pollution and its effects during the past 40 years. The **Clean Air Act** has reduced pollution by requiring that new industrial sites contain pollution-control technology. These technologies avoid or minimize the negative effects on the environment. For example, new coal-fired power plants are fitted with pollution-control devices that greatly reduce and nearly eliminate sulfur dioxide and nitrogen oxide emissions. This greatly reduces acid rain, improves water quality, and improves the overall health of ecosystems. Reducing acid rain improves soil quality, which in turn improves the health of producers, which consequently improves the health of consumers, essentially strengthening the entire ecosystem. Reduced greenhouse gas emissions have lessened the impact of global warming such as rising sea levels due to melting glaciers and the resulting loss of habitats and biodiversity. Reduced smog and haze improves the intensity of sunlight required for photosynthesis.

Resource Management

Resource management such as waste management and recycling greatly impacts the environment. **Waste management** is the monitoring, collection, transportation, and recycling of waste products. Well-managed landfills include using clay or another lining material to prevent liquid leachate and layers of soil on top to reduce odors and vermin. Wastes, including hazardous biomedical waste, can also be incinerated to reduce waste volume. However, incineration does emit pollutants and greenhouse gases. Proper waste management always includes recycling. **Recycling** is a method to recover resources. Recycled materials can be reprocessed into new products. Metals such as aluminum, copper, and steel are recycled. Plastics, glass, and paper products can also be recycled. In addition, organic materials such as plant materials and food scraps can be composted. The current trend is to shift from waste management to resource recovery. Wastes should be minimized and reduced to minimize the need for disposal. Unavoidable nonrecyclable wastes should be converted to energy by combustion if at all possible.

Impact of Global Warming, Rising Sea Levels, and Flooding on Society

Global warming caused largely by greenhouse gas emission will greatly affect society in the next several years. The increase in global temperature leads to more extreme levels of otherwise normal weather events such hurricanes, tornadoes, floods, and droughts. Rising temperatures cause weather patterns to shift, leading to even more floods and droughts. Rising temperatures mean a decrease in glaciers, sea ice, ice sheets, and snow cover, which contributes to rising sea levels. Rising sea levels lead to habitat change or loss, which greatly affects numerous species, but could also mean higher storm surges and related issues. Some motile species are already moving north to cooler climates. Earlier annual snowmelt and runoff may overwhelm water management systems.

Endangered Species Act

The **Endangered Species Act** (ESA) of 1973 has had a positive impact on many species. The law was designed to protect "imperiled species" from extinction due to factors such as loss of habitat, overhunting, and lack of conservation. The ESA also protects the species' ecosystems and removes threats to those ecosystems. If an animal is placed on the endangered or threatened list, it is prohibited to "harass, harm, pursue, hunt, shoot, wound, kill, trap, capture, or collect, or to attempt to engage in any such conduct" with the endangered animal. The populations of many imperiled species have increased significantly, including the whooping crane, the gray wolf, the red wolf, and the Hawaiian goose. Some species have even been removed from the endangered species list, including the bald eagle, the peregrine falcon, the gray whale, and the grizzly bear. The ESA has protected numerous species while balancing human economic needs and rights to private property.

National Park System

The purpose of the **National Park System** is to "conserve the scenery and the natural and historic objects and the wildlife therein and to provide for the enjoyment of the same in such manner and by such means as will leave them unimpaired for the enjoyment of future generations." The National Park System protects complete ecosystems and houses great biodiversity. National parks are an integral part of the survival of many species. National parks provide a home to hundreds of endangered or threatened species. Studies show that preserved habitats near national parks help many species better survive with the resources they need. This will prevent fragmentation and further habitat loss. Nevertheless, National parks may be threatened by invasion species or pressure for use of land along park boundaries. Biodiversity is threatened even within national parks. Even though many are vast, they are often not large enough to support a species population on their own.

Effects of Extraction of Minerals and Oil Drilling

The extraction of mineral and energy resources by mining and drilling has harmful effects on the environment including pollution and alterations to ecosystems. **Mining** often requires large amounts of deforestation, which harms habitats and affects biodiversity. Mining also causes water pollution. Toxic chemicals such as mercury and sulfuric acid are used in the mining process and are released into bodies of water, harming the aquatic life. If these toxic chemicals are leaked, the ground water is polluted. Rainwater mixes with the heavy metals in mines and produces an acid runoff that harms aquatic life, birds, and mammals. The pollution is especially bad in countries without proper mining regulations. Open-pit mines and mountaintop removal techniques are especially harsh to the environment, and reclamation is often not regulated in developing countries. Oil drilling is controversial due to habitat disruption or loss as well as the potential of an oil spill occurring. Oil spills are toxic to wildlife and difficult to clean up. Offshore drilling uses seismic waves to locate oil, which disturbs whales and dolphins and has been tied to hundreds of beached whales.

Sustainable Agriculture

The management of natural resources and the renewability or **sustainability** of those natural resources greatly impact society. Sustainable agriculture involves growing foods in economical ways that do not harm resources. If left unchecked, farming can deplete the soil of valuable nutrients. Crops grown in these depleted soils are less healthy and more susceptible to disease. Sustainable agriculture uses more effective pest control such as insect-resistant corn, which reduces runoff and water pollution in the surrounding area. Sustainable forestry involves replenishing trees as trees are being harvested, which maintains the environment.

Renewable and Nonrenewable Energy Resources

Energy sources such as wind, solar power, and biomass energy are all **renewable**. Wind power is clean with no pollution and no greenhouse gas emissions. Disadvantages of wind power include the use of land for wind farms, threats to birds, and the expense to build. Solar power has no greenhouse gas emissions, but some toxic metal wastes result in the production of photovoltaic cells, and solar power requires large areas of land. Biomass energy is sustainable, but its combustion produces greenhouse emissions. Farming biomass requires large areas of land. Fossil fuels, which are **nonrenewable**, cause substantially more air pollution and greenhouse gas emissions, contributing to habitat loss and global warming.

> **Review Video: Renewable and Nonrenewable Resources**
> Visit mometrix.com/academy and enter code: 840194

Global and Local Ecology

Flow of Biotic Material Between Ecosystems

Various events can cause the **flow of materials and energy** from one ecosystem to another. In this sense, the local ecosystem is related to the global ecosystem. Both biotic and abiotic elements of an ecosystem can flow into another environment. **Abiotic factors** move through natural processes, such as erosion and deposition of sediment and transportation of those materials by rivers and weather systems. Harvesting of materials such as water, natural gas, and trees also plays a large role, as many materials used for building and survival and may be transported from one ecosystem to another. Plants are often moved through similar processes, whether by harvesting and planting by humans, or by passive systems of seed dispersal through rivers and animals. Animal movement is usually referred to as **migration**, and it is primarily driven by the pursuit of food, safety from predators and harsh environmental conditions, and reproductive opportunity. Ecosystems function through the interaction and balance of biotic and abiotic factors, such as competition and predation and reliance on water supply. As biotic and abiotic factors constantly flow from one local ecosystem to another, the balance has to shift constantly to accommodate ecological change on a global scale.

Chapter Quiz

Ready to see how well you retained what you just read? Scan the QR code to go directly to the chapter quiz interface for this study guide. If you're using a computer, simply visit the online resources page at **mometrix.com/resources719/mttcbiology** and click the Chapter Quizzes link.

MTTC Practice Test

Want to take this practice test in an online interactive format?
Check out the online resources page, which includes interactive practice questions and much more: **mometrix.com/resources719/mttcbiology**

Molecular and Cellular Biology

1. How do the hydrogen bonds in water affect its characteristics?

a. Hydrogen bonds are so polar that they can attract non-polar molecules.
b. Hydrogen bonds cause water to be denser when it is a solid than when it is a liquid.
c. Hydrogen bonds cause water to have a high enough surface tension that some organisms can move across it.
d. Hydrogen bonds cause water to be a poor solvent.
e. Hydrogen bonds make water an excellent buffer.

2. The breakdown of a disaccharide releases energy, which is stored as ATP. This is an example of a(n):

a. Combination reaction
b. Replacement reaction
c. Endothermic reaction
d. Exothermic reaction
e. Thermodynamic reaction

3. Which of the following metabolic compounds is composed of only carbon, oxygen, and hydrogen?

a. Phospholipids
b. Glycogen
c. Peptides
d. RNA
e. Amino acids

4. When an animal takes in more energy than it uses over an extended time, the extra chemical energy is stored as:

a. Fat
b. Starch
c. Protein
d. Enzymes
e. Cholesterol

5. Which of the following molecules is thought to have acted as the first enzyme in early life on earth?

a. Protein
b. RNA
c. DNA
d. Triglycerides
e. Phospholipids

6. Which of the following are formed when the plasma membrane surrounds a particle outside of the cell?

a. Golgi bodies
b. Rough endoplasmic reticulum
c. Lysosomes
d. Endocytic vesicles

7. Which of the following plant organelles contain the pigment that gives green leaves their color?

a. Centrioles
b. Cell walls
c. Chloroplasts
d. Central vacuole
e. Golgi apparatus

8. All but which of the following processes are ways of moving solutes across a plasma membrane?

a. Osmosis
b. Passive transport
c. Active transport
d. Facilitated diffusion
e. Endocytosis

9. Prokaryotic and eukaryotic cells are similar in having which of the following?

a. Membrane-bound organelles
b. Protein-studded DNA
c. Presence of a nucleus
d. Integral membrane proteins in the plasma membrane
e. Flagella composed of microtubules

10. Which of the following cell types has a peptidoglycan cell wall?

a. Algae
b. Bacteria
c. Fungi
d. Land plants
e. Protists

11. Enzymes catalyze biochemical reactions by

a. Lowering the potential energy of the products
b. Separating inhibitors from products
c. Forming a complex with the products
d. Lowering the activation energy of the reaction
e. Providing energy to the reaction

12. Which of the following is an example of a cofactor?

a. Zinc
b. Actin
c. Cholesterol
d. GTP
e. Chlorophyll

13. Cyanide is a poison that binds to the active site of the enzyme cytochrome c oxidase and prevents its activity. Cyanide is a(n)

a. Prosthetic group
b. Cofactor
c. Coenzyme
d. Inhibitor
e. Reverse regulator

14. The graph below shows the potential energy of molecules during the process of a chemical reaction. All of the following may be true EXCEPT

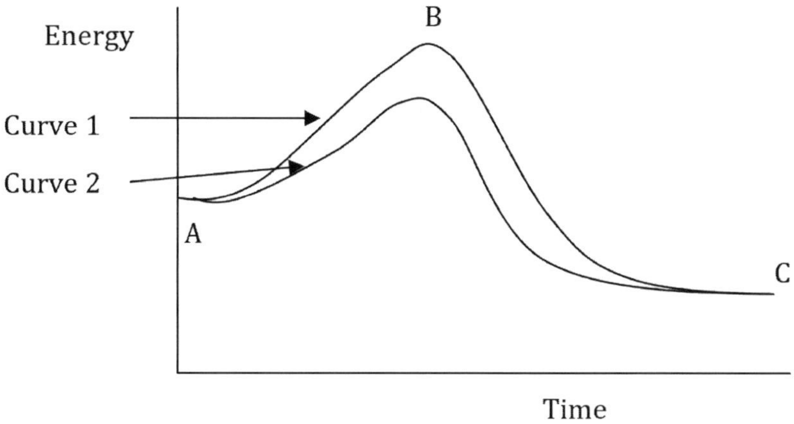

a. This is an endergonic reaction
b. The activation energy in curve 2 is less than the activation energy in curve 1
c. The energy of the products is less than the energy of the substrate
d. Curve 2 shows the reaction in the presence of an enzyme
e. The reaction required ATP

15. Which of the following is NOT a characteristic of enzymes?

a. They change shape when they bind their substrates.
b. They can catalyze reactions in both forward and reverse directions.
c. Their activity is sensitive to changes in temperature.
d. They are always active on more than one kind of substrate.
e. They may have more than one binding site.

16. In a strenuously exercising muscle, NADH begins to accumulate in high concentration. Which of the following metabolic processes will be activated to reduce the concentration of NADH?

a. Glycolysis
b. The Krebs cycle
c. Lactic acid fermentation
d. Oxidative phosphorylation
e. Acetyl CoA synthesis

17. Which of the following statements regarding chemiosmosis in mitochondria is NOT correct?

a. ATP synthase is powered by protons flowing through membrane channels.
b. Energy from ATP is used to transport protons to the intermembrane space.
c. Energy from the electron transport chain is used to transport protons to the intermembrane space.
d. An electrical gradient and a pH gradient both exist across the inner membrane.
e. The waste product of chemiosmosis is water.

18. In photosynthesis, high-energy electrons move through electron transport chains to produce ATP and NADPH. Which of the following provides the energy to create high energy electrons?

a. NADH
b. $NADP^+$
c. O_2
d. Water
e. Light

19. Which of the following kinds of plants is most likely to perform CAM photosynthesis?

a. Mosses
b. Grasses
c. Deciduous trees
d. Cacti
e. Legumes

20. The combination of DNA with histones is called

a. A centromere
b. Chromatin
c. A chromatid
d. Nucleoli
e. A plasmid

21. How many chromosomes does a human cell have after meiosis I?

a. 92
b. 46
c. 23
d. 22
e. 12

22. In plants and animals, genetic variation is introduced during

a. Crossing over in mitosis
b. Chromosome segregation in mitosis
c. Cytokinesis of meiosis
d. Prophase I of meiosis
e. Anaphase II of meiosis

23. DNA replication occurs during which of the following phases?

a. Prophase I
b. Prophase II
c. Interphase I
d. Interphase II
e. Telophase I

24. The synaptonemal complex is present in which of the following phases of the cell cycle?

a. Metaphase of mitosis
b. Prophase of meiosis I
c. Metaphase of meiosis I
d. Prophase of meiosis II
e. Anaphase of meiosis II

25. A length of DNA coding for a particular protein is called a(n)

a. Allele
b. Genome
c. Gene
d. Transcript
e. Codon

26. In DNA replication, which of the following enzymes is required for separating the DNA molecule into two strands?

a. DNA polymerase
b. Single-strand binding protein
c. DNA gyrase
d. Helicase
e. Primase

27. Which of the following chemical moieties forms the backbone of DNA?

a. Nitrogenous bases
b. Glycerol
c. Amino groups
d. Pentose and phosphate
e. Glucose and phosphate

28. Which of the following is required for the activity of DNA polymerase?

a. Okazaki fragments
b. RNA primer
c. Single-strand binding protein
d. Leading strand
e. Replication fork

29. Which of the following is the substrate for DNA ligase?

a. Okazaki fragments
b. RNA primer
c. Single-strand binding protein
d. Leading strand
e. Replication fork

30. Which of the following is true of the enzyme telomerase?

a. It is active on the leading strand during DNA synthesis
b. It requires a chromosomal DNA template
c. It acts in the $3' \rightarrow 5'$ direction
d. It adds a repetitive DNA sequence to the end of chromosomes
e. It takes the place of primase at the ends of chromosomes

31. Which enzyme in DNA replication is a potential source of new mutations?

a. DNA ligase
b. Primase
c. DNA gyrase
d. DNA polymerase
e. Topoisomerase

32. Which of the following mutations is most likely to have a dramatic effect on the sequence of a protein?

a. A point mutation
b. A missense mutation
c. A deletion
d. A silent mutation
e. A proofreading mutation

33. Which of the following could be an end product of transcription?

a. rRNA
b. DNA
c. Protein
d. snRNP
e. Amino acids

34. The *lac* operon controls

a. Conjugation between bacteria
b. Chromatin organization
c. Gene transcription
d. Excision repair
c. Termination of translation

35. All of the following are common ways of controlling eukaryotic gene expression EXCEPT

a. Regulatory proteins
b. Nucleosome packing
c. Methylation of DNA
d. RNA interference
e. Operons

36. Transfer of DNA between bacteria using a narrow tube called a pilus is known as:

a. Transformation
b. Transduction
c. Operation
d. Conjugation
e. Conformation

37. A virus that has incorporated into the DNA of its host

a. Lysogenic cycle
b. Lytic cycle
c. Retrovirus
d. Provirus
e. Bacteriophage

38. A virus is actively replicating DNA in what stage?

a. Lysogenic cycle
b. Lytic cycle
c. Retrovirus
d. Provirus
e. Bacteriophage

39. A bacterial mini-chromosome used in recombinant DNA technology is called a

a. Centromere
b. Telomere
c. Plasmid
d. Transposon
e. cDNA

Organismal Biology

40. Which of the following parts of an angiosperm gives rise to the fruit?

a. Pedicel
b. Filament
c. Sepal
d. Ovary
e. Meristem

41. Which of the following structures is NOT present in gymnosperms?

a. Leaves
b. Pollen
c. Flowers
d. Stomata
e. Roots

42. Which of the following plant structures allows for gas exchange?

a. Xylem
b. Phloem
c. Cuticle
d. Meristem
e. Stomata

43. Which type of plant has leaves with parallel veins?

a. Monocots
b. Dicots
c. Angiosperms
d. Gymnosperms
e. Nonvascular plants

44. Which type of plant does NOT produce seeds?

a. Monocots
b. Dicots
c. Angiosperms
d. Gymnosperms
e. Nonvascular plants

45. Which type of plant produces seeds that are housed inside a fruit?

a. Monocots
b. Dicots
c. Angiosperms
d. Gymnosperms
e. Nonvascular plants

46. Which structure of a tree contains tissue that is dead at maturity?

a. Heartwood
b. Sapwood
c. Cork cambium
d. Phloem (inner bark)
e. Roots

Refer to the following for question 47:

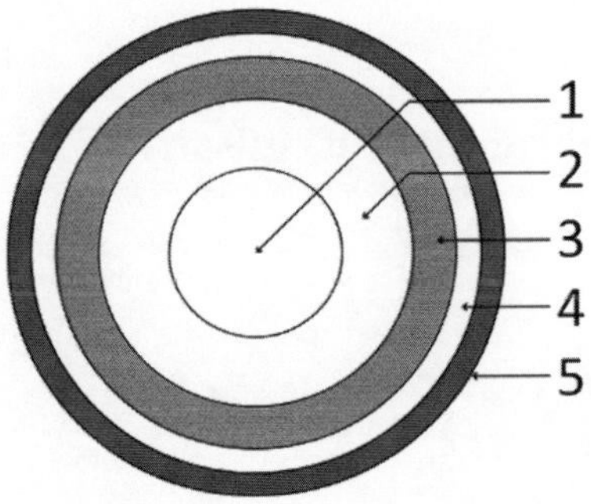

47. Which structure transports carbohydrates to the roots?

a. 1
b. 2
c. 3
d. 4
e. 5

48. In ferns, the joining of egg and sperm produces a zygote, which will grow into the

a. Gametophyte
b. Sporophyte
c. Spore
d. Sporangium
e. Seedling

49. Which of the following is an example of the alternation of generations life cycle?

a. Asexual reproduction of strawberries by runners
b. Annual plants that live through a single growing season
c. Ferns that have a large diploid and a diminutive haploid stage
d. Insects that have distinct larval and adult stages
e. Reptiles that have long periods of dormancy and metabolic inactivity

Refer to the following for questions 50–51:

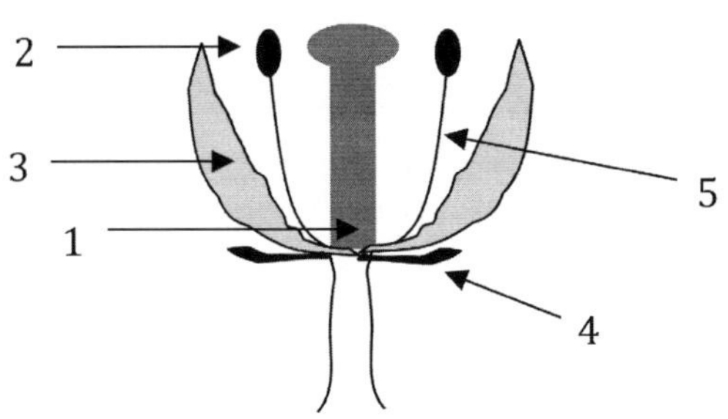

50. The structure in which microspores are produced is:

a. 1
b. 2
c. 3
d. 4
e. 5

51. The structures composed solely of diploid cells are:

a. 1, 2, and 3
b. 2, 3, and 4
c. 3, 4, and 5
d. 1, 4, and 5
e. 1, 2, and 4

52. Auxins are plant hormones that are involved in all but which of the following processes?

a. Fruit ripening
b. Gravitropism
c. Growth
d. Phototropism
e. Seed germination

53. Which of the following plant hormones is most likely to delay aging when sprayed on cut flowers and fruit?

a. Ethylene
b. Gibberellins
c. Cytokinins
d. Abscisic acid
e. Jasmonic acid

54. Which of the following would most likely be disruptive to the flowering time of a day-neutral plant?

a. Daylight interrupted by a brief dark period
b. Daylight interrupted by a long dark period
c. High daytime temperatures
d. Night interrupted by a brief exposure to red light
e. Night interrupted by a long exposure to red light

55. Animals exchange gases with the environment in all of the following ways EXCEPT

a. Direct exchange through the skin
b. Exchange through gills
c. Stomata
d. Tracheae
e. Lungs

56. Which of the following blood components is involved in blood clotting?

a. Red blood cells
b. Platelets
c. White blood cells
d. Leukocytes
e. Plasma

57. Which section of the digestive system is responsible for water reabsorption?

a. The large intestine
b. The duodenum
c. The small intestine
d. The gallbladder
e. The stomach

58. When Ca^{2+} channels open in a presynaptic cell

a. The cell depolarizes
b. The cell hyperpolarizes
c. An action potential is propagated
d. Synaptic vesicles release neurotransmitter
e. The nerve signal is propagated by salutatory conduction

59. Which of the following processes is an example of positive feedback?

a. High CO_2 blood levels stimulate respiration which decreases blood CO_2 levels
b. High blood glucose levels stimulate insulin release, which makes muscle and liver cells take in glucose
c. Increased nursing stimulates increased milk production in mammary glands
d. Low blood oxygen levels stimulate erythropoietin production which increases red blood cell production by bone marrow
e. Low blood calcium levels stimulate parathyroid hormone release from the parathyroid gland. Parathyroid hormone stimulates calcium release from bones.

60. Which of the following would be the most likely means of thermoregulation for a mammal in a cold environment?

a. Adjusting body surface area
b. Sweating
c. Countercurrent exchange
d. Muscle contractions
e. Increased blood flow to extremities

61. Which hormone is *not* secreted by a gland in the brain?

a. Human chorionic gonadotropin (hCG)
b. Gonadotropin-releasing hormone (GnRH)
c. Luteinizing hormone (LH)
d. Follicle-stimulating hormone (FSH)
e. None of these

62. Which hormone is secreted consistently by the placenta throughout pregnancy once established?

a. Human chorionic gonadotropin (hCG)
b. Gonadotropin-releasing hormone (GnRH)
c. Luteinizing hormone (LH)
d. Follicle-stimulating hormone (FSH)
e. Progesterone

63. Polar bodies are a by-product of

a. Meiosis I
b. Meiosis II
c. Both meiosis I and II
d. Zygote formation
e. Mitosis of the morula

64. Which of the following hormones triggers ovulation in females?

a. Estrogen
b. Progesterone
c. Serotonin
d. Luteinizing hormone
e. Testosterone

65. Spermatogenesis occurs in the

a. Prostate gland
b. Vas deferens
c. Seminal vesicles
d. Penis
e. Seminiferous tubules

66. In which of the following stages of embryo development are the three primary germ layers first present?

a. Zygote
b. Gastrula
c. Morula
d. Blastula
e. Coelomate

67. Which of the following extraembryonic membranes is an important source of nutrition in many nonhuman animal species but NOT in humans?

a. Amnion
b. Allantois
c. Yolk sac
d. Chorion
e. Placenta

68. Which of the following is NOT a mechanism that contributes to cell differentiation and development in embryos?

a. Asymmetrical cell division
b. Asymmetrical cytoplasm distribution
c. Organizer cells
d. Location of cells on the lineage map
e. Homeotic genes

69. Which of the following is true of the gastrula?

a. It is a solid ball of cells.
b. It has three germ layers.
c. It is an extraembryonic membrane.
d. It gives rise to the blastula.
e. It derives from the zona pellucida.

70. In birds, gastrulation occurs along the

a. Dorsal lip of the embryo
b. Embryonic disc
c. Primitive streak
d. Circular blastopore
e. Inner cell mass

71. In snapdragons, the red (R) allele is incompletely dominant to the white (r) allele. If you saw a pink snapdragon, you would know:

a. Its phenotypes for both parents
b. Its genotypes for both parents
c. Its genotype for one parent
d. Its genotype
e. Its phenotype but not its genotype

72. In peas, purple flower color (P) is dominant to white (p) and tall stature (T) is dominant to dwarf (t). If the genes are unlinked, how many tall plants will be purple in the progeny of a $PpTt \times PpTT$ cross?

a. 0
b. $\frac{1}{4}$
c. $\frac{1}{2}$
d. $\frac{3}{4}$
e. 1

73. Which of the following does NOT obey the law of independent assortment?

a. Two genes on opposite ends of a chromosome
b. Flower color and height in snapdragons
c. Two genes on separate chromosomes
d. Seed color and flower color in peas
e. Two genes next to each other on a chromosome

74. In a dihybrid cross between bean plants with red (R) wrinkled (w) seeds and white (r) smooth (W) seeds, the F1 progeny is all red and smooth. If the F1 plants are selfed, what proportion of the F2 will also be red and smooth if the genes are linked?

a. All of them
b. $\frac{1}{4}$
c. $\frac{1}{2}$
d. $\frac{9}{16}$
e. None of them

75. Red-green color blindness is an X-linked trait. If a mother is heterozygous for this trait and a father has this trait, what is the probability that their child will have this trait?

a. 0
b. $\frac{1}{4}$
c. $\frac{1}{2}$
d. $\frac{3}{4}$
e. 1

76. An individual with an AB blood type needs a blood transfusion. Which of the following types could NOT be a donor?

a. O
b. AB
c. A
d. B
e. All of the above types can be donors

77. In humans, more than one gene contributes to the trait of hair color. What is this an example of?

a. Pleiotropy
b. Polygenic inheritance
c. Codominance
d. Linkage
e. Epistasis

78. A child is born with type A blood and his mother has type A. Which of the following is a possible combination of genotypes for the mother and father?

a. I^AI^B and ii
b. I^Ai and ii
c. I^AI^A and I^BI^B
d. I^Ai and I^BI^B
e. I^AI^B and I^Bi

Population Biology

79. Which of the following ecosystems is most likely to have an inverted biomass pyramid?

a. Forest ecosystem
b. Tundra ecosystem
c. Desert ecosystem
d. Aquatic ecosystem
e. Grassland ecosystem

80. In the food chain below, what do vultures represent?

$$grass \rightarrow cow \rightarrow wolf \rightarrow vulture$$

a. Scavengers
b. Detritivores
c. Primary carnivores
d. Herbivores
e. Secondary consumers

81. Which of the following is the major way in which carbon is released into the environment?

a. Transpiration
b. Respiration
c. Fixation
d. Sedimentation
e. Absorption

82. What is the largest reservoir of nitrogen on the planet?

a. The ocean
b. Plants
c. Soil
d. The atmosphere
e. Sediments, including fossil fuels

83. The diagram below represents the three types of survivorship curves, describing how mortality varies as species age. Which of the following species is most likely to exhibit Type I survivorship?

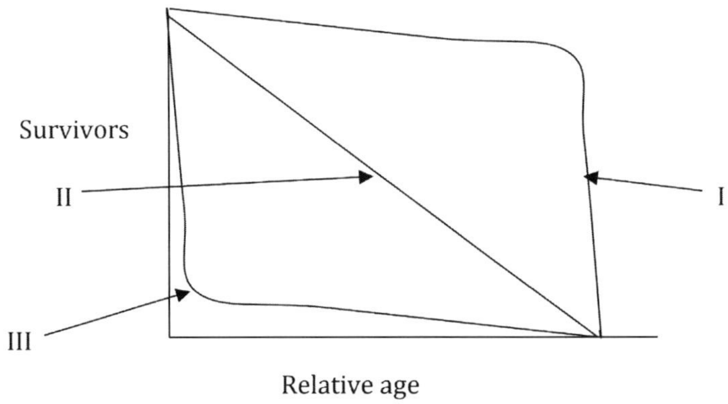

a. Frogs
b. Oysters
c. Salmon
d. Dolphins
e. Shrimp

84. A population of 1,000 individuals has 110 births and 10 deaths in a year. Its growth rate (r) is equal to

a. 0.01 per year
b. 0.1 per year
c. 0.09 per year
d. 0.11 per year
e. 0.009 per year

85. During primary succession, which species would most likely be a pioneer species?

a. Lichens
b. Fir trees
c. Mosquitoes
d. Dragonflies
e. Mushrooms

86. Which of the following habitats would provide an opportunity for secondary succession?

a. A retreating glacier
b. Burned cropland
c. A newly formed volcanic island
d. A 500-year-old forest
e. A sand dune

87. Which biome is most likely to support the growth of epiphytes?

a. Deserts
b. Tropical rain forests
c. Temperate deciduous forests
d. Taigas
e. Savannas

88. Which of the following is NOT a natural dispersal process that would lead to species colonization on an island?

a. Mussels carried into a lake on the hull of a ship
b. Drought connecting an island to other land
c. Floating seeds
d. Animals swimming long distances
e. Birds adapted to flying long distances

89. When a population reaches its carrying capacity:

a. Other populations will be forced out of the habitat
b. Density-dependent factors no longer play a role
c. Density-independent factors no longer play a role
d. The population growth rate approaches zero
e. The population size begins to decrease

90. Which of the following is an example of a density-dependent limiting factor?

a. Air pollution by a factory
b. The toxic effect of waste products
c. Nearby volcanic eruptions
d. Frosts
e. Fires

91. Two species of finches are able to utilize the same food supply, but their beaks are different. They are able to coexist on an island because of

a. Niche overlap
b. Character displacement
c. Resource partitioning
d. Competitive exclusion
e. Realized niches

92. Lichens consist of fungi and algae. The algae supply sugars through performing photosynthesis while the fungi provide minerals and a place to attach. This is an example of

a. Mutualism
b. Commensalism
c. Parasitism
d. Coevolution
e. Resource partitioning

93. Which of the following of Lamarck's evolutionary ideas turned out to be true?

a. Natural selection
b. Organisms naturally transform into increasingly complex organisms
c. Inheritance of acquired characters
d. Body parts develop with increased usage and weaken with disuse
e. Genes are the basic units of inheritance

94. The weight of adult wolves is within a fairly narrow range, even if they are well-fed in zoos. This is an example of

a. Stabilizing selection
b. Directional selection
c. Disruptive selection
d. Sexual selection
e. Artificial selection

95. Which of the following is a trait that results from disruptive selection?

a. Insecticide resistance
b. Only male peacocks having colorful plumage
c. Some birds having significantly large bills than others within the same species
d. Human height
e. Different varieties of wheat

96. Which of the following conditions would promote evolutionary change?

a. Gene flow
b. No selection
c. Random mating
d. A large population

97. Which of the following would create the greatest amount of genetic variation for a diploid species in a single generation?

a. Crossing over
b. Mutation
c. Hybridization
d. Independent assortment of homologs
e. Random joining of gametes

98. A population of pea plants has 25% dwarf plants and 75% tall plants. The tall allele, T is dominant to the dwarf allele, t. What is the frequency of the T allele?

a. 0.75
b. 0.67
c. 0.5
d. 0.25
e. 0.16

99. Darwin's idea that evolution occurs by the gradual accumulation of small changes can be described as:

a. Punctuated equilibrium
b. Phyletic gradualism
c. Convergent evolution
d. Adaptive radiation
e. Sympatric speciation

100. Which of the following processes of speciation would most likely occur if a species of bird were introduced into a group of islands that were previously uninhabited by animals?

a. Allopatric speciation
b. Adaptive radiation
c. Sympatric speciation
d. Artificial speciation
e. Hybridizing speciation

101. Hummingbirds drink nectar from *Ipomopsis* flowers. *Ipomopsis* are trumpet-shaped, and hummingbirds have long narrow beaks to access the nectar. These adaptations could best be described as

a. Divergent evolution
b. Convergent evolution
c. Parallel evolution
d. Coevolution
e. Macroevolution

102. All of the following are homologous structures EXCEPT

a. Bird feathers
b. Elephant eyelashes
c. Human fingernails
d. Dog fur
e. Insect exoskeleton

103. Human predation has cause the population of cheetahs to decline dramatically. Changes in allele frequencies in the remaining population of cheetahs would most likely be due to

a. Mutation
b. The bottleneck effect
c. The founder effect
d. Gene flow
e. Natural selection

104. The first living cells on earth were most likely

a. Heterotrophs
b. Autotrophs
c. Aerobic
d. Eukaryotes
e. Photosynthetic

105. Evidence that humans share a common ancestor with other primates includes all of the following EXCEPT

a. DNA sequence
b. Fossil evidence of intermediate species
c. Analogous structures
d. Homologous structures
e. Radiometric dating of fossils

106. Sea anemones pull food into their mouths by withdrawing their tentacles. If the tentacles are stimulated with a non-food item, they will ignore the stimulus after a few futile attempts to capture the food. This is known as which of the following?

a. Associative learning
b. Imprinting
c. Habituation
d. Chemical communication
e. Territoriality

107. Queen bees secrete pheromones that are eaten by workers and prevent the workers from being able to reproduce. This is known as which of the following?

a. Associative learning
b. Imprinting
c. Habituation
d. Chemical communication
e. Territoriality

108. Salmon hatch in freshwater streams and then migrate to the ocean to mature. When they are mature, they swim upstream to their birthplace to spawn. This is known as which of the following?

a. Associative learning
b. Imprinting
c. Habituation
d. Chemical communication
e. Territoriality

109. The species *Homo sapiens* first appeared in the fossil record approximately

a. 10 million years ago
b. 1 million years ago
c. 100,000 years ago
d. 10,000 years ago
e. 6,000 years ago

110. Which of the following demographic changes would lead to a population with an older age composition?

a. Increased birth rate
b. Environmental pollution
c. Increased availability of food
d. Medical advancements that increase life expectancy
e. Introduction of contraceptives

111. Which of the following factors has the greatest impact on birth rate in humans?

a. The carrying capacity of the earth
b. Age at reproductive maturity
c. Reproductive lifetime
d. Survivorship of offspring to reproductive maturity
e. Socioeconomic factors

112. Which of the following organisms is likely to have the greatest quantity of mercury in its body?

a. Mosquitoes
b. Carnivorous insects
c. Frogs
d. Filter-feeding fish
e. Fish-eating birds

113. Which of the following consequences is NOT a direct result of clear-cutting rain forests?

a. Climate change
b. Erosion
c. Reduction in species diversity
d. Air pollution
e. Desertification

114. Burning fossil fuels releases sulfur dioxide and nitrogen dioxide. These pollutants lead to which environmental problem?

a. Denitrification
b. Acid rain
c. Global climate change
d. Ozone depletion
e. Eutrophication

115. Genetic engineering:

a. Is a form of human reproduction
b. Always involves using restriction enzymes to cut DNA
c. Often involves transient expression of genes
d. Always involves introducing new proteins to a cell
e. Often involves using nucleases to cut DNA

Answer Key and Explanations

Molecular and Cellular Biology

1. C: Hydrogen bonds are a special type of dipole-dipole interaction between molecules that causes a strong attraction (negative dipole to positive dipole). This interaction gives water such a high surface tension that some small organisms, such as water striders, can move across its surface. Although water molecules are polar, they do not attract non-polar molecules, such as fats or oils. Thus, choice A is incorrect. Solid water is less dense than liquid water, which is why ice floats in water and why choice B is incorrect. Choice D is incorrect because water is generally a very good solvent, especially for substances whose molecules have polar or ionic bonds. Choice E is incorrect because water cannot produce more of either H^+ or OH^-, since both would be made in equal amounts from H_2O, making it a terrible buffer.

2. D: An exothermic reaction releases energy, whereas an endothermic reaction requires energy. The breakdown of a chemical compound is an example of a decomposition reaction ($AB \rightarrow A + B$). A combination reaction ($A + B \rightarrow AB$) is the reverse of a decomposition reaction, and a replacement (displacement) reaction is one where a compound breaks apart and forms a new compound plus a free reactant ($AB + C \rightarrow AC + B$ or $AB + CD \rightarrow AD + CB$).

3. B: Glycogen is a polysaccharide, a molecule composed of many bonded glucose molecules. Glucose is a carbohydrate, and most simple carbohydrates are composed of only carbon, oxygen, and hydrogen. Most other metabolic compounds contain other atoms, particularly nitrogen, phosphorus, and sulfur.

4. A: Long-term energy storage in animals takes the form of fat. Animals also store energy as glycogen, and plants store energy as starch, but these substances are for shorter-term use. Fats are a good storage form for chemical energy because fatty acids bond to glycerol in a condensation reaction to form fats (triglycerides). This reaction, which releases water, allows for the compacting of high-energy fatty acids in a concentrated form.

5. B: Some RNA molecules in extant organisms have enzymatic activity; for example, the formation of peptide bonds on ribosomes is catalyzed by an RNA molecule. This and other information have led scientists to believe that the most likely molecules to first demonstrate enzymatic activity were RNA molecules.

6. D: Endocytosis is a process by which cells absorb larger molecules (or even tiny organisms, such as bacteria) than would be able to pass through the plasma membrane. Endocytic vesicles containing molecules from the extracellular environment often undergo further processing once they enter the cell.

7. C: Chloroplasts contain the light-absorbing compound chlorophyll, which is essential in photosynthesis. This gives leaves their green color. Chloroplasts also contain yellow and red carotenoid pigments, which give leaves red and yellow colors in the fall as chloroplasts lose their chlorophyll.

8. A: Osmosis is the movement of water molecules (not solutes) across a semi-permeable membrane. Water moves from a region of higher concentration to a region of lower concentration. Osmosis occurs when the concentrations of a solute differ on either side of a semi-permeable membrane. For example, a cell (containing a higher concentration of water) in a salty solution (containing a lower concentration of water) will lose water as water leaves the cell. This continues until the solution outside the cell has the same salt concentration as the cytoplasm.

9. D: Both prokaryotes and eukaryotes interact with the extracellular environment and use membrane-bound or membrane-associated proteins to achieve this. They both use diffusion and active transport to move materials in and out of their cells. Prokaryotes have very few proteins associated with their DNA, whereas eukaryotes' DNA is richly studded with proteins. Both types of living things can have flagella, although with different structural characteristics in the two groups. The most important differences between prokaryotes and eukaryotes are the lack of a nucleus and membrane-bound organelles in prokaryotes.

10. B: Bacteria and cyanobacteria have cell walls constructed from peptidoglycans—a polysaccharide and protein molecule. Other types of organisms with cell walls, for instance, plants and fungi, have cell walls composed of different polysaccharides. Plant cell walls are composed of cellulose, and fungal cell walls are composed of chitin.

11. D: Enzymes act as catalysts for biochemical reactions. A catalyst is not consumed in a reaction, but rather lowers the activation energy for that reaction. The potential energy of the substrate and the product remain the same, but the activation energy—the energy needed to make the reaction progress—can be lowered with the help of an enzyme.

12. A: A cofactor is an inorganic substance that is required for an enzymatic reaction to occur. Cofactors bind to the active site of the enzyme and enable the substrate to fit properly. Many cofactors are metal ions, such as zinc, iron, and copper.

13. D: Enzyme inhibitors attach to an enzyme and block substrates from entering the active site, thereby preventing enzyme activity. Cyanide irreversibly binds to the enzyme cytochrome c oxidase and blocks its active site. Cyanide therefore fits the definition of an enzyme inhibitor.

14. A: Because the energy of the products is less than the energy of the substrate, the reaction releases energy and is an exergonic reaction.

15. D: Enzymes are substrate-specific. Most enzymes catalyze only one biochemical reaction. Their active sites are specific for a certain type of substrate and do not bind to other substrates and catalyze other reactions.

16. C: Lactic acid fermentation converts pyruvate into lactate using high-energy electrons from NADH. This process allows ATP production to continue in anaerobic conditions by providing NAD^+ so that ATP can be made in glycolysis.

17. B: Proteins in the inner membrane of the mitochondrion accept high-energy electrons from NAD and $FADH_2$, and in turn transport protons from the matrix to the intermembrane space. The high proton concentration in the intermembrane space creates a gradient, which is harnessed by ATP synthase to produce ATP.

18. E: Electrons trapped by the chlorophyll P680 molecule in photosystem II are energized by light. They are then transferred to electron acceptors in an electron transport chain.

19. D: Crassulacean acid metabolism (CAM) photosynthesis occurs in plants that grow where water loss must be minimized, such as cacti. These plants open their stomata and fix CO_2 at night. During the day, stomata are closed, reducing water loss. Thus, photosynthesis can proceed without water loss.

20. B: DNA wrapped around histone proteins is called chromatin. In a eukaryotic cell, DNA is always associated with protein; it is not "naked" as with prokaryotic cells.

21. C: The diploid chromosome number for humans is 46. After DNA duplication but before the first cell division of meiosis, there are 92 chromatids (46 chromosomes). After meiosis I is completed, the chromosome number is halved and equals 23. Each daughter cell is haploid, but the chromosomes are still paired (sister chromatids). During meiosis II, the two sister chromatids of each chromosome separate, resulting in 23 haploid chromosomes per germ cell.

22. D: In prophase I, homologous chromosomes pair up and form tetrads. The arms of the chromosomes can break and recombine to create new genetic variations, a process called crossing over. At the end of meiosis, in telophase I and cytokinesis, the tetrads split up. The cell divides into two daughter cells that each contain one chromosome from each pair. Each daughter cell contains a unique combination of chromosomes that is different from both the mother cell and its cognate daughter cell.

23. C: Although there are two cell divisions in meiosis, DNA replication occurs only once. It occurs in interphase I, before M phase begins.

24. B: The synaptonemal complex is a protein-based structure that is required for synapsis and recombination of homologous chromosomes. It provides a framework that aligns and stabilizes the chromosomes during synapsis. It is also required for the formation of chiasmata, where crossing over occurs. It is formed in the zygotene phase of prophase I (the second of five phases of prophase I) and disassembled during the diplotene stage (the fourth phase of prophase I). Therefore, it only exists during prophase I, which can also be referred to as prophase of meiosis I.

25. C: Genes code for proteins, and genes are discrete lengths of DNA on chromosomes. An allele is a variant of a gene (different DNA sequence). In diploid organisms, there may be two versions of each gene.

26. D: The enzyme helicase unwinds DNA. It depends on several other proteins to make the unwinding run smoothly, however. Single-strand binding protein holds the single-stranded DNA in place, and topoisomerase helps relieve tension at the replication fork.

27. D: DNA is composed of nucleotides joined together in long chains. Nucleotides are composed of a pentose sugar, a phosphate group, and a nitrogenous base. The bases form the "rungs" of the ladder at the core of the DNA helix, and the pentose-phosphates are on its outside, or backbone.

28. B: DNA replication begins with a short segment of RNA (not DNA). DNA polymerase cannot begin adding nucleotides without an existing piece of RNA (a primer).

29. A: DNA synthesis on the lagging strand forms short segments called Okazaki fragments. Because DNA polymerase can only add nucleotides in the $5' \rightarrow 3'$ direction, lagging strand synthesis is discontinuous. The final product is formed when DNA ligase joins Okazaki fragments together.

30. D: Each time a cell divides, a few base pairs of DNA at the end of each chromosome are lost. Telomerase is an enzyme that uses a built-in template to add a short sequence of DNA over and over at the end of chromosomes—a sort of protective "cap". This prevents the loss of genetic material with each round of DNA replication.

31. D: DNA polymerase does not match base pairs with 100% fidelity. Some level of mismatching is present for all DNA polymerases, and this is a source of mutation in nature. Cells have mechanisms of correcting base pair mismatches, but they do not fix all of them.

32. C: Insertions and deletions cause frameshift mutations. These mutations cause all subsequent nucleotides to be displaced by one position, and thereby cause all the amino acids to be different than they would have been if the mutation had not occurred.

33. A: Transcription is the process of creating an RNA strand from a DNA template. All forms of RNA—for example, mRNA, tRNA, and rRNA—are products of transcription.

34. C: The *lac* operon controls transcription of the gene that allows bacteria to metabolize lactose. It codes for both structural and regulatory proteins and includes promoter and operator sequences.

35. E: Operons are common in prokaryotes. They are units of DNA that control the transcription of DNA and code for their own regulatory proteins as well as structural proteins.

36. D: Conjugation is direct transfer of plasmid DNA between bacteria through a pilus. The F plasmid contains genes that enable bacteria to produce pili and is often the DNA that is transferred between bacteria.

37. D: In the lysogenic cycle, viral DNA gets incorporated into the DNA of the host. A virus in this dormant stage is called a provirus. Eventually, an external cue may trigger the virus to excise itself and begin the lytic cycle.

38. B: In the lytic cycle, viruses use host resources to produce viral DNA and proteins in order to create new viruses. In the process, they destroy the host cell by lysing it. For this reason, actively replicating viruses are said to be in the lytic cycle.

39. C: Plasmids are small circular pieces of DNA found in bacteria. Plasmids are widely used in recombinant DNA technology. They are cut with restriction enzymes and DNA of interest is ligated to them. They can then easily be used to transform bacteria.

Organismal Biology

40. D: The ovary houses the ovules in a flower. Pollen grains fertilize ovules to create seeds, and the ovary matures into a fruit.

41. C: Gymnosperms reproduce by producing pollen and ovules, but they do not have flowers. Instead, their reproductive structures are cones or cone-like structures.

42. E: Stomata are openings on leaves that allow for gas exchange, which is essential for photosynthesis. Stomata are surrounded by guard cells, which open and close based on their turgidity.

43. A: Monocots differ from dicots in that they have one cotyledon, or embryonic leaf in their embryos. They also have parallel veination, fibrous roots, petals in multiples of three, and a random arrangement of vascular bundles in their stems.

44. E: Nonvascular plants do not produce seeds like angiosperms and gymnosperms do. They generally reproduce sexually, but produce spores instead of seeds.

45. C: Angiosperms produce flowers, with ovules inside of ovaries. The ovaries become a fruit, with seeds inside. Gymnosperms have naked seeds that are produced in cones or cone like structures. Monocots and dicots/eudicots are subgroups within angiosperms. While they are technically a correct answer, the best answer is angiosperms.

46. A: The central, supporting pillar of the tree is known as heartwood. Heartwood does not function in the transport of water, and even though it is dead, it will not decay or lose strength as long as the outer layers remain intact.

47. D: The phloem is the pipeline through which carbohydrates are transported to the roots. It is located outside of the xylem and lives for only a short time before becoming part of the outer bark.

48. B: In ferns, the mature diploid plant is called a sporophyte. Sporophytes undergo meiosis to produce spores, which develop into gametophytes, which produce gametes.

49. C: Alternation of generations means the alternation between the diploid and haploid phases in plants.

50. B: Anthers produce microspores (the male gametophytes of flowering plants), which undergo meiosis to produce pollen grains.

51. C: In flowering plants, the anthers house the male gametophytes (which produce sperm) and the pistils house the female gametophytes (which produce eggs). Eggs and sperm are haploid. All other tissues are solely diploid.

52. A: The plant hormone ethylene is responsible for fruit ripening. Auxins are involved in a range of processes involving growth and development.

53. C: Cytokinins stimulate cell division (cytokinesis) and have been found to delay senescence (aging). They are often sprayed on cut flowers and fruit to prolong their shelf life.

54. C: Day-neutral plants are not affected by day length in their flowering times. Rather, they respond to other environmental cues, like temperature and water.

55. C: Plants exchange gases with the environment through pores in their leaves called stomata. Animals exchange gases with the environment in many different ways: small animals like flatworms exchange gases through their skin; insects use tracheae; and many species use lungs.

56. B: Platelets are cell fragments that are involved in blood clotting. Platelets are the site for the blood coagulation cascade. Its final steps are the formation of fibrinogen, which, when cleaved, forms fibrin, the "skeleton" of the blood clot.

57. A: The large intestine's main function is the reabsorption of water into the body to form solid waste. It also allows for the absorption of vitamin K produced by microbes living inside the large intestine.

58. D: When Ca^{2+} channels open, calcium enters the axon terminal and causes synaptic vesicles to release neurotransmitter into the synaptic cleft.

59. C: In a positive feedback loop, an action intensifies a chain of events that, in turn, intensify the conditions that caused the action beyond normal limits. Nursing stimulates lactation, which promotes nursing. Contractions during childbirth and sexual orgasm are examples of positive feedback.

60. D: Mammals often warm themselves by altering their metabolism. Shivering warms animals due to the heat generated by contractions in trunk muscles.

61. A: HCG (human chorionic gonadotropin) is secreted by the trophoblast, part of the early embryo, following implantation in the uterus. GnRH (gonadotropin-releasing hormone) is secreted by the hypothalamus, while LH (luteinizing hormone) and FSH (follicle-stimulating hormone) are secreted by the pituitary gland. GnRH stimulates the production of LH and FSH. LH stimulates ovulation and the production of estrogen and progesterone by the ovary in females, and testosterone production in males. FSH stimulates maturation of the ovarian follicle and estrogen production in females and sperm production in males.

62. E: The placenta secretes progesterone and estrogen once a pregnancy is established. The placenta secretes hCG early in pregnancy and in small doses throughout the pregnancy.

63. C: In oogenesis, meiosis I produces a secondary oocyte and a polar body. Both the first polar body and the secondary oocyte undergo meiosis II. The secondary oocyte divides to produce the ovum and the second polar body.

64. D: Positive feedback from rising levels of estrogen in the menstrual cycle produces a sudden surge of luteinizing hormone (LH). This high level triggers ovulation.

65. E: The testes contain hundreds of seminiferous tubules for the production of sperm, or spermatogenesis. This requires 64-72 days. Leydig cells surround the seminiferous tubules and produce male sex hormones called androgens, the most important of which is testosterone. Semen is made in the seminal vesicles, prostate gland, and other glands. Sperm are transferred to the penis via the epididymis, where they become motile, and thence through the vas deferens.

66. B: The gastrula is formed from the blastocyst, which contains a bilayered embryonic disc. One layer of this disc's inner cell mass further subdivides into the epiblast and the hypoblast, resulting in the three primary germ layers (endoderm, mesoderm, ectoderm).

67. C: In birds and reptiles, the yolk sac contains the yolk, the main source of nutrients for the embryo. In humans, the yolk sac is empty and embryos receive nutrition through the placenta. However, the yolk sac forms part of the digestive system and is where the earliest blood cells and blood vessels are formed.

68. D: A lineage map describes the fates of cells in the early embryo; in other words, it tells which germ layer different cells will occupy. In some small organisms such as the nematode *Caenorhabditis elegans*, all of the adult cells can be traced back to the egg. A lineage map is not a mechanism of embryo development, but rather a tool for describing it.

69. B: The gastrula is the first three-layered stage of the embryo, containing the ectoderm, mesoderm, and endoderm.

70. C: In birds, the invagination of gastrulation occurs along a line called the primitive streak. Cells migrate to the primitive streak, and the embryo becomes elongated.

71. D: You would know the snapdragon has an Rr genotype, but you would not know whether its parents had an Rr genotype or a combination of Rr and rr or RR and rr.

72. D: All the plants will be tall, and flower color will assort independently of stature. In a $Pp \times Pp$ cross, $\frac{3}{4}$ of the progeny will be purple.

73. E: Two genes next to each other (or within a specified distance) are said to be linked. Linked genes do not follow the law of independent assortment because they are too close together to be segregated from each other in meiosis.

74. C: If the genes are linked, there would be only two kinds of alleles produced by the F1 plants: Rw and rW. A Punnett square with these alleles reveals that half the progeny will have both an R and a W allele.

75. C: Half of the boys will receive the color-blind allele from the mother, and the other half will receive the normal one. All the girls will receive the color-blind allele from the father; half of them will also get one from the mother, while the other half will get the normal one. Therefore, half the children will be colorblind.

76. E: An individual with AB blood is tolerant to both the A carbohydrate on red blood cells and the B carbohydrate as "self" and can therefore accept any of the 4 different blood types.

77. B: When more than one gene contributes to a trait, inheritance of that trait is said to be polygenic. This type of inheritance does not follow the rules of Mendelian genetics.

78. B: For this situation, one of the parental genotypes must be either I^Ai or I^AI^A. This rules out options A and E. Of the remaining options, the only one that would work is the one where the type A parent is paired with a parent with at least one i in their genotype. This leaves option B as the only possible combination from this selection.

Population Biology

79. D: Biomass pyramids are graphical representations of the total amount of organic matter present within an ecosystem. Most terrestrial ecosystems have the traditional pyramid presentation with the smallest point at the top. In aquatic ecosystems however, the pyramid is often inverted with the major producer within the system having a smaller biomass than the consumers above it. This is generally because the producers, often phytoplankton in these cases, produce multiple generations quickly while having shorter individual lives. These are then quickly devoured by the substantially larger mass of zooplankton.

80. A: Vultures eat carrion, or dead animals, so they are considered scavengers. Detritivores are heterotrophs that eat decomposing organic matter such as leaf litter. They are usually small.

81. B: Carbon is released in the form of CO_2 through respiration, burning, and decomposition.

82. D: Most nitrogen is in the atmosphere in the form of N_2. In order for it to be used by living things, it must be fixed by nitrogen-fixing bacteria. These microorganisms convert N_2 to ammonia, which then forms NH_4^+ (ammonium).

83. D: Type I curves describe species in which most individuals survive to middle age, after which deaths increase. Dolphins have few offspring, provide extended care to the young, and live a long time.

84. B: The growth rate is equal to the difference between births and deaths divided by population size. In this case, $r = \frac{110-10}{1,000} = 0.1$.

85. A: Pioneer species colonize vacant habitats, and the first such species in a habitat demonstrate primary succession. Succession on rock or lava often begins with lichens. Lichens need very little organic material and can erode rock into soil to provide a growth substrate for other organisms.

86. B: Secondary succession occurs when a habitat has been entirely or partially disturbed or destroyed by abandonment, burning, storms, etc.

87. B: Epiphytes are plants that grow in the canopy of trees, and the tropical rain forest has a rich canopy because of its density and extensive moisture.

88. A: Transportation by humans or human-associated means is not considered a natural dispersal process.

89. D: Within a habitat, there is a maximum number of individuals that can continue to thrive, known as the habitat's carrying capacity. When the population size approaches this number, population growth will stop.

90. B: Density-dependent limiting factors on population growth are factors that vary with population density. Pollution from a factory, volcanic eruptions, frosts, and fires do not vary as a function of population size. Waste products, however, increase with population density and could limit further population increases.

91. B: Character displacement means that, although similar, species in the same habitat have evolved characteristics that reduce competition between them. It occurs as a result of resource partitioning.

92. A: Because both species benefit, lichens constitute an example of mutualism.

93. D: Natural selection was Darwin's idea, not Lamarck's. Mendel discovered that genes are the basic units of inheritance. Lamarck's observation about use and disuse is true, although he did not connect it with the underlying mechanism of natural selection.

94. A: Stabilizing selection is a form of selection in which a particular trait, such as weight, becomes stable within a population. It results in reduced genetic variability, and the disappearance of alleles for extreme traits. Over time, the most common phenotypes survive.

95. C: Disruptive selection occurs when the environment favors alleles for extreme traits. In the example, seasonal changes can make different types of food available at different times of the year, favoring the large or small bills.

96. A: Gene flow, which is the movement of alleles between populations through migration and interbreeding, can change allele frequencies and promote evolutionary change. Options B-D all describe conditions that would lead to genetic equilibrium, where no evolution would occur.

97. C: Hybridization between two different species would result in more genetic variation than sexual reproduction within a species.

98. C: According to Hardy-Weinberg equilibrium, $p + q = 1$ and $p^2 + 2pq + q^2 = 1$. In this scenario, $q^2 = 0.25$, so $q = 0.5$. p must also be 0.5.

99. B: Phyletic gradualism is the view that evolution occurs at a more or less constant rate. Contrary to this view, punctuated equilibrium holds that evolutionary history consists of long periods of stasis punctuated by geologically short periods of evolution. This theory predicts that there will be few fossils revealing intermediate stages of evolution, whereas phyletic gradualism views the lack of intermediate-stage fossils as a deficit in the fossil record that will resolve when enough specimens are collected.

100. B: Adaptive radiation is the evolution of several species from a single ancestor. It occurs when a species colonizes a new area and members diverge geographically as they adapt to somewhat different conditions.

101. D: In coevolution, one species responds to new adaptations in another. Coevolution occurs between predator and prey, pathogens and the immune systems of animals, and plants and their pollinators.

102. E: Structures are homologous because they derive from a common ancestor. Insects do not share a common ancestor with birds and mammals. Birds and mammals share a reptile ancestor.

103. B: The bottleneck effect occurs when populations undergo a dramatic decrease in size. It could be due to natural or artificial causes.

104. A: The first living organisms probably had not yet evolved the ability to synthesize their own organic molecules for food. They were probably heterotrophs that consumed nutrition from the "organic soup."

105. C: Analogous structures do not reveal anything about common ancestors between species. They are simply features that arise due to adapting to similar ecological conditions.

106. C: Habituation is a learned behavior that teaches an animal to ignore meaningless or neutral stimuli.

107. D: Pheromones are chemicals used by animals for communication. They are released by certain individuals and elicit behavioral changes in other individuals.

108. B: Imprinting is a program for acquiring a behavior if an appropriate stimulus is given during a critical time period early in life. Salmon are imprinted with the odors of their birthplace after hatching.

109. C: *Homo sapiens* are thought to have evolved in Africa approximately 100,000 years ago.

110. D: Prolonging the life of individuals in a current population will lead to an older age composition. An increased birth rate will cause population growth, but a greater proportion will be younger, not older.

111. E: With many species, factors like food, space, and predation have large effects on reproduction. Humans are able to control or at least affect many of these challenges, as well as the reproductive process itself, so other factors like education, religion, wealth, and access to health care are more significant factors in birth rates.

112. E: Mercury is a fat-soluble pollutant and can be stored in body tissues. Animals higher up the food chain, which eat other animals, are most likely to accumulate mercury in their bodies.

113. D: Air pollution would not be a direct result of clear-cutting forests. Air pollution would be an indirect consequence, because the CO_2 contained in the wood is released when the wood is either burnt or decomposed. Deforestation contributes to an estimated ten percent of all emissions. With less trees to reduce CO_2 already present in the air, clear-cutting results in increased atmospheric

CO_2, as well as localized climate change. Due to deforestation roots lose strength and cause the soil to become loose, this combined with the lack of trees and shrubs to absorb water during heavy rainfall, rapid runoff occurs causing flooding and erosion. This can develop into mudslides such as the 2017 Sierra Leone mudslide disaster which resulted in the death of 1,141 people and left 3,000 homeless. Transpiration from trees in the tropical rain forest contributes largely to cloud formation and rain, so rainfall decreases because of clear-cutting, resulting in desertification.

114. B: When sulfur dioxide and nitrogen dioxide mix with water and other substances in the atmosphere, they produce sulfuric acid and nitric acid. These acids kill plants and animals when they reach the surface of the earth.

115. E: *Genetic engineering* is a general term to describe altering DNA sequences through adding or removing pieces of DNA from a native sequence. In the earliest genetic engineering processes, restriction enzymes were used to perform this "clipping" function, but other methods have been devised and are in use today. Current technologies include those using nucleases (such as CRISPR-Cas9, zinc-finger nucleases, or TALENs) or site-specific recombinases.

How to Overcome Test Anxiety

Just the thought of taking a test is enough to make most people a little nervous. A test is an important event that can have a long-term impact on your future, so it's important to take it seriously and it's natural to feel anxious about performing well. But just because anxiety is normal, that doesn't mean that it's helpful in test taking, or that you should simply accept it as part of your life. Anxiety can have a variety of effects. These effects can be mild, like making you feel slightly nervous, or severe, like blocking your ability to focus or remember even a simple detail.

If you experience test anxiety—whether severe or mild—it's important to know how to beat it. To discover this, first you need to understand what causes test anxiety.

Causes of Test Anxiety

While we often think of anxiety as an uncontrollable emotional state, it can actually be caused by simple, practical things. One of the most common causes of test anxiety is that a person does not feel adequately prepared for their test. This feeling can be the result of many different issues such as poor study habits or lack of organization, but the most common culprit is time management. Starting to study too late, failing to organize your study time to cover all of the material, or being distracted while you study will mean that you're not well prepared for the test. This may lead to cramming the night before, which will cause you to be physically and mentally exhausted for the test. Poor time management also contributes to feelings of stress, fear, and hopelessness as you realize you are not well prepared but don't know what to do about it.

Other times, test anxiety is not related to your preparation for the test but comes from unresolved fear. This may be a past failure on a test, or poor performance on tests in general. It may come from comparing yourself to others who seem to be performing better or from the stress of living up to expectations. Anxiety may be driven by fears of the future—how failure on this test would affect your educational and career goals. These fears are often completely irrational, but they can still negatively impact your test performance.

Elements of Test Anxiety

As mentioned earlier, test anxiety is considered to be an emotional state, but it has physical and mental components as well. Sometimes you may not even realize that you are suffering from test anxiety until you notice the physical symptoms. These can include trembling hands, rapid heartbeat, sweating, nausea, and tense muscles. Extreme anxiety may lead to fainting or vomiting. Obviously, any of these symptoms can have a negative impact on testing. It is important to recognize them as soon as they begin to occur so that you can address the problem before it damages your performance.

The mental components of test anxiety include trouble focusing and inability to remember learned information. During a test, your mind is on high alert, which can help you recall information and stay focused for an extended period of time. However, anxiety interferes with your mind's natural processes, causing you to blank out, even on the questions you know well. The strain of testing during anxiety makes it difficult to stay focused, especially on a test that may take several hours. Extreme anxiety can take a huge mental toll, making it difficult not only to recall test information but even to understand the test questions or pull your thoughts together.

Effects of Test Anxiety

Test anxiety is like a disease—if left untreated, it will get progressively worse. Anxiety leads to poor performance, and this reinforces the feelings of fear and failure, which in turn lead to poor performances on subsequent tests. It can grow from a mild nervousness to a crippling condition. If allowed to progress, test anxiety can have a big impact on your schooling, and consequently on your future.

Test anxiety can spread to other parts of your life. Anxiety on tests can become anxiety in any stressful situation, and blanking on a test can turn into panicking in a job situation. But fortunately, you don't have to let anxiety rule your testing and determine your grades. There are a number of relatively simple steps you can take to move past anxiety and function normally on a test and in the rest of life.

Physical Steps for Beating Test Anxiety

While test anxiety is a serious problem, the good news is that it can be overcome. It doesn't have to control your ability to think and remember information. While it may take time, you can begin taking steps today to beat anxiety.

Just as your first hint that you may be struggling with anxiety comes from the physical symptoms, the first step to treating it is also physical. Rest is crucial for having a clear, strong mind. If you are tired, it is much easier to give in to anxiety. But if you establish good sleep habits, your body and mind will be ready to perform optimally, without the strain of exhaustion. Additionally, sleeping well helps you to retain information better, so you're more likely to recall the answers when you see the test questions.

Getting good sleep means more than going to bed on time. It's important to allow your brain time to relax. Take study breaks from time to time so it doesn't get overworked, and don't study right before bed. Take time to rest your mind before trying to rest your body, or you may find it difficult to fall asleep.

Along with sleep, other aspects of physical health are important in preparing for a test. Good nutrition is vital for good brain function. Sugary foods and drinks may give a burst of energy but this burst is followed by a crash, both physically and emotionally. Instead, fuel your body with protein and vitamin-rich foods.

Also, drink plenty of water. Dehydration can lead to headaches and exhaustion, especially if your brain is already under stress from the rigors of the test. Particularly if your test is a long one, drink water during the breaks. And if possible, take an energy-boosting snack to eat between sections.

Along with sleep and diet, a third important part of physical health is exercise. Maintaining a steady workout schedule is helpful, but even taking 5-minute study breaks to walk can help get your blood pumping faster and clear your head. Exercise also releases endorphins, which contribute to a positive feeling and can help combat test anxiety.

When you nurture your physical health, you are also contributing to your mental health. If your body is healthy, your mind is much more likely to be healthy as well. So take time to rest, nourish your body with healthy food and water, and get moving as much as possible. Taking these physical steps will make you stronger and more able to take the mental steps necessary to overcome test anxiety.

Mental Steps for Beating Test Anxiety

Working on the mental side of test anxiety can be more challenging, but as with the physical side, there are clear steps you can take to overcome it. As mentioned earlier, test anxiety often stems from lack of preparation, so the obvious solution is to prepare for the test. Effective studying may be the most important weapon you have for beating test anxiety, but you can and should employ several other mental tools to combat fear.

First, boost your confidence by reminding yourself of past success—tests or projects that you aced. If you're putting as much effort into preparing for this test as you did for those, there's no reason you should expect to fail here. Work hard to prepare; then trust your preparation.

Second, surround yourself with encouraging people. It can be helpful to find a study group, but be sure that the people you're around will encourage a positive attitude. If you spend time with others who are anxious or cynical, this will only contribute to your own anxiety. Look for others who are motivated to study hard from a desire to succeed, not from a fear of failure.

Third, reward yourself. A test is physically and mentally tiring, even without anxiety, and it can be helpful to have something to look forward to. Plan an activity following the test, regardless of the outcome, such as going to a movie or getting ice cream.

When you are taking the test, if you find yourself beginning to feel anxious, remind yourself that you know the material. Visualize successfully completing the test. Then take a few deep, relaxing breaths and return to it. Work through the questions carefully but with confidence, knowing that you are capable of succeeding.

Developing a healthy mental approach to test taking will also aid in other areas of life. Test anxiety affects more than just the actual test—it can be damaging to your mental health and even contribute to depression. It's important to beat test anxiety before it becomes a problem for more than testing.

Study Strategy

Being prepared for the test is necessary to combat anxiety, but what does being prepared look like? You may study for hours on end and still not feel prepared. What you need is a strategy for test prep. The next few pages outline our recommended steps to help you plan out and conquer the challenge of preparation.

Step 1: Scope Out the Test

Learn everything you can about the format (multiple choice, essay, etc.) and what will be on the test. Gather any study materials, course outlines, or sample exams that may be available. Not only will this help you to prepare, but knowing what to expect can help to alleviate test anxiety.

Step 2: Map Out the Material

Look through the textbook or study guide and make note of how many chapters or sections it has. Then divide these over the time you have. For example, if a book has 15 chapters and you have five days to study, you need to cover three chapters each day. Even better, if you have the time, leave an extra day at the end for overall review after you have gone through the material in depth.

If time is limited, you may need to prioritize the material. Look through it and make note of which sections you think you already have a good grasp on, and which need review. While you are studying, skim quickly through the familiar sections and take more time on the challenging parts.

Write out your plan so you don't get lost as you go. Having a written plan also helps you feel more in control of the study, so anxiety is less likely to arise from feeling overwhelmed at the amount to cover.

Step 3: Gather Your Tools

Decide what study method works best for you. Do you prefer to highlight in the book as you study and then go back over the highlighted portions? Or do you type out notes of the important information? Or is it helpful to make flashcards that you can carry with you? Assemble the pens, index cards, highlighters, post-it notes, and any other materials you may need so you won't be distracted by getting up to find things while you study.

If you're having a hard time retaining the information or organizing your notes, experiment with different methods. For example, try color-coding by subject with colored pens, highlighters, or post-it notes. If you learn better by hearing, try recording yourself reading your notes so you can listen while in the car, working out, or simply sitting at your desk. Ask a friend to quiz you from your flashcards, or try teaching someone the material to solidify it in your mind.

Step 4: Create Your Environment

It's important to avoid distractions while you study. This includes both the obvious distractions like visitors and the subtle distractions like an uncomfortable chair (or a too-comfortable couch that makes you want to fall asleep). Set up the best study environment possible: good lighting and a comfortable work area. If background music helps you focus, you may want to turn it on, but otherwise keep the room quiet. If you are using a computer to take notes, be sure you don't have any other windows open, especially applications like social media, games, or anything else that could distract you. Silence your phone and turn off notifications. Be sure to keep water close by so you stay hydrated while you study (but avoid unhealthy drinks and snacks).

Also, take into account the best time of day to study. Are you freshest first thing in the morning? Try to set aside some time then to work through the material. Is your mind clearer in the afternoon or evening? Schedule your study session then. Another method is to study at the same time of day that you will take the test, so that your brain gets used to working on the material at that time and will be ready to focus at test time.

Step 5: Study!

Once you have done all the study preparation, it's time to settle into the actual studying. Sit down, take a few moments to settle your mind so you can focus, and begin to follow your study plan. Don't give in to distractions or let yourself procrastinate. This is your time to prepare so you'll be ready to fearlessly approach the test. Make the most of the time and stay focused.

Of course, you don't want to burn out. If you study too long you may find that you're not retaining the information very well. Take regular study breaks. For example, taking five minutes out of every hour to walk briskly, breathing deeply and swinging your arms, can help your mind stay fresh.

As you get to the end of each chapter or section, it's a good idea to do a quick review. Remind yourself of what you learned and work on any difficult parts. When you feel that you've mastered the material, move on to the next part. At the end of your study session, briefly skim through your notes again.

But while review is helpful, cramming last minute is NOT. If at all possible, work ahead so that you won't need to fit all your study into the last day. Cramming overloads your brain with more information than it can process and retain, and your tired mind may struggle to recall even previously learned information when it is overwhelmed with last-minute study. Also, the urgent nature of cramming and the stress placed on your brain contribute to anxiety. You'll be more likely to go to the test feeling unprepared and having trouble thinking clearly.

So don't cram, and don't stay up late before the test, even just to review your notes at a leisurely pace. Your brain needs rest more than it needs to go over the information again. In fact, plan to finish your studies by noon or early afternoon the day before the test. Give your brain the rest of the day to relax or focus on other things, and get a good night's sleep. Then you will be fresh for the test and better able to recall what you've studied.

Step 6: Take a Practice Test

Many courses offer sample tests, either online or in the study materials. This is an excellent resource to check whether you have mastered the material, as well as to prepare for the test format and environment.

Check the test format ahead of time: the number of questions, the type (multiple choice, free response, etc.), and the time limit. Then create a plan for working through them. For example, if you have 30 minutes to take a 60-question test, your limit is 30 seconds per question. Spend less time on the questions you know well so that you can take more time on the difficult ones.

If you have time to take several practice tests, take the first one open book, with no time limit. Work through the questions at your own pace and make sure you fully understand them. Gradually work up to taking a test under test conditions: sit at a desk with all study materials put away and set a timer. Pace yourself to make sure you finish the test with time to spare and go back to check your answers if you have time.

After each test, check your answers. On the questions you missed, be sure you understand why you missed them. Did you misread the question (tests can use tricky wording)? Did you forget the information? Or was it something you hadn't learned? Go back and study any shaky areas that the practice tests reveal.

Taking these tests not only helps with your grade, but also aids in combating test anxiety. If you're already used to the test conditions, you're less likely to worry about it, and working through tests until you're scoring well gives you a confidence boost. Go through the practice tests until you feel comfortable, and then you can go into the test knowing that you're ready for it.

Test Tips

On test day, you should be confident, knowing that you've prepared well and are ready to answer the questions. But aside from preparation, there are several test day strategies you can employ to maximize your performance.

First, as stated before, get a good night's sleep the night before the test (and for several nights before that, if possible). Go into the test with a fresh, alert mind rather than staying up late to study.

Try not to change too much about your normal routine on the day of the test. It's important to eat a nutritious breakfast, but if you normally don't eat breakfast at all, consider eating just a protein bar. If you're a coffee drinker, go ahead and have your normal coffee. Just make sure you time it so that the caffeine doesn't wear off right in the middle of your test. Avoid sugary beverages, and drink enough water to stay hydrated but not so much that you need a restroom break 10 minutes into the test. If your test isn't first thing in the morning, consider going for a walk or doing a light workout before the test to get your blood flowing.

Allow yourself enough time to get ready, and leave for the test with plenty of time to spare so you won't have the anxiety of scrambling to arrive in time. Another reason to be early is to select a good seat. It's helpful to sit away from doors and windows, which can be distracting. Find a good seat, get out your supplies, and settle your mind before the test begins.

When the test begins, start by going over the instructions carefully, even if you already know what to expect. Make sure you avoid any careless mistakes by following the directions.

Then begin working through the questions, pacing yourself as you've practiced. If you're not sure on an answer, don't spend too much time on it, and don't let it shake your confidence. Either skip it and come back later, or eliminate as many wrong answers as possible and guess among the remaining ones. Don't dwell on these questions as you continue—put them out of your mind and focus on what lies ahead.

Be sure to read all of the answer choices, even if you're sure the first one is the right answer. Sometimes you'll find a better one if you keep reading. But don't second-guess yourself if you do immediately know the answer. Your gut instinct is usually right. Don't let test anxiety rob you of the information you know.

If you have time at the end of the test (and if the test format allows), go back and review your answers. Be cautious about changing any, since your first instinct tends to be correct, but make sure you didn't misread any of the questions or accidentally mark the wrong answer choice. Look over any you skipped and make an educated guess.

At the end, leave the test feeling confident. You've done your best, so don't waste time worrying about your performance or wishing you could change anything. Instead, celebrate the successful completion of this test. And finally, use this test to learn how to deal with anxiety even better next time.

Review Video: Test Anxiety
Visit mometrix.com/academy and enter code: 100340

Important Qualification

Not all anxiety is created equal. If your test anxiety is causing major issues in your life beyond the classroom or testing center, or if you are experiencing troubling physical symptoms related to your anxiety, it may be a sign of a serious physiological or psychological condition. If this sounds like your situation, we strongly encourage you to seek professional help.

Online Resources

Due to our efforts to try to keep this book to a manageable length, we've created a link that will give you access to all of your online resources:

mometrix.com/resources719/mttcbiology

It's Your Moment, Let's Celebrate It!

Share your story @mometrixtestpreparation

Mometrix
TEST PREPARATION

NPS

Exam Secrets
Study Guide

DEAR FUTURE EXAM SUCCESS STORY

First of all, **THANK YOU** for purchasing Mometrix study materials!

Second, congratulations! You are one of the few determined test-takers who are committed to doing whatever it takes to excel on your exam. **You have come to the right place.** We developed these study materials with one goal in mind: to deliver you the information you need in a format that's concise and easy to use.

In addition to optimizing your guide for the content of the test, we've outlined our recommended steps for breaking down the preparation process into small, attainable goals so you can make sure you stay on track.

We've also analyzed the entire test-taking process, identifying the most common pitfalls and showing how you can overcome them and be ready for any curveball the test throws you.

Standardized testing is one of the biggest obstacles on your road to success, which only increases the importance of doing well in the high-pressure, high-stakes environment of test day. Your results on this test could have a significant impact on your future, and this guide provides the information and practical advice to help you achieve your full potential on test day.

Your success is our success

We would love to hear from you! If you would like to share the story of your exam success or if you have any questions or comments in regard to our products, please contact us at **800-673-8175** or **support@mometrix.com**.

Thanks again for your business and we wish you continued success!

Sincerely,
The Mometrix Test Preparation Team

Need more help? Check out our flashcards at:
http://mometrixflashcards.com/NPS

Written and edited by the Mometrix Exam Secrets Test Prep Team
Printed in the United States of America

TABLE OF CONTENTS

Introduction

Thank you for purchasing this resource! You have made the choice to prepare yourself for a test that could have a huge impact on your future, and this guide is designed to help you be fully ready for test day. Obviously, it's important to have a solid understanding of the test material, but you also need to be prepared for the unique environment and stressors of the test, so that you can perform to the best of your abilities.

For this purpose, the first section that appears in this guide is the **Secret Keys**. We've devoted countless hours to meticulously researching what works and what doesn't, and we've boiled down our findings to the five most impactful steps you can take to improve your performance on the test. We start at the beginning with study planning and move through the preparation process, all the way to the testing strategies that will help you get the most out of what you know when you're finally sitting in front of the test.

We recommend that you start preparing for your test as far in advance as possible. However, if you've bought this guide as a last-minute study resource and only have a few days before your test, we recommend that you skip over the first two Secret Keys since they address a long-term study plan.

If you struggle with **test anxiety**, we strongly encourage you to check out our recommendations for how you can overcome it. Test anxiety is a formidable foe, but it can be beaten, and we want to make sure you have the tools you need to defeat it.

Secret Key #1 – Plan Big, Study Small

There's a lot riding on your performance. If you want to ace this test, you're going to need to keep your skills sharp and the material fresh in your mind. You need a plan that lets you review everything you need to know while still fitting in your schedule. We'll break this strategy down into three categories.

Information Organization

Start with the information you already have: the official test outline. From this, you can make a complete list of all the concepts you need to cover before the test. Organize these concepts into groups that can be studied together, and create a list of any related vocabulary you need to learn so you can brush up on any difficult terms. You'll want to keep this vocabulary list handy once you actually start studying since you may need to add to it along the way.

Time Management

Once you have your set of study concepts, decide how to spread them out over the time you have left before the test. Break your study plan into small, clear goals so you have a manageable task for each day and know exactly what you're doing. Then just focus on one small step at a time. When you manage your time this way, you don't need to spend hours at a time studying. Studying a small block of content for a short period each day helps you retain information better and avoid stressing over how much you have left to do. You can relax knowing that you have a plan to cover everything in time. In order for this strategy to be effective though, you have to start studying early and stick to your schedule. Avoid the exhaustion and futility that comes from last-minute cramming!

Study Environment

The environment you study in has a big impact on your learning. Studying in a coffee shop, while probably more enjoyable, is not likely to be as fruitful as studying in a quiet room. It's important to keep distractions to a minimum. You're only planning to study for a short block of time, so make the most of it. Don't pause to check your phone or get up to find a snack. It's also important to **avoid multitasking**. Research has consistently shown that multitasking will make your studying dramatically less effective. Your study area should also be comfortable and well-lit so you don't have the distraction of straining your eyes or sitting on an uncomfortable chair.

The time of day you study is also important. You want to be rested and alert. Don't wait until just before bedtime. Study when you'll be most likely to comprehend and remember. Even better, if you know what time of day your test will be, set that time aside for study. That way your brain will be used to working on that subject at that specific time and you'll have a better chance of recalling information.

Finally, it can be helpful to team up with others who are studying for the same test. Your actual studying should be done in as isolated an environment as possible, but the work of organizing the information and setting up the study plan can be divided up. In between study sessions, you can discuss with your teammates the concepts that you're all studying and quiz each other on the details. Just be sure that your teammates are as serious about the test as you are. If you find that your study time is being replaced with social time, you might need to find a new team.

Secret Key #2 – Make Your Studying Count

You're devoting a lot of time and effort to preparing for this test, so you want to be absolutely certain it will pay off. This means doing more than just reading the content and hoping you can remember it on test day. It's important to make every minute of study count. There are two main areas you can focus on to make your studying count.

Retention

It doesn't matter how much time you study if you can't remember the material. You need to make sure you are retaining the concepts. To check your retention of the information you're learning, try recalling it at later times with minimal prompting. Try carrying around flashcards and glance at one or two from time to time or ask a friend who's also studying for the test to quiz you.

To enhance your retention, look for ways to put the information into practice so that you can apply it rather than simply recalling it. If you're using the information in practical ways, it will be much easier to remember. Similarly, it helps to solidify a concept in your mind if you're not only reading it to yourself but also explaining it to someone else. Ask a friend to let you teach them about a concept you're a little shaky on (or speak aloud to an imaginary audience if necessary). As you try to summarize, define, give examples, and answer your friend's questions, you'll understand the concepts better and they will stay with you longer. Finally, step back for a big picture view and ask yourself how each piece of information fits with the whole subject. When you link the different concepts together and see them working together as a whole, it's easier to remember the individual components.

Finally, practice showing your work on any multi-step problems, even if you're just studying. Writing out each step you take to solve a problem will help solidify the process in your mind, and you'll be more likely to remember it during the test.

Modality

Modality simply refers to the means or method by which you study. Choosing a study modality that fits your own individual learning style is crucial. No two people learn best in exactly the same way, so it's important to know your strengths and use them to your advantage.

For example, if you learn best by visualization, focus on visualizing a concept in your mind and draw an image or a diagram. Try color-coding your notes, illustrating them, or creating symbols that will trigger your mind to recall a learned concept. If you learn best by hearing or discussing information, find a study partner who learns the same way or read aloud to yourself. Think about how to put the information in your own words. Imagine that you are giving a lecture on the topic and record yourself so you can listen to it later.

For any learning style, flashcards can be helpful. Organize the information so you can take advantage of spare moments to review. Underline key words or phrases. Use different colors for different categories. Mnemonic devices (such as creating a short list in which every item starts with the same letter) can also help with retention. Find what works best for you and use it to store the information in your mind most effectively and easily.

Secret Key #3 – Practice the Right Way

Your success on test day depends not only on how many hours you put into preparing, but also on whether you prepared the right way. It's good to check along the way to see if your studying is paying off. One of the most effective ways to do this is by taking practice tests to evaluate your progress. Practice tests are useful because they show exactly where you need to improve. Every time you take a practice test, pay special attention to these three groups of questions:

- The questions you got wrong
- The questions you had to guess on, even if you guessed right
- The questions you found difficult or slow to work through

This will show you exactly what your weak areas are, and where you need to devote more study time. Ask yourself why each of these questions gave you trouble. Was it because you didn't understand the material? Was it because you didn't remember the vocabulary? Do you need more repetitions on this type of question to build speed and confidence? Dig into those questions and figure out how you can strengthen your weak areas as you go back to review the material.

Additionally, many practice tests have a section explaining the answer choices. It can be tempting to read the explanation and think that you now have a good understanding of the concept. However, an explanation likely only covers part of the question's broader context. Even if the explanation makes perfect sense, **go back and investigate** every concept related to the question until you're positive you have a thorough understanding.

As you go along, keep in mind that the practice test is just that: practice. Memorizing these questions and answers will not be very helpful on the actual test because it is unlikely to have any of the same exact questions. If you only know the right answers to the sample questions, you won't be prepared for the real thing. **Study the concepts** until you understand them fully, and then you'll be able to answer any question that shows up on the test.

It's important to wait on the practice tests until you're ready. If you take a test on your first day of study, you may be overwhelmed by the amount of material covered and how much you need to learn. Work up to it gradually.

On test day, you'll need to be prepared for answering questions, managing your time, and using the test-taking strategies you've learned. It's a lot to balance, like a mental marathon that will have a big impact on your future. Like training for a marathon, you'll need to start slowly and work your way up. When test day arrives, you'll be ready.

Start with the strategies you've read in the first two Secret Keys—plan your course and study in the way that works best for you. If you have time, consider using multiple study resources to get different approaches to the same concepts. It can be helpful to see difficult concepts from more than one angle. Then find a good source for practice tests. Many times, the test website will suggest potential study resources or provide sample tests.

Practice Test Strategy

If you're able to find at least three practice tests, we recommend this strategy:

Untimed and Open-Book Practice

Take the first test with no time constraints and with your notes and study guide handy. Take your time and focus on applying the strategies you've learned.

Timed and Open-Book Practice

Take the second practice test open-book as well, but set a timer and practice pacing yourself to finish in time.

Timed and Closed-Book Practice

Take any other practice tests as if it were test day. Set a timer and put away your study materials. Sit at a table or desk in a quiet room, imagine yourself at the testing center, and answer questions as quickly and accurately as possible.

Keep repeating timed and closed-book tests on a regular basis until you run out of practice tests or it's time for the actual test. Your mind will be ready for the schedule and stress of test day, and you'll be able to focus on recalling the material you've learned.

Secret Key #4 – Pace Yourself

Once you're fully prepared for the material on the test, your biggest challenge on test day will be managing your time. Just knowing that the clock is ticking can make you panic even if you have plenty of time left. Work on pacing yourself so you can build confidence against the time constraints of the exam. Pacing is a difficult skill to master, especially in a high-pressure environment, so **practice is vital**.

Set time expectations for your pace based on how much time is available. For example, if a section has 60 questions and the time limit is 30 minutes, you know you have to average 30 seconds or less per question in order to answer them all. Although 30 seconds is the hard limit, set 25 seconds per question as your goal, so you reserve extra time to spend on harder questions. When you budget extra time for the harder questions, you no longer have any reason to stress when those questions take longer to answer.

Don't let this time expectation distract you from working through the test at a calm, steady pace, but keep it in mind so you don't spend too much time on any one question. Recognize that taking extra time on one question you don't understand may keep you from answering two that you do understand later in the test. If your time limit for a question is up and you're still not sure of the answer, mark it and move on, and come back to it later if the time and the test format allow. If the testing format doesn't allow you to return to earlier questions, just make an educated guess; then put it out of your mind and move on.

On the easier questions, be careful not to rush. It may seem wise to hurry through them so you have more time for the challenging ones, but it's not worth missing one if you know the concept and just didn't take the time to read the question fully. Work efficiently but make sure you understand the question and have looked at all of the answer choices, since more than one may seem right at first.

Even if you're paying attention to the time, you may find yourself a little behind at some point. You should speed up to get back on track, but do so wisely. Don't panic; just take a few seconds less on each question until you're caught up. Don't guess without thinking, but do look through the answer choices and eliminate any you know are wrong. If you can get down to two choices, it is often worthwhile to guess from those. Once you've chosen an answer, move on and don't dwell on any that you skipped or had to hurry through. If a question was taking too long, chances are it was one of the harder ones, so you weren't as likely to get it right anyway.

On the other hand, if you find yourself getting ahead of schedule, it may be beneficial to slow down a little. The more quickly you work, the more likely you are to make a careless mistake that will affect your score. You've budgeted time for each question, so don't be afraid to spend that time. Practice an efficient but careful pace to get the most out of the time you have.

Secret Key #5 – Have a Plan for Guessing

When you're taking the test, you may find yourself stuck on a question. Some of the answer choices seem better than others, but you don't see the one answer choice that is obviously correct. What do you do?

The scenario described above is very common, yet most test takers have not effectively prepared for it. Developing and practicing a plan for guessing may be one of the single most effective uses of your time as you get ready for the exam.

In developing your plan for guessing, there are three questions to address:

- When should you start the guessing process?
- How should you narrow down the choices?
- Which answer should you choose?

When to Start the Guessing Process

Unless your plan for guessing is to select C every time (which, despite its merits, is not what we recommend), you need to leave yourself enough time to apply your answer elimination strategies. Since you have a limited amount of time for each question, that means that if you're going to give yourself the best shot at guessing correctly, you have to decide quickly whether or not you will guess.

Of course, the best-case scenario is that you don't have to guess at all, so first, see if you can answer the question based on your knowledge of the subject and basic reasoning skills. Focus on the key words in the question and try to jog your memory of related topics. Give yourself a chance to bring the knowledge to mind, but once you realize that you don't have (or you can't access) the knowledge you need to answer the question, it's time to start the guessing process.

It's almost always better to start the guessing process too early than too late. It only takes a few seconds to remember something and answer the question from knowledge. Carefully eliminating wrong answer choices takes longer. Plus, going through the process of eliminating answer choices can actually help jog your memory.

Summary: Start the guessing process as soon as you decide that you can't answer the question based on your knowledge.

How to Narrow Down the Choices

The next chapter in this book (**Test-Taking Strategies**) includes a wide range of strategies for how to approach questions and how to look for answer choices to eliminate. You will definitely want to read those carefully, practice them, and figure out which ones work best for you. Here though, we're going to address a mindset rather than a particular strategy.

Your odds of guessing an answer correctly depend on how many options you are choosing from.

Number of options left	5	4	3	2	1
Odds of guessing correctly	20%	25%	33%	50%	100%

You can see from this chart just how valuable it is to be able to eliminate incorrect answers and make an educated guess, but there are two things that many test takers do that cause them to miss out on the benefits of guessing:

- Accidentally eliminating the correct answer
- Selecting an answer based on an impression

We'll look at the first one here, and the second one in the next section.

To avoid accidentally eliminating the correct answer, we recommend a thought exercise called **the $5 challenge**. In this challenge, you only eliminate an answer choice from contention if you are willing to bet $5 on it being wrong. Why $5? Five dollars is a small but not insignificant amount of money. It's an amount you could afford to lose but wouldn't want to throw away. And while losing $5 once might not hurt too much, doing it twenty times will set you back $100. In the same way, each small decision you make—eliminating a choice here, guessing on a question there—won't by itself impact your score very much, but when you put them all together, they can make a big difference. By holding each answer choice elimination decision to a higher standard, you can reduce the risk of accidentally eliminating the correct answer.

The $5 challenge can also be applied in a positive sense: If you are willing to bet $5 that an answer choice *is* correct, go ahead and mark it as correct.

Summary: Only eliminate an answer choice if you are willing to bet $5 that it is wrong.

Which Answer to Choose

You're taking the test. You've run into a hard question and decided you'll have to guess. You've eliminated all the answer choices you're willing to bet $5 on. Now you have to pick an answer. Why do we even need to talk about this? Why can't you just pick whichever one you feel like when the time comes?

The answer to these questions is that if you don't come into the test with a plan, you'll rely on your impression to select an answer choice, and if you do that, you risk falling into a trap. The test writers know that everyone who takes their test will be guessing on some of the questions, so they intentionally write wrong answer choices to seem plausible. You still have to pick an answer though, and if the wrong answer choices are designed to look right, how can you ever be sure that you're not falling for their trap? The best solution we've found to this dilemma is to take the decision out of your hands entirely. Here is the process we recommend:

Once you've eliminated any choices that you are confident (willing to bet $5) are wrong, select the first remaining choice as your answer.

Whether you choose to select the first remaining choice, the second, or the last, the important thing is that you use some preselected standard. Using this approach guarantees that you will not be enticed into selecting an answer choice that looks right, because you are not basing your decision on how the answer choices look.

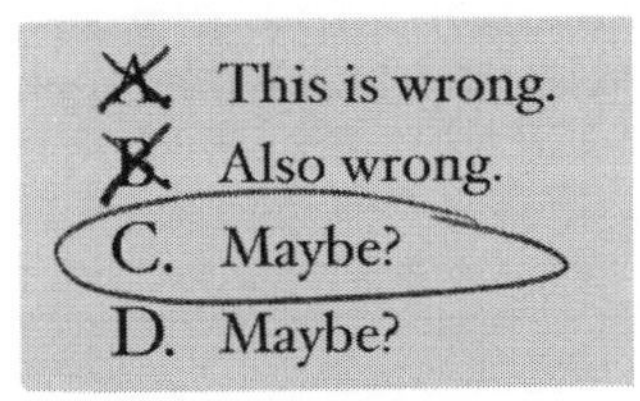

This is not meant to make you question your knowledge. Instead, it is to help you recognize the difference between your knowledge and your impressions. There's a huge difference between thinking an answer is right because of what you know, and thinking an answer is right because it looks or sounds like it should be right.

Summary: To ensure that your selection is appropriately random, make a predetermined selection from among all answer choices you have not eliminated.

Test-Taking Strategies

This section contains a list of test-taking strategies that you may find helpful as you work through the test. By taking what you know and applying logical thought, you can maximize your chances of answering any question correctly!

It is very important to realize that every question is different and every person is different: no single strategy will work on every question, and no single strategy will work for every person. That's why we've included all of them here, so you can try them out and determine which ones work best for different types of questions and which ones work best for you.

Question Strategies

✓ Read Carefully

Read the question and the answer choices carefully. Don't miss the question because you misread the terms. You have plenty of time to read each question thoroughly and make sure you understand what is being asked. Yet a happy medium must be attained, so don't waste too much time. You must read carefully and efficiently.

✓ Contextual Clues

Look for contextual clues. If the question includes a word you are not familiar with, look at the immediate context for some indication of what the word might mean. Contextual clues can often give you all the information you need to decipher the meaning of an unfamiliar word. Even if you can't determine the meaning, you may be able to narrow down the possibilities enough to make a solid guess at the answer to the question.

✓ Prefixes

If you're having trouble with a word in the question or answer choices, try dissecting it. Take advantage of every clue that the word might include. Prefixes can be a huge help. Usually, they allow you to determine a basic meaning. *Pre-* means before, *post-* means after, *pro-* is positive, *de-* is negative. From prefixes, you can get an idea of the general meaning of the word and try to put it into context.

✓ Hedge Words

Watch out for critical hedge words, such as *likely, may, can, often, almost, mostly, usually, generally, rarely*, and *sometimes*. Question writers insert these hedge phrases to cover every possibility. Often an answer choice will be wrong simply because it leaves no room for exception. Be on guard for answer choices that have definitive words such as *exactly* and *always*.

✓ Switchback Words

Stay alert for *switchbacks*. These are the words and phrases frequently used to alert you to shifts in thought. The most common switchback words are *but, although*, and *however*. Others include *nevertheless, on the other hand, even though, while, in spite of, despite*, and *regardless of*. Switchback words are important to catch because they can change the direction of the question or an answer choice.

✓ Face Value

When in doubt, use common sense. Accept the situation in the problem at face value. Don't read too much into it. These problems will not require you to make wild assumptions. If you have to go beyond creativity and warp time or space in order to have an answer choice fit the question, then you should move on and consider the other answer choices. These are normal problems rooted in reality. The applicable relationship or explanation may not be readily apparent, but it is there for you to figure out. Use your common sense to interpret anything that isn't clear.

Answer Choice Strategies

✓ Answer Selection

The most thorough way to pick an answer choice is to identify and eliminate wrong answers until only one is left, then confirm it is the correct answer. Sometimes an answer choice may immediately seem right, but be careful. The test writers will usually put more than one reasonable answer choice on each question, so take a second to read all of them and make sure that the other choices are not equally obvious. As long as you have time left, it is better to read every answer choice than to pick the first one that looks right without checking the others.

✓ Answer Choice Families

An answer choice family consists of two (in rare cases, three) answer choices that are very similar in construction and cannot all be true at the same time. If you see two answer choices that are direct opposites or parallels, one of them is usually the correct answer. For instance, if one answer choice says that quantity *x* increases and another either says that quantity *x* decreases (opposite) or says that quantity *y* increases (parallel), then those answer choices would fall into the same family. An answer choice that doesn't match the construction of the answer choice family is more likely to be incorrect. Most questions will not have answer choice families, but when they do appear, you should be prepared to recognize them.

✓ Eliminate Answers

Eliminate answer choices as soon as you realize they are wrong, but make sure you consider all possibilities. If you are eliminating answer choices and realize that the last one you are left with is also wrong, don't panic. Start over and consider each choice again. There may be something you missed the first time that you will realize on the second pass.

✓ Avoid Fact Traps

Don't be distracted by an answer choice that is factually true but doesn't answer the question. You are looking for the choice that answers the question. Stay focused on what the question is asking for so you don't accidentally pick an answer that is true but incorrect. Always go back to the question and make sure the answer choice you've selected actually answers the question and is not merely a true statement.

✓ Extreme Statements

In general, you should avoid answers that put forth extreme actions as standard practice or proclaim controversial ideas as established fact. An answer choice that states the "process should be used in certain situations, if..." is much more likely to be correct than one that states the "process should be discontinued completely." The first is a calm rational statement and doesn't even make a definitive, uncompromising stance, using a hedge word *if* to provide wiggle room, whereas the second choice is far more extreme.

⊘ BENCHMARK

As you read through the answer choices and you come across one that seems to answer the question well, mentally select that answer choice. This is not your final answer, but it's the one that will help you evaluate the other answer choices. The one that you selected is your benchmark or standard for judging each of the other answer choices. Every other answer choice must be compared to your benchmark. That choice is correct until proven otherwise by another answer choice beating it. If you find a better answer, then that one becomes your new benchmark. Once you've decided that no other choice answers the question as well as your benchmark, you have your final answer.

⊘ PREDICT THE ANSWER

Before you even start looking at the answer choices, it is often best to try to predict the answer. When you come up with the answer on your own, it is easier to avoid distractions and traps because you will know exactly what to look for. The right answer choice is unlikely to be word-for-word what you came up with, but it should be a close match. Even if you are confident that you have the right answer, you should still take the time to read each option before moving on.

General Strategies

⊘ TOUGH QUESTIONS

If you are stumped on a problem or it appears too hard or too difficult, don't waste time. Move on! Remember though, if you can quickly check for obviously incorrect answer choices, your chances of guessing correctly are greatly improved. Before you completely give up, at least try to knock out a couple of possible answers. Eliminate what you can and then guess at the remaining answer choices before moving on.

⊘ CHECK YOUR WORK

Since you will probably not know every term listed and the answer to every question, it is important that you get credit for the ones that you do know. Don't miss any questions through careless mistakes. If at all possible, try to take a second to look back over your answer selection and make sure you've selected the correct answer choice and haven't made a costly careless mistake (such as marking an answer choice that you didn't mean to mark). This quick double check should more than pay for itself in caught mistakes for the time it costs.

⊘ PACE YOURSELF

It's easy to be overwhelmed when you're looking at a page full of questions; your mind is confused and full of random thoughts, and the clock is ticking down faster than you would like. Calm down and maintain the pace that you have set for yourself. Especially as you get down to the last few minutes of the test, don't let the small numbers on the clock make you panic. As long as you are on track by monitoring your pace, you are guaranteed to have time for each question.

⊘ DON'T RUSH

It is very easy to make errors when you are in a hurry. Maintaining a fast pace in answering questions is pointless if it makes you miss questions that you would have gotten right otherwise. Test writers like to include distracting information and wrong answers that seem right. Taking a little extra time to avoid careless mistakes can make all the difference in your test score. Find a pace that allows you to be confident in the answers that you select.

⊘ Keep Moving

Panicking will not help you pass the test, so do your best to stay calm and keep moving. Taking deep breaths and going through the answer elimination steps you practiced can help to break through a stress barrier and keep your pace.

Final Notes

The combination of a solid foundation of content knowledge and the confidence that comes from practicing your plan for applying that knowledge is the key to maximizing your performance on test day. As your foundation of content knowledge is built up and strengthened, you'll find that the strategies included in this chapter become more and more effective in helping you quickly sift through the distractions and traps of the test to isolate the correct answer.

Now that you're preparing to move forward into the test content chapters of this book, be sure to keep your goal in mind. As you read, think about how you will be able to apply this information on the test. If you've already seen sample questions for the test and you have an idea of the question format and style, try to come up with questions of your own that you can answer based on what you're reading. This will give you valuable practice applying your knowledge in the same ways you can expect to on test day.

Good luck and good studying!

Competencies Shared Between Critical and General Care

Assess Patient Information

Patient History and Physical Examination

The foundation of a complete patient assessment rests with physical examination findings and obtaining a full past medical history. Without this basic information, further assessment cannot take place. When performing a patient assessment, the respiratory therapist must first complete a full physical examination of the patient. This includes obtaining vital signs such as the patient's heart rate, respiratory rate, blood pressure, breath sounds, and oxygen saturation (SpO_2). Next, the clinician must ask the patient or caregiver pertinent questions regarding their past medical history. The respiratory therapist must ask the patient or caregiver about the patient's past immunization history including yearly influenza vaccines and wellness vaccines, ensuring that the patient is up to date on any required immunizations. The respiratory therapist should screen the patient for any preexisting conditions such as asthma, sleep apnea, allergies, and congenital anomalies. Finally, the respiratory therapist must ask the patient or caregiver about any pertinent environmental history of the illness, such as exposure to secondhand smoke, allergens, fumes, infectious diseases, and other potential respiratory triggers.

Laboratory Tests

Laboratory and diagnostic imaging are of critical value to a respiratory therapist during a patient assessment. A laboratory test such as blood gas analysis provides the clinician with the patient's blood pH, pO_2, pCO_2, bicarbonate, and O_2. This information can identify possible ventilatory problems such as impending respiratory failure, poor oxygenation, CO_2 retention, metabolic ketoacidosis, and other serious ventilatory issues that require treatment. Other tests, such as a complete blood count, measure values such as white blood cell count as well as their components, hemoglobin, and red blood cell count. An increased white blood cell count can reflect an infectious disease process in the body, whereas increased eosinophils (a type of white blood cell) can indicate a potential allergic reaction or asthma exacerbation. Low hemoglobin or red blood cell levels can demonstrate a reduction in the ability of the patient to maintain oxygen saturation because these cells are responsible for carrying oxygen throughout the body.

Imaging Tests

Imaging studies can reveal many clues about a patient's condition, especially for those who have a respiratory history. A chest X-ray is a noninvasive test that can show various disease processes such as pneumonia, asthma, and pneumothorax, and it can also confirm endotracheal tube or chest tube placement. Echocardiography, another noninvasive imaging study, can be used to determine the integrity of the heart's structures and diagnose any abnormalities that require intervention. Chest X-rays and echocardiography are used exclusively for diagnostic and investigational purposes, whereas tests such as cardiac catheterization and angiography are used for diagnostic and therapeutic purposes. For example, the patient might undergo cardiac catheterization and angiography for informational purposes such as investigating the heart's anatomy and/or measuring pressures within the heart's structures. Other patients might require this procedure for therapeutic purposes such as repairing a congenital heart defect, opening a blockage, or inserting medical devices such as mesh filters.

Identify the purpose of fluoroscopy, magnetic resonance imaging (MRI), and computed tomography (CT) imaging studies for neonatal and pediatric respiratory patients.

Imaging studies such as fluoroscopy, magnetic resonance imaging (MRI), and computed tomography (CT) are used in neonatal and pediatric populations for diagnostic and therapeutic reasons. A fluoroscopy imaging study can be used to diagnose various heart conditions by administering a dose of a radiological agent to the patient and then observing the heart's structures as it beats. The radiological agent helps to highlight the structures of the heart and allows the clinician to observe its blood flow and muscle contraction. Imaging studies such as CT and MRI are noninvasive scans that provide clinicians with an internal cross-sectional view of the patient's body and organs. These tests can be performed with or without contrast, depending on the reason for testing. If blood vessels are to be examined, then contrast is often administered via intravenous infusion or injection. These imaging studies can help to diagnose congenital defects and disease processes.

Indices of Respiratory Physiology and Mechanics Including Oxygenation

A patient's respiratory status is determined in part by measuring the patient's oxygenation and work of breathing. Oxygenation can be measured in several ways, both invasively and noninvasively. A noninvasive oxygen saturation measurement can be obtained via an SpO_2 monitor, either continuously or as a spot check. The pulse oximeter's sensor measures the oxygen in the patient's blood through a red light which penetrates the nail bed and measures the amount of hemoglobin that is saturated with oxygen. If a pulse oximeter is not measuring functioning properly, several invasive methods of measuring oxygen saturation are available. Respiratory therapists may obtain arterial blood gases or capillary blood gases. The arterial blood gas is obtained via an arterial blood sample through the radial, brachial, or femoral artery. Capillary blood gases are obtained through a heel prick on infants.

Work of Breathing

Work of breathing refers to the effort required during inspiration. Increased work of breathing occurs when a patient's lung compliance drops (the lungs become stiffer) or the patient's airway resistance increases due to bronchospasm, intubation, or airway obstruction. Signs of increased work of breathing in neonates and pediatric patients include nasal flaring, intercostal and subcostal retractions, tracheal tugging, and grunting during respiration. These symptoms are subconscious efforts by the patient to relieve airway resistance and improve lung compliance. For example, accessory muscle use such as tracheal tugging, intercostal retractions, and nasal flaring help compensate for reduced compliance or increased resistance. Nasal flaring helps to open the airway and reduce airway resistance. All these signs of increased work of breathing must be addressed promptly before ventilatory failure and subsequent respiratory arrest occurs. Increased work of breathing must not be confused with dyspnea. Dyspnea is subjective; it is a patient's perception of shortness of breath, whereas work of breathing is an objective measurement.

Sleep Study Results

A sleep study is a test conducted overnight in a hospital, clinic, or the patient's home. These tests are ordered for patients who are suspected of having a sleep disorder such as sleep apnea. Symptoms including a history of snoring, obesity, and/or morning headaches are often consistent with a diagnosis of sleep apnea, but polysomnography (sleep study testing) is the only way to confirm this diagnosis. Patients may undergo this testing in a variety of settings, and testing is always performed during the overnight hours. The patient checks into the facility and is fitted with several sensors that each measure a different vital sign or activity. The sensors are placed on the patient's head, chest, and finger in order to measure criteria such as heart rate, respiratory rate, periods of apnea, and electroencephalographic parameters. The physician then compiles these data and makes a diagnosis based on the test's findings.

Sleep studies, or polysomnography, measure several criteria such as heart rate, respiratory rate, respiratory events, apneas, oxygen saturation, duration of sleep, awakenings, and snoring. The periods of apnea, if found, are further broken down into types of apnea. This can include obstructive (blockage of the airway due to structural issues), central (absence of breathing due to the brain's failure to trigger breathing), or mixed (a combination of obstructive and central). Sleep studies also measure the quality and quantity of a patient's sleep, including arousals and awakenings, restlessness and movement, and sleep efficiency. Sleep efficiency refers to the ratio of time between the total testing time and actual sleeping time of the patient. This measures the quality of a patient's sleep. A patient's sleep stages are also measured and timed to identify any sleep disorders such as night terrors and rapid eye movement sleep behavior disorders.

If a patient is found to have a sleep disorder such as sleep apnea, the physician will then determine the type of sleep apnea and design an appropriate treatment plan. For patients with obstructive sleep apnea, home continuous positive airway pressure (CPAP) machines are particularly helpful. These machines deliver constant positive pressure to the airway, alleviating obstructions due to structural problems such as poor muscle tone of the airway, excess tissue blocking the airway, and the tongue falling back into the oral cavity. This treatment is delivered via face mask or nasal prongs and is generally well tolerated. For other patients with more extensive structural problems such as congenital defects, surgery might be required in some instances. For central sleep apnea, patients often require noninvasive mechanical ventilation during sleep because their central nervous systems do not trigger the act of breathing during sleep. Therefore, the patient requires assistance in the form of mechanical ventilation. This therapy is most often delivered via face mask.

Neurological Status Including Respiratory Function and Level of Consciousness

A patient's neurological status reveals important ventilatory information to the clinician. Neuromuscular weakness can require a patient to be intubated to fully support their respiratory efforts and needs. Central nervous system failure can require full ventilatory support of the patient, including mechanical ventilation and intubation or tracheotomy. A patient's neurological status is directly related to their ventilatory status. Prior to intubation, a physician will administer a neuromuscular blocking agent to relax the patient and allow for intubation with endotracheal tube. In addition, neurological disorders can also cause loss of consciousness, changes in breathing patterns and effort, and reduction in muscle strength that can contribute to inadequate ventilation as well as ventilatory failure and potential respiratory arrest. A patient's neurological status must be assessed and monitored to ensure that the patient is breathing effectively. Support measures such as invasive or noninvasive ventilation may be required for some of these patients.

Cardiovascular Status

All neonatal patients must be assessed for any cardiac sources of ventilatory problems, including altered hemodynamics and congenital heart defects such as persistent pulmonary hypertension of the newborn, a disorder in which the patient does not fully transition from prenatal pulmonary circulation to postnatal pulmonary circulation. In these neonatal patients, the pressure inside the pulmonary vasculature is increased, causing right to left blood shunting. The patient's ductus arteriosus does not close as it should, and blood is funneled back through the heart without being oxygenated. This causes cyanosis, desaturation, and increased pulmonary vascular resistance. This disorder has a high rate of mortality, even with treatment. Other congenital heart defects can also cause periods of desaturation, cyanosis, and respiratory failure. When neonatal patients present with unexplained cyanosis, poor perfusion, and oxygen desaturation, congenital heart defects such as persistent pulmonary hypertension of the newborn must be ruled out.

Recognition of Respiratory Failure Mechanisms

Primary Pulmonary and Airway Diseases

Recognizing causes of respiratory failure can help the clinician successfully treat the underlying disease process and improve the patient's ventilatory status. Several common diseases can cause respiratory failure, including asthma, croup, and pneumonia. Asthma is a chronic obstructive disease of the lungs in which bronchoconstriction, airway inflammation, and bronchial mucus production occur cyclically in response to allergens, irritants, or other external factors. Croup is an acute disease of the upper airway in which constriction and swelling occur, causing increased work of breathing and respiratory distress. This disease is often caused by viral illness. Pneumonia, another potentially serious respiratory disease, is an acute infection of the lungs that is characterized by areas of atelectasis often in the bases of the lung fields. These areas of consolidation prevent adequate gas exchange in the alveoli, causing hypoxia and increased work of breathing.

Other Respiratory Issues

Flail chest and apnea of prematurity are two possible sources of respiratory failure in pediatric and neonatal patients. Flail chest is a disorder in which blunt force trauma to the chest causes a section of the ribs to fracture and become displaced from the rest of the rib cage and sternum. This fracture and displacement can occur on one side of the rib cage, or it can be bilateral. The blunt trauma can cause pulmonary contusions that change the patient's lung compliance and cause respiratory failure. In addition, the fracture itself causes a limitation in the affected lung's inflation, causing reduced lung capacity, areas of atelectasis and subsequent pneumonia, and ventilatory failure. This disorder is confirmed via chest X-ray, and it is treated by preventing the development of pneumonia, intubating and providing mechanical ventilation, and corrective surgery. Flail chest is not common in the pediatric population.

Apnea of prematurity is a very common disorder found in newborns. All neonatal patients are monitored for apnea in the neonatal intensive care unit (NICU), and many premature patients experience periods of apnea. These patients have periods of apnea, bradycardia, desaturation, and cyanosis. Apnea is defined as an absence of breathing for more than 20 seconds, but this time frame can be adjusted if the patient also displays signs of ventilatory failure such as cyanosis and bradycardia. The patient's apnea can be central, obstructive, or mixed. There are many root causes of apnea of prematurity, including central nervous system immaturity, infection, airway obstruction, metabolic disorders, congenital heart defects, and drug use. Apnea of prematurity treatment can include supplemental oxygen, invasive or noninvasive mechanical ventilation as needed, nasal CPAP, administration of methylxanthines, physical stimulation, and treatment of any underlying disease or factor that could be causing the disorder.

Renal, Metabolic, Endocrine, and Nutrition Status

Neonates with respiratory distress require careful monitoring of their fluid and nutrition status to manage their current respiratory condition and to prevent further decline. Patients with respiratory distress syndrome require careful fluid management because fluid overload can cause bronchopulmonary dysplasia. Neonatal patients who hold excessive fluid, such as in bronchopulmonary dysplasia with pulmonary edema, are often prescribed diuretics to prevent fluid overload. An overload of fluid can in turn cause electrolyte imbalances as well as respiratory failure due to the increased work of breathing. In addition to careful fluid balance, a neonate's nutrition status must also be assessed and monitored. All patients must be monitored for nutrition deficits, but patients with inborn errors of metabolism are much more susceptible to poor nutrition and inability to manufacture energy from food sources. These patients often present with respiratory distress due in part to metabolic acidosis secondary to the underlying metabolic disorder.

An acid–base balance disruption can cause respiratory distress and respiratory failure in neonatal, pediatric, and adult populations. Respiratory acidosis, a common cause of respiratory failure, is caused by alveolar hypoventilation. During alveolar hypoventilation, a patient's carbon dioxide levels rise and oxygenation falls, causing a decrease in pH. Left untreated, this condition can result in respiratory failure. Other acid–base imbalances, such as diabetic ketoacidosis, can also be causes of respiratory failure. In diabetic ketoacidosis, a patient's high blood sugar causes the release of ketones, which in turn causes an acid–base mismatch. In this disorder, the patient's pH rises, carbon dioxide rises, and pO_2 falls. Patients with ketoacidosis require immediate intervention to prevent or treat subsequent respiratory failure and possible mechanical ventilation. Early identification of acid–base imbalances via an arterial blood gas sample can identify impending respiratory failure and prevent complete respiratory arrest.

Gastrointestinal Anomalies

Several gastrointestinal anomalies can be present at birth. These abnormalities often need immediate surgical intervention to prevent respiratory failure and other complications. In cases such as diaphragmatic hernias, the diaphragm muscle does not close during fetal development and the organs of the digestive system migrate into the chest cavity. This causes restriction of the lungs and subsequent respiratory distress. Other gastrointestinal anomalies, such as esophageal atresia with tracheoesophageal fistula, also require immediate intervention. In this disorder, a fistula is present in the esophagus due to improper fetal development. These patients often suffer from aspiration pneumonia, hypoxia, respiratory distress, and distension of the abdomen due to air passing through the tracheal fistula into the stomach through the esophagus. This airflow causes cough, excess mucus production, poor feeding, and hypoxia. In gastrointestinal anomalies such as gastroschisis, patients are born with their intestines, liver, and/or stomach outside of their body. This is caused by failure of the abdominal wall to close in utero. This condition, like diaphragmatic hernias and esophageal atresia, requires surgical correction as well as respiratory support as needed.

Some neonates are born with inadequate feeding ability, causing an increased risk of aspiration. These patients can subsequently suffer from aspiration pneumonia, coughing, excess mucus production, and respiratory distress. To prevent these complications, feeding tubes should be placed. These tubes provide nutrition to infants until they gain the necessary strength and skill for feeding. The underlying feeding problems may be the result of inadequate sucking or inability to swallow effectively. When these issues are corrected, the patient's feeding tube can be removed and regular feeding can take place. Meanwhile, the oral or nasogastric tube can help not only to provide nutrition to the patient but also to protect the airway from possible aspiration and infection. However, the pros and cons of feeding tube use must be carefully weighed before placement. Some studies indicate that feeding tubes are related to an increased risk of necrotizing enterocolitis, a bacterial infection of the intestines found in the premature neonatal population. This disease is characterized by respiratory distress, abdominal distension, bloody stools, and gas presence in the stomach on chest X-rays.

Musculoskeletal

Spinal cord injuries can occur at birth due to breech positioning of the fetus, compression of the spinal cord due to bleeding in the epidural space, or excessive force placed on the spine during delivery. The level of respiratory distress associated with this disorder ranges from mild to complete respiratory failure. The resulting impairment is dependent upon the location of the spinal cord injury: The higher the injury on the spinal cord, the more severe the respiratory impairment. If the injury is below C5, the common impairment includes aspiration pneumonia and other respiratory infections due to insufficient respiratory efforts. However, if the injury is higher than C5, the patient often experiences complete respiratory arrest due to paralysis of the diaphragm and other respiratory muscles in the chest and abdomen. Depending on the level of impairment, mechanical ventilation may be required.

Neonatal congenital myopathies refers to a wide range of neuromuscular diseases and disorders in the neonatal population. Some of these disorders include muscular dystrophy, myotonic dystrophy, and neuromyotonia. These diseases affect the proteins within muscle fibers and are characterized by poorly functioning musculature that is weak and/or contracted. Neonatal congenital myopathies can result in scoliosis and other skeletal abnormalities that can restrict the patient's lungs and increase their work of breathing, causing the breathing to become labored. Other patients experience respiratory failure due to respiratory muscle insufficiency. Some patients with neonatal congenital myopathies require supplemental oxygen and/or mechanical ventilatory support such as positive pressure ventilation and mechanical ventilation. Other neonatal congenital abnormalities such as myelomeningocele may also require supplemental oxygen and ventilatory support. Myelomeningocele is a type of spina bifida. In this form of the disease, the patient's spinal canal is malformed, causing an exposed spinal cord and meninges outside of the patient's body.

Evaluate Pulmonary Status

Gas Exchange

Measuring a patient's oxygen saturation is of vital importance in the NICU because oxygen levels can rise and plummet quickly in the neonatal population. Constant noninvasive monitoring of SpO_2 is essential to clinicians in the NICU because quick decisions can be made regarding titration of supplemental oxygen and/or beginning the administration of supplemental oxygen. It is important for the clinician to remove and reposition the sensor periodically (according to their facility's policy and procedure) to minimize skin breakdown and irritation from the adhesive, pressure, and light. Respiratory therapists should strive for a saturation of approximately 90% to 95% when administering supplemental oxygen to a neonate because hyperoxia is a common problem in the NICU. Hyperoxia can cause serious medical problems such as blindness; therefore, supplemental oxygen should be used sparingly and only when clinically necessary. However, it is important to remember that the guideline of 90% to 95% SpO_2 is not necessarily appropriate for every patient. Some patients will require a higher or lower SpO_2 depending upon their disease process.

End-tidal CO_2 monitoring, also known as capnography, is commonly used on intubated and mechanically ventilated neonates. The CO_2 sensor is placed in line with the ventilator, and CO_2 is measured continuously. The position of the sensor depends on the type of end-tidal CO_2 equipment used because there are several different end-tidal CO_2 systems including sidestream, mainstream, and colorimetric systems. Although end-tidal CO_2 measurement is a helpful tool for clinicians who want a fairly accurate measurement of alveolar CO_2, end-tidal CO_2 measurement can be impeded due to tachypnea, lung diseases, and patients in full cardiac arrest. These conditions can affect the accuracy of the end-tidal CO_2 measurement, limiting its efficacy, especially in the neonatal population. End-tidal CO_2 monitoring can also be used to determine the position and adequate placement of an endotracheal tube in conjunction with standard procedures such as breath sound evaluation and chest X-ray.

If an end-tidal CO_2 monitor is not registering correctly, the clinician must troubleshoot the equipment to determine the cause of the problem and correct it quickly. The clinician should refer to the manufacturer's guidelines regarding troubleshooting because all machines are different. Generally speaking, the clinician must first assess the patient for any changes in condition that might be reflecting on the machine's readings such as apnea, hypoventilation, airway obstruction, or other respiratory status changes. Metabolic changes can also affect the readings. These conditions can include poor perfusion and diabetic ketoacidosis. Once those issues are ruled out, the clinician must then ensure that the sensor is fully attached and clean, with no debris covering the sensor. Condensation from a humidifier may also affect the sensor's ability to register accurate results. The clinician must also evaluate all of the connections to ensure that they are fully tightened and in the correct positions. Any disconnects must be quickly resolved.

Arterial blood gas interpretation is a complicated process of analysis by the clinician. An acceptable range for neonatal PaO_2 is often 50 to 80 mm Hg. In adults and children, the normal PaO_2 range is 80 to 100 mm Hg. A normal pH range is 7.35 to 7.45. If the pH measurement is lower than 7.35, the arterial blood gas is considered to be in acidosis. If it is higher than 7.45, it is considered to be in alkalosis. Then the clinician must determine if the cause is metabolic or respiratory. In metabolic disorders, the pH and $PaCO_2$ are either both high or both low. In respiratory disorders, the pH and $PaCO_2$ directions are opposites. In other words, the pH rises while the $PaCO_2$ falls (respiratory alkalosis) or the pH falls while the $PaCO_2$ rises (respiratory acidosis). Next, the clinician must determine if the blood gas results are compensated or uncompensated. Compensation refers to the body's ability to try to normalize the blood gas. The clinician must look at the HCO_3 and CO_2 levels to determine compensation. The HCO_3 can rise or fall to metabolically compensate for a respiratory disorder. The CO_2 level can rise or fall to compensate for a metabolic disorder.

Arterial blood gas results are the direct measurement of important ventilatory information including the PaO_2, pCO_2, and pH of the patient's blood. This measurement can be performed either by obtaining a sample from the patient's artery or through continuous sampling via catheter. Although the catheter is an invasive option, it prevents patient discomfort by reducing the need for obtaining the sample through percutaneous puncture and provides constant monitoring of the patient's ventilatory status. In this procedure, the clinician removes the cap from the three-way valve on the end of the patient's catheter and cleans the port. A 5 mL syringe is inserted, and the tap is turned to open the port. The clinician then obtains a sample of blood, removes the syringe, and closes the port. The clinician disposes of this syringe. This "wasting" of blood ensures that the arterial blood gas sample has no debris in it. Next, the clinician repeats the procedure with a heparinized syringe and obtains a blood sample for blood gas analysis. The clinician closes the port and removes the syringe. The clinician then attaches a saline flush, opens the port, and injects saline into the port to flush the system. Finally, the clinician closes the port, places the blood gas sample on ice, and sends it to the lab for analysis.

In a subcutaneous puncture, the clinician palpates the arterial site (the radial artery is often the first choice, with the brachial artery as an alternative option) to determine the location of the artery. The patient's arm is positioned wrist-up with a rolled towel beneath the wrist to help extend it. An Allen's test is performed, in which the clinician places pressure on the radial and ulnar arteries until the hand blanches. Then the ulnar artery is released, and the clinician watches the hand to ensure that it returns to its natural color. This ensures adequate collateral blood flow in case of injury to the radial artery during the puncture. The clinician then cleans the site, punctures the artery with either a 23 G needle with a heparinized 5 mL syringe or a butterfly needle with a heparinized 5 mL syringe, and the blood sample is obtained. The clinician holds pressure on the wound and covers it with a bandage. Finally, the clinician puts the sample on ice and sends it to the lab for analysis. Arterial blood gas results require careful assessment to determine the patient's ventilatory status.

Capillary blood gas sampling is used to determine a patient's PcO_2 and pH. It does not accurately measure a patient's PaO_2. To obtain a capillary blood sample, the clinician warms the neonate's heel by using a "hot pack" heel warmer for several minutes. The clinician cleans the lateral side of the patient's heel where the puncture will take place, punctures the heel with a lancet, and allows the blood droplet to fall into the heparinized capillary tube without interference. Squeezing the patient's heel is strongly discouraged because the blood will not yield accurate capillary blood gas results. The clinician must ensure that the capillary tube does not contain any air bubbles or blood clots. If the tube does contain these substances, the clinician must remove them by discharging them onto gauze. If the resulting sample is too small, a new sample must be obtained. Finally, the clinician places the sample on ice and transports it to the lab for analysis.

Blood samples for venous blood gases are not commonly obtained by respiratory therapists because these clinicians are not trained in venous blood draws. Often, the sample is obtained by phlebotomy and delivered to the respiratory therapist who then analyzes the specimen. Venous blood gases are used to measure a patient's pH, CO_2, and HCO_3. Venous blood gases are not used to evaluate a patient's oxygenation because venous blood is unoxygenated. Therefore, any PaO_2 value is inaccurate. This test is valuable when trying to minimize excessive puncture sites on compromised or sensitive patients because blood specimens can often be obtained during other routine venous blood draws for other blood tests. This reduces the need for additional punctures. However, if a respiratory therapist needs to fully evaluate a patient's respiratory status, an arterial blood gas is the only test that will give complete and accurate results.

PULMONARY FUNCTION

Spirometry refers to a series of pulmonary function tests that measure a patient's lung volumes and inspiratory and/or expiratory flows to diagnose or treat respiratory disorders. These tests are commonly performed on patients 5 years of age and older, but the test results depend exclusively on the patient's willingness and ability to perform the testing. Therefore, age limitations are negotiable based on the patient's maturity and ability to follow commands. During the testing, the patient breathes in and out in specific patterns while a pulmonary function testing machine measures the patient's volumes and flows. Some of the more common pulmonary function testing maneuvers include forced vital capacity, forced expiratory volume in one second, exhaled nitric oxide measurement, and diffusion capacity. Other more specialized pulmonary function tests can also be performed depending on the patient's disease process and ventilatory status.

Mean inspiratory pressure, or MIP, is a parameter that is measured in pulmonary function testing. This measurement indicates the negative pressure that the patient draws when trying to inhale against a closed circuit. In other words, MIP is the maximum negative force that a patient can expend when attempting to inhale against an occluded circuit. This measures a patient's respiratory muscle strength on inspiration and can be an important tool in the process of weaning a patient from a ventilator. It is also used to help identify respiratory deficits associated with some muscular disorders. When performing a MIP maneuver, the clinician takes three measurements and records the best (most negative) effort. To be reproducible, the values of each effort must be within 10% of each other. When performing this maneuver in children, it is uncommon for children younger than 4 or 5 years of age to be cooperative enough to participate. This test is effort dependent, and the patient must be willing and able to perform the maneuver.

When performing a peak flow measurement, the clinician provides the patient with a peak flow meter. This is a handheld device that measures a patient's peak expiratory flow rate. The clinician instructs the patient to exhale completely. Then the patient puts the peak flow meter mouthpiece into their mouth, closing their lips tightly around it and avoiding any obstructions such as their tongue or teeth positioned near the opening. The patient takes a maximum inhalation and exhales as hard and fast as possible. The maneuver is completed two more times, and the highest number is recorded. The patient must measure the peak flows daily and observe any drops in peak flow or patterns of symptoms. Reduced peak flow levels indicate a current or impending asthma exacerbation. Sometimes, patients will notice a reduction in peak flow readings before they feel any asthma symptoms.

Peak flow monitoring is a tool used to help patients with asthma identify impending asthma exacerbations and manage their daily symptoms. Patients record their peak flows daily and compare them to either their personal best reading or their predicted value. Then, the patient takes action depending on his or her level of impairment indicated by the peak flow meter readings. When first diagnosed, a patient will refer to his or her predicted peak flow value, which is a target number based on his or her height and sex. This number is calculated by using a chart that is included in every peak flow meter package. If the patient has a personal best peak flow reading (the highest peak flow reading they have ever achieved), he or she would compare the current peak flow reading to that number. A personal best number is a more accurate measurement of the patient's prior health as opposed to the predicted number. This is because a predicted value is based on a healthy individual with no underlying lung disease. Many patients, even when healthy, cannot achieve this number.

The measurement of peak flow zones acts as a benchmark for asthmatic patients to refer to when trying to determine their level of respiratory impairment. The patient's peak flow measurements are organized into a zone system, which is designed around a traffic light. The system uses green, yellow, and red zones to indicate a patient's level of respiratory impairment. In the green zone, the patient is between 80% and 100% of their personal best or predicted value (a personal best value must be used if available because this is the most accurate value for that particular patient). In the green zone, the patient's asthma is well controlled and no action needs to be taken. In the yellow zone, the patient's peak flows are between 79% and 50% of their personal best or predicted value. This is the most important zone in asthma management because this is often the first indicator of an asthma exacerbation. If action is taken while the patient is in the yellow zone, he or she may not deteriorate further. In the yellow zone, the patient refers to his or her written asthma action plan, which is provided by their physician. This plan may include the use of bronchodilators, inhaled or systemic corticosteroids, and following up with their physician. In the red zone, the patient is at less than 50% of their personal best or predicted value and must seek emergency assistance.

If a peak flow meter is not registering accurately, the clinician must carefully check the meter for leaks, damage, and obstructions. If the peak flow meter has visible damage such as cracks, missing pieces, or other damage, it must be replaced. If there is no visible damage, the clinician should then inspect the peak flow meter for obstructions such as displaced pieces of the meter or foreign bodies inside the mouthpiece or the body of the peak flow meter. If no obstruction is found, the clinician should then ensure that the peak flow meter is cleaned in accordance with the manufacturer's specifications. Once that is complete, the clinician should ask the patient for a return demonstration of the peak flow meter because poor patient effort or incorrect form can alter a peak flow meter's readings and result in inaccurate information.

Assess and Manage Airways

Airway Devices

A tracheostomy tube is a tool used to bypass the upper airway and provide ventilation and airway protection in patients with airway obstructions or injuries or in patients who require long-term mechanical ventilation. Adults are often more likely to receive a tracheostomy for long-term mechanical ventilation, whereas children and neonates are more likely to need a tracheostomy for obstructions originating in the upper airway. Patients requiring long-term mechanical ventilation can benefit from a tracheostomy because endotracheal intubation and ventilation can cause trauma and possibly permanent damage to the airway. Using a smaller, shorter tracheostomy tube can prevent this adverse event. Another benefit associated with tracheostomies is that patients can be mechanically ventilated at home with a tracheostomy tube and have shorter hospital stays and increased patient comfort. Tracheostomy tubes also allow for airway clearance, but aspiration and infection are risks associated with respiratory tube placements of all kinds.

Tracheostomy tubes come in various sizes and styles. This can include different materials (metal versus plastic), styles (uncuffed versus cuffed), and sizes. Tracheostomy tubes come in sizes from 00 for the smallest neonates, up to much larger sizes. The chosen size depends on the diameter and length of the patient's airway as well as their ventilatory needs. Pediatric tracheostomy tubes are generally not fenestrated. Patients with tracheostomy tubes must be suctioned frequently, using either a sterile technique or a closed-suction system. This prevents infection. Conversely, if a tracheostomy tube must be changed, it can be done in the clean technique rather than sterile. This includes hand hygiene; personal protective equipment use such as gloves, gown, and/or mask; as well as ensuring the cleanliness of the tracheostomy tube by avoiding touching the end or sides of the tube. To change or replace the tube, the clinician must place the patient in the supine position with the patient's neck slightly extended to ensure unobstructed access to the stoma. The new tube is carefully and slowly inserted, ensuring that the clinician follows the curve of the airway. Tracheostomy care must be provided frequently to ensure a patent airway.

Oral airways are inserted into the mouth to help prevent airway obstruction by either bypassing a structural obstruction or preventing the patient from biting down on an endotracheal tube and preventing ventilation. Some structural airway obstructions can include but are not limited to the tongue falling back into the oral cavity and large or infected tonsils. The oral airway is placed in the patient's mouth and into the airway, providing a pathway for gas delivery, manual breaths via a resuscitation bag, or spontaneous breathing. These tubes also have a center channel through which suction catheters can pass. This allows for easy suctioning of the airway, maintaining airway patency in the unconscious or sedated patient. The oral airway may be taped in place for long-term use. Frequent suctioning and inspection of the oral airway is necessary to ensure a patent airway.

Nasopharyngeal airways are tubes that are placed in the nares and down to the top of the patient's glottis. The purpose of the nasopharyngeal airway is to ensure a patent airway by bypassing or treating an airway obstruction. These obstructions can include but are not limited to the tongue falling back into the oral cavity and blocking the airway or reduced muscle tone in the upper airway resulting in a "floppy" airway. Nasopharyngeal airways can be used on conscious and unconscious patients and are particularly useful on patients who either cannot open their mouths or have facial or oral trauma. A nasopharyngeal airway often stays in place with no additional support needed and can fit under an oxygen mask or resuscitation mask. These tubes also have a center channel through which suction catheters can pass. This allows for easy suctioning of the airway, maintaining airway patency in the unconscious or sedated patient. Frequent suctioning and inspection of the oral airway are necessary to ensure a patent airway.

Oral hygiene is an intervention that can help to prevent the acquisition of ventilator-associated pneumonia and other nosocomial infections. Bacteria thrive in the oral cavity, and these organisms can be transmitted to the lower airway via secretions. This action often results in ventilator-associated pneumonia. To combat this common adverse event, clinicians must perform facility-approved oral care procedures. This might include moist swabs, tooth brushing, and mouthwash (such as chlorhexidine antiseptic solution) swabs for the oral cavity. Oral suctioning is also helpful on an as-needed or scheduled basis, depending on the facility's policy and procedure. Oral care is implemented in both mechanically ventilated patients using a tracheostomy or endotracheal tube as well as in unconscious patients or patients using other artificial airways. Although there is no evidence of a direct link between oral care and patient mortality or morbidity, studies indicate that oral care can help to prevent nosocomial infections such as ventilator-associated pneumonia, which directly affect a patient's prognosis.

Airway Clearance Devices and Techniques

Cystic fibrosis is an inherited disorder that is genetic in nature. This disease is progressive, and the constant infections associated with excessive mucus pooling eventually cause respiratory failure and subsequent death. Patients with cystic fibrosis produce an excessive amount of secretions in the lungs that lead to increased dyspnea, respiratory distress, and frequent infections. This disease is characterized by a persistent, productive cough, frequent pulmonary infections, dyspnea, and failure to thrive. Patients with cystic fibrosis need enzyme supplements because the pancreas is unable to release the enzymes necessary to metabolize certain foods. This causes weight loss, poor nutrition, and low muscle mass. These patients are diagnosed in childhood, and with the help of medical intervention, they are able to live into adulthood in most cases. Respiratory therapists often treat the same cystic fibrosis patients over their career because these patients have a high readmission rate due to the nature of their illness.

High-frequency chest wall oscillation is a therapeutic intervention that is commonly used in the cystic fibrosis population, but it also has value for other patients with excessive respiratory secretions. In high-frequency chest wall oscillation, a patient wears an inflatable vest that vibrates using a pneumatic mechanism. The vest provides percussion therapy to the chest wall, mobilizing secretions and allowing the patient to expectorate. This intervention is often used in addition to bronchodilators and muscarinic antagonist therapy in order to maximize the mobilization of secretions. Although the patient's physician may specify a particular order in which to deliver this therapy, the common practice is to administer the nebulized treatment first, followed by high-frequency chest wall oscillation. Administering a nebulized treatment during high frequency chest wall oscillation is not recommended because the drug deposition in the lungs may be reduced due to the percussion delivered to the chest wall.

High-frequency chest wall oscillation machines vary among manufacturers and facilities. When this equipment is not functioning correctly, the clinician should follow the manufacturer's guidelines for troubleshooting. Depending on the problem, the guidelines might instruct the clinician to check the power source, connections, and fit of the vest or chest wrapper. The clinician must ensure that all connections are secure and that the machine is plugged into an adequate power source. The clinician should inspect the machine for any visible damage, and if any is found, he or she should contact the manufacturer or home-care company directly. The clinician must also assess the equipment for any leaks, kinks, or obstructions in the tubing. If the clinician is not able to resolve the equipment failure, he or she should contact the manufacturer or home-care company as soon as possible to schedule a service call or replacement order.

Positive expiratory pressure (PEP) therapy, also known as "flutter therapy," is an intervention used to help mobilize secretions in patients who have excess mucus production. This therapy provides PEP as the patient exhales. This helps the patient's airways to remain open and facilitates expectoration of secretions. The most commonly used version of PEP therapy is oscillatory PEP therapy. In this therapy, the patient exhales into a handheld device that provides resistance and oscillation to the airway. This internal "percussion" helps to release mucus, and it allows the patient to expectorate when coughing. The respiratory therapist instructs the patient to exhale into the device for several seconds, repeating the maneuver for 10–20 breaths. The patient then is instructed to huff cough. The goal of treatment is to expectorate any secretions and resolve any mucus-related dyspnea. The treatment can be performed as many times as the patient wishes, if care is taken to minimize hyperventilation and/or dizziness.

When troubleshooting a positive expiratory pressure (PEP) therapy device, the clinician should first inspect the PEP equipment for any visible damage including cracks or other signs of defect. If visible damage is found, the clinician should either replace the device (if the patient is an inpatient) and/or contact the home-care company to order a replacement. PEP devices vary between manufacturers and facilities, so the clinician should refer to the manufacturer's guidelines and the facility's policy and procedure for exact troubleshooting steps. Generally speaking, after inspecting the PEP device for visible damage, the clinician should then assess the device for any obstructions or foreign bodies inside the body or mouthpiece of the device. The clinician should also instruct the patient to demonstrate use of the device to ensure correct technique. If the clinician is still unable to address the issue, the PEP device should be replaced or reordered as soon as possible.

Chest physical therapy refers to the practice of percussing the patient's chest and back. This can be done either by using palm cups or a cupped hand. The clinician then taps on the patient's back and chest, during which the patient changes positions periodically to ensure that the clinician has treated every lung field. This intervention is painless, due in part to using a cupped hand rather than a flat hand. The cupped position allows for an air cushion during the chest physical therapy. The goal of chest physical therapy is secretion mobilization. This intervention is used in patients with excessive pulmonary secretions such as in those with cystic fibrosis. This therapy should not be performed if the patient just ate a large meal because stomach upset can occur. Percussion should not take place on any sore or irritated areas or on any injured areas. Chest physical therapy is contraindicated in patients with rib fractures, chest tube placement, or on other potentially painful areas of the body.

Chest physical therapy and postural drainage are mucus mobilization interventions that are often performed in tandem. During chest physical therapy, the patient is moved into different positions to facilitate secretion mobilization. To drain the upper lobes, the patient should be seated in the upright position after percussion is complete in this position; the patient should lean slightly forward for more percussion and drainage of the upper lobes. Then the clinician can begin percussing the front of the chest while the patient lays supine. The patient should be positioned flat for part of the percussion, rolled onto one side for more percussion, and then rolled onto the opposite side for the remainder of the percussion therapy. The lower lung lobes are targeted by having the patient lay prone while the clinician percusses the patient's lower back. Be sure to avoid the kidney area because pain will develop. The patient can then move side to side again to percuss the lower lobes of the lungs.

Intrapulmonary percussive ventilation (IPV) is a therapy modality in which saline mist and pressure are delivered to the airway in small bursts to aid secretion mobilization. The saline mist is delivered via nebulizer in line with the IPV machine. Other drugs such as bronchodilators can also be added to the saline treatment, especially for the asthmatic population who can experience bronchospasm due to humidity delivered to the airway. IPV machines vary by manufacturer and facility; however, generally speaking, the nebulizer is in line with the IPV machine, in which a set pressure is dialed in and subsequently administered. Patients trigger the mist and positive pressure by pushing a button or moving a lever. The patient continues to inhale the pressure and mist for the duration of the set treatment. The patient will likely experience coughing and should be encouraged to huff cough frequently throughout the treatment. The goal of therapy is to help the patient expectorate any pulmonary secretions. Contraindications include but are not limited to pneumothorax, chest tube placement, recent thoracic or oral surgeries, or eating within an hour prior to treatment.

When troubleshooting an intrapulmonary percussive ventilation (IPV) machine, the clinician should refer to the manufacturer's guidelines and his or her facility's policy and procedure. IPV machines vary among manufacturers and facilities. Generally speaking, the clinician should first inspect the machine for any visible damage and ensure that the machine is turned on and plugged into an adequate and functional power source. The clinician then checks all connections to ensure a tight fit. The clinician should look for leaks, kinks, and other obstructions in the tubing and/or mouthpiece. The clinician should perform the same inspections on the nebulizer equipment that is used in conjunction with this machine. If the machine is still not functional or is not delivering the proper therapy, the therapy should be discontinued and the machine should be sent to the appropriate department for service according to the facility's policy. If the patient is an outpatient, the home-care company or manufacturer should be contacted to schedule a service call.

Cough assist can mean different things to different clinicians. Some physicians use the term cough assist to order bronchial hygiene such as PEP therapy or insufflator-exsufflator therapy. Manual cough assist is the process of helping a patient to cough effectively by using the clinician's hands and body to facilitate airway secretion clearance. In a manual cough assist, the clinician places the palms of his or her hands on each side of the patient's navel. The clinician then instructs the patient to perform a maximum inhalation, and then the clinician pushes the patient's abdomen with an in and up motion (similar to the Heimlich maneuver) while the patient attempts to cough. This process is repeated until the patient's airway clears. This process can be performed with the patient either sitting up or lying down. Contraindications for cough assist include but are not limited to vomiting, abdominal pain, eating within 2 hours of treatment, and abdominal surgery or injury.

Airway Challenges

Upper airway obstructions can impair a patient's ventilation by partially or completing blocking the airway. Some possible causes of acute upper airway obstruction include but are not limited to a foreign body obstruction, the tongue falling back into the oral cavity, poor muscle tone of the airway, and other structural obstructions. The clinician must first evaluate and assess the patient to determine the cause of the upper airway obstruction, and then the clinician can then treat the patient. In the event of a foreign body obstruction, the clinician can suction the airway via the nares using sterile technique. If the foreign body is not able to be removed via suction, other interventions such as surgical intervention may be required. In that case, a clinician must support the patient's ventilation until the obstruction is removed. For obstruction due to the tongue falling back into the airway or structural abnormalities, the clinician can insert either a nasopharyngeal airway or oral airway to bypass the upper airway and facilitate effective ventilation.

Unplanned extubation refers to the action of displacement or removal of a patient's endotracheal tube before it is deemed clinically indicated. This can occur due to intentional removal by the patient or accidental displacement. Accidental displacement can occur due to repositioning the patient, spontaneous movements of the patient, or improperly securing the tube. The risks associated with unplanned extubation include damage to the airway, airway stenosis, infection, hypoxia, respiratory insufficiency or failure, and death. Some studies indicate that the rate of unplanned extubation is higher in the neonatal intensive care unit (NICU) than in the pediatric ICU possibly because patients in the NICU are being removed from their beds for various reasons, requiring more repositioning than older patients. Extra care must be taken to ensure that a patient's endotracheal tube remains in place during any movement into or out of bed. The tube must be properly secured according to the facility's policies and procedures, using either an endotracheal tube holder or adhesive tape. In addition, it is helpful to have two clinicians at the bedside during any procedures that require movement and disruption of the patient. Clinicians must also document the depth of the endotracheal tube (example: "23 at the lip"), which can help them identify patterns of endotracheal tube displacement before total extubation occurs.

When a patient has an unexpected extubation, the clinical team must first assess the patient for signs of respiratory distress or hypoxia and address those clinical findings. The patient must be ventilated with a resuscitation bag and mask with supplemental oxygen while the team gathers the equipment to reintubate. This equipment can include suction, supplemental oxygen, and a laryngoscope. The clinician will place the patient in a supine position, extend the neck, and insert a laryngoscope into the mouth to visualize the airway. The tube is then gently and carefully advanced into the patient's mouth and trachea. The tube cuff is then inflated with a syringe (neonatal tubes are not cuffed, so this step would be skipped for that patient population). The tube is then secured using the process approved by the facility's policy and procedure, either with an endotracheal tube holder or adhesive tape. The tube position can then be confirmed by assessing breath sounds (they should be equal and bilateral) and obtaining a chest X-ray.

Unplanned decannulation refers to the action of displacement or removal of a patient's tracheostomy tube before it is deemed clinically indicated. This can occur due to intentional removal by the patient or accidental displacement. Accidental displacement can occur due to repositioning the patient, spontaneous movements of the patient, or improperly securing the tube. The risks associated with unplanned extubation includes damage to the airway, bleeding, airway swelling, tracheoesophageal fistula, granulomas, airway stenosis, tissue necrosis, infection, hypoxia, respiratory insufficiency or failure, and death. Many facilities have policies and procedures in place for the reduction of accidental decannulation including securing the tracheostomy tube with facility-approved ties, requiring continuous oxygen saturation monitoring, requiring two clinicians at the bedside during any procedures that require movement and disruption of the patient, and giving a report at the patient's bedside during a change of shift. It is also recommended that extra tracheostomy tubes be stocked at the bedside in the patient's current size plus one size smaller in case the larger tube cannot be reinserted.

After unplanned decannulation, the clinician must follow the facility's policy and procedure for emergency replacement of the tracheostomy tube. Generally speaking, when decannulation occurs, the clinician will call for help and assess the patient for signs of respiratory distress. The tracheostomy tube must be replaced as quickly as possible because the patient will likely be in respiratory distress. Using a clean technique (this may be optional in some emergency situations), the clinician will suction the airway if needed and attempt to insert a tracheostomy tube of the patient's current size. If this is unsuccessful, the clinician can attempt insertion of the smaller size tracheostomy tube. The cuff should be inflated, if applicable. The patient is then reconnected to any supplemental oxygen or ventilation equipment that was previously in use. Then the tube placement must be confirmed by listening for equal and bilateral breath sounds in all lung fields.

Some patients may have a critical or difficult airway, either due to congenital defects, structural damage, or other respiratory conditions. These patients are often difficult to intubate and have hard-to-manage airways. To manage these patients, the clinician must first determine the cause of the impairment and choose a treatment option that is appropriate for that condition. Many patients with difficult-to-manage airways benefit from the use of a laryngeal mask airway. This specialized endotracheal tube has a mask on the end that fits above the larynx. This tube is easier to place than a traditional endotracheal tube and is designed for emergency situations. It is especially helpful for patients with facial deformities and/or airway obstructions. Other patients may require noninvasive ventilation or modified intubation techniques such as the use of a fiber-optic scope for visualization of the airway during intubation.

Difficult airway refers to many different types of patients with various defects. Patients with omphalocele and congenital diaphragmatic hernia often have difficult to manage airways due to congenital defects. Facial abnormalities such as Pierre Robin sequence and Treacher Collins syndrome also have critical airway defects that can affect the jaw, which in turn makes traditional means of intubation difficult or impossible. These facial deformities can also cause a reduction in the ability to ventilate with resuscitation bag and mask, resulting in a potentially emergent clinical scenario. Other patients may have congenital upper airway obstructions due to structural abnormalities. These congenital defects can result in the need for a surgical intervention such as tracheostomy in order to bypass the obstruction and restore adequate ventilation. Some patients may have been intubated for an extended period of time, causing an airway stenosis or swelling. This can result in a difficult reintubation or long-term structural changes of the airway.

Select and Manage Equipment

Oxygen Administration Devices

A heated high-flow nasal cannula differs in many ways from a conventional nasal cannula. A conventional nasal cannula is a piece of flexible tubing with nose prongs that is attached to an oxygen flowmeter. The conventional nasal cannula is a low-flow system, with only a few liters of oxygen being delivered to the airway. Conversely, a heated high-flow cannula is a high-flow oxygen system, delivering much higher liter flows to the airway via heated and humidified oxygen. Heated high-flow nasal cannulas can be used in several clinical scenarios, including during weaning from mechanical ventilation, continuous positive airway pressure (CPAP), and bilevel positive airway pressure (BIPAP), or noninvasive mechanical ventilation. It is also useful for neonatal and pediatric patients with respiratory distress syndrome and/or as an alternative to nasal CPAP. The benefits of this intervention include better bonding and feeding outcomes, less skin and tissue breakdown around and inside the nares, and better mobility.

When troubleshooting a heated high-flow nasal cannula, the clinician should refer to the manufacturer's guidelines and the facility's policy and procedure because these machines vary between manufacturers. Generally speaking, the clinician will first assess the patient for any signs of distress. If distress is noted, the patient should be removed from the heated high-flow nasal cannula and either manually ventilated, if necessary, or placed on an alternate oxygen source at the same FiO_2. The clinician should then inspect the equipment for kinks, obstructions, and/or leaks in the tubing and circuit. All connections must be tight and secure. The oxygen flowmeter must be turned on, functional, and set at the proper liter flow. The heater must be inspected for any cracks or visible damage. If damage is found in any of the system's components, the equipment should be removed from the patient and replaced, while the patient is placed on an alternate oxygen source at the same FiO_2.

Heated high-flow nasal cannulas work by delivering higher flow rates to the patient, thereby providing positive pressure to the airway, reducing dead space and carbon dioxide within the lungs, and increasing PaO_2. This action helps to decrease dyspnea and improve oxygenation in compromised patients. Care must be taken to choose the appropriate size cannula for the patient's nares. Sizing procedures vary based on the equipment used, manufacturer's guidelines, and the facility's policy and procedure; however, generally speaking, heated high-flow nasal cannulas come in various sizes from neonatal to pediatric sizes. Some systems require measurement of the nares using measurement tools, whereas others are sized based on weight. An appropriately sized nasal cannula is needed to reduce skin and tissue breakdown and allow for adequate exhalation and air flow. When the cannula is inserted in the nares, the nares should not be flared out or obstructed by the prongs.

Aerosol Delivery Devices

Small-volume nebulizers are handheld tools that deliver intermittent or continuous aerosol therapy and medication delivery to respiratory patients. Small-volume nebulizers are comprised of a nebulizer cup, which is filled with a mixture of medication and saline, as well as a mouthpiece or mask, and oxygen tubing. Most inpatient and outpatient nebulizers are jet nebulizers. The oxygen tubing for these nebulizers is attached to an oxygen flowmeter and set at the recommended flow rate for that particular type of nebulizer. The patient then breathes in the mist, inhaling humidity, oxygen, and medication intermittently. Small-volume nebulizers come in many different styles, including those that run on a continuous basis and those that only deliver the mist on inspiration. Other small-volume nebulizers, such as mesh nebulizers, use electricity to create vibrations that deliver the mist to the patient. Similarly, ultrasonic nebulizers use electrically sourced vibrations to deliver the mist to the patient's airway.

When troubleshooting small-volume jet nebulizers, clinicians should instruct patients to refer to the manufacturer's guidelines for the care and cleaning of their nebulizers. Generally speaking, small-volume jet nebulizers used in the home environment must be cleaned periodically with soap and water or other approved cleaning solution and rinsed with water. A consistent cleaning schedule ensures that the nebulizer is free from damage and obstructions because the patient will be inspecting and disassembling it during the cleaning process. If a nebulizer is properly maintained but still not functioning, the patient should be instructed to first ensure that the nebulizer has been reassembled correctly after cleaning and then check all system connections. Lastly, the clinician should rinse out the nebulizer cup and components, ensuring that there is no obstruction to the nebulizer cone (this is where the mist is released into the face mask or mouthpiece). The patient should also assess the gas source to make sure it is adequate. If the oxygen tank is empty or if the oxygen concentrator is not functioning, it should be serviced or replaced as soon as possible. If the patient still has a malfunctioning nebulizer after performing the troubleshooting steps, it should be replaced or serviced.

When troubleshooting mesh and ultrasonic jet nebulizers, clinicians should instruct patients to refer to the manufacturer's guidelines for the care and cleaning of the nebulizer. Generally speaking, mesh and ultrasonic jet nebulizers used in the home environment must be cleaned periodically in accordance with the manufacturer's guidelines to ensure that it is free from damage and obstructions because the patient will be inspecting and disassembling the nebulizer during the cleaning process. If mist is not coming out of the nebulizer, the patient should disassemble the system and rinse the components with distilled water in case any clogs are present in the system. The patient should also assess the medication level in the cup, ensuring that there is adequate medication volume. The patient should check all system connections, ensuring a tight fit with no leaks, kinks, or obstructions. The patient should also assess the gas source to make sure it is adequate. The patient must also ensure an adequate power source for the nebulizer. Finally, if the patient still has a malfunctioning nebulizer after performing the troubleshooting steps, it should be replaced or serviced.

Airway Devices

Oral airways, also known as bite blocks, are C-shaped pieces of plastic that have a hole in the center. These tools are inserted into the mouth to help keep the tongue from falling back into the oral cavity and obstructing the airway. They can also be used to stop the patient from unconsciously biting down on the endotracheal tube, which then obstructs the tube and prevents ventilation. Care must be taken to choose the correct oral airway size. If the oral airway is too small, the tongue will not be moved into the correct position, further obstructing the airway. If the oral airway is too large, it can also obstruct the airway and/or cause the patient discomfort and distress. Oral airways come in various sizes, with diameter measurements in millimeters. These tools are helpful for patients with oral airway obstructions, excessive biting of the endotracheal tube, and congenital abnormalities that affect the patient's oral airway patency.

Oral airways are often placed to relieve an obstruction of the airway either due to the tongue falling back in the oral cavity or the patient biting down on the endotracheal tube. These airways are rarely associated with adverse events; however, displacement or improper sizing of the oral airway can result in further airway obstruction and respiratory distress with subsequent respiratory arrest. When troubleshooting an oral airway, the clinician must first ensure that the airway is the correct size for the patient. This is determined by measuring the distance from the mouth to the jaw. An oral airway that is shorter than that distance will not open the airway adequately, whereas an oral airway that is longer than that distance can potentially cause further airway obstruction. The clinician must ensure that the oral airway is in the correct position, with the curve of the airway following the curve of the tongue in the oral cavity and the end of the oral airway resting just outside the patient's lips.

Nasopharyngeal airways, also known as nasal trumpets, are plastic tubes that are placed in the nares, with the end resting just above the glottis. The nasopharyngeal airway must be coated with hospital-approved lubricant prior to insertion to prevent nasal trauma. Some bleeding is common with the placement of nasal airways, due to the delicate nature of nasal structures, so care must be taken to choose the correct size and insert the airway slowly and cautiously while the patient is in the sniffing position. Nasal airways come in various sizes, with diameter and length measurements in millimeters. The correct size is chosen by measuring the distance between the patient's nare and jaw. This distance in millimeters is then converted to French measurement, and an airway is chosen. Often these airways range from size 12 to 36 French. Nasopharyngeal airways can cause patients discomfort and are often better tolerated in patients who are unconscious or sedated; however, consciousness is not a contraindication to their use.

Nasopharyngeal airways are often placed to relieve an obstruction of the airway often due to the tongue falling back in the oral cavity. Aside from bleeding and damage to the nasal mucosa, these airways are rarely associated with adverse events; however, displacement or improper sizing of the nasopharyngeal airway can result in further airway obstruction and respiratory distress with subsequent respiratory arrest. When troubleshooting a nasopharyngeal airway, the clinician must first ensure that the airway is the correct size for the patient. Then the clinician must ensure that the nasopharyngeal airway is in the correct position. The nasopharyngeal airway should be carefully inserted into the nare, following the curve of the airway. The end of the oral airway should rest just outside the patient's nare. Supplemental oxygen can be provided in conjunction with airway placement if desaturation occurs.

Endotracheal tubes are long, plastic tubes that are placed in the patient's airway to facilitate ventilation. These tubes come in various diameters and lengths. The clinician evaluates the size of the patient's airway, and an appropriately sized tube is chosen. Endotracheal tubes have inflatable cuffs at the distal end, which are inflated to prevent oral secretions and other substances from traveling into the patient's lungs around the endotracheal tube. Endotracheal tubes require frequent suctioning using either a sterile technique or a closed-suction system to ensure patency of the airway. Endotracheal lavage is not commonly used today because some studies indicate that this can increase a patient's risk for ventilator-acquired pneumonia. An endotracheal tube is placed by positioning the patient in a supine position, extending the neck, and using a laryngoscope to visualize the airway. The tube is then gently and carefully advanced into the patient's mouth and trachea. The tube cuff is then inflated with a syringe (this step is skipped for the neonatal population because their tubes are uncuffed). The tube is then secured using the process approved by your facility's policy and procedure, either with an endotracheal tube holder or adhesive tape. Tube position can then be confirmed by assessing breath sounds (they should be equal and bilateral) and obtaining a chest X-ray.

If a clinician suspects an endotracheal tube displacement or obstruction, he or she must first assess the patient. If the patient demonstrates any signs of respiratory distress, the clinician should remove the patient from the ventilator and attempt to bag ventilate them. If ventilation is not successful, or if an obstruction in the tube is suspected, the clinician should first suction the tube to alleviate any foreign bodies or secretions in the endotracheal tube. If unable to pass a suction catheter, the clinician should assess for possible biting of the tube, in which case a bite block or oral airway may be needed. If the clinician suspects a tube displacement, they should first check the charting to see what position the tube was in prior (example: "23 at the lip"). If the tube is positioned outside of that parameter, the tube has become displaced and needs to be repositioned. The endotracheal tube placement can also be confirmed via chest X-ray and assessing the patient for equal and bilateral breath sounds.

When suctioning an endotracheal tube, sterile technique is required. If a patient has a closed-suction system, the clinician performs hand hygiene and then advances the catheter into the endotracheal tube to the preapproved depth and applies suction as he or she slowly pulls the catheter out of the endotracheal tube. The suctioning process should be performed over only a few seconds because the patient is unable to take a breath while the procedure is taking place. The process can be repeated as needed until secretions are cleared. When using an open-suctioning system, the clinician must use sterile technique with a sterile dominant hand and a dirty nondominant hand. The clinician will put on sterile gloves by touching only the folded top portion of the glove. Once the gloves are on, the dirty hand can attach the suction tubing to the sterile catheter held by the sterile hand. The sterile hand then advances the catheter into the endotracheal tube to a preset length, applies suction, and removes the catheter from the endotracheal tube. The procedure is then repeated as needed. Follow your facility's policy and procedure for lavage because this intervention is linked to an increased incidence of ventilator-associated pneumonia.

Speaking valves are tools that attach to the end of a tracheostomy tube and allow a patient to speak by providing one-way airflow with exhalation through the patient's upper airway rather than out the tracheostomy tube. These valves come in many different styles and vary by facility. When placing a speaking valve, the clinician suctions the airway (the lower airway and the oral cavity) as needed and then deflates the tracheostomy tube cuff. The valve is then attached to the end of the tracheostomy tube by twisting it into place. While the speaking valve is in use, the patient can still receive supplemental oxygen and humidity through the valve and tracheostomy tube; however, the valve should be removed during nebulizer treatments to prevent the buildup of medication and subsequent occlusion. The valve is cleaned periodically according to the facility's policy and procedure.

When troubleshooting a speaking valve, the clinician must first ensure that the valve is in the correct position. If a patient is experiencing respiratory distress with the valve in place, the clinician must first remove the valve and then address the patient's shortness of breath. Then the clinician can further assess the speaking valve. The patient should be positioned sitting up when using the valve. If the tracheostomy tube is cuffed, the cuff should be deflated for speaking valve therapy. The patient's tracheostomy tube and oral cavity should be suctioned to ensure that there are no airway obstructions. The tracheostomy tube size should also be evaluated because speaking valves are often not tolerated on tracheostomy tubes that are too large for the patient. The clinician should also ensure that the speaking valve is firmly attached to the tracheostomy tube and that the valve or tube has not been displaced. Speaking valves must also be cleaned periodically according to the manufacturer's guidelines to ensure a patent airway and fully functioning speaking valve.

A laryngeal mask airway (LMA) is a temporary airway placed in the patient's mouth and throat to protect the airway and provide ventilation during transport or surgery. An LMA resembles a traditional endotracheal tube; however, rather than a conventional cuff at the end of the tube, the LMA has a small mask that fits over the larynx. This tool is used mainly in patients with airways free from congenital defects because a proper fit is necessary for successful ventilation. LMAs are available in disposable and nondisposable varieties; however, most facilities use disposable airways to ensure infection control. The placement of an LMA can vary slightly between manufacturers and varieties. When placing an LMA, the clinician places the patient in the sniffing position, coats the mask end of the airway in a facility-approved lubricant, and inserts the LMA into the mouth with the mask pointing down. The clinician feeds the tube through the oral cavity, into the airway until he or she feels resistance and then inflates the cuff.

Transcutaneous Monitoring Systems

Transcutaneous monitoring systems are used in the neonatal intensive care unit for the measurement and monitoring of PaO_2 and $PaCO_2$. These measurements are estimates and are not as accurate as blood gas analysis; however, the benefit to these monitoring systems is that the measurements are taken noninvasively through the skin, therefore minimizing pain. To set up the transcutaneous monitors, the clinician first ensures that the machine is cleaned and calibrated according to the manufacturer's instructions and his or her facility's policy and procedure. Then, the clinician prepares the transcutaneous monitoring site either on the patient's chest or abdomen. Other sites, such as the legs or arms, are rarely used for transcutaneous monitoring. To prepare the skin, the clinician cleans the site with a gentle soap or other facility-approved skin cleanser. This ensures adequate contact and adhesion of the sensor and skin. The sensor temperature should be titrated to minimize heat damage to the patient's skin, especially in the neonatal population. Contact solution is applied to the sensor, allowing for proper measurement of oxygen and carbon dioxide. The sensor is then affixed to the patient's skin.

Transcutaneous monitoring systems are used for constant noninvasive measurement and monitoring of a patient's PaO_2 and $PaCO_2$. These systems are used for extended periods of time and have reliability issues when used short term. Relative contraindications to this monitoring system include allergy to adhesives and chemicals and skin breakdown such as burns or lesions. Transcutaneous monitoring of PaO_2 and/or $PaCO_2$ is generally well tolerated but is associated with some negative effects. The skin probe can cause burns due to excessive temperatures. Clinicians must titrate the sensor temperature to ensure adequate measurement of gas diffusion while minimizing the risk for skin breakdown. This monitoring system can also provide inaccurate results due to a variety of factors including incorrect sensor placement, edema, the sensor's lack of adhesion to the skin, and disorders or diseases that result in poor perfusion.

Airway Clearance Devices

An insufflator-exsufflator is a machine that facilitates secretion clearance by applying positive and negative pressure to the airway. This therapy is commonly used in patients who have insufficient respiratory muscle strength such as those with neuromuscular disorders. Insufflation refers to the act of applying positive pressure to the airway on inhalation, whereas exsufflation refers to the act of applying negative pressure to the airway on exhalation, which triggers a patient to cough. Equipment varies between manufacturers and facilities; generally speaking, an insufflator-exsufflator looks like a small tabletop machine with corrugated tubing and a mask, mouthpiece, or adapter for an artificial airway. The pressures are dialed in by the clinician prior to the initialization of treatment. Serious complications are unlikely with insufflator-exsufflator use; however, some adverse events associated with its use can include bleeding, pneumothorax, chest pain, hyperventilation, increased acid reflux, and abdominal pain. This therapy should not be used immediately after a patient eats because this can cause stomach discomfort.

Insufflator-exsufflator machines are used at the patient's bedside to help the patient cough and expectorate pooled secretions in the airway. Policies and procedures vary based on the equipment's manufacturer and the care facility's guidelines; generally speaking, the clinician will set the inspiratory pressure, expiratory pressure, flow rate, and time parameters in accordance with the physician's order. The clinician positions the patient sitting up (if able) and applies the face mask, mouthpiece, or artificial airway adapter. The clinician triggers the machine to deliver positive pressure during the patient's inhalation for approximately 3 seconds, and then he or she switches to negative pressure for up to three seconds. This triggers the cough. The maneuver can be repeated up to five times. Follow your facility's policy and procedure for the exact steps in this process. This intervention has several contraindications including but not limited to pneumothorax, blood in the sputum, and head trauma or cranial surgery.

When troubleshooting an insufflator-exsufflator machine, the clinician should refer to the manufacturer's guidelines because these machines vary among different models and manufacturers. Generally speaking, the clinician should first ensure that all connections are secure and that there are no leaks, kinks, or obstructions in the circuit. The clinician must ensure that the machine is turned on and plugged into an adequate power source. The clinician should check for adequate air flow and ensure that all machine settings are dialed in according to the physician's order. The clinician must also visually inspect the machine for any visible signs of damage. If the clinician suspects a pressure leak, he or she can obstruct the face mask with a hand while cycling through the treatment. If the pressure dial does not reach the ordered pressure, a leak or machine malfunction is occurring. If the machine is not delivering the proper pressure and flow despite following the manufacturer's troubleshooting procedure, the therapy must be stopped, and the machine must be sent for service.

Home-Care Devices

Mechanical ventilators can be used in the intensive care unit and in the patient's home. Some patients require long-term mechanical ventilation due to congenital defects or other disorders and can use these machines in their homes. Mechanical ventilation can be applied invasively or noninvasively in the home setting. This can include patients who have tracheostomies or patients who use noninvasive ventilation via a face mask. When a patient has orders for mechanical ventilation at home, the clinician along with the healthcare team will provide comprehensive patient education for the family. Consult with your facility's policy and procedure and the equipment manufacturer for exact guidelines on the education session requirements; however, most education sessions include a hands-on demonstration of the equipment, training on suctioning and airway management, and instruction on oral care. The family must also be instructed on how to identify an emergency.

A continuous positive airway pressure (CPAP) machine can be used in both the inpatient and outpatient settings. This machine delivers constant positive pressure to the patient's airway, preventing airway obstruction from disorders such as obstructive sleep apnea. This machine is used in spontaneously breathing patients and uses facial or nasal masks to deliver the positive pressure to the airway. (Some patients prefer a full-face mask, but this option does pose a risk of aspiration if the patient vomits and is unable to remove the mask quickly.) The clinician will set the pressure according to the physician's order and will help the patient apply the mask. Some machines offer a "ramp" option in which pressure is steadily increased over several minutes until it reaches the set pressure designated by the physician. This helps to increase patient comfort by easing into the therapy. Often, CPAP machines have humidifiers. This helps to prevent tissue breakdown due to dehydration of the mucus membranes.

When troubleshooting CPAP machines, the assessment procedure can vary among manufacturers and models. Clinicians should refer to their facility's policy and procedure as well as the manufacturer's guidelines for troubleshooting procedures. Generally speaking, CPAP machines should be disassembled, cleaned, disinfected, and inspected periodically in accordance with the manufacturer's guidelines. This ensures that the machine is free from visible damage and obstructions due to clogs in the system. If the machine is not functioning correctly, the clinician or patient should assess the system for leaks, kinks, and obstructions. All connections should be tight, and the machine must be plugged into an adequate power source and turned on. The patient or clinician should ensure that the correct pressure level is set and that flow is being delivered. The patient or clinician should schedule a service call for any machine that malfunctions despite completing the manufacturer's suggested troubleshooting procedure.

CPAP machines are generally well tolerated by patients; however, some patients have significant obstacles to using their CPAP machines. This often requires a clinician's assessment and intervention to ensure that the patient is able to use their machine as ordered by the physician. A common patient complaint is that the patient can't tolerate the pressure delivered by the CPAP machine. If a patient complains of this issue, the clinician can set the "ramp" feature (if applicable on the patient's CPAP model). This useful feature slowly ramps up the delivered pressure, giving the patient time to acclimate to the pressure change over time rather than all at once. Some patients even fall asleep before the ramping is complete. Another common complaint associated with the use of CPAP machines is an uncomfortable or painful face mask or mouthpiece. If the patient complains of pain or irritation from the mask or nose prongs, the patient can either apply gauze to the edges of the mask or inquire about other styles of mask with the manufacturer or home-care company. If a patient complains of mucosal dryness in the nose or mouth, a humidifier may be helpful.

Humidifiers are often used in tandem with other respiratory devices in the home. Mechanical ventilators, CPAP machines, bilevel positive airway pressure (BIPAP), and nasal cannulas are all commonly used with humidifiers. These tools help to keep the patient's airway moist and patent, which is especially important when delivering oxygen and flow to a patient's airway. This action can be very drying, which has a negative impact on the patient's airway mucosa. Using a humidifier with either saline or sterile water (depending on the machine and the manufacturer's guidelines) is essential when providing high levels of flow to the patient's airway. However, room humidifiers should not be used for asthmatic patients. Often, a physician will suggest the use of a humidifier for respiratory infections in young children; however, this is particularly dangerous for children with asthma and reactive airway disease because humidity can be a trigger for those diseases.

Oxygen therapy humidifiers vary among manufacturers and models. The clinician should refer to the manufacturer's guidelines for troubleshooting their particular model of humidifier. Generally speaking, the clinician should ensure tight connections in the system, as well as an adequate power source for the humidifier. The humidifier should be free from visible damage; if damage is found, the clinician must remove the humidifier and send it for service. The clinician must ensure that there is an adequate water source for the humidifier, with no kinks or obstructions in the tubing. The water bag must have an adequate volume of water, or it must be replaced. If condensation is found in the system tubing, the humidity level and temperature should be titrated to minimize this effect. Excessive "rainout" in the tubing can lead to aspiration by the patient. The humidifier should also be checked to ensure that the temperature level is not too high or too low.

Apnea monitors are machines that continuously measure a patient's heart rate and respiratory rate. When a patient experiences apnea, or absence of breathing for several seconds, an alarm will sound. This type of monitor is commonly used for patients with severe refractory gastroesophageal reflux disease, patients who require supplemental oxygen at home, patients who use mechanical ventilation in the home environment, and patients with respiratory abnormalities that have resulted in prior periods of apnea. This monitoring equipment is commonly used in children under one year of age but might be appropriate in other limited clinical scenarios. Apnea monitors are commonly used during sleeping hours, but they may be used while the patient is awake in some cases. Parents of patients who use apnea monitors in the home setting must also be aware that some machines do not include battery backup systems, and if there is a power outage, the machine will not function. Careful monitoring of the patient may be required in that instance.

When setting up a home apnea monitor, clinicians must refer to the manufacturer's directions. Policies and procedures will vary among manufacturers and facilities; however, setup of an apnea monitor generally includes only a few steps. First, the clinician ensures the machine is clean and properly calibrated in accordance with the manufacturer's guidelines. The clinician then cleans the patient's skin with an approved cleanser as needed. The clinician attaches the heart rate sensor to the patient's chest and attaches the respiratory rate sensor to the patient's abdomen. The machine is then turned on and monitored to ensure that it is reading accurately. No serious adverse events are related to apnea monitor use, but some patients may experience irritation of the skin due to the adhesive material on the electrodes. Changing electrode sites periodically can combat this problem. Other patients may use a chest wrap that eliminates the use of adhesives.

When troubleshooting an apnea monitor, the clinician should refer to the manufacturer's guidelines because these machines vary among models and manufacturers. Generally speaking, the clinician must ensure that all wire and sensor connections are tight and that the machine is turned on and plugged into an adequate power source. If the machine indicates apnea, but the patient is not apneic, the clinician should ensure that the sensors or electrode belt is firmly attached to the patient and positioned correctly. Sensors might need to be replaced or repositioned if the machine is not reading correctly. Nondisposable sensors may need to be cleaned periodically in accordance with the manufacturer's guidelines for use. If the machine continues to be nonoperational or malfunctioning despite following the manufacturer's troubleshooting guidelines, it should be sent for service either through the facility's biomed department or through the home-care company (if used in the home setting).

Some patients are ready to be discharged from the neonatal intensive care unit or pediatric intensive care unit but may still require oxygen. In these cases, oxygen can be ordered for home use.

The indications for home oxygen use include respiratory diseases such as bronchopulmonary dysplasia; periods of hypoxia at rest or during activity; and periods of apnea, dyspnea, and/or mechanical ventilation use. Oxygen can be delivered using many different pieces of equipment depending on a patient's needs and respiratory status, including mechanical ventilators, nasal cannulas, and tracheostomy collars. Oxygen is sourced in multiple ways, including compressed oxygen in tanks, oxygen concentrators that extract oxygen from ambient air, and liquid oxygen in which oxygen is liquified using a cooling process. Each form of oxygen is associated with its own list of challenges including running out of gas, loss of electrical power source due to power outage, or the high cost of therapy; however, the clinician must work with the patient to prepare him or her for these challenges and ensure that the patient has an adequate supply of oxygen. The clinician must also stress the importance of keeping all flames and heat away from oxygen sources because oxygen is highly flammable and combustible.

Nasal cannulas are a common form of oxygen therapy in the home environment. These pieces of equipment are useful for patients of all ages and are comfortable and well tolerated. Nasal cannulas look like small prongs attached to a clear oxygen tube. The nasal cannula is then attached to a gas source and a liter flow is set. The liter flow is set according to the physician's order, but it may be titrated as needed to achieve the ultimate goal of weaning the patient off oxygen. A weaning protocol will be ordered by the healthcare team and is commonly given in written instructions to the patient's family. The patient must wear the nasal cannula at all times unless directed otherwise by the physician and health care team.

When educating a parent or caregiver on troubleshooting a nasal cannula, the clinician must ensure that the family first knows how to properly set up the equipment. After that instruction takes place, the clinician then describes how to troubleshoot the equipment. This can include checking for disconnections, ensuring that there is an adequate gas source (full oxygen tank), identifying obstructions to the tubing such as kinks or mucus plugs, making sure that the oxygen tank or concentrator is turned on, and ensuring that the correct flow rate is set on the machine or flowmeter. Parents and caregivers must be instructed on approximately how long a tank of oxygen will last so they don't inadvertently run out of oxygen. Kinks in the tubing or disconnections must be corrected quickly, and any mucus plugs can be either wiped clean or the tubing may need to be replaced. Extra tubing and/or nasal cannulas should always be available at the bedside for emergencies. Adverse events are not commonly associated with nasal cannula use, except for possible mucosal dryness in the nares. This can be remedied by adding a humidifier to the nasal cannula.

Portable oxygen concentrators are a common source of oxygen for home use. These machines come in various forms and sizes and vary among manufacturers. Some oxygen concentrators are midsize tabletop machines, whereas others are smaller portable machines that can be carried with the patient on outings. One of the great benefits of an oxygen concentrator is its mobility, as well as its ability to manufacture oxygen without the use of tanks. Oxygen concentrators work by extracting oxygen from ambient air and delivering that concentrated oxygen to the patient via a nasal cannula or other oxygen delivery device. These machines do require a power source, either by plugging the machine into an electrical outlet or by using its internal battery. Batteries last a finite amount of time and must be recharged according to the manufacturer's specifications. Patients who use oxygen concentrators may require a backup oxygen tank for emergencies such as power failures, inadequate battery life, or other mechanical failures.

When an oxygen concentrator is not operational, the clinician must troubleshoot the equipment to find the source of the problem. First, the clinician must check all connections to ensure a tight fit and then evaluate the tubing and oxygen delivery equipment for any kinks, obstructions, or leaks.

Once that is complete, the clinician checks the machine itself. If the machine is turned on but is not delivering oxygen, the clinician should check to see if an attached humidifier might be the problem. If there is an obstruction or leak that originates in the humidifier, a new humidifier may need to be ordered. The clinician also needs to ensure that the correct liter flow is dialed into the machine because sometimes machines can become jostled or tampered with, changing the airflow. If the machine does not have any power, then the power source must be checked. Ensure that the unit is plugged in and turned on and that the circuit breaker for that outlet is on and functional. If the unit is still not operational, then the home-care company must be contacted, and the patient must be placed on an alternate oxygen source.

Facilitate Procedures and Evaluate Efficacy

Bronchoscopy and Associated Procedures

Bronchoscopy refers to a procedure in which a physician visually inspects a patient's lungs with the use of a specialized flexible lighted scope. The bronchoscope components include a camera, light, and various tools that are used for the visual inspection, lavage, biopsy, and mucus clearance of the lungs. The bronchoscope can be inserted either into the patient's mouth or nare and is advanced through the trachea into the bronchi. Bronchoscopy procedures can be used to determine the cause of an obstruction, presence of an infection, abnormality of the structure of the airways, and to biopsy tumors in the bronchi. Numbing agents are administered to the airway, and the patient is sedated for the procedure. Common adverse events associated with bronchoscopy include throat pain, loss of voice, cough, and bronchospasm. Other less common adverse events include pneumothorax, refractory bronchospasm, and nosocomial infection.

Bronchial lavage, or bronchial rinsing, is a therapy used in specialized respiratory cases. Indications for bronchial lavage include but are not limited to patients with chronic refractory pneumonia, suspected lung cancer, chronic respiratory infections, bleeding of the airways, and scattered infiltrates throughout the lung fields. Bronchial lavage takes place during the bronchoscopy procedure in which the patient's airways are visually inspected via bronchoscope. With the bronchoscope in the affected area of the bronchi, the physician will insert saline into the bronchoscope port. The physician then suctions out the saline, performing a bronchial wash or lavage. The steps are repeated as needed to ensure that an adequate specimen is collected and that the lungs are clear of either mucus or obstruction. The saline specimen is then tested for possible pathogens, malignancy, cell count, and foreign bodies.

Bronchoscopy is useful for many interventions, including the biopsy of airway tissue. During a bronchoscopy procedure, the physician advances the bronchoscope into the affected portion of the bronchi. Here, the physician removes a tissue sample from the airway and collects it for further testing. This intervention can help to diagnose conditions such as malignancy and various types of infections. In addition to performing a biopsy on affected tissue, the bronchoscope can also collect smaller samples of cells using a bronchoscopy brush tool. This tool allows the physician to take microscopic cellular samples from the lining of the bronchi. These samples are then analyzed to determine the presence of infection, malignancy, and other respiratory conditions. The bronchoscope's brush tool is often used in conjunction with bronchial lavage because saline is often required as a medium for the cellular sample.

Sputum Culture

A nasal swab is a procedure in which a sample of mucus is collected from the patient's nares. The sample is tested for pathogens such as methicillin-resistant *Staphylococcus aureus* and influenza. A nasal swab can be completed in various ways, so it is important for the clinician to follow the facility's policy and procedure for the collection of these specimens. Generally speaking, the clinician will use a facility-approved dry nasal swab (similar to a common cotton swab) to collect the specimen. The clinician inserts the swab into the patient's nare, up to the approximate level of the nasopharynx. The clinician then rotates the swab and ensures contact with the mucus membranes of the inside of the nares. The clinician then performs the same process with the same swab in the other nare. Then the sample is packaged in accordance with the facility's policy and procedure, labeled, and sent for testing.

A nasal wash is a procedure in which a sample of mucus is collected from the patient's nares using a wet medium. The sample is then tested for pathogens such as respiratory syncytial virus. A nasal wash can be completed in various ways, so it is important for the clinician to follow the facility's policy and procedure for the collection of these specimens. Generally speaking, the clinician will use a facility-approved nasal wash system to collect the specimen. This can include a saline-filled 3 cc syringe with a flexible catheter or tubing. The clinician inserts the tubing into the patient's nare and then injects a small amount of saline into the nare while quickly pulling back on the plunger. This provides a lavage-type action in the nare. The syringe is then labeled, packaged, and processed in the lab.

Tracheal aspiration is a diagnostic procedure in a patient's airway is lavaged through their artificial airway. This procedure is similar to bronchial lavage via bronchoscopy; however, the bronchoscope is not used during this type of tracheal aspiration procedure. The tracheal aspiration procedure varies among facilities, so it is important for the clinician to follow the facility's policy and procedure for this intervention. Generally speaking, the clinician will use a sputum trap with one end attached to suction and the other end attached to the suction catheter. Using sterile technique, instill saline into the endotracheal tube or tracheostomy tube while quickly suctioning the saline back out. Ensure that the sputum trap is held upright and is not tipped over, or the sputum sample may bypass the trap and fall into the wall suction receptacle. Then the clinician labels and packages the specimen and transports it for testing.

Manage and/or Anticipate Effects of Medication Administration

Neuromuscular Blocking Agents

When preparing for intubation, the physician will order several drugs that will relax, paralyze, and sedate the patient. Some of these drugs also alter the patient's memory, allowing them to forget the procedure if they are indeed aware of it as it is happening. It is important to note that each physician performs an intubation differently, and there is no one correct way to medicate a patient. Medications and dosages vary according to the patient's condition, medical history, and physician preference. Often, a physician will order an opioid such as fentanyl to block the vagal response of the patient during intubation. The physician may also order a hypnotic medication such as propofol, which sedates the patient and offers memory-altering effects. A paralytic or neuromuscular blocking agent such as succinylcholine is a useful paralytic agent for intubation because it prevents any and all movement by the patient. Succinylcholine must always be administered with a sedative because patients will be paralyzed but fully aware of the procedure if a paralytic agent is used alone.

Reversal Agents

Reversal agents are medications that are used to reverse the effects of sedative and paralytic drugs used in the healthcare setting. For example, these drugs can be used to reverse the effects of drugs used during intubation, general sedation, surgery, and other medical procedures. Naloxone, also known as Narcan, reverses the effects of opioids. It is important to note that naloxone has a short duration of action, and more doses may be required to fully reverse the effects of administered opioids. Constant monitoring of the patient is required even if the naloxone administration appears to have reversed all sedative effects due to its short duration of action. Side effects associated with naloxone include but are not limited to withdrawal symptoms in opioid-addicted patients, allergic reaction, stomach upset, seizure, anxiety, and recurrence of pain. Naloxone is administered via intravenous injection. Dosing varies depending on the clinical situation with dosing ranging from 0.01 mg/kg for anesthesia reversal to 0.001 to 0.015 for opioid effect reversal.

Neostigmine is a reversal agent used to reverse the effects of paralytic agents and neuromuscular blocking agents in the healthcare setting. It can be used to reverse the effects of drugs used in various medical procedures including surgery and endotracheal intubation. Neostigmine is commonly administered via intravenous injection. Side effects associated with the use of neostigmine include but are not limited to dizziness, sleepiness, rash, irregular heartbeat, and allergic reaction. Neostigmine is available in 0.5 and 1 mg/mL strengths. The correct dosing of neostigmine for pediatric patients is from 0.03 to 0.07 mg/kg depending on the patient's level of consciousness, the neuromuscular blocking agent given, and the patient's overall health. This drug works by binding to the same receptor site as the paralytic agent administered, therefore interrupting the neuromuscular blocking agent's effects.

Vasoactive and Inotropic Agents

Vasoactive and inotropic agents are in a family of medications that improve cardiac output in compromised patients. These patients may have medical conditions such as sepsis or congenital heart defects such as patent ductus arteriosus. These medications improve cardiac output, thereby increasing oxygen delivery to the tissues of the body. This results in better oxygen saturations. Some examples of inotropic agents used in the neonatal and pediatric populations include dopamine and dobutamine. Dosing varies depending on the medication ordered as well as the patient's weight, condition, medical history, and overall health. Therapy should be initiated with a low dose; titrate the dosage as needed to maintain adequate cardiac output and oxygenation. Careful monitoring of the patient is required to avoid any adverse events associated with the use of these medications. Vasoactive and inotropic agents are often administered via intravenous infusion.

Diuretics

Diuretics are a classification of medication that causes excess fluid to be released from the cells of the body. For example, this type of medication may be administered to neonates with respiratory distress syndrome or transient tachypnea of the newborn. Diuretics such as furosemide (Lasix) release the excess fluid buildup from the lungs, resulting in improved respiration and oxygenation. Careful monitoring of the patient is necessary to prevent adverse events associated with the use of this medication including but not limited to dehydration and electrolyte imbalance. Dosing depends on the medication ordered. For example, furosemide is dosed as 1 mg/kg and is often administered via intravenous or intramuscular injection; however, the medication can also be given by mouth when appropriate. Dosing and schedules can be titrated as needed. Generally speaking, furosemide is often administered to neonates daily or on an every-12-hour schedule.

Systemic Smooth Muscle Relaxants

Magnesium sulfate is a smooth-muscle relaxant that is given to a pregnant woman for the prevention of seizures. This medication is commonly used in patients who have preeclampsia because this patient population has a high risk for seizures during pregnancy. Magnesium sulfate can also be used to treat preterm labor because this medication can slow or stop contractions. Magnesium sulfate is commonly administered via intravenous infusion or injection. Patients taking magnesium sulfate are also often given steroids to help increase the fetus' lung maturity. The use of magnesium sulfate is associated with several risks and adverse events for the mother and the fetus. When taking magnesium sulfate, the mother may notice symptoms such as sleepiness, nausea, visual disturbances, and headache. Magnesium sulfate can affect the newborn by causing poor muscle tone, reduced respiratory drive, and sleepiness. Neonates who have magnesium sulfate in their system may require supplemental oxygen, resuscitation, and/or mechanical ventilation in some cases.

Terbutaline is a systemic smooth muscle relaxant that is administered to a pregnant patient for the treatment of preterm labor. Terbutaline can slow or stop contractions and help to delay a preterm delivery. This medication is commonly delivered via intravenous infusion or injection at a dose of 0.25 mg per dose for up to two doses per day. Terbutaline is commonly used for up to three days. During that time, patients are often given steroids to help increase the fetus' lung maturity. Patients taking terbutaline should be monitored carefully for cardiac abnormalities or arrhythmias and changes in blood sugar. Some common adverse effects associated with the use of terbutaline include anxiety, shakiness, and increased heart rate in the mother. Newborns with terbutaline in their system can suffer from changes in blood sugar and tachycardia. Some studies also indicate that terbutaline can cause neurological disorders in children who were born to mothers using terbutaline during pregnancy and delivery.

Drug Interactions

The neonatal perinatal specialist is responsible for ensuring the safety and efficacy of respiratory treatments administered to the patient. Although numerous medication interactions can occur, respiratory therapists must be aware of the most common interactions among respiratory drugs. These can include proper dosage (i.e., preventing overdose and subsequent adverse events) and interactions with common respiratory drugs. For example, respiratory therapists should be aware that bronchodilators, common respiratory drugs, can interact with cardiovascular drugs such as beta blockers. This interaction occurs because bronchodilators or beta agonists work on the same mechanism as beta blockers; the resulting combination of the two drugs is an example of a classic drug interaction in respiratory care. It is the respiratory therapist's responsibility, which is also shared with the pharmacy, nursing, and other medical staff, to anticipate these interactions and offer alternative choices for the treatment of respiratory conditions.

Influence of Comorbid Conditions, Renal Failure, and Hepatic Failure

Neonatal patients have a low glomerular filtration rate, which can cause kidney failure when the patient's kidney is stressed. The already low glomerular filtration rate drops as the patient's kidneys are stressed, and kidney failure develops. These patients are unable to regulate their electrolytes, serum creatinine and nitrogen, and fluid status. These patients often have reduced urine output and fluid overload. Neonatal kidney failure can be treated with dialysis and diuretics, which decrease fluid overload and subsequently increase urine output. Due to the patient's fluid overload, pulmonary edema and subsequent hypoxia is a common finding in this patient population. Patients may present with an acidosis or other abnormalities in blood gas analysis due to the interrupted acid–base balance that kidney failure causes. Depending on the clinical findings, patients may need respiratory interventions such as supplemental oxygen and mechanical ventilation.

Hepatic failure is a relatively rare but very serious condition affecting some neonates. Patients with hepatic failure present with several complications including but not limited to multiple organ failure or compromise, immune system deficiencies, problems with blood clotting, inadequate oxygenation and subsequent respiratory distress syndrome, swelling of the brain, and kidney failure. There are several main causes of hepatic failure including injury, toxicity, metabolic disorders, vascular abnormalities, and infection; however, neonates often present with either a metabolic or an infectious cause. These patients often eventually require a liver transplant. Meanwhile, careful monitoring of the patient is required. Respiratory therapists must be prepared to treat hypoxia and respiratory distress syndrome associated with hepatic failure, including administering supplemental oxygen and/or mechanical ventilation as needed. Clinicians must also be aware that although many patients present with hypovolemia due to hepatic failure, care must be taken when supplementing fluids because patients who develop renal failure in addition to hepatic failure can experience fluid overload.

Anticipate Care Based on Laboratory Results

Hematologic Findings

Complete blood count (CBC) and Hgb electrophoresis are blood tests that measure the components of a patient's blood (CBC) and the patient's hemoglobin (Hgb electrophoresis). The CBC measures the patient's red and white blood cell counts, hemoglobin, hematocrit, mean corpuscular volume, and platelets. In addition, the test can further break down the white blood cells into types, including neutrophils, basophils, eosinophils, monocytes, and lymphocytes. This information can indicate whether a patient is experiencing allergies, asthma, infection, or another type of inflammatory response. A CBC is especially helpful in testing for sepsis, which is a severe form of infection that can result in multisystem failure including respiratory and cardiac arrest. Hemoglobin electrophoresis, another type of blood test, can also reveal problems with the patient's blood, such as anemia, hemoglobin defects, and other blood disorders. Patients with reduced hemoglobin levels often have hypoxia, which must be treated with supplemental oxygen as needed.

Chemistry

Serum electrolyte measurement can help the clinician determine whether a patient's acid–base balance is compromised due to disorders such as metabolic diseases, renal failure, and hypoventilation. Electrolyte replacement therapy may be necessary to support and maintain a patient's acid–base and fluid balances. Neonates in the NICU often require fluid replacement therapy, and they require careful monitoring of their fluid balance and electrolytes; however, patients with respiratory disorders such as bronchopulmonary dysplasia or patent ductus arteriosus require especially careful titration of supplemental fluids because these patients are prone to fluid overload and subsequent respiratory distress. Electrolyte imbalances, including high or low potassium, high or low sodium, and high or low calcium, can cause changes in the patient's blood gas values. Therefore, a comprehensive assessment must take place on respiratory patients who have a metabolic component to their disease process.

Albumin is a blood test in which the patient's levels of albumin protein are measured. This protein originates in the liver, and its measurement can indicate disorders such as hypobilirubinemia or hyperbilirubinemia. In hypobilirubinemia, a patient's albumin levels are low due to renal or hepatic disease. This disorder is related to sepsis and subsequent respiratory distress syndrome in neonates. The treatment for hypobilirubinemia varies depending on the cause of the disorder and the patient's overall condition. Some patients benefit from albumin infusion therapy. In hyperbilirubinemia, another albumin-related disorder of the neonate, patients appear jaundiced due to increased levels of bilirubin in the blood. Phototherapy is commonly ordered for these patients, and, in some cases, albumin is administered to assist in bringing down the patient's bilirubin levels and preventing subsequent bilirubin toxicity.

Glucose testing refers to a simple blood test in which the patient's blood sugar levels are measured. This is often performed as a heel prick on neonatal patients. Indications for glucose testing in neonates include but are not limited to being born to a gestational, type 1 or type 2 diabetic mother, premature birth, endocrine system deficiencies, congenital heart defects, sepsis, and increased work of breathing. All of these disorders can affect a patient's blood sugar levels due to stress, increased use of glucose (energy), and metabolic changes. Low blood sugar, also known as hypoglycemia, is a common problem in neonates with these disorders. Signs of low blood sugar in neonates include lethargy, apnea, and respiratory distress. Treatment for hypoglycemia includes glucose supplement therapy in accordance with your facility's policy and procedure depending on the patient's condition.

A sweat test is a medical test in which chloride levels in a patient's sweat are measured to determine if a patient has cystic fibrosis. In cystic fibrosis, a patient's lungs go through phases of cyclical infections and excessive mucus production, which leads to increased dyspnea and respiratory distress. This disease is characterized by a persistent productive cough, frequent pulmonary infections, dyspnea, and failure to thrive. Patients with cystic fibrosis excrete excessive amounts of chloride through their sweat glands. A sweat test measures the chloride levels in a patient's sweat by first provoking the sweating response and then collecting and analyzing the sweat sample. The test is painless and noninvasive, with the sweat response being initiated by electrical stimulation of the patient's extremity, and the sweat is collected in accordance with the facility's policy and procedure. Collection vessels can vary.

Microbiology

In Gram stain testing, a fluid or tissue sample is tested for the presence of bacteria as well as the type of bacteria present. In respiratory patients, the Gram stain technique is used to evaluate a patient's sputum sample for infectious bacteria. A sputum sample is obtained using various techniques. In a conscious and cooperative patient, the patient may simply cough and expectorate into a sterile cup. Other patients may require suctioning of the airway either by closed or open suction techniques. Once a sufficient sample is obtained, it is labeled and transported to the lab. The laboratory staff then prepares a slide with the sputum sample and applies a facility-approved stain to the sample. The sample is then visually inspected using a microscope to differentiate between the different types of bacteria that may be present.

A sputum culture is a test in which a sputum sample is evaluated for the presence of bacteria, fungi, and other pathogens. Patients with chronic or recurring respiratory symptoms may require this test to determine the cause of their symptoms. First, a sputum sample must be obtained by either coughing and expectorating into a sterile cup or by suctioning the patient's airway using either a closed or an open suction technique. Once an adequate sample is obtained, it is labeled and transported to the lab. The laboratory staff then takes a portion of the sample and places it in a medium that encourages pathogen growth. After a set period of time elapses, the sample is assessed and the presence and type of pathogens are determined. The clinician can then treat the patient's respiratory symptoms efficiently because he or she will know the likely cause of the patient's illness.

Toxicology

Toxicology testing is an important tool for the determination of the cause of a patient's respiratory arrest or distress. Patients who have overdosed on medications may present to the emergency room as unresponsive or minimally responsive with depressed respiratory effort, faint or weak pulses, and impending respiratory failure. In a suspected drug overdose, a blood sample is obtained via venous puncture. The blood sample is then packaged and labeled according to the facility's policy and procedure and is transported to the lab. The laboratory staff then prepares and analyzes the blood sample for the presence of opioids, alcohol, prescription medications, over-the-counter medications such as Tylenol, and other drugs. The clinicians can then attempt to reverse the effects of the drugs (in cases of opioid overdose) by administering reversal agents such as naloxone.

Neonatal abstinence syndromes refer to a collection of symptoms or disorders that are a direct result of neonatal withdrawal from medication that was abused during the mother's pregnancy. Multiple organ systems are affected by neonatal abstinence syndromes, including the cardiac and respiratory systems. Patients with suspected neonatal abstinence syndromes often present with symptoms such as irritability, seizures, crying, digestive upset, and respiratory distress or subsequent arrest. Toxicology testing can be used to determine the medication causing the withdrawal symptoms. This information can help clinicians determine if administering a reversal agent would be beneficial to the patient. In addition, patients may be treated with pharmacological agents such as morphine to help relieve the symptoms of withdrawal, or they may use comfort care measures to help calm the newborn such as swaddling, holding, and feeding on demand.

Blood Gas Analyses and Hemoximetry

When assessing arterial blood gas samples, some blood gas analyzers provide CO-oximetry but others do not. CO-oximetry is a specialized method of analyzing blood gas samples using spectrophotometry. This light-based tool analyzes the hemoglobin portions of the blood, including oxyhemoglobin, methemoglobin, and carboxyhemoglobin. These measurements can indicate conditions such as carbon monoxide poisoning and methemoglobinemia. In both conditions, the patient's hemoglobin is unable to carry oxygen throughout the body, resulting in the need for supplemental oxygen. In the case of carbon monoxide poisoning, the patient's saturation on a pulse oximeter is normal; however, the patient's hemoglobin is carrying carbon monoxide through the blood rather than oxygen. A false high result in the pulse oximeter is a result of the carbon monoxide binding to the hemoglobin rather than oxygen. Without CO-oximetry, the clinician is unable to differentiate between a normal oxygen saturation and a false high due to carbon monoxide poisoning.

Anticipate Care Based on Imaging and/or Reports of Imaging

Radiographs

There are two types of sail signs in pediatric and neonatal chest radiographs. The term sail sign refers to the triangular or sail-shaped thymus gland that is present on chest X-rays. A normal sail sign is characterized by a triangle-shaped thymus, whereas an abnormal sail sign is characterized by a larger thymic outline similar to the appearance of a large ship's sails blowing in the wind. This abnormally large sail sign indicates a pneumomediastinum, also known as trapped air in the center of the chest cavity. This condition can be the result of barotrauma during mechanical ventilation or resuscitation, meconium aspiration, injury to the chest, and infections. Neonatal patients with a pneumomediastinum often present with increased work of breathing including retractions and nasal flaring, grunting, tachypnea, and low tidal volumes. The underlying cause of the pneumomediastinum must be treated to resolve the condition, and the patient must be carefully monitored until the pneumomediastinum resolves.

Chest X-rays or chest radiographs are noninvasive tests that provide imaging of the chest's structures and organs. The most common chest X-rays are the anterior and posterior (front and back) views; however, some suspected patient conditions may require a lateral (side) view of the chest. These clinical situations and conditions may include a suspected pneumothorax, foreign body or mass, inspection of the heart, confirmation of drain or chest tube placement, or inspection of umbilical artery catheter or umbilical vein catheter placement. Alternatively, some physicians prefer to have the anterior and posterior views as well as the lateral view because this multiview approach allows for optimal inspection of the chest and its structures. Some facilities and physicians routinely perform lateral and anterior and posterior views. A lateral view can provide the physician with a three-dimensional look at the affected area by comparing the anterior and posterior views with the lateral view.

Tetralogy of Fallot is a combination of four separate heart defects that are present in a patient. Tetralogy of Fallot includes ventricular hypertrophy, enlarged aorta that connects both ventricles, a ventricular septal defect, and pulmonary stenosis. In this condition, the heart pumps unoxygenated blood throughout the body, causing hypoxia and respiratory distress. The patient often appears cyanotic, and the clinician may identify a heart murmur during their assessment. Echocardiograms and chest X-rays can be used to confirm the presence of tetralogy of Fallot. The patient's chest radiograph will show a boot- or shoe-shaped heart, with an upturned cardiac apex or toe part of the boot. Tetralogy of Fallot is a life-threatening condition that requires immediate surgery, which is often conducted moments after birth. The condition is surgically repaired by closing the ventricular septal defect, opening the pulmonary valve, and possibly replacing the pulmonary valve entirely.

Transposition of the great vessels is a congenital heart defect in which the blood vessels of the heart, including the aorta and the pulmonary artery, are found in the opposite position as expected. In this condition, the pulmonary artery is attached to the left ventricle, whereas the aorta is attached to the right ventricle. Patients with transposition of the great vessels have insufficient blood oxygenation due to one of two scenarios: Either the blood flow is traveling only between the lungs and heart, or it is traveling only between the body and heart. Either way, the body is not receiving oxygenated blood due to the transposed vessels of the heart. The patient's chest X-ray will show an egg-on-a-string view, with the heart appearing oval or egg-shaped, bulbous, and enlarged. Surgical correction is needed; however, some surgeries are delayed until the patient is in a more stable condition. In these cases, the patient may undergo cardiac catheterization treatment in which the atria are enlarged to allow for blood flow and some oxygenation.

OTHER TESTS

CT scans are noninvasive diagnostic tests in which the structures of a patient's body are inspected via cross-sectional views. The tests can be performed with or without contrast medium infusion, depending on the reason for the testing. If, for example, the physician requires a view of the patient's blood vessels or urine flow, contrast may be used to help highlight these areas or processes. Contrast medium is given via intravenous injection, and the patient may feel warm or flushed during the infusion process. CT scans are commonly used to investigate or rule out suspected foreign bodies, masses, disease processes, congenital defects, infections, structural abnormalities, damage or obstructions in blood vessels, and confirmation or investigation of other clinical scenarios. During the test, the patient lies on a table and is transported into a circular donut-shaped machine. The CT machine then takes cross sectional views of the internal structures of the affected area, using radiation similar to that in an X-ray.

MRI testing is a noninvasive diagnostic test in which the structures of a patient's body are inspected via cross-sectional views. This test can be performed with or without contrast medium infusion, depending on the reason for the testing. If, for example, the physician requires a view of the blood vessels in an area of the body, contrast may be used to help highlight these areas. Contrast medium is given via intravenous injection, and the patient often feels no flushing or warmth (unlike the use of contrast medium in CT scans). MRI testing is commonly used to investigate or rule out suspected foreign bodies, masses, disease processes, congenital defects, heart defects, infections, structural abnormalities, damage or obstructions in blood vessels, and confirmation or investigation of other clinical scenarios. During the test, the patient lies on a table and is transported into a tube-shaped machine. The MRI machine then images cross-sectional views of the internal structures of the affected area, using magnetic fields rather than radiation. MRI testing is quite loud, and the patient will require hearing protection especially if undergoing an MRI of the head.

Ultrasound testing is a noninvasive diagnostic imaging test in which the structures of a patient's body are inspected. This test does not require contrast medium infusion, and it uses sound waves rather than magnetic waves or radiation. The test is painless and safe, and it takes several minutes to one hour to perform, depending on the area(s) of the body being tested. Ultrasound testing is commonly used to investigate or rule out suspected foreign bodies, masses, disease processes, congenital defects, infections, structural abnormalities, damage or obstructions in blood vessels, blood or urine flow, confirmation or ruling out of appendicitis, and confirmation or investigation of other clinical scenarios. During the test, the patient lies on a table and ultrasound gel is applied to the affected area. The clinician performing the test then uses a wand or probe to provide gentle pressure on the affected area. The patient's internal structures are then visible on the clinician's ultrasound machine screen.

Manage Care Based on Nutritional Status

Complications of Feedings

Neonatal patients with low birth weights can suffer from feeding intolerance, which is the inability of the newborn to accept and digest feedings. This can result in complications such as apnea, gastroesophageal reflux, aspiration and subsequent pneumonia, vomiting, abdominal distension, and other clinical symptoms. Patients with feeding intolerance may also fail to thrive, resulting in longer hospital stays. Respiratory therapists treating neonates with feeding intolerance must be prepared for possible apneic spells with bradycardia. These patients may require respiratory intervention including but not limited to supplemental oxygen and mechanical ventilation interventions. Patients with feeding intolerance may also require tube feedings, which can further complicate the patient's respiratory status because disruption or displacement of the feeding tube, especially a nasogastric feeding tube, can result in aspiration and subsequent nosocomial pneumonia infection.

Morbid Obesity

Morbid obesity refers to patients who have a body mass index (BMI) of 40 or higher. These patients carry excess weight, which can affect their airway patency and increase their risk of respiratory diseases. Patients with morbid obesity often have airway management challenges in the critical care setting due to excess weight on the chest and neck, causing airway partial obstructions. Some patients with morbid obesity may require special concessions during mechanical ventilation and the use of artificial airways, such as extended-length tracheostomy tubes. Manually ventilating morbidly obese patients can be difficult, with challenges such as poorly fitting and subsequently inadequately sealed masks during manual mask-bag ventilation, difficult intubations due to excess tissue on the patient's neck, and airway obstruction due to the tongue falling back in the oral cavity. The use of bite blocks or oral airways can be helpful for airway obstructions due to structural or tissue blockage of the airway, and laryngeal mask airways can be useful in difficult-to-intubate patients.

Patients with a high BMI often suffer from sleep-disordered breathing due to the excessive weight carried in the patient's airway. Sleep disorders such as obstructive sleep apnea can occur because of failures in airway patency due to a variety of factors. This obstructive effect commonly occurs during sleep when the patient's airway musculature relaxes and the excess weight of the tissues of the neck obstructs the airway and causes the patient to momentarily stop breathing. The patient's tongue may also fall back into the oral cavity during sleep, causing an airway obstruction and subsequent period of apnea. This cyclic disorder, resulting in multiple periods of apnea per night, can have adverse effects on the patient's health. In addition to weight loss management techniques, these patients often benefit from the use of a CPAP machine. These machines provide continuous airflow to the patient's airway via a mask or mouthpiece, maintaining airway patency during sleep.

Assist with or Perform Resuscitation

Selection of Appropriate Equipment

T-piece resuscitators are machines that provide manual breaths as well as peak end expiratory pressure (PEEP) to a neonate's airway during resuscitation. The setup of T-piece resuscitators varies among manufacturers, and the clinician should check their facility's policy and procedure for correct setup instructions. Generally speaking, when setting up a T-piece resuscitator machine, the unit is first plugged into an adequate gas source. The patient circuit and T-piece is attached to the machine, ensuring adequate gas flow through the T-piece. The oxygen flowmeter is set at the desired liter flow, and the clinician obstructs the PEEP port to ensure that the desired pressure is delivered to the T-piece. Then the peak inspiratory pressure is set by continuing to obstruct the PEEP port and dialing in the peak inspiratory pressure. The PEEP level is then adjusted according to the physician's order, and the T-piece attaches to the neonatal mask, which is placed over the patient's nose and mouth

T-piece resuscitators are resuscitative tools that provide manual pressure-regulated breaths as well as PEEP to a neonate's airway during resuscitation. The use of T-piece resuscitators varies among manufacturers, and the clinician should check the facility's policy and procedure for correct usage instructions. Generally speaking, the clinician will ensure the adequate setup and calibration of the machine and place the resuscitation T-piece and mask on the patient's face, providing an adequate seal. Manual breaths are provided by occluding the PEEP port with the clinician's thumb for inhalation, and removal of the thumb from the port for exhalation. The benefits to the use of T-piece resuscitators as opposed to flow-inflating resuscitation bags or self-inflating resuscitation bags include the ability for the clinician to deliver exact pressures for the duration of the respiratory cycle (PEEP) while also delivering set pressures for inhalation. This prevents barotrauma associated with high or varying inspiratory pressures during manual resuscitation. Patients may also benefit from better alveolar recruitment and ventilation with this dual-pressure system.

Following the Appropriate Protocol

When performing neonatal resuscitation in the delivery room, it is imperative that clinicians are familiar with current Neonatal Resuscitation Program (NRP) guidelines. Practitioners are encouraged to become NRP certified because this ensures that the care team is aware of the latest guidelines. Clinicians must be aware that NRP guidelines change periodically; therefore, clinicians must follow the most recent edition of the NRP guidelines when performing resuscitation. Generally speaking, clinicians will perform resuscitation when a patient has inadequate and/or an absence of breathing or pulse. The clinician will follow the NRP algorithm and provide manual breaths as needed via mask-bag ventilation at a rate of 40–60 breaths per minute. PEEP may be administered if needed. Chest compressions will be performed as needed at a rate of 100–120 compressions per minute. Compressions are performed by placing the clinician's index and middle fingers between the nipple line in the center of the patient's chest and depressing to a depth of one-third of the chest's width from front to back. Current NRP guidelines suggest a ratio of three compressions to one ventilation when using a team of resuscitating clinicians.

When performing pediatric resuscitation, it is imperative that clinicians are familiar with the Pediatric Advanced Life Support (PALS) guidelines. Practitioners are encouraged to become PALS certified because this ensures that the care team is aware of the latest guidelines. Clinicians must be aware that PALS guidelines change periodically; therefore, clinicians must follow the most recent edition of the PALS guidelines when performing resuscitation. Generally speaking, clinicians will perform resuscitation when a patient has inadequate and/or an absence of breathing or pulse. The clinician will follow the PALS algorithm and provide manual breaths as needed via mask-bag ventilation at a rate of 40–60 breaths per minute. PEEP may be administered if needed. Chest compressions will be performed as needed at a rate of 100–120 compressions per minute. Compressions are performed by placing the heel of the clinician's hand between the nipple line in the center of the patient's chest and depressing to a depth of one-third of the chest's width from front to back. Current PALS guidelines suggest a ratio of 15 compressions to 2 breaths when using a team of resuscitating clinicians.

Prepare for Disaster and Mass Casualty Events

Procedures for Patient Movement and Protection

Disasters, either man-made or natural, can occur at any time. The healthcare team, especially those in critical care units, must be prepared for the evacuation of critical patients if the need arises. Follow your facility's policy and procedure for mass casualty and disaster preparedness because these processes vary among facilities. In the event of dangerous weather, patients may simply be moved away from windows, into the hallways or to the center of the patient's room. In these cases, patients using oxygen will need extension tubing from their new location to the oxygen source. If the oxygen source is too far away from the patient's new safe location, the clinician may need to use oxygen tanks to provide supplemental oxygen in the interim. In the event of an evacuation, clinicians will need to dispatch the healthcare team, including nursing, respiratory therapy, and other clinicians to assist in moving critical patients. Clinicians will need to gather appropriate equipment for the transfer or transport of patients during a disaster event. This can include resuscitative equipment, oxygen tanks, portable heart and respiratory monitors, and other clinical tools.

Triage Procedures

In the event of a disaster or mass casualty event, clinicians must be prepared to triage the patients who present to the emergency room. Clinicians should follow their facility's policy and procedure because processes vary among facilities. The healthcare team will congregate in one area, often the emergency department, and wait for further instruction. Often, the team will be required to assess patients to determine severity of injuries. This process is known as triage. The most critical patients are treated first, and patients with less severe injuries are treated last. This process keeps the emergency department functional during mass influxes of patients. It also helps to ensure that the most critical patients are treated before those with minimal or minor injuries. This process results in the highest rate of survival for victims.

Equipment and Supply Management

Clinicians should follow their facility's policy and procedure for the management of equipment during a mass casualty or disaster event because these processes vary among facilities. Generally speaking, members of the healthcare team are responsible for stocking and maintaining their equipment stores in their respective departments. This can include resuscitative equipment such as resuscitation bag and mask; mechanical ventilators; isolettes; oxygen tanks; heart rate and respiratory monitors; as well as first aid equipment such as gauze, bandages, and other tools. The healthcare team must ensure that they remain well stocked with these items in the event of a disaster. The triage process of assessing and treating the most critical patients first helps with the appropriate use of medical supplies. Additional supplies may be delivered by governmental aid agencies during mass casualty or disaster events, depending on the situation.

Interact with Members of an Interdisciplinary Team

Suggested Modifications to the Care Plan Based on the Respiratory Assessment and Responses to Proposed Care Plan Modifications from Other Team Members

Critical care patients are often treated by a multidisciplinary team comprised of many different branches of medicine. The members of the team can include the respiratory therapist, physician, nurse, pharmacy, physical therapy, and other healthcare disciplines. It is the respiratory therapist's responsibility to work in collaboration with the interdisciplinary healthcare team, participating in patient rounds, round-table discussion, care planning, and other meetings of the healthcare team. The respiratory therapist is expected to offer suggestions and solutions based on their assessment of the patient as well as their professional experience. Respiratory therapists must work together with the rest of the healthcare team, modifying their delivered interventions to help create a cohesive team and ensure that the patient is being treated optimally. For example, the respiratory therapist may alter his or her rounding schedule to provide cluster care to critical neonatal patients because this type of consolidated care involving several practitioners providing their treatments simultaneously can prevent unnecessary disruption of the patient's rest.

Evaluate Patient and Family Understanding of Education

Discharge and Home

Patients are often able to be discharged to their home while using a tracheostomy tube. Special care must be taken to ensure that the airway remains patent, secure, and clean. Patients and caregivers must perform tracheostomy care up to several times per day, depending on the physician's instructions and the age of the patient's tracheostomy (for example, newly placed tracheostomy as opposed to an established tracheostomy). Generally speaking, tracheostomy care at home is similar to the procedure performed in the hospital. However, in the home setting, sterile technique is not required. Clean technique, including proper hand hygiene and limiting contamination of the tube, is appropriate for home use. The patient or caregiver should carefully clean the patient's skin around the tracheostomy with mild soap and warm water. Then the skin should be dried thoroughly with a clean cloth. Tracheostomy ties should be clean. If soiled, replace them promptly. Suctioning using clean technique is required several times per day as needed.

At some point after the patient's discharge, the patient's tracheostomy tube may need to be changed. This can be due to displacement or accidental decannulation, obstruction, or scheduled time for the tube change. When changing a tracheostomy in the home environment, the patient and caregiver should follow any instructions given by the physician, hospital staff, and home-care company. Generally speaking, the caregiver will first perform hand hygiene and suction the tube using clean technique. Assemble the tracheostomy tube in accordance with the manufacturer's guidelines for the model of tracheostomy tube that is used. If using a cuffed tracheostomy tube, ensure that the cuff is functional on the new tube by inflating and deflating it once. Untie the tracheostomy tube ties on the existing tracheostomy tube. Deflate the cuff if applicable. Carefully remove the existing tracheostomy tube. Apply lubricant to the end of the new tracheostomy tube, and insert it quickly and carefully into the stoma. Then secure the tracheostomy tube with ties or other equipment. If applicable, clean the old tracheostomy tube according to the manufacturer's directions for future use.

When suctioning a tracheostomy tube in the home setting, the caregiver should first ensure that the patient has not eaten recently because suctioning after meals can cause stomach upset and vomiting. This can increase the chance of aspiration or infection. The caregiver can use clean suctioning technique as opposed to sterile technique, which is required in the clinical setting. First, the caregiver will perform hand hygiene. The caregiver will ensure that all equipment is set up and ready and will test the suction catheter for functionality prior to starting the procedure. Then the caregiver will advance the catheter into the tracheostomy tube up to a predetermined length. The caregiver will then apply suction while pulling the catheter slowly out of the tracheostomy tube. This should be performed quickly, only a few seconds in duration. Repeat the procedure as needed until secretions have been cleared. Lavage may be required for thick secretions, but the caregiver should follow the physician's guidelines on its use.

When suctioning a tracheostomy tube in the hospital setting, sterile technique is required. If a patient has a closed-suction system, the clinician performs hand hygiene, and then he or she advances the catheter into the tracheostomy to the preapproved depth and applies suction while slowly pulling the catheter out of the tracheostomy tube. The suctioning process should be performed over only a few seconds because the patient is unable to take a breath while the procedure is taking place. The process can be repeated as needed until secretions are cleared. When using an open-suctioning system, the clinician must use sterile technique with a sterile dominant hand and a dirty nondominant hand. The clinician will put on sterile gloves by touching only the folded top portion of the glove. Once the gloves are on, the dirty hand can attach the suction tubing to the sterile catheter held by the sterile hand. The sterile hand then advances the catheter into the tracheostomy tube to a preset length, applies suction, and removes the catheter from the tracheostomy tube. The procedure is then repeated as needed. Follow the facility's policy and procedure for lavage because this intervention is linked to an increased incidence of infection.

When trying to determine if a patient with an artificial airway requires suctioning, the clinician should look for several signs and symptoms. If the patient is mechanically ventilated, the clinician may notice a high-pressure alarm sounding. This can indicate an airway obstruction. The clinician might also observe the patient coughing frequently or forcefully. If secretions are seen in the artificial airway or in the patient's mouth, suctioning is often required. Suctioning may also be required of any patient demonstrating signs of respiratory distress. In older children, this can include but is not limited to coughing, increased respiratory rate, use of accessory muscles, and flushed or pale skin tone. In infants and neonates, signs of respiratory distress include grunting, nasal flaring, intercostal and/or subcostal retractions, flushed or pale skin tone, cough, and increased respiratory rate.

Patients with a history of cardiac or respiratory disorders may require further monitoring in the home environment. Some common monitoring options for home include apnea monitoring and oxygen saturation monitoring. Apnea monitors are machines that continuously measure a patient's heart rate and respiratory rate, watching for periods of apnea, which is the absence of breathing for several seconds. Apnea monitors are commonly used during sleeping hours but may be used while the patient is awake in some cases, especially during times that the parent or caregiver is not supervising the patient. Oxygen saturation monitors are also used to monitor a patient's respiratory status. This noninvasive monitor measures the oxygen in the patient's blood through a sensor attached to the patient's finger or toe (other sites may be used in special cases). The sensor has a red light that penetrates the nail bed. The pulse oximeter's sensor measures the amount of hemoglobin that is saturated with oxygen. These measurements can be taken continuously or intermittently.

For parents of children with chronic respiratory disease and/or impairment, cardiopulmonary resuscitation (CPR) training may be beneficial. Some facilities require this training prior to discharge. The training can take place either at the hospital or in a community center or fire station. CPR education is of vital importance to parents of patients with respiratory compromise because patients with a history of apnea or respiratory insufficiency often have a higher incidence of respiratory distress and subsequent respiratory arrest. Educating the patient's family and caregivers can ensure a safe transition to the home environment while offering the patient an emergency plan of action if respiratory arrest does take place. Patients should be sent home with emergency resuscitative equipment in accordance with your facility's policy and procedure. This can include supplemental oxygen, replacement artificial airways, and a resuscitation bag.

In a car seat challenge, a preterm infant is placed into a car seat for a set period of time while he or she is monitored. This test is used to determine if it is safe to transport the child home via a traditional infant car seat. Often, a car seat challenge is conducted on patients who are considered preterm, with a gestational age of 37 weeks or less. This patient population is at a higher risk for cardiopulmonary complications, and extra care must be taken when discharging these patients. The parents often bring the car seat into the hospital, and the patient is placed in it for a set period of time, often an hour and a half to two hours. The patient is observed to see any signs of respiratory distress, and he or she is monitored for any change in heart rate, respiratory rate, or oxygen saturation. If these changes are observed, the patient fails the test and it is repeated at a later date. Other arrangements might be made for patients who are unable to successfully complete a car seat challenge but need to be discharged from the hospital.

Equipment and Procedure Instruction

When discharging a patient to their home, the healthcare team will assign a home-care company to the patient for their home-care needs. This can include suction equipment, supplemental oxygen via tank or concentrator, and cardiopulmonary monitors. Prior to discharge, the home-care company or inpatient healthcare team will educate the patient and caregiver on the setup and use of any equipment that will be used en route to the patient's home. More education on other home-care equipment might take place while the patient is still admitted, but this practice varies among facilities. Clinicians should refer to their facility's policy and procedure for home-care education and equipment setup. Generally speaking, the home-care company will visit the patient at home and educate the parent or caregiver on any monitoring or therapeutic equipment ordered, including setup, troubleshooting, and general operational topics.

Medication Administration

When a respiratory patient is discharged from the hospital, many different home therapy modalities may be ordered. These can include respiratory interventions such as inhalers and nebulizer treatments. Upon discharge, the patient should be educated on their home medication regimen including the medication dosage and schedule and any special technique required to deliver the medication. Inhaler technique varies among models, with several different types of inhalers available. Breath-actuated inhalers require a quick, even inhalation to actuate the inhaler. The same is true for dry powder inhalers because these inhalers do not release the medication until the patient inhales. For traditional metered-dose inhalers, the patient will require a valved holding chamber (spacer). Spacers come in multiple styles including chambers with a mouthpiece or mask. They also come in different sizes to accommodate patients of all ages. When using an inhaler with a spacer, the patient must take a slow, deep breath in through the chamber after actuating the inhaler. The spacer holds the puff of medication and suspends it so that the patient can inhale slowly and deeply, maximizing medication deposition in the lower airway.

Competencies Specific to Critical Care

Evaluate Pertinent Information

Maternal History

The amniotic fluid index of a mother is the level of amniotic fluid found in the four quadrants of the uterus. The measurement is taken in each of the four quadrants in areas in which there is no structures present (including the fetal body and/or umbilical cord). The test adds the readings of each quadrant together, and that resulting number is the mother's amniotic fluid index. If the amniotic fluid index is less than 5 cm, this indicates that there is insufficient amniotic fluid to support the fetus. Depending on the fetus's gestational age, the fetus may be delivered early. Reduced amniotic fluid is associated with poor prognosis including fetal death and must be evaluated and treated promptly. A reduced amniotic fluid index can be caused by conditions such as early rupture of the membranes, fetal abnormalities such as trisomy disorders, renal defects, and other medical disorders.

Many pregnant patients take medications during pregnancy that have no adverse effects on the fetus; however, some medications are not safe for use in pregnancy. For example, patients who abuse illegal drugs or prescription opioids can have fetuses with low birth weight, congenital defects, respiratory distress, and withdrawal symptoms. These neonates may require emergency interventions such as mechanical ventilation and resuscitation depending on the severity of their condition and the medication taken by the mother. Pregnant mothers who abuse drugs must be treated and monitored throughout the pregnancy to minimize the effects on the fetus. Pregnant patients should be advised to check with their doctor regarding the safety and efficacy of all medications (prescribed or over the counter) used during pregnancy. Some medications, such as those that treat asthma, are usually continued throughout pregnancy because the benefits of the medications for the mother outweigh the risks to the fetus.

Fetal and Neonatal Assessments

Biophysical profile testing is a painless, noninvasive series of tests that measure the overall health of a fetus. During the ultrasound portion of the test, the clinician measures the amount of amniotic fluid present in the uterus, the fetus's muscle tone, and the fetus's movements. During the nonstress test component of the biophysical profile, the mother wears a monitor on her abdomen that measures the fetus's heart rate. The mother clicks a button when she feels fetal movement, which is then notated. A healthy fetus will have a brief increase in heart rate during fetal movement, which then returns to baseline. The absence of this increase can indicate that the fetus is stressed. The overall biophysical profile is scored on a scale of 1 to 10. Scores at or above 8 indicate a healthy fetus, whereas low scores can indicate fetal distress.

Apgar testing, named after Dr. Virginia Apgar, is a test that assesses a newborn for signs of distress. The test is performed twice: once immediately after birth (within 1 minute) and once 5 minutes after birth. The components of the test include appearance, pulse, grimace, activity, and respiration. Each criterion is rated on a scale of 0 to 2 where 2 is the best score. The appearance portion of the test refers to the presence of cyanosis. For example, pink neonates are given a score of 2 whereas cyanotic infants may be given a score of zero. Neonates receive two scores, and often the second score (after 5 minutes) improves or normalizes in healthy neonates. Scores of less than 7, however, require reassessments every 5 minutes until 20 minutes have passed. These patients may require treatment including supplemental oxygen or resuscitation if the Apgar scores do not increase.

Fetal lung maturity indices are criteria that clinicians measure to determine the relative maturity of a fetus's lungs. Assessing the maturity of a fetus's lungs can help the healthcare team anticipate the medical needs of the neonate after birth. Surfactant, the group of phospholipids that reduce the surface tension of the alveoli, is naturally occurring in the lungs of term infants. However, insufficient levels of surfactant are often found in preterm infants, resulting in the need for supplemental oxygen, mechanical ventilation, and surfactant replacement therapy. To measure the levels of surfactant, the mother undergoes amniocentesis, in which a sample of amniotic fluid is obtained and tested to determine the level of surfactant present. This test, which measures the ratio of the two phospholipid components of surfactant (sphingomyelin and lecithin), can help measure fetal lung maturity.

OTHER DIAGNOSTIC PROCEDURES

Transillumination is a noninvasive procedure in which the patient's room is darkened, and a fiber-optic light source is held up to a neonate's chest. This can identify the presence of a pneumothorax or pneumopericardium, or other disorders causing air to collect in the pleural space. The light source is held against the midaxillary line on the front of the patient's chest. On the area of air leakage due to pneumothorax or pneumopericardium, the transmitted light will appear in a diffuse pattern around the light source. In unaffected areas, the clinician will notice only a small circumference of light around the light source. Air in the pleural space can also be confirmed using a chest X-ray in conjunction with clinical assessment. Transillumination can also be helpful for assessing and locating blood vessels for insertion of cannulas and catheters or the sampling of blood.

When neonates appear cyanotic, the clinician must determine if the cause is respiratory or cardiac. Part of this assessment includes an oxygen challenge test or hyperoxia test. During this evaluation, the neonate undergoes blood gas testing via the right radial artery. No supplemental oxygen can be used during that measurement. Then, the patient is placed on 100% oxygen for 10 minutes. After that time, the clinician draws a second blood gas reading. The two blood gas values are then compared. Normally, the patient will have a PaO_2 of between 40 and 25 mm Hg while not using any supplemental oxygen. The patient will also have a PaO_2 of greater than 80 mm Hg while breathing 100% oxygen if they do not have a cardiac defect. If the patient's PaO_2 does not rise dramatically after inspiring 100% oxygen, then the clinician can deduce that the cause of the patient's hypoxia and cyanosis is cardiac in nature.

Assess and Manage Airways

ESTABLISHMENT OF A PATENT AIRWAY

Bag-mask resuscitation is a common form of resuscitation in critical care areas of the hospital. Resuscitation masks come in various sizes, including adult, pediatric, infant, and neonate. The correct size must be chosen to ensure a tight fit. During resuscitation, the clinician stands at the head of the bed and holds the mask on the patient's face with the nondominant hand in a C and E position around the face mask. The clinician's dominant hand squeezes the resuscitation bag to deliver breaths. The C and E position refers to the hand positioning of the clinician performing bag-mask ventilation. The C refers to the C shape that the clinician's thumb and index finger make as they encircle the mask and hold it in place on the patient's face. The E refers to the clinician's remaining three fingers holding the patient's jaw just under their chin. This hand positioning helps to maintain a tight seal on the mask for ventilation as well as the appropriate chin lift and head tilt patient positioning.

Some resuscitation bags can be self-inflating, whereas others require an attached gas source's flow to inflate. Flow-inflating bags are commonly used in the neonatal intensive care unit because neonates can have immature lungs that require careful pressure titration during ventilation. Excessive airway pressures can cause barotrauma to the lungs. Some flow-inflating resuscitation bags have pressure-limiting dials built into the system, which prevents excessive pressure delivered to the airway. Other flow-inflating bags have a flow adjustment dial, which allows the clinician to titrate the flow and subsequently keep the delivered pressure constant. To use flow-inflating bags, the clinician must ensure an adequate gas source (often an oxygen flowmeter attached to a wall or oxygen tank), pressure manometer (unless using a bag that has a pressure-limiting feature), and facility-approved flow-inflating resuscitation bag. The clinician will titrate the bag's flow while watching the pressure manometer during resuscitation. The clinician will ensure that the delivered breaths do not exceed the pressure ordered by the physician.

When choosing a resuscitation bag, the clinician must first determine the patient population being served. If the population is neonatal, a pressure-limiting flow inflating bag system is required for resuscitation. However, if the patient population is comprised of older pediatric patients, a self-inflating bag is appropriate. Self-inflating bags often do not have pressure-limiting capabilities, which is why they are not commonly used in neonatal resuscitation. When using self-inflating resuscitation bags, the bag will be attached to a supplemental oxygen flowmeter, often at the wall of the bedside or on an oxygen tank. The flowmeter is set at 15 l/min at 100% oxygen unless otherwise specified by the physician. Then resuscitation can take place. Some self-inflating bags also feature PEEP valve connections, where a PEEP valve can be attached.

Performing or Assisting Intubation

When assisting with intubation for a neonatal patient, the clinician must gather and prepare the necessary equipment. This can include correctly sized laryngoscopes and endotracheal tubes, suction equipment, resuscitation bag and mask, oxygen source, and pressure manometer. The clinician must assemble the laryngoscope and ensure that the light is functioning. If not, the batteries must be replaced, or the clinician can replace the entire laryngoscope. An appropriately sized resuscitation mask must be gathered and attached to the resuscitation bag, and the bag must be attached to an adequate gas source with the oxygen set at either 100% or the FiO_2 ordered by the physician. The clinician should titrate the flow (neonates often require flow-inflating bags due to the pressure-limiting features) while occluding the mask and watching the pressure manometer to ensure that the set airway pressure equals the pressure ordered by the physician. Suction equipment including catheters and oral suctioning tools should be attached and functioning.

When assisting with intubation for a pediatric patient, the clinician must gather and prepare the necessary equipment. This can include correctly sized laryngoscopes and endotracheal tubes, suction equipment, resuscitation bag and mask, oxygen source, 10ml syringe, and stylet. The clinician must assemble the laryngoscope and ensure that the light is functioning. If not, the batteries must be replaced, or the clinician can replace the entire laryngoscope. An appropriately sized resuscitation mask must be gathered and attached to the resuscitation bag, and the bag must be attached to an adequate gas source with the oxygen set at 100% FiO_2. Suction equipment including catheters and oral suctioning tools should be attached and functioning. The 10 ml syringe is used for inflation of an endotracheal tube cuff; however, if the chosen endotracheal tube is cuffless, then the syringe is no longer necessary.

CO_2 verification after intubation can be performed using a CO_2 detector. These tools are often small pieces of plastic with litmus paper placed in a viewing window. They are attached to the endotracheal tube immediately after intubation, and the clinician provides the patient with several manual positive-pressure breaths via a resuscitation bag. When CO_2 passes through the system, the litmus paper changes color. This provides a visual clue to the clinician that the endotracheal tube is in the correct position because exhaled CO_2 is present in the system. Although these tools are very helpful in critical clinical situations, their use does not replace the need for a physical assessment of the patient including checking for equal bilateral breath sounds and a chest X-ray. CO_2 detectors can vary among manufacturers, so the clinician must refer to their facility's policy and procedure on their use and features.

Performing or Assisting Advanced Intubation Techniques

When intubating a patient, visualization of the glottis and vocal chords is necessary to pass the endotracheal tube through the airway. In some patients, visualization is reduced either due to structural defects, excess secretions, or other abnormalities. Clinicians can use various tools to help with visualization, including a traditional laryngoscope; however, some laryngoscopes are not able to provide adequate visualization for intubation. In these cases, some clinicians choose to attempt intubation with a straight laryngoscope blade rather than the traditional curved blade. The straight blade offers better visualization in some patients because straight blades often provide better tongue control and help to displace the epiglottis. Other clinicians use tools such as video laryngoscopes for the direct visualization of the airway. These pieces of equipment use either a camera or fiber-optic technology to directly inspect the patient's airway, depending on the model of video laryngoscope chosen.

Artificial Airways

Endotracheal Tube Including Securing and Positioning

When securing an endotracheal tube, the clinician should follow the facility's policy and procedure. The process of securing a tube varies among facilities. Endotracheal tubes can be secured by either using a tube holder or by using tape. Endotracheal tube holders are helpful in neonatal and pediatric populations, and clinicians should refer to the manufacturer's guidelines for the use of the tube holder. Tube holders vary among manufacturers, with many different styles to choose from. Generally speaking, endotracheal tube holders are often plastic grips that clamp onto the end of an endotracheal tube at the lip position. The holder is attached to a soft fabric strap that wraps around from behind the patient's neck to either side of the patient's face. Endotracheal tube holders are often associated with a lower incidence of skin breakdown than with the use of tape for securing endotracheal tubes.

When securing an endotracheal tube, the clinician should follow the facility's policy and procedure. The process of securing a tube varies among facilities. Endotracheal tubes can be secured by either using a tube holder or by using tape. Generally speaking, when using the behind-the-neck process for taping an endotracheal tube, the clinician feeds a long piece of tape behind the patient's neck, with both sides resting beside the patient's face. Both sides of the tape are each split partway down the length of the tape, so that one piece of the split goes across the patient's chin or lip and the other piece winds around the endotracheal tube, taking care to overlap the tape on the tube and not obstructing the view of the depth measurement. The same is true for the opposite piece of tape, but the process is reversed.

When securing an endotracheal tube, the clinician should follow the facility's policy and procedure. The process of securing a tube varies among facilities. Endotracheal tubes can be secured by either using a tube holder or by using tape. Generally speaking, when securing an endotracheal tube on a neonate, the clinician will use two small pieces of tape on the patient's face, without wrapping around the neck as in the adult population. The clinician then prepares two lengths of tape and trims them to fit. Both pieces of the tape are split partway down the length of the tape, so that one piece of the split goes across the patient's chin or lip and the other piece winds around the endotracheal tube, taking care to overlap the tape on the tube and not obstructing the view of the depth measurement. The same is true for the opposite piece of tape, but the process is reversed. In the neonatal population, skin protective barriers may be used under the tape to prevent skin breakdown.

After intubation, it is imperative that the healthcare team immediately confirm correct endotracheal tube placement. Incorrect placement is associated with serious adverse events such as hypoxia, hypoventilation, barotrauma, and death. Correct endotracheal tube placement is defined as the distal end of the tube sitting 5 cm above the patient's carina. The carina is the point at which the trachea bifurcates into the left and right mainstem bronchus. In neonatal patients, the criterion for correct endotracheal tube placement is different. The Neonatal Resuscitation Program states that the clinician should take the patient's weight in kilograms and add 6. The sum of these numbers is appropriate for the depth measurement for the endotracheal tube. In micropreemies (neonates weighing less than 1 lb), the correct tube placement is more difficult to predict. Correct endotracheal tube positioning can be confirmed by auscultating equal bilateral breath sounds, returned carbon dioxide in a CO_2 detector, and chest X-ray.

Newly Placed Tracheostomy Tubes

Tracheostomy tubes are artificial airways inserted through the skin and neck structures at the base of the neck via surgical incision. Tracheostomy tubes are used for patients who have long-term ventilatory needs as well as patients who have upper airway obstructions or other upper airway defects. Newly placed tracheostomy tubes require special care because these are fresh surgical sites in the neck with healing wounds. Caregivers and clinicians should refer to the instructions given by the physician, surgical team, and home-care team for tracheostomy care in a newly placed tracheostomy. Generally speaking, wound care will be a significant component of early tracheostomy care. This can include inspection and future removal of stitches and skin care techniques to keep the wound clean and dry. These wound care interventions will be performed in tandem with general tracheostomy care, including but not limited to suctioning, cleaning the tracheostomy components, and replacing them as needed.

Manage Specialty Gas Administration

Nitric Oxide

Nitric oxide (NO) is a gas used to treat pulmonary hypertension in patients with respiratory distress syndrome, congenital lung or heart defects, or persistent pulmonary hypertension of the newborn. The gas is commonly delivered via mechanical ventilator, and the patient is carefully monitored during therapy. NO dilates the pulmonary vasculature, allowing for better oxygen uptake. The goal of NO therapy is to improve the patient's oxygenation while lowering the patient's required FiO_2. Weaning off the NO can be attempted after a minimum of 48 hours; however, the process of using NO can vary among facilities. Side effects associated with the use of NO include methemoglobinemia and toxicity. NO is approved in patients of 35 weeks' gestation and older. NO may be used in younger patients in some cases, but the risk of hemorrhages in the brain increases in this population.

Helium-Oxygen

Heliox, a helium and oxygen blend, is a gas that is used to treat patients with respiratory distress and airway obstruction, either due to a disease process or congenital defect. Patients who benefit from heliox include those with asthma, reactive airway disease, and other obstructive airway diseases. Patients with severe bronchoconstriction benefit from heliox, because heliox is a lighter gas than plain oxygen. The heliox is delivered through the restricted airways, allowing for better oxygen saturation and reduction of respiratory distress. Patients who benefit from heliox often show improvement after a short period of time. Heliox can be delivered through a mechanical ventilator or via a mask. The heliox tank flowmeter is either attached to a mask via oxygen tubing or a mechanical ventilator and is used on a continuous basis until improvement in the patient's condition is noted. Heliox is appropriate for all patient ages, from neonates to adults.

Other Anesthetics

Isoflurane and sevoflurane are gases used for general anesthesia. Isoflurane and sevoflurane are administered via mask and are used for their anesthetic and muscle-relaxing effects. Adverse events associated with the use of isoflurane and sevoflurane include but are not limited to bronchospasm, respiratory depression, myocardial ischemia, respiratory failure, and death. Careful, continuous monitoring of the patient is necessary when using these anesthetic gases. Care should be taken when administering these drugs to patients with reactive airways, such as those with asthma or reactive airway disease because gases can be a trigger for bronchospasm in these sensitive patients. Bronchodilators may be needed when administering anesthetic gases to patients with reactive airways, and/or alternative anesthetics may be considered.

Subambient oxygen refers to the administration of oxygen at levels less than 21% (room air). Patients with congenital heart diseases may benefit from this unorthodox treatment because hyperoxia in cardiac-compromised patients can cause further adverse cardiac events such as tricuspid atresia, congestive heart failure, and hypoplastic left heart syndrome. Therefore, some patients with these conditions may require an FiO_2 that is lower than ambient air. This subambient air, at concentrations less than 21%, can help provide the patient with supplemental oxygen and support their oxygen needs while protecting their cardiovascular status. This is achieved by blending oxygen with nitrogen to get the desired FiO_2 using oxygen and nitrogen blenders in the critical care units of the hospital. Subambient oxygen equipment setup can vary among facilities depending on the equipment available, and clinicians should refer to their facility's policy and procedure for correct subambient oxygen delivery.

Manage Ventilation and Oxygenation

Selection of Initial Settings

Oxygen, classified as a drug by the US Food and Drug Administration, must have a physician's order to be administered. Once a physician's order is obtained, the clinician can begin to administer the drug. Oxygen can be administered via many different pieces of equipment including traditional nasal cannulas, high-flow nasal cannulas, oxygen masks of various types, mechanical ventilators, tracheostomy collars, face tents, croup tents, and other administration routes. Regardless of the route of administration, oxygen should be delivered at the lowest possible FiO_2 to maintain the patient's oxygen saturation. Patients who receive too much supplemental oxygen, especially those who are preterm, can suffer from serious adverse events including but not limited to cardiac insufficiency, oxygen toxicity, and retinopathy. Therefore, oxygen should be used with care, starting with the lowest possible FiO_2 and titrating as needed.

Initial ventilator settings can vary depending on the mode of mechanical ventilation chosen, the patient's condition and disease process, the patient's oxygenation and ventilatory needs, available equipment, and physician preference. Generally speaking, physicians will order ventilator settings at the patient's bedside. In pressure ventilation modes such as pressure control, the peak inspiratory pressure (PIP), rate, inspiratory (I) time, and FiO_2 are set. Often the I time for a neonatal patient is 0.3 to 0. 6 for rates up to 40 breaths per minute, whereas keeping the inspiratory to expiratory (I:E) ratio at 1:2 or 1:1 depending on the patient's compliance and ventilatory needs. A 1:1 I:E ratio might be required for patients with poor lung compliance such as those with respiratory distress syndrome. PIP is usually set between 15 to 20 cmH_2O and can be titrated as needed. For spontaneous pressure ventilation modes such as CPAP, only the pressure value and FiO_2 are set. In volume ventilation modes, such as synchronized intermittent mandatory ventilation (SIMV), the tidal volume, FiO_2, rate, and PEEP (if applicable) are set. Tidal volumes for neonates are often 5–10 ml/kg, whereas tidal volumes for preterm neonates are closer to 4–6 ml/kg. Respiratory rates are often set at between 30 and 60 breaths per minute for neonates.

Initial ventilator settings can vary depending on the mode of mechanical ventilation chosen, the patient's condition and disease process, the patient's oxygenation and ventilatory needs, available equipment, and physician preference. Generally speaking, physicians will order ventilator settings at the patient's bedside. In pressure ventilation modes such as the pressure control, PIP, rate, I time, and FiO_2 are set. Often, the I time for a pediatric patient is approximately 0.5 to 1 second. PIP settings for pediatric patients can range from 18 to 35 cmH_2O depending on the patient's compliance and ventilatory needs. The I:E ratio should be maintained at 1:2 or 1:1 depending on the patient's compliance and ventilatory needs. A 1:1 I:E ratio might be required for patients with poor lung compliance such as those with respiratory distress syndrome. For spontaneous pressure ventilation modes such as CPAP, only a pressure value and FiO_2 are set. In volume ventilation modes, such as SIMV, the tidal volume, FiO_2, rate, and PEEP (if applicable) are set. Tidal volumes for neonates are often 10 ml/kg. Respiratory rates are often set at between 15 and 30 breaths per minute for pediatric patients.

Conventional Modes

Modes of mechanical ventilation can vary between facilities depending on the types of ventilators used and their available modes. Generally speaking, there are two main types of ventilation including pressure ventilation and volume ventilation. Pressure ventilation refers to ventilator modes that have a set pressure and varying tidal volumes. Volume ventilation refers to ventilator modes that have a set tidal volume but varying pressures. Often, neonates are placed on pressure-limiting ventilation modes to prevent barotrauma in immature lungs. Older children may benefit from volume-control ventilation. These types of mechanical ventilation are further broken down into modes. There are two main types of mechanical ventilation modes, including spontaneous modes and nonspontaneous modes. A spontaneous mode is a mode in which the patient is able to take breaths as needed at varying tidal volumes. Nonspontaneous modes are modes in which the patient is only receiving machine-delivered breaths at a set rate and predetermined pressure or tidal volume.

Traditional mechanical ventilation includes volume ventilation and pressure ventilation. Volume ventilation modes include but are not limited to SIMV and assist control. These modes deliver a set tidal volume with varying airway pressures. Pressure ventilation modes include but are not limited to CPAP and pressure control. These modes deliver a set pressure with varying tidal volumes. It is important to note that there are numerous modes of ventilation available today, and the modes vary depending on the equipment used. Not all ventilators offer the same modes, and new modes are developing rapidly in the healthcare marketplace. It is important to follow your facility's policy and procedure for volume and pressure ventilation depending on the ventilator available at your location. Generally speaking, the more common types of mechanical ventilation modes in the neonatal and pediatric population include SIMV, CPAP, and pressure control.

Modes of ventilation vary among equipment manufacturers. Some common spontaneous modes of ventilation in the pediatric and neonatal population include SIMV with or without pressure support and CPAP. SIMV is a mode in which a set tidal volume and rate are set but the patient is able to take additional spontaneous breaths in addition to the set rate. The patient's spontaneous breaths are delivered at varying tidal volumes determined by the patient. This mode ensures a constant minute volume while offering flexibility for patients who require additional spontaneous breaths above the set rate. SIMV can be used with or without pressure support. Pressure support is an additional setting in which a set pressure is delivered during spontaneous breaths. This helps to reduce the patient's work of breathing when triggering spontaneous breaths while on the ventilator. SIMV is often used for patients who are conscious or being weaned from sedation. Volume ventilation such as SIMV is less common in the neonatal population because these patients are particularly susceptible to barotrauma. Therefore, pressure control ventilation is more common in the neonatal population.

Modes of ventilation vary among equipment manufacturers. Some common spontaneous modes of ventilation in the pediatric and neonatal population include SIMV with or without pressure support and CPAP. CPAP is a spontaneous mode used in patients who are conscious and not sedated. The patient must be alert to trigger breaths. This mode does not deliver any breaths, pressure, or volume until the patient triggers the machine. Therefore, care must be taken to ensure that the patient is clinically ready for CPAP initiation. CPAP can be used as ventilatory support or as a weaning mode. Some patients move from SIMV to CPAP prior to extubation. In CPAP mode, a set pressure is delivered during each spontaneous breath. Similar to pressure support, CPAP mode often results in less work of breathing because the extra pressure offers the patient support during spontaneous breaths.

Modes of ventilation vary among equipment manufacturers. A common mode of ventilation, especially in the neonatal population, is pressure-control ventilation. In this mode, a set pressure and rate are delivered to the patient, with varying tidal volumes. This mode prevents barotrauma in compromised patients such as those who are preterm. The tidal volume in pressure-control ventilation depends upon the set PIP. In order to change a patient's minute ventilation, the clinician must titrate the PIP or rate. Changes to the PIP should be limited because increased PIPs can cause barotrauma in some cases. These changes are often ordered by a physician depending on the patient's overall condition and respiratory status. In addition, some ventilators may offer pressure control with a "volume guarantee" or volume-regulated pressure control. In these modes, the patient receives a set pressure as well as a set volume.

Assist control mode is a volume-cycled mode of mechanical ventilation in which a set respiratory rate, FIO_2, and tidal volume are delivered, with varying airway pressures. The difference between the SIMV and assist control modes lies in the ability of the patient to trigger breaths. The patient may trigger spontaneous breaths in both modes, but the breaths in the assist control mode are delivered at the set tidal volume with no variance. In SIMV, the patient may trigger a breath that delivers a tidal volume determined by the patient. Assist control should be used with care in patients who trigger many spontaneous breaths. These patients may hyperventilate, or their lungs may hyperinflate due to the larger tidal volumes delivered with each additional breath delivered over the set rate. This can increase the minute volume and cause respiratory alkalosis.

Review Video: Mechanical Ventilators
Visit mometrix.com/academy and enter code: 679637

High-Frequency Ventilation

High-frequency oscillatory ventilation (HFOV) and high-frequency jet ventilation (HFJV) are very similar modes of mechanical ventilation. Both use small tidal volumes and high rates to ventilate compromised patients, such as those with respiratory distress syndrome. The differences between these modes of ventilation lie in the delivery of the breaths and the mechanics of the ventilator. HFJVs are used in addition to traditional mechanical ventilators. The ventilators are connected via the endotracheal tube because a special port is attached to the tube, allowing for both ventilators to ventilate simultaneously. PEEP is provided by the mechanical ventilator, and the tidal volumes and rate are delivered by the jet ventilator. In HFOV, only the oscillator ventilator is used to support the patient's respiratory needs. The HFOV provides the tidal volume and rate to the patient, and it initiates the inspiration and expiration. In HFJV, only inspiration is initiated by the ventilator.

In HFJV, the initial ventilator settings vary depending on the patient's condition, the available equipment, and the facility's policy and procedures. Clinicians should follow their facility's policy and procedure for selecting initial ventilator settings. Generally speaking, jet ventilation requires two ventilators, including a jet ventilator and a traditional mechanical ventilator. For the jet ventilator, an I time value is set and titrated as needed to support the patient's ventilatory needs. Additionally, the clinician will need to set the rate in hertz or breaths per minute, depending on the equipment used. The clinician will also set the I time, while monitoring the I:E ratio for changes and maintaining an appropriate ratio value. For the mechanical ventilator, depending on the mode chosen, the clinician will set the PEEP, PIP, and FIO_2. The clinician may also set sigh breaths as needed to help with alveolar recruitment.

The goals of high-frequency ventilation, either via oscillation or jet, include alveolar recruitment, improvements in oxygenation, and increased functional residual capacity. These goals are met by delivering small tidal volumes at high rates to the diseased or compromised lung. Patients with poor compliance are more likely to benefit from this unique style of mechanical ventilation. Although there are many benefits associated with high-frequency ventilation, there are several risks associated with its use. Some adverse events associated with high-frequency ventilation include but are not limited to overinflation of the lungs, intraventricular hemorrhage and other cerebral bleeds, hyperventilation, tracheal inflammation, infection, and barotrauma. To prevent ventilator-associated pneumonia, clinicians should not change the ventilator circuits unless they are soiled and the humidifiers used with mechanical ventilation should be optimized to reduce any condensation in the ventilator circuit.

High-frequency oscillatory ventilation (HFOV) is a mode of ventilation in which low tidal volumes and high respiratory rates are used to ventilate patients with severe lung disease. This is not a conventional form of ventilation and is used only in very serious cases. HFOV is associated with less barotrauma than traditional mechanical ventilators due to the very small tidal volumes delivered. Clinicians will set the frequency in hertz, mean airway pressure (MAP), and amplitude (delta P). The MAP can be titrated to improve oxygenation and alveolar recruitment. Often, the MAP needs to be increased in these cases until lung compliance improves. Overinflation of the lungs is a possible adverse event associated with HFOV use. This condition can be evaluated by ordering periodic chest X-rays, including one radiograph up to two hours post initiation of ventilation.

If a patient has increasing CO_2 levels, the delta P can be titrated to keep the PCO_2 at approximately 40–50 mm Hg. (This range can vary and may change depending on the patient's condition and the physician's preference.) An increase in delta P or a decrease in frequency will causes the patient's CO_2 to fall. It is important to note that changing one setting on a HFOV will inevitably change all other settings. There is a careful balance between settings, and each setting interacts with the others. Therefore, care must be taken to ensure that all settings are checked and titrated appropriately after any ventilator setting change. The oxygen saturation must be carefully monitored in patients receiving HFOV. If a decrease in saturation is noted, the clinician can adjust the MAP and/or FiO_2; however, maintaining low FiO_2s is preferable. The MAP is often initially set at 8–12 mm Hg depending on the compliance of the lungs and the disease process of the patient.

Alternative Modes

In volume-targeted mechanical ventilation, patients receive a set peak inspiratory pressure as well as a consistent tidal volume. The mechanics and settings of this mode of ventilation depend upon the equipment being used because different ventilators offer different versions of this mode. Clinicians should follow their facility's policy and procedure as well as the manufacturer's guidelines for their particular machine and available volume-targeted mode of ventilation. Generally speaking, the clinician will set the peak inspiratory pressure (PIP), FiO_2, rate, and target tidal volume. Sometimes the PIP will vary slightly from the set pressure in order to deliver the targeted tidal volume. The set PIP is the highest pressure that will be delivered to the patient. The pressure may drop as needed to ensure that the target tidal volume is delivered. This mode is helpful because it allows patients to control some of their ventilatory needs while offering lung protection from barotrauma.

Airway pressure release ventilation (APRV) is a mode of mechanical ventilation characterized by inverse I:E ratios. In this mode, the pressures are preset while the delivered tidal volumes vary. A set rate is delivered, and the patient may also take additional spontaneous breaths as needed. Patients breathe "between" two set pressures, including a high- and a low-pressure setting, with time cycling the ventilator. The name of the APRV mode can vary among ventilator models and manufacturers, and it may be called other names such as BiVent. Clinicians must be familiar with their facility's APRV availability because not all ventilators offer this mode of ventilation. The APRV mode is commonly used in patients with respiratory distress syndrome and subsequent hypoxemia. Possible adverse events associated with this mode of ventilation include increased work of breathing and hyperinflation due to excessive delivered volumes and subsequent trauma to the lungs.

NAVA refers to neutrally adjusted ventilatory assist, which is a mode in mechanical ventilation. This mode is not common and may not be available in all facilities or on all ventilators. Ventilation modes vary among ventilator manufacturers. In NAVA mode, the patient's diaphragmatic activity is monitored via the mechanical ventilator, allowing the clinician to assess the patient's respiratory muscle strength and respiratory effort. This can also indicate the level of work of breathing that a patient might be experiencing. Using NAVA can help prevent patient-ventilator asynchrony, which in turn improves a patient's sleep, respiratory status, and comfort level. When using NAVA, a patient's delivered ventilation depends upon the electrical activity in the patient's diaphragm. When there is more activity in the diaphragm, the ventilator delivers less ventilatory support. This mode of ventilation can help to prevent overdistension of the lungs and subsequent barotrauma. This mode is not always useful, however, because some patients have impaired neurological function due to injury or sedation, which can cause the electrical activity measurement of the diaphragm to be inaccurate.

When using the NAVA mode of ventilation, the electrical diaphragmatic activity (Edi) is measured via a catheter that is inserted to a predetermined depth via either the nose or mouth. The catheter comes in various sizes, and the correct size is determined by the patient's weight and height. Next, the clinician must determine the depth at which to place the catheter. This process may vary among manufacturers. Generally speaking, the clinician determines the insertion depth by first measuring from the nare to the ear and adding the distance of the ear to the xiphoid process. This sum is known as the NEX calculation. The clinician then uses the NEX value to calculate the insertion depth using a chart based on the size of the catheter and route of administration (oral or nasal). Use the chart included in your equipment setup to calculate the catheter's insertion depth.

When inserting a NAVA catheter, the clinician must first ensure that the correct size catheter has been chosen. Then the clinician should moisten the end of the catheter with sterile water. No lubricants should be used on NAVA catheters. Insert the catheter into the patient's nare or mouth to the predetermined depth, and secure it in accordance with your facility's policy and procedure. The catheter then needs to be evaluated for correct positioning. This is achieved by ensuring that the Edi catheter waveforms are uniform. If the waveforms show deflections, the catheter may need to be repositioned and reevaluated. The clinician must reevaluate and confirm the position of the catheter periodically as needed to ensure an adequate waveform. The patient's ventilation depends upon the Edi catheter's ability to properly register the patient's diaphragmatic electrical activity.

When applying NAVA ventilator settings, the clinician must first set an initial NAVA level. NAVA ventilation settings can vary among manufacturers, so it is important for clinicians to refer to their facility's policy and procedure for NAVA setup. Generally speaking, a clinician will start with a NAVA setting of 1 cm H_2O/ μV and titrate as needed. A predetermined FiO_2 will also be dialed into the ventilator and will be titrated to maintain oxygen saturation. The Edi max or Edi peak should read between 5 and 15μV depending on the patient's condition. NAVA can be titrated by 0.1 or 0.2 cm H_2O/ μV if required. Apnea time may be set at 5 seconds or less, depending on the patient's respiratory status. The Edi min setting is commonly set to less than 3 cm H_2O/ μV, but this can vary among patients. PEEP can be set if needed, and the Edi trigger starts at 0.5 cm H_2O/ μV, but it can be titrated if needed.

Noninvasive Ventilation

CPAP is a therapy modality in which constant pressure and FiO_2 are delivered to the patient's airway via a mask or nasal prongs. This intervention helps to decrease the work of breathing, increase oxygenation, and provide respiratory support for compromised patients. Neonates born preterm (prior to 36 weeks) often have immature lungs that require additional respiratory support. Nasal CPAP is commonly used in preterm neonates with respiratory distress syndrome, airway obstructions, apnea of prematurity, and other respiratory conditions. It can also be used in pediatric patients with respiratory disorders such as obstructive sleep apnea. CPAP is only used in spontaneously breathing patients because this is a spontaneous mode of ventilation and no tidal volume breaths will be delivered to the patient. Patients may require CPAP constantly or intermittently depending on their condition and underlying disease process. In disorders such as obstructive sleep apnea, CPAP is used only during sleep, whereas other disorders such as respiratory distress syndrome often require constant use of CPAP.

CPAP delivery options can vary depending on the facility and the available equipment. Clinicians should refer to their facility's policy and procedure for the use of CPAP in their neonatal and pediatric populations. One option for CPAP delivery is a bubble CPAP setup. This setup can also vary among manufacturers, but it generally includes an oxygen flowmeter, heated humidifier, oxygen analyzer, nasal prongs, pressure gauge, respiratory circuit, and water canister. The water canister is filled with water, and the expiratory limb of the breathing circuit is inserted into the canister. The flowmeter is set at a predetermined flow rate and turned on. The pressure gauge will read the level of CPAP delivered by measuring the back pressure created by submerging the expiratory limb into the water canister. The nasal prongs (previously evaluated for correct sizing according to the manufacturer's guidelines) are then inserted into the patient's nares and secured in accordance with the facility's policy and procedure.

CPAP delivery options can vary depending on the facility and the available equipment. Clinicians should refer to their facility's policy and procedure for the use of CPAP in their neonatal and pediatric populations. One option for CPAP delivery is a traditional nasal CPAP setup. This setup can also vary among manufacturers, but it generally includes an oxygen flowmeter, heated humidifier, oxygen analyzer, nasal prongs, pressure line, respiratory circuit, and hat or other device for securing the prongs on the patient. The circuit is attached to the CPAP machine, flow meter, and humidifier in accordance with the manufacturer's guidelines. The patient is measured for the correct size nasal prongs and cap. Nasal prongs should not be large enough to distend the patient's nares. This can cause tissue breakdown and future deformities. The ordered CPAP level is dialed into the machine and tested for accuracy. The nasal prongs are then inserted into the patient's nares and secured in accordance with your facility's policy and procedure.

Bilevel ventilation, also known as BIPAP, is a spontaneous mode of ventilation in which the patient breathes "between" two set pressures. These pressures are known as inspiratory positive airway pressure (IPAP) and expiratory positive airway pressure (EPAP) or PEEP low and PEEP high. The clinician dials in a predetermined IPAP and EPAP level, and the patient breathes between those levels. In other words, the patient's airway pressure will never drop below the PEEP, and the patient will always receive the IPAP level of pressure during spontaneous breaths. The BIPAP machine delivers a "boost" of IPAP with every breath. This intervention improves alveolar recruitment, reduces hypercapnia, and treats impending respiratory failure. Bilevel ventilation can be used in patients who are both conscious and unconscious because a mandatory rate can be dialed in if needed. The pressure is delivered to the airway either via a full face mask, nasal mask, or sometimes nasal prongs.

Adjunct Techniques

Lung Recruitment Maneuvers

Lung recruitment maneuvers are therapeutic interventions in which a clinician attempts to open the patient's alveoli and expand the lungs using various techniques. This intervention is currently being studied to determine its efficacy and safety in the pediatric and neonatal populations, although many clinicians have found that patients respond positively to this therapy. Some patients who might benefit from lung recruitment include those who have respiratory distress syndrome. Lung recruitment maneuvers can be performed in different ways and varies among facilities. Clinicians should follow their facility's policy and procedure for lung recruitment. One common recruitment maneuver involves increasing PIP and PEEP for short periods of time, attempting to "pop open" the patient's alveoli and recruit lung tissue. Lung recruitment maneuvers are associated with some adverse events including barotrauma and respiratory distress; however, in some very severe respiratory cases, the potential benefits outweigh the risks.

Prone Positioning

Patients with respiratory distress syndrome often have areas of lung consolidation and atelectasis. In some severe cases, prone positioning of the patient can be helpful. This position can help to reduce atelectasis in the posterior areas of the lung lobes and recruit alveoli in these areas. This can improve oxygenation and respiratory status while decreasing the work of breathing. The act of positioning the patient prone reduces the pressure forces on the lungs from the weight of the abdomen, helping to recruit more lung tissue. Some studies also indicate that prone positioning can help to mobilize airway secretions in some cases. The goals of prone positioning are lung recruitment, reduction in atelectasis, and improved oxygenation. Prone positioning should be avoided or used with care in patients with facial injuries, cardiovascular insufficiency, and abdominal injury or surgery. Some patients in the prone position may experience edema and changes in blood pressure.

Extracorporeal Life Support

In extracorporeal membrane oxygenation (ECMO), a machine provides oxygenation and perfusion to the patient while bypassing the heart and lungs. The patient is placed on the patient, where their blood is circulated into the machine. The machine then sends the blood through a specialized membrane that provides oxygen and removes carbon dioxide from the blood. The blood is then warmed and circulated back into the patient's body via a port. ECMO can be delivered either arterially or venously. In venovenous ECMO, the patient's blood is circulated into and out of the machine via a catheter in the right atrium. Only patients without cardiovascular compromise can use this version of ECMO. Conversely, venoarterial ECMO, the patient's blood is circulated into the machine via a catheter in the right jugular artery. This catheter removes blood from the patient's right atrium and returns it to the body through a catheter in the right carotid artery.

When using ECMO therapy, the patient's blood is circulated through a machine that oxygenates the patient's blood while removing carbon dioxide (CO_2). Patients can remain on mechanical ventilation during ECMO, but the settings may change slightly depending on the patient's condition and response to ECMO treatment. Often, ventilatory support is decreased over time, but set PEEP levels may be increased to maintain alveolar recruitment. Arterial blood gas testing is performed periodically to ensure an adequate acid–base balance, including measurements of CO_2 in the patient's blood. This information helps the clinician to determine if CO_2 is being successfully removed from the blood during ECMO. Carbon dioxide must be kept at appropriate levels to avoid either blood acidosis or alkalosis from too much or too little CO_2 in the blood.

Patients who are using ECMO must be monitored carefully for coagulation because this can interrupt ECMO service and cause injury to the patient. Anticoagulation policies in the use of ECMO can vary among facilities. Clinicians should refer to their facility's policy and procedure for anticoagulation therapy in patients using ECMO. In many facilities, heparin is used for anticoagulation therapy in ECMO patients. Heparin dosage varies among patients, and some patients require additional anticoagulation medications on an as-needed basis. When using heparin and other anticoagulation medications, clinicians should measure the patient's activated clotting time periodically to ensure adequate but not excessive anticoagulation levels while the patient is using ECMO. Patients may require infusions of packed red blood cells or plasma during ECMO treatment. Anticoagulation and blood transfusion needs vary depending on the patients' condition, and therefore the patient should be monitored very carefully and consistently during ECMO therapy.

Only select patients are good candidates for ECMO because this therapeutic intervention is associated with several potentially serious risks. The requirements for ECMO patients can vary among facilities. Generally speaking, ECMO is indicated in patients who are not responding to traditional treatment, and those who have a high incidence of death associated with their condition. These patients are often more than 34 weeks of gestational age or older, and their disease process and condition are expected to be resolved with treatment. In addition, the patient should have been mechanically ventilated for a relatively short period of time and have an adequate body weight (a minimum of 2 kg). Patients also often require several preoperative tests (ECMO is considered an invasive procedure due to placement of catheters by surgeons). These tests vary depending on the patient's condition but may include chest X-rays, blood draws for metabolic panels and complete blood counts, arterial blood gas puncture, echocardiograms, and other diagnostic tests.

When using ECMO, patients are carefully monitored for cardiovascular, respiratory, and neurological status. Patients often undergo frequent, periodic arterial blood gas draws to ensure an adequate acid–base status as well as adequate oxygenation, saturation, and blood pressure. Patients may also undergo blood draws for a complete blood count and/or metabolic panel as well as anticoagulation studies to ensure that their clotting factors are adequate for ECMO usage. Patients with ECMO may require blood transfusions as needed, and this decision is partly based on the patient's blood test results. The patient's hemodynamics are also carefully and consistently monitored to ensure the patient's safety while using ECMO. Pain levels are monitored and evaluated continuously, and sedation levels are titrated as needed for patient comfort. Patients are on ECMO for only a short period of time, often for several days.

ECMO is a therapeutic intervention that is associated with many potentially serious risks and adverse events. Some adverse events associated with ECMO can include but are not limited to cardiac arrhythmias, various organ failure, infection, equipment failure, air embolism, blood clotting, edema, bloodborne pathogen exposure (however, this is a very rare event due to meticulous blood processing procedures in the hospital setting), neurological dysfunction including stroke, and hemorrhaging in the brain, lungs, abdominal organs, or other organ systems. The risk of bleeding is associated with the use of heparin and other anticoagulation agents that are required to prevent clotting of the blood in the ECMO machine circuitry. Despite the many risks involved with the implementation of ECMO, this intervention is a life-saving intervention for many patients with severe cardiac or respiratory insufficiencies and disorders. Often, the benefits outweigh the risks.

Monitoring

Measures of Lung Disease Severity

The PaO_2/FiO_2 ratio shows the relationship between the partial pressure of arterial oxygen content to the fraction of inspired oxygen. A patient's PaO_2/FiO_2 ratio is measured via arterial blood gas analysis, in which a blood sample is evaluated to determine the levels of oxygen, carbon dioxide, pH, and other respiratory status indicators. A normal PaO_2/FiO_2 ratio is 300–500. A reduced PaO_2/FiO_2 ratio is consistent with gas exchange impairment and shunting such as in cases of sepsis, lung injury, respiratory distress syndrome, and other respiratory compromised patients. The ratio can be used to determine the level of severity of lung injury or disease because a lower ratio is associated with hypoxemia, respiratory distress or failure, and poor patient outcomes. The clinician's goal is to support the patient's respiratory needs while striving for a normal PaO_2/FiO_2 ratio.

The SaO_2/FiO_2 ratio shows the relationship between the oxygen saturation in the patient's blood and the current fraction of inspired oxygen used. In other words, the SaO_2/FiO_2 ratio compares the patient's oxygen saturation to the amount of oxygen being delivered to the patient via nasal cannula, mechanical ventilator, or other oxygen delivery equipment. A reduced SaO_2/FiO_2 ratio indicates gas exchange impairment and shunting, such as in cases of sepsis, lung injury, respiratory distress syndrome, and other respiratory-compromised patients. The ratio can be used to determine the level of severity of lung injury or disease because a lower ratio is associated with hypoxemia, respiratory distress or failure, and poor patient outcomes. The clinician's goal is to support the patient's respiratory needs while striving for a normal SaO_2/FiO_2 ratio.

OI, or oxygen index, is the result of the following equation: $OI = MAP \times FiO_2 \times 100 / PaO_2$, where MAP refers to the mean airway pressure, FiO_2 refers to the fraction of inspired oxygen delivered to the patient via oxygen-delivery devices, and PaO_2 refers to the arterial oxygen content in the patient's blood. This equation determines the patient's oxygen index, or the ventilatory support that is required for adequate oxygenation. The higher the ratio, the higher the level of ventilatory support that is needed. An increased OI is associated with lung diseases such as respiratory distress syndrome, persistent pulmonary hypertension of the newborn, and other respiratory disorders. A very high OI can be indicative of a need for ECMO because these patients are often unable to adequately oxygenate on standard mechanical ventilation. An OI of 40 or higher can indicate a need for ECMO intervention.

Airway Pressures and Volumes

A patient's mean airway pressure (MAP) is directly related to the patient's oxygen saturation, PaO_2, and I:E ratio. Adequate MAPs are associated with better oxygenation and less atelectasis in the lungs; however, excessive MAPs can cause adverse events such as barotrauma, air trapping, pneumothorax, overdistension, and overinflation. Therefore, the MAP should be minimized and titrated accordingly while maintaining oxygenation. A drop-in oxygen saturation may indicate a reduced MAP on a mechanically ventilated patient. The MAP can be manipulated during conventional mechanical ventilation by altering the patient's delivered I time. In high-frequency oscillatory ventilation, the MAP is manipulated by directly changing the MAP value on the ventilator.

Minute ventilation is defined as the volume of air and oxygen delivered to the patient during one minute of respiration. A patient's minute ventilation is directly related to the levels of CO_2 in his or her blood and the acid–base balance. Increased minute ventilation is associated with hyperventilation and subsequent hypercapnia, whereas decreased minute ventilation is associated with hypoventilation and subsequent hypocapnia. A patient's minute ventilation is often calculated automatically by a mechanical ventilator; however, the clinician may calculate this value manually by multiplying the patient's tidal volume by the patient's respiratory rate. The minute ventilation must be adequate to ensure oxygenation and adequate CO_2 removal. The minute ventilation may be manipulated on mechanically ventilated patients by titrating the set tidal volume and/or respiratory rate. If a clinician needs to optimize the patient's oxygenation, it is often more beneficial to change the patient's tidal volume because this allows for more gas exchange than simply increasing the rate. This effect is due to anatomical dead space, which is the volume of air that does not reach the alveoli in each breath. Increasing the tidal volume can help to improve oxygenation by increasing the amount of air that reaches the alveoli after the anatomical dead space is fulfilled.

Ventilator Waveforms

The purpose of a neutrally adjusted ventilatory assist (NAVA) catheter is to measure the patient's diaphragmatic electrical activity so that ventilation can take place. NAVA is a mode of ventilation available on specialized mechanical ventilators. The NAVA catheter (also called an Edi catheter) is placed according to the facility's policies and procedures, and then the waveforms are inspected on the corresponding monitor. The waveforms should be uniform with a consistent pattern. If the waveforms show deflections, the catheter position will need to be evaluated. The catheter may need to be repositioned to ensure a consistent waveform pattern because the patient's ventilation depends upon the catheter's ability to properly register. When functioning correctly, the NAVA catheter's corresponding waveforms will help the clinician to adequately ventilate the patient as well as facilitate weaning from the mechanical ventilator.

Ventilator–Patient Interaction

Ventilator synchrony is an issue that affects all patients on mechanical ventilation. Ventilator synchrony is defined as a harmonious relationship between the patient and the mechanical ventilator. In other words, in ventilator synchrony, a patient is able to obtain respiratory support from the ventilator without "fighting" the ventilator or its settings. Conversely, ventilator asynchrony is a situation in which the ventilator is not supporting the patient's respiratory needs either due to problems with the rate, tidal volume, or mode of ventilation. In these cases, the patient may be seen coughing, triggering extra breaths, and breath stacking and there may be inadequate flow and inadequate breath triggering. Many ventilator settings, adverse events, and underlying disease processes can contribute to ventilator asynchrony; therefore, a full assessment must be performed on patients who are unable to be adequately and comfortably mechanically ventilated.

During ventilator asynchrony, the ventilator is not supporting the patient's respiratory needs either due to problems with the rate, tidal volume, flow, mode of ventilation, or other factors. Patients with ventilator asynchrony are often agitated and anxious, air hungry, and coughing due to fighting the ventilator. During ventilator asynchrony, the clinician must first examine the patient to determine if there is an underlying health condition causing ventilator asynchrony such as changes in lung compliance or resistance, airway obstruction, need for suctioning, and other clinical conditions. The clinician should also check the sedation level of the patient and titrate the dose of sedatives as needed to ensure patient comfort. Ventilator changes, such as changing the sensitivity, flow rate, tidal volume, rate, or mode, can be helpful in the mitigation of ventilator asynchrony. The patient's condition and type of asynchrony (for example, flow, triggering, or effort asynchrony) will determine the changes that are needed in the mechanical ventilator settings.

Ventilator asynchrony, the act of fighting or breathing out of sync with the mechanical ventilator, is associated with an increased incidence of adverse events and poor patient outcomes. Common adverse events associated with ventilator asynchrony can include but are not limited to hypoxia, hypoventilation or hyperventilation, barotrauma, increased length of stay in the hospital, extra unanticipated time intubated on the mechanical ventilator, increased mortality rate, poor weaning outcomes, and poor sleep. All of these conditions can adversely affect a patient's overall health and well-being. Some studies indicate that ventilator asynchrony can have adverse effects on the patients' respiratory system and respiratory muscles, causing future episodes of ventilator asynchrony. Careful titration of ventilator settings as well as treatment of underlying health conditions are essential components in minimizing and mitigating ventilator asynchrony in all patient populations. Ventilator asynchrony can affect patients of all ages.

Pulmonary Mechanics

Lung compliance is defined as the stiffness of the patient's lungs. In other words, lung compliance refers to the amount of effort it takes to expand the patient's lungs during respiration. Lungs with poor compliance are stiff and difficult to expand. Similar to a balloon that is difficult to blow up until you stretch it first, lungs with poor compliance may require recruitment maneuvers that help to "pop open" the alveoli and make the lungs less stiff. Then, the patient's compliance improves. Poor lung compliance can be the result of underlying lung disease or injury such as respiratory distress syndrome, blunt trauma, and other airway disorders. These patients may present with increased work of breathing such as grunting, nasal flaring, and intercostal or subcostal retractions. These actions are a patient's subconscious efforts to improve lung compliance and reduce the work of breathing.

A mechanically ventilated patient's lung compliance, or lung stiffness, is directly related to their ventilator settings. Ventilator settings are often dependent on the patient's lung compliance, and clinicians must titrate settings as needed to adequately ventilate the patient. Compliance can change rapidly, and clinicians must be prepared to make additional changes to the ventilator at that time. When a patient's lung compliance changes, the patient's values on the ventilator and the patient's physical symptoms will change. For example, ventilator settings such as plateau pressure will rise or fall depending on the patient's compliance. Patients may show signs of improved oxygenation and decreased work of breathing when their compliance improves and may show symptoms of dyspnea and respiratory distress when their compliance drops. Some patients with poor lung compliance that is not responsive to traditional treatment may require specialized ventilatory support such as high-frequency oscillatory ventilation.

Lung resistance can be defined as the narrowing of the airways and disruption of laminar flow through the patient's bronchioles. In lungs with increased airway resistance, the patient has a difficult time inhaling an adequate volume of air due to reduced flow through the bronchioles. The airflow is disturbed in these narrowed airways, which can be best described as breathing through a straw. More respiratory effort is required of these patients, who often have underlying health conditions such as asthma, reactive airway disease, airway obstruction, and other airway disorders. These patients may present with increased work of breathing such as grunting, nasal flaring, and intercostal or subcostal retractions. These actions are a patient's subconscious efforts to reduce lung resistance and reduce their work of breathing. Pursed-lip breathing can also be helpful for these patients because this action slows the breathing process and helps to deliver small amounts of PEEP to the affected airways.

A mechanically ventilated patient's lung resistance, airway narrowing, is directly related to their ventilator settings. Ventilator settings are often dependent on the patient's lung resistance, and clinicians must titrate the settings as needed to adequately ventilate the patient. Resistance can change rapidly, either due to medication delivery such as bronchodilators or to improvement in the patient's lung disease. Clinicians must be prepared to make additional changes to the ventilator as needed depending on the patient's airway resistance. When a patient's lung resistance changes, the patient's values on the ventilator and the patient's physical symptoms will change. For example, ventilator settings such as PIP will rise or fall depending on the patient's resistance. Patients may show signs of improved oxygenation and decreased work of breathing when their resistance drops and may show symptoms of dyspnea and respiratory distress when their resistance rises.

The patient's lung compliance (the stiffness of the lungs) and the patient's airway resistance (the interruption of laminar flow through the airways) can cause adverse effects and poor patient outcomes if not treated. Mechanically ventilated patients with poor lung compliance and airway resistance may have increased work of breathing, dyspnea, symptoms of respiratory distress (grunting, flaring, retractions), hypoxia, desaturation, and respiratory failure. Mechanically ventilated patients may present with ventilator asynchrony, in which the patient fights the ventilator or is out of sync with the ventilator's delivered settings. Patients with increased airway resistance such as those with asthma or reactive airway disease may present with air trapping, breath stacking, and asynchrony on a mechanical ventilator. These effects can be dangerous and are associated with poor patient outcomes. Treatment such as bronchodilator therapy can be useful in reversing bronchospasm and relieving increased airway resistance in these patients.

The VD/VT ratio is defined as the comparison of dead space to tidal volume. A normal VD/VT ratio is between 0.28 and 0.33, or 150 ml of dead space to 500 ml of tidal volume. The patient's VD/VT ratio can be determined by the following equation:

Discuss $PaCO_2 - PeCO_2 / PaCO_2 = VD/VT$.

A patient's VD/VT ratio can go up or down depending on the patient's current dead space and tidal volume. For example, if the patient's dead space increases, the ratio will go up. Similarly, if the patient's tidal volume goes down, the ratio will increase. Both of these events can cause the patient's VD/VT ratio to increase, resulting in decreased ventilation and poor patient outcomes. Therefore, the clinician must pay careful attention to the patient's VD/VT ratio to ensure adequate oxygenation and CO_2 removal during respiration. Mechanical ventilator settings may need to be altered to fully support a patient with a poor VD/VT ratio.

Describe the significance of a patient's VD/VT ratio.

A patient's VD/VT ratio, or the comparison of dead space to tidal volume, is directly related to the adequacy of a patient's ventilation. A patient's dead space is the volume of air in each breath that does not reach the alveoli for oxygenation. A patient's tidal volume is the amount of air inspired during respiration. A high VD/VT ratio indicates a reduction in oxygenation and CO_2 removal. This inadequate ventilation can cause adverse effects and poor patient outcomes. High VD/VT ratios result in increased levels of carbon dioxide in the blood and reduced oxygenation. This disrupts a patient's acid–base balance, as determined by arterial blood gas analysis. Mechanical ventilator settings may require adjustment to fully support a patient's ventilation when the patient has a high VD/VT ratio. Some possible ventilator setting changes might include increasing the tidal volume or increasing the rate. However, in cases of desaturation, increasing the tidal volume (and, therefore, increasing the amount of air delivered to the alveoli) can be more beneficial.

A patient's maximal inspiratory pressure (MIP) is also referred to as negative inspiratory pressure (NIP). This value can be measured either via a maneuver on a mechanical ventilator or a bedside test with a manometer. The patient's maximal inspiratory pressure is an important respiratory parameter and indicator. This value indicates the strength of the patient's respiratory effort, including the health of the diaphragm and inspiratory muscles. The patient's MIP is a negative number because it measures the negative force required to inhale. A normal MIP is between −80 and −100 mm Hg. An MIP test can be performed to determine patterns in a patient's respiratory strength, such as patients with muscular or neurological diseases such as myasthenia gravis or Guillain-Barré syndrome. These patients can lose respiratory muscle strength over time, reducing respiratory effort, and requiring ventilatory support. An MIP test can also be performed as part of a mechanical ventilation weaning procedure, in which the clinician measures a patient's respiratory effort to determine their ability to breathe spontaneously without support.

A patient's MIP is the negative force required to inhale. This value reflects the patient's respiratory muscle strength and is indicative of the patient's ability to adequately breathe on their own. An MIP test can be performed two ways, either via a mechanical ventilation maneuver or via a manometer in a spontaneously breathing patient. To measure MIP via a ventilator, the clinician must follow their facility's policy and procedure for the test because the steps of the test vary depending on the equipment used and the ventilator mode. Generally speaking, the clinician will set the ventilator to occlude the airway at the end of an expiration and instruct the patient to inhale as hard as possible. The clinician must continuously monitor the patient's vital signs for signs of distress during the test, at which time the maneuvers must be terminated. The clinician may perform 10 maneuvers of 20 seconds duration. The clinician looks at the ventilator readings to determine the patient's MIP value (this can vary based on the equipment used).

A patient's MIP is the negative force required to inhale. This value reflects the patient's respiratory muscle strength and is indicative of the patient's ability to adequately breathe on their own. An MIP test can be performed two ways, either via mechanical ventilation maneuver or via a manometer in a spontaneously breathing patient. To measure MIP in a spontaneously breathing patient using a manometer, the clinician must follow the facility's policy and procedure for the test because the steps of the test vary depending on the available equipment. Generally speaking, the clinician will gather the necessary equipment including a circuit with one-way valves and the appropriate pressure manometer and will set up the equipment. Then the clinician will place nose clips on the patient and instruct the patient to put the mouthpiece in his or her mouth, ensuring a tight seal with the lips. The clinician occludes the circuit and instructs the patient to inhale as hard as possible. The maneuver can be repeated for 10 inhalations in 20 seconds or until the patient is unable to continue. The clinician must monitor the patient for signs of respiratory distress throughout the test and terminate the test if adverse events occur.

Effects of Mechanical Ventilation on Cardiac Function

Mechanical ventilation, also known as positive pressure ventilation, changes the pressure within the chest wall to facilitate respiration. These changing pressures can result in cardiac effects such as reduced venous return, positive intrathoracic pressure, and reduced cardiac output due to reduced right atrial filling. These effects can result in hypotension and increased vascular resistance, which affects the patient's perfusion. In addition, vagal stimulation due to mechanical ventilation's effects on the cardiac system can result in fluctuations of the heart rate as well as cardiac arrhythmias. Clinicians must carefully monitor the patient's cardiac status during mechanical ventilation, and any cardiac effects must be treated and/or reported to the physician and healthcare team. Some patients may require fluid-based interventions or pharmacological intervention to help support their cardiac status while being mechanically ventilated. Other patients, such as those with pulmonary edema and pulmonary hypertension, may present with fluid overload. Careful management of fluids can help to stabilize a patient with cardiac insufficiency.

Cerebral Oximetry Including Near-Infrared Spectroscopy

Cerebral oximetry refers to the measurement of oxygen within the patient's brain tissue. Near-infrared spectroscopy is used to measure the patient's cerebral oxygen saturation noninvasively via continuous monitoring. This technology uses lighted probes that are attached to the patient's head. The light passes through the cranium into the patient's brain, and the light is reabsorbed by the probe on its way back out of the brain. The saturation of oxygen within the brain is determined by the amount of light that is sent into the brain and the returned light that is received by the probe on the patient's forehead. The difference in these two numbers determines the patient's percentage of cerebral oxygen saturation. This phenomenon is supported by the Beer–Lambert law, which states that the brightness of light decreases as it passes through higher concentrations of matter.

Cerebral oximetry, the process of monitoring oxygen levels in the brain, can be monitored in two different ways: trend or absolute monitoring. In absolute monitoring, the clinician bases clinical decisions on the exact percentage of cerebral oxygen saturation. This is similar to the practice of continuous pulse oximetry in which the clinician offers supplemental oxygen to the patient based on exact saturation levels. Conversely, in trend monitoring, the clinician bases clinical decisions on the saturation trends such as decreases or increases over time. In other words, the clinician is more concerned about patterns of desaturation rather than the actual oxygen saturation value. The type of monitoring chosen depends upon the equipment available because different oximeters offer different types of monitoring. If the patient needs trend monitoring, a specialized trend oximeter must be used. Conversely, if the patient needs absolute monitoring, then the clinician must obtain an absolute monitor.

Cerebral oximeters, monitors that measure the oxygen saturation in a patient's brain, can vary among manufacturers. Clinicians should refer to their facility's policy and procedure as well as the manufacturer's guidelines for use before setting up the monitor. Generally speaking, cerebral oximeter setup includes the monitor, lighted probes, and an adequate power source. The monitor is plugged into the power source and turned on. Appropriately sized sensors are chosen, often based on the patient's weight in kilograms. Then the clinician applies the sensors in accordance with the manufacturer's instructions on the patient's head or forehead. Placing the probes on hairless areas of the head often results in better readings. The probes are connected to the monitor cables, and the cerebral oximetry measurement begins. The clinician will see the patient's cerebral oximetry levels on the monitor.

STRATEGIES

WEANING FROM MECHANICAL VENTILATION

Spontaneous breathing trials are used on mechanically ventilated patients to predict the ability of the patient to be weaned from the ventilator. Prior to spontaneous breathing trials being initiated, the patient must first meet other clinical parameters for weaning, including but not limited to stable vital signs, muscle strength and tone, low level of ventilatory support (i.e., reduced ventilator settings), reduced or discontinued sedation, no fever, adequate oxygen saturation, and appropriate arterial blood gas values. Once these criteria are met, the spontaneous breathing trials can begin. The clinician should follow the facility's policy and procedure for spontaneous breathing trials because they may vary among facilities. These various choices include CPAP trials, pressure support trials, or T-piece trials. In each of these procedures, the patient is placed on a spontaneous mode of ventilation (or no mechanical ventilation at all, in the case of the T-piece trial) and the patient is monitored for a set period of time. If signs of respiratory distress are evident during that time, the trial is terminated, and the patient is placed back on their previous ventilator settings. If the trial is successful, the clinician may consider starting the weaning process.

CPAP trials can be performed on patients of all ages as part of a mechanical ventilator weaning procedure. CPAP trials can be performed in different ways depending on the equipment available. Clinicians should follow the facility's policy and procedure as well as the manufacturer's guidelines for CPAP trials. The clinician will first determine the patient's readiness to wean based on criteria such as stable vital signs, muscle strength and tone, a low level of ventilatory support (i.e., reduced ventilator settings), reduced or discontinued sedation, no fever, adequate oxygen saturation, and appropriate arterial blood gas values. Once these criteria are met, the CPAP trial can begin. Generally speaking, the clinician will change the patient's ventilator mode to CPAP and enter a CPAP value that is predetermined by the physician and the facility's policy. The patient is observed for a set period of time during which the clinician monitors the patient's respiration, tidal volumes, oxygenation, vital signs, and appearance for signs of respiratory distress or insufficiency. The trial is terminated if the patient shows signs of respiratory distress during the procedure. If the trial is successful, the clinician may consider starting the weaning process.

Pressure support trials can be performed on patients of all ages as part of a mechanical ventilator weaning procedures. Pressure support trials can be performed in different ways depending on the equipment available. Clinicians should follow their facility's policy and procedure as well as the manufacturers' guidelines for pressure support trials. The clinician will first determine the patient's readiness to wean based on criteria such as stable vital signs, muscle strength and tone, a low level of ventilatory support (i.e., reduced ventilator settings), reduced or discontinued sedation, no fever, adequate oxygen saturation, and appropriate arterial blood gas values. Once these criteria are met, the pressure support trial can begin. Generally speaking, the clinician will change the patient's ventilator mode to pressure support ventilation and enter a pressure support value that is predetermined by the physician and the facility's policy. The patient is observed for a set period of time during which the clinician monitors the patient's respiration, tidal volumes, oxygenation, vital signs, and appearance for signs of respiratory distress or insufficiency. The trial is terminated if the patient shows signs of respiratory distress during the procedure. If the trial is successful, the clinician may consider starting the weaning process.

T-piece trials can be performed on patients of all ages as part of mechanical ventilator weaning procedures. These procedures can take place with an endotracheal tube or with a tracheostomy tube. Clinicians should follow the facility's policy and procedure as well as the manufacturer's guidelines for T-piece trials. The clinician will first determine the patient's readiness to wean based on criteria such as stable vital signs, muscle strength and tone, a low level of ventilatory support (i.e., reduced ventilator settings), reduced or discontinued sedation, no fever, adequate oxygen saturation, and appropriate arterial blood gas values. Once these criteria are met, the T-piece trial can begin. Generally speaking, the clinician will change the patient's ventilator mode to either CPAP or pressure support ventilation and enter in a CPAP or pressure support value that is predetermined by the physician and the facility's policy. The patient is then placed on the T-piece. This equipment includes an endotracheal or tracheostomy tube adapter, corrugated tubing attached to one end of the adapter that leads to a humidified oxygen source, and an open exhalation end on the opposite side of the adapter. The patient is observed for a set period of time during which the clinician monitors the patient's respiration, tidal volumes, oxygenation, vital signs, and appearance for signs of respiratory distress or insufficiency. The trial is terminated if the patient shows signs of respiratory distress during the procedure. If the trial is successful, the clinician may consider starting the weaning process.

Weaning protocols for mechanically ventilated patients vary widely among facilities. Many protocols begin with readiness criteria such as stable vital signs, muscle strength and tone, a low level of ventilatory support (i.e., reduced ventilator settings), reduced or discontinued sedation, no fever, adequate oxygen saturation, and appropriate arterial blood gas values. Next, the protocols often include instructions on the form of weaning to be initiated such as T-piece trials, CPAP trials, and pressure support trials. The choice of trial may be determined by the facility, or it may be chosen by the physician or clinician depending on the patient's overall condition and available equipment. Protocols also include information on when to terminate the weaning process and what to do once termination begins. This can include placing the patient back on previous ventilator settings or instituting new settings. Some protocols are in algorithm form, whereas others are in outline form. Many different styles of protocols exist, and the clinician should refer to the facility's policy and procedure for the weaning protocols used at his or her institution.

Lung-Protective Ventilation Including Permissive Hypercapnia

Permissive hypercapnia is defined as maintaining intentionally high levels of carbon dioxide in the blood while a patient is mechanically ventilated. Often, permissive hypercapnia is the result of very severe respiratory disease and disorders that require high levels of mechanical ventilation. In these cases, the patient's ventilator settings are at a maximum level in order to maintain oxygenation but are still not able to successfully remove carbon dioxide from the patient's blood. Clinicians will allow permissive hypercapnia in an effort to protect the patient's lungs from overinflation and barotrauma due to excessive ventilator-delivered pressures and volumes. If the clinician increases the patient's ventilator settings (often the tidal volume and peak inspiratory pressure) any further, the patient will experience barotrauma and lung injury. This in turn would cause an emergency situation, whereas the benefits of permissive hypercapnia outweigh the risks associated with increased ventilator-delivered pressures and volumes.

Facilitate Procedures and Evaluate Efficacy

Needle Decompression of a Tension Pneumothorax

A tension pneumothorax, or collapsed lung, is a very serious condition in which portions of a patient's lung deflate due to air from the lungs passing into the pleural space. This leak causes a tension pneumothorax. The treatment for this condition is a needle decompression procedure to release the air and subsequent pressure from the pleural space, resulting in reinflation of the lung. When using needle decompression for the treatment of a pneumothorax, the clinician should follow the facility's policy and procedure because the process may vary slightly among different facilities. Generally speaking, the clinician will prep the patient's skin in accordance with his or her facility's policy. He or she will then administer supplemental oxygen to the patient, often at 100% FiO_2. Next, the clinician inserts an appropriately sized needle (depending on the size and age of the patient) into the second rib space at the midclavicular line. The clinician may then aspirate the trapped air using a syringe and place a chest tube in accordance with the facility's policy.

Therapeutic Hypothermia

Therapeutic hypothermia is defined as the process of cooling the body of an unconscious patient to below normal body temperature. The patient is kept at the lower body temperature for a set period of time in an effort to slow the patient's metabolism and preserve brain cells and brain function after cardiac surgery, CPR, acute brain injury, and other clinical scenarios. Therapeutic hypothermia prevents cell death and improves a patient's mortality and morbidity, resulting in increased numbers of unimpaired survivors of cardiopulmonary arrest and other conditions. In the event of CPR, the patient is cooled to between 32 and 34 degrees Celsius for 24 hours or more, depending on the facility's policy and procedure. The cooling process occurs after an adequate pulse and perfusion are restored to the patient, but while the patient is still unconscious. Patients who regain consciousness after cardiac arrest are not good candidates for therapeutic hypothermia.

The process of initiating therapeutic hypothermia can vary among facilities. Clinicians should follow their facility's policy and procedure for the initiation of therapeutic hypothermia in the pediatric patient. Generally speaking, the patient is sedated and paralyzed to minimize the possibility of shivering. The act of shivering can change a patient's metabolism and negate the effects of the therapeutic hypothermia. Next, the patient is placed on cardiopulmonary monitoring equipment that will measure the patient's heart rate, respiratory rate, oxygen saturation, blood pressure, and other vital signs. A temperature probe is also used to continuously measure the patient's body temperature. This process can vary among institutions, but often a rectal probe is used. The patient is gradually cooled to a set temperature (between 32 and 34 degrees Celsius) either via cooling blankets or a cooling cap in accordance with their facility's policy and procedure.

The process of maintaining and rewarming a patient with therapeutic hypothermia can vary among different facilities. Clinicians should follow their facility's policy and procedure for the maintaining and rewarming of pediatric patients with therapeutic hypothermia. Generally speaking, after hypothermia is initiated, the patient will be constantly monitored for cardiac status, respiratory status, and body temperature. The clinician will then maintain the patient's body temperature at the ordered temperature by titrating the settings on the cooling equipment. After the ordered time period has passed for therapeutic hypothermia, the clinician will begin to gradually rewarm the patient over several hours either by increasing the temperature on the cooling blankets or cap or by providing the patient with warming blankets. A gradual temperature increase is vital because shivering or quick temperature increases can result in metabolic changes and adverse events. The patient is constantly monitored during the entire cooling, maintaining, and warming phases of therapeutic hypothermia. In addition to cardiopulmonary monitoring, the patient will also be monitored for electrolyte imbalances, metabolic changes, fluid level changes, and blood sugar fluctuations.

When performing therapeutic hypothermia in the neonatal population, clinicians must first determine the patient's ability to participate in the intervention. Studies indicate that patients who are less than 36 weeks of gestational age, weigh less than 2.2 lbs, have chromosomal or other congenital abnormalities, or patients who have cardiac or respiratory defects are not good candidates for this therapy. To initiate therapeutic hypothermia, the patient must be older than 35 weeks of gestational age and have a 10-minute Apgar score of 5 or less and require ventilation or resuscitation. Neonates must also meet neurological criteria such as encephalopathy or seizure activity. Other criteria may be included in the facility's policy and procedure because the therapeutic requirements can vary among various facilities. Clinicians should refer to their facility's policy and procedure for therapeutic hypothermia inclusion and exclusion factors for neonates.

Manage and/or Anticipate Effects of Medication Administration

Surfactant Replacement Therapy

Healthy lungs produce a substance called surfactant, which reduces the surface tension of the alveoli, keeping them open and available for gas exchange during respiration. In very preterm neonates, surfactant levels are inadequate, resulting in poor gas exchange, hypoxia, and respiratory distress or arrest. Surfactant replacement therapy allows the patient to receive replacement surfactant via instillation into the endotracheal tube. The surfactant then acts as a lubricant, opening the alveoli and restoring oxygenation. Surfactant instillation technique can vary among facilities. Clinicians should follow their facility's policy and procedure regarding surfactant instillation. Generally speaking, the clinician will first deliver supplemental oxygen to the patient to keep saturations at greater than 95%. Then the clinician will suction the airway and instill the predetermined dose of surfactant via catheter in the endotracheal tube. The patient may be repositioned side to side during administration depending on the facility's policy and procedure. Manual ventilation with a bag and mask is then resumed and the patient is placed back on mechanical ventilation. Continuous monitoring of the patient's vital signs is imperative during this procedure.

Surfactant, a naturally occurring lipid- and protein-containing substance in the lungs, reduces the surface tension of the alveoli. This action results in the ability of the alveoli to remain open and maintain adequate gas exchange and oxygenation. The administration of supplemental surfactant in preterm neonates has dramatic, and often quick, effects on the patient's lung compliance. Lung compliance is defined as the "stiffness" of the lungs or the ease of inhalation. Changes in compliance can cause dramatic changes in the patient's pulmonary status because the lungs are quickly becoming less "stiff" and easier to mechanically ventilate. Therefore, constant monitoring of the patient is required during this procedure because almost immediate mechanical ventilator setting changes may need to occur. Failure to adjust mechanical ventilator settings as the patients' lung compliance improves can result in lung injury and barotrauma.

Although surfactant is a naturally occurring lipid- and protein-containing substance in the lungs, the administration of surfactant can cause adverse effects. Surfactant is a thick, slippery substance that can easily clog tiny endotracheal tubes, such as those used in very preterm infants. Airway obstructions due to surfactant administration can cause hypoxia and respiratory distress. Therefore, the risk of surfactant obstruction in the endotracheal tube must be mitigated by careful and methodical instillation of the substance per the facility's policy and procedure, followed by manual resuscitation bag breaths delivered to the airway after instillation. Other techniques may be used, and the clinician should refer to the facility's policy and procedure for proper surfactant instillation. Other adverse events associated with the administration of surfactant can include but are not limited to bleeding in the airway, bradycardia, and changes in the electrical activity or blood flow of the brain. Barotrauma and hyperventilation can also occur in patients who have rapid improvements in lung compliance secondary to surfactant administration.

Airway Instillations

When undergoing medical procedures such as bronchoscopy and fiber-optic intubation, some patients benefit from having the airway itself anesthetized. This is accomplished by instilling 2% lidocaine into the trachea to numb the airway during the procedure. The technique for lidocaine instillation can vary among different facilities. Clinicians should follow their facility's policy and procedure for lidocaine instillation. Generally speaking, the clinician will intubate the patient and instill a predetermined dose of 2% lidocaine into the endotracheal tube or port. Vital signs must be constantly monitored during this procedure to prevent adverse events. These criteria include blood pressure, respiratory rate, heart rate, and oxygen saturation. If signs of distress occur, the procedure is terminated, and the patient's condition is treated. In addition, lidocaine is a numbing agent, and it is therefore associated with a higher aspiration risk. Instruct conscious patients to not eat or drink anything for at least 60 minutes after the procedure, or follow your facility's policy and procedure for an appropriate NPO (nothing by mouth) duration.

During CPR, epinephrine (a vasopressor) is often administered to stimulate the heart and regain a pulse in patients who have arrested. Epinephrine is commonly administered via intravenous injection during CPR; however, it can also be administered via intracardiac injection or tracheal instillation. Intracardiac injection is associated with several potentially serious side effects; therefore, tracheal instillation is often preferred over intracardiac injection. In tracheal instillation of epinephrine, a predetermined dose of epinephrine is administered via an endotracheal tube in an unconscious patient. The epinephrine is absorbed into the tissues and begins its vasopressor effects on the body. This technique can be used in patients of all ages, and it is often well tolerated and successful, especially in neonatal patients who require CPR but do not have vascular access yet. The technique for instillation of epinephrine can vary by facility. Clinicians should follow their facility's policy and procedure for the proper instillation of epinephrine.

Prevent Hospital-Acquired Conditions

Ventilator-Associated Pneumonia

Bed Position

Ventilator-associated pneumonia is a common health risk in the intensive care unit. The act of intubation or surgical placement of a tracheostomy tube can introduce new bacteria into the airway, increasing the patient's risk of infection. While on the ventilator, several factors can contribute to an increased risk of ventilator-associated pneumonia. Condensation in the ventilator circuit tubing, also known as "rainout," is a common problem for patients on mechanical ventilators. The condensation droplets can fall back into the endotracheal tube or tracheostomy tube, transporting bacteria and other pathogens into the lungs. To prevent rainout, the clinician must carefully titrate the ventilator's humidifier temperature and any condensation must be drained back into the humidifier away from the patient end of the circuit. In addition, oral secretions containing bacteria and pathogens can pass from the mouth into the airway, increasing the patient's risk of infection. Oral care, including interventions such as antiseptic swabs and tooth brushing, can help prevent ventilator-associated pneumonia in susceptible patients. Lastly, keeping the patient's head of the bed elevated to 30 to 45 degrees can also help secretions from pooling in the airways.

Minimizing Intubation Time

Assessing a patient's readiness to be weaned from a mechanical ventilator depends on several criteria. First, the patient must be hemodynamically stable, with normal vital signs and an adequate level of consciousness. Next, the patient must be assessed for underlying health conditions, ensuring that the medical reason for their mechanical ventilation is either reversed or adequately treated. The clinical team can then begin a weaning protocol and a weaning assessment. These tools can vary among facilities. Clinicians should follow their facility's policy and procedure for weaning patients from mechanical ventilation. Generally speaking, weaning protocols and assessments can include interventions such as spontaneous breathing trials, NIP or MIP, CPAP trials, and/or pressure support trials. Some weaning protocols incorporate several of the aforementioned interventions, whereas others only rely on one or two. Weaning protocols often vary among patient populations as well, with different protocols and requirements for neonatal, pediatric, and adult populations.

Noninvasive positive pressure ventilation (NPPV) is a form of mechanical ventilation in which a patient is ventilated without the use of an endotracheal tube or tracheostomy tube. These patients are instead ventilated via a mechanical ventilator with a face mask. The mask is often a full-face mask as opposed to a nasal mask because this type of mask reduces the possibility of leaks in the circuit. Clinicians must be aware, however, that full-face masks can be associated with a higher risk of aspiration if the patient is unable to remove the mask quickly enough when vomiting. Therefore, the full-face mask should be used in areas of the hospital in which patients are monitored more closely, such as critical care areas and telemetry or step-down units. NPPV can be used as a weaning tool for mechanically ventilated patients, or it can be used for patients who need full ventilatory support. In addition, this type of mechanical ventilation can be used constantly or intermittently depending on the patient's needs. For example, some patients with central sleep apnea may require NPPV only during sleep.

Ventilator Circuit Care

Clinicians in critical care settings often incorporate closed-suction systems into the mechanical ventilator circuit. Closed-suction systems have several benefits for patients, including a lower risk of infection and reduction of ventilator-associated pneumonia. These systems are truly closed, meaning that the ventilator circuit does not have to be broken or opened in order to suction a patient's airway. Care techniques for closed-suction systems vary among facilities, and clinicians should follow their facility's policy and procedure for the care of their particular brand and style of closed-suction system. Many facilities do not change closed-suction systems unless they are visibly soiled or damaged. This action further helps to prevent ventilator associated pneumonia by not breaking the ventilator circuit for equipment changes unless it is absolutely necessary. Clinicians often keep the closed-suction system patent by using sterile saline "bullets" to instill sterile saline into the system while applying suction. This type of lavage can help to keep the suction catheter clear of secretions and other debris. Saline bullets should not be reused: These are one-time-use items.

Some mechanical ventilator circuits are equipped with heated wires within the circuit tubing. The wires are coiled throughout the ventilator circuit, providing the patient with a consistent gas temperature. The constant temperature control helps to minimize the possibility of condensation or rainout within the circuit. This in turn helps to reduce ventilator-associated pneumonia; condensation that drips back into the patient's airway from the ventilator circuit is a common ventilator-associated pneumonia trigger. The condensation delivers pathogens to the patient's airway, resulting in potentially serious infections. In addition to infection-control benefits, heated-wire circuits are also beneficial to patients because of the consistent temperature delivery that this type of circuit offers. These circuits are also often disposable and are changed if visibly soiled. Replacement of heated-wire circuitry varies among facilities. Clinicals should refer to their facility's policy and procedure for the implementation and care of heated-wire ventilator circuits. Heated-wire circuits are commonly used in neonatal and pediatric intensive care units, but they are also used in the adult population.

Device-Related Pressure Ulcers

Patients with respiratory insufficiencies often require long-term use of respiratory equipment. The various types of equipment, including BIPAP and CPAP machine masks, nasal CPAP prongs, noninvasive mechanical ventilation masks, and heated high-flow nasal cannulas, can all cause pressure ulcers from overuse. It is imperative for the clinician to ensure a tight fit for these masks and prongs to prevent leaks in the system, but they must also be aware of the risk of skin breakdown and pressure ulcer formation. To combat these issues, several interventions can be incorporated into the patient's care plan. Skin-protective devices such as DuoDERM or other protective pads and strips can be applied to the skin around the areas where the equipment will be applying pressure. Changing the style of the mask or adjusting the tightness of fit can also be helpful. In the case of heated high-flow nasal cannulas and other nasal prongs, accurate measurements must be taken prior to the initiation of therapy to ensure that the prongs are not too large for the patient's nares. Constant pressure from prongs on the inside of the patient's nares can cause pressure ulcers and eventual tissue necrosis.

Manage End-of-Life Care

Types of End-of-Life Care

Palliative care refers to a type of care provided to a patient with a terminal or progressive and irreversible illness. The patient may not be near death; in fact, if a patient is within the last 6 months of predicted life, they are offered hospice care as opposed to palliative care. Respiratory patients requiring palliative care can include patients with diseases such as chronic obstructive pulmonary disorder, pulmonary fibrosis, and other chronic irreversible pulmonary diseases. Patients receiving palliative care will participate in goal-setting meetings with an interdisciplinary team, with the patient setting their own goals for therapy and treatment. Patients in palliative care can stay in their own homes or move to a palliative care facility depending on their condition and preferences. Palliative care is designed to be supportive care for patients with chronic, irreversible diseases. This can include services such as medication delivery, grocery delivery, in-home medical services, and caregiver support services for the patient's family.

Patients who are at 6 months or fewer of their expected life span due to disease or illness can be eligible for hospice care. Hospice care is also known as comfort care and is offered to patients with terminal illnesses that are incurable. When treatment is futile, hospice care is considered. Patients receiving hospice care can do so either in their homes or in a hospice or hospital facility, depending on their condition, preferences, and other factors. Hospice care incorporates various comfort measures at the end of a patient's life. These interventions can include pain management; caregiver support services; and in-home medical care including nursing care, respiratory therapy, and help with daily responsibilities. Patients and their caregivers work with the hospice team to ensure that the patient is comfortable and well cared for in their last days of life.

Advance directives are the legal documents that outline a patient's wishes for treatment, especially for end-of-life issues or emergency care. Advance directives can include information such as the patient's medical power of attorney, who is responsible for making end-of-life and emergency care decisions, do-not-resuscitate orders, do-not-intubate orders, and other interventional preferences. Advance directive laws vary by state, and clinicians should be familiar with their state's rules and regulations regarding medical decision making. The patient's medical power of attorney or designated decision maker is the person in charge of all decisions regarding a patient's care. Family and friends may be consulted by the medical power of attorney, but the final decisions lie with him or her. It is also important to note that in some instances, a medical power of attorney or appointed decision maker can choose not to follow a patient's preferences in healthcare decision making.

Determination of Brain Death

Brain death, also known as the state of being clinically dead, is determined by several factors. The American Academy of Neurology has set several criteria that must be met for a patient to be considered brain dead. First, the patient must be in an irreversible coma unrelated to sedation, other medications, therapeutic hypothermia, pH or electrolyte changes, or other metabolic issues. The patient must be unresponsive, with no eye, tracheal, or facial movement, including the absence of a gag reflex. The patient's blood pressure must be stable, with a systolic blood pressure of 100 mm Hg, to ensure an accurate patient assessment and neurological testing. Third, at least two neurological tests must be performed. The patient must be unable to breathe on their own, which can be confirmed with a CO_2 challenge test. Other testing including but not limited to electroencephalogram, cerebral scintigraphy, and transcranial Doppler can also be performed to help confirm brain death.

Withdrawal of Life Support

When determining when to remove a patient from life-sustaining equipment such as mechanical ventilation, the clinician must first assess the patient's wishes. If the patient has advance directives that outline their preferences for care, or if the patient has a medical power of attorney or designated decision maker, the clinician should defer to them. In the absence of these criteria, the clinician must rely on legal and clinical requirements for the withdrawal of life support. It is important to note that despite a clinician's professional assessment and opinion that indicates that further treatment is futile, if the patient's designated decision maker or next of kin requests full life support, that preference must be carried out. Clinicians can appeal to local courts for an unbiased assessment and decision if there is a dispute between the healthcare team and family regarding the patient's care. Clinicians should also follow their facility's policy and procedure for end-of-life decision making.

When determining when to remove a patient from life-sustaining equipment such as mechanical ventilation, the clinician must first assess the patient's wishes. If the patient's wishes are unknown, and the next of kin is unwilling or unable to make end-of-life decisions, the clinician must rely on legal, clinical, and facility-based requirements for the withdrawal of life support. The clinician should refer to the facility's policy and procedure for end-of-life decision making. The decision to withdraw care is based on the patient's clinical presentation. The patient's condition must be severe enough that further treatment is considered futile. In other words, the patient's condition is irreversible, the patient is not likely to make a meaningful recovery, and no further treatment will be beneficial. The decision to withdraw life support interventions is one that is easily debated, and, unfortunately, it is not easily defined. Clinicians must make the best ethical decision they can, based on the patient's clinical presentation, likelihood of meaningful survival, and the patient's wishes (if applicable).

Care of Organ Donor

Misinformation is common in the discussion of organ donors because many myths regarding their care are communicated among the community. Organ donors are not treated differently than non-organ donors. Treatment is not withheld or withdrawn early in an attempt to harvest needed organs. Organ donors receive the same standard of care as any other patient in the healthcare system. Once the organ donor is determined to be brain dead, the healthcare team follows the facility's policy and procedure for organ harvesting and subsequent matching. This often results in an outside company taking charge of the patient's care, including the harvesting and matching of organs. The company may change ventilator settings, withdraw various types of support and care, and initiate other interventions as needed for optimal organ health. The patient is treated with the utmost respect even after brain death because this patient is saving the lives of countless others.

Conditions and Disorders

Neopulmonary (Neonatal Pulmonary Including Meconium Aspiration and Pneumonia)

In meconium aspiration syndrome, a fetus inhales fetal stool (meconium) in utero. Meconium is a very sticky, tar-like substance that causes respiratory distress upon aspiration. Clinicians attending the delivery of a meconium aspiration syndrome neonate will notice stained amniotic fluid, and the neonate will present with respiratory distress. In suspected or confirmed meconium aspiration, it is critical that the healthcare team suction the patient FIRST prior to ventilating the patient. If the patient is ventilated first via resuscitation bag and mask, the meconium can be pushed further into the bronchioles, causing severe respiratory distress that is much more difficult to treat. Suctioning the meconium out of the patient's airway will help to remove the airway obstruction caused by the meconium and result in better rescue ventilation of the patient. Patients with meconium aspiration syndrome may require resuscitation, supplemental oxygen, and/or mechanical ventilation depending on the patient's condition and the extent of meconium aspiration.

Epiglottitis is a very serious, life-threatening respiratory condition affecting mostly children. In this disorder, the patient's epiglottis becomes inflamed and painful, resulting in partial or complete blockage of the patient's airway. Patients with epiglottitis often present with signs of respiratory distress, excessive drooling, fever, and stridor. (Stridorous breath sounds originate in the neck, and, therefore, the clinician should auscultate the side of the patient's neck listening for whistling or coarse breath sounds. Stridor is indicative of an upper airway obstruction.) An artificial airway, such as an endotracheal tube or tracheostomy tube, may be required for the relief of airway obstruction; however, intubation with an endotracheal tube can be risky due to the epiglottitis swelling. A short-term tracheostomy may be more beneficial for patients with life-threatening epiglottitis. Other treatment interventions can include humidified supplemental oxygen, antibiotics, and repositioning the patient to a sitting-up position, which can improve respiratory effort and relieve some of the dyspnea.

Chronic Lung (Chronic Lung Disease of Prematurity)

Neonates who are born prematurely are at an increased risk for continued lung disease later in life. Many of these patients present with pulmonary diseases such as asthma and reactive airway disease in childhood. In cases of reactive airway disease, in which patients have cyclic episodes of wheezing and dyspnea in early childhood, the child often outgrows the condition by the time he or she reaches school age. Some children never outgrow reactive airway disease, and in those cases, the patients are often diagnosed with asthma. Asthma is a chronic health condition characterized by bronchoconstriction, mucus production, and airway inflammation. Although the symptoms of reactive airway disease and asthma are similar, the main difference between the two disorders lies in the reversibility and ability to "grow out of" the disease. Asthma is a lifelong health condition that can have episodes of varying severity depending on various triggers and the patient's overall health.

Bronchiolitis

Bronchiolitis, an acute infection of the small airways in the lungs (bronchioles), is a common infection found in pediatric patients, especially during cold and flu season. Bronchiolitis is characterized by mucus production and wheezing, which can become severe. Patients are often febrile and can require suctioning of the airway to relieve the mucus within the airway. Patients with bronchiolitis can present with a combination of wheezing, intercostal or subcostal retractions, tracheal tugging, nasal flaring, hypoxia, increased respiratory rate, and cough. Treatment for bronchiolitis includes supplemental oxygen for hypoxemia and bronchodilators via nebulizer or metered-dose inhaler for bronchospasm. Antibiotics can be administered if the cause is presumed to be bacterial; however, many cases of bronchiolitis are viral in nature. Very young children and premature infants are particularly susceptible to severe cases of bronchiolitis that can require mechanical ventilation.

Ped Airway (Pediatric Airway Including Tracheomalacia, Vocal Cord Paralysis, and Vascular Ring)

Vocal cord paralysis is a condition in which a patient's vocal cords are unable to move. The paralysis can be one sided (affecting only one cord), or it may affect both sides. The impaired movement of the vocal cords can result in respiratory distress because the cords are unable to open and close properly. Patients with vocal cord paralysis often present with a weak cry or diminished ability to speak, stridorous breath sounds, and varying levels of respiratory difficulty. These patients may have trouble swallowing and may therefore aspirate when swallowing. Patients with aspiration are at increased risk for aspiration pneumonia and should be treated promptly to avoid this complication. Treatment for vocal cord paralysis can include surgical procedures in severe cases or watchful waiting in less severe cases. Vocal cord paralysis can be caused by congenital defects, vocal cord injury, or tumor growth.

Tracheomalacia, also known as a floppy windpipe, is a condition in which a patient's tracheal cartilage is unstable, resulting in premature closure of the airway. Patients with tracheomalacia are born with the condition, and symptoms are apparent from a young age. Some common symptoms associated with tracheomalacia include noisy breathing, including stridor or coarse breath sounds; periods of apnea; orthopnea (difficulty breathing while lying flat); and dyspnea with feeding, crying, or exertion. Symptoms of tracheomalacia are often noticed more during exhalation because this is when the airway collapses prematurely. Tracheomalacia can be diagnosed by using several different procedures including CT scans, bronchoscopy, airway fluoroscopy, and pulmonary function testing. Tracheomalacia can be serious if left untreated because the patient's ability to breathe is hindered by the malformed tracheal cartilage. Surgical interventions can resolve the anatomical issue and restore natural breathing.

A vascular ring is a condition in which a patient's aorta surrounds and encloses the trachea and esophagus. This is a congenital heart defect present at birth. Patients with vascular rings can present with acid reflux and trouble swallowing due to pressure on the esophagus, as well as dyspnea with feeding and exertion, coughing, and vomiting. Vascular rings can cause severe symptoms or more mild symptoms. In some cases, the symptoms associated with vascular rings are so mild that the patient isn't diagnosed until later in life. Vascular rings are diagnosed with the help of radiological studies such as esophagography, MRI, and CT scan. In severe cases, surgical intervention is required to repair the defect. The surgical intervention required can vary based on the severity and type of vascular ring present.

Immunocompromised

Immunocompromised patients, such as preterm neonates, patients taking systemic corticosteroids, patients with inherited immune system deficiencies, and patients with organ transplants, are at an increased risk for infections due to their underdeveloped immune systems. Infection control procedures must be followed to minimize the risk to these fragile patients. Infection control procedures for intensive care units can vary among facilities. Clinicians should follow their facility's policy and procedure for infection control measures in critical care units. Generally speaking, clinicians should practice good hand hygiene including scrubbing in and out when entering and leaving the unit. Personal protective equipment such as gloves, gown, and mask may also be required to prevent the spread of illness to preterm neonates and other immunocompromised patients.

SHOCK

The term shock can refer to several different disorders. There are several main types of shock, including but not limited to anaphylactic (allergic), hypovolemic (low fluid), septic (infectious), and cardiogenic (cardiac) shock. Each form of shock has its own specific standard of care; clinicians should refer to their facility's policy and procedure for treating the various types of shock. Generally speaking, shock is treated by stabilizing the patient and treating the underlying cause. For example, in anaphylactic shock, patients with food allergies or other allergies present with swollen airways, rapid and weak pulses, poor perfusion, respiratory distress or arrest, stomachache, hives, and other serious symptoms. The treatment for anaphylactic shock is to reverse the underlying allergic reaction by administering epinephrine. It is important to note that even when shock is adequately treated, additional life-saving measures may be required in the interim. This can include mechanical ventilation, supplemental oxygen, and resuscitation.

HEART FAILURE

Heart failure, the inability of the heart to adequately perfuse the body, can have several causes. Structural abnormalities within the heart, such as congenital heart defects, are the main cause of heart failure in neonates. Patent ductus arteriosus, aortic stenosis, coarctation of the aorta, ventricular septal defect, and other congenital heart defects are all possible causes of heart failure in neonates. Neonates with heart failure often present with symptoms such as hypoxia, poor feeding, lethargy, edema, and signs of respiratory distress such as grunting, intercostal or subcostal retractions, nasal flaring, and tracheal tugging. Infants and older children with heart failure may present with any of the aforementioned symptoms as well as failure to thrive and inability to meet developmental milestones. The diagnosis of heart disease in neonates relies on imaging studies such as chest X-rays and echocardiograms, as well as patient assessment findings. The treatment of heart failure depends upon the underlying cause of the disorder, which is often structural in neonatal patients. These patients often require surgical correction of the congenital heart defects that are causing the heart failure.

INHALATION (INHALATION INJURIES)

Inhalation injury is damage to a patient's respiratory tract caused by inspiring gases, particulates, and other irritants. Inhaling smoke can cause burns to the airway, whereas inhaling fumes and particulates can cause an airway obstruction due to irritant-induced bronchospasm. A common source of inhalation injury is smoke inhalation. Patients with inhalation injury from smoke exposure often present with swelling and inflammation in the airway tissues, including the mouth, throat, and trachea. These patients require supplemental oxygen, often at a high FiO_2, in order to combat carbon monoxide poisoning from the smoke exposure. Some patients may have extensive injuries to the airway that can result in respiratory distress or failure. In cases of respiratory failure, the clinician must be prepared to intubate and ventilate the patient. Tracheostomy tube placement may be required for patients with extensive facial burns or trauma, or severe upper airway obstructions due to swelling or foreign bodies.

NBRC-NPS Practice Questions

1. All of the following criteria are components of a comprehensive initial patient assessment EXCEPT

a. Breath sounds and respiratory rate
b. Medical history and history of present illness
c. Laboratory results and SPO_2
d. Allergies and recent exposures

2. What is the purpose of imaging studies performed on neonatal and pediatric patients?

a. Diagnostic
b. Therapeutic
c. Interventional
d. All of the above

3. A respiratory therapist is called to the emergency room to evaluate a neonatal patient's respiratory status. All of the following symptoms are signs of respiratory distress in an infant EXCEPT

a. Accessory muscle use
b. Intercostal retractions
c. Grunting
d. Nasal flaring

4. Which one of the following statements is true regarding sleep studies?

a. Sleep studies are conducted in the daytime and nighttime hours.
b. Sleep studies are only performed on adult patients.
c. Sleep studies are the only way to diagnose sleep apnea.
d. Sleep studies only measure occurrences of airway obstruction.

5. All of the following statements are true regarding neurological function and respiratory status EXCEPT

a. Central nervous system insufficiency can result in respiratory failure.
b. Neurological status is not directly related to respiratory status.
c. Neurological disorders can cause abnormal breathing patterns.
d. Neurological status directly affects the successful intubation of a patient.

6. Congenital heart defects of the newborn can cause all of the following signs and symptoms EXCEPT

a. Desaturation
b. Cyanosis
c. Respiratory failure
d. Wheezing

7. A 4-year-old female presents to the ER with the following vital signs: respiratory rate 36, heart rate 157, and oxygen saturation 88%. The patient has had a viral illness for several days and is currently experiencing a high-pitched "seal's bark" cough. The healthcare team suspects croup. Which of the following actions would help the team make that diagnosis?

a. Listening to breath sounds at the patient's neck
b. Performing a peak flow measurement
c. Performing a huff cough maneuver
d. Obtaining a chest X-ray

8. All of the following are signs and symptoms of an asthma exacerbation EXCEPT

a. Persistent cough
b. Orthopnea
c. Throat clearing
d. Rhonchi

9. The respiratory therapist is called to the ER for a trauma alert due to a motor vehicle accident. A 14-year-old boy experienced blunt-force trauma to the chest during the accident and is currently being transported to the ER for evaluation. As a result of the accident, the respiratory therapist should anticipate treating all of the following conditions EXCEPT

a. Pneumothorax
b. Bronchospasm
c. Pulmonary contusion
d. Ventilatory failure

10. Apnea is defined as the absence of breathing for

a. At least 10 seconds
b. At least 15 seconds
c. At least 20 seconds
d. At least 30 seconds

11. All of the following neonatal disorders are characterized by excessive fluid EXCEPT

a. Bronchopulmonary dysplasia
b. Apnea of prematurity
c. Pulmonary hypertension
d. Kidney failure

12. Which of the following choices best describes the effects of diabetic ketoacidosis on respiratory status?

a. Diabetic ketoacidosis does not cause respiratory failure but can cause changes in neurological status.
b. In diabetic ketoacidosis, the patient's pH falls, carbon dioxide rises, and PO_2 falls.
c. High blood sugar causes the release of ketones, acid–base mismatch, and respiratory failure.
d. The acid–base balance has no effects on respiratory status.

13. All of the following congenital abnormalities of the digestive system require immediate surgical intervention EXCEPT

a. Umbilical hernia
b. Diaphragmatic hernia
c. Esophageal atresia
d. Tracheoesophageal fistula

14. A 33-week-gestation infant is admitted to the neonatal intensive care unit (NICU). The patient is experiencing aspiration, poor latch, desaturation, and coughing during feeds. Which one of the following interventions is appropriate to initiate at this time?

a. Place the patient on 100% oxygen during feeds.
b. Change the patient's formula.
c. Increase the frequency and duration of feeds.
d. Place a feeding tube.

15. All of the following complications are associated with necrotizing enterocolitis in the neonate EXCEPT

a. Abdominal distension
b. Respiratory distress
c. Jaundice
d. Bloody stools

16. The respiratory therapist is called to the delivery room for the birth of a full-term infant. The fetus is determined to be in the breech position. The physician attempts to turn the infant and delivers the infant with the aid of forceps. The newborn is cyanotic and apneic. The physician suspects a spinal cord injury due to the difficult delivery. Which of the following choices is the likely location of the injury?

a. Above C5
b. Above C6
c. Below C5
d. Below C3

17. All of the following conditions can impede the accurate measurement of end-tidal CO_2 EXCEPT

a. Apnea
b. Hypoventilation
c. Airway obstruction
d. Oxygen delivery

18. Which one of the following choices is not a step in drawing a blood gas from an indwelling catheter in a neonatal patient?

a. Obtain a sample of blood to discard with a heparinized syringe.
b. Flush the port with normal saline.
c. Place the blood gas sample in an ice slurry for transport.
d. Remove the cap from the three-way valve and clean the port.

19. Which of the following choices is not a step in drawing a capillary blood gas from a neonatal patient?

a. Place a heel warmer on the patient several minutes before beginning the procedure.
b. Squeeze the heel to release a drop of blood.
c. Remove any clots in the capillary tube.
d. Prick the heel with a hospital-approved lancet.

20. A respiratory therapist is called to the pulmonary function lab to perform simple spirometry on a 4-year-old patient. The patient has a history of unexplained cough that worsens at night. The patient is talkative and cooperative with the hospital staff. Which one of the following choices is not a step in the preparation of a 4-year-old patient for spirometry?

a. The respiratory therapist should notify the doctor that the patient is too young for spirometry.
b. The respiratory therapist should ensure that the equipment is calibrated.
c. The respiratory therapist should introduce themselves to the patient and family.
d. The respiratory therapist should explain the procedure.

21. What is the purpose of mean inspiratory pressure testing?

a. To measure the mean airway pressure (MAP) during synchronized intermittent mandatory ventilation (SIMV) ventilation
b. To measure the patient's static compliance
c. To measure the strength of the patient's inspiratory muscles
d. To measure the effects of bronchospasm during an asthma episode

22. Which one of the following statements is true regarding peak flow meter use in asthmatic patients?

a. Peak flow zones are most accurate when based on a patient's predicted number.
b. Many patients never achieve their predicted peak flow number when asymptomatic.
c. A patient's predicted peak flow value is based on his or her weight and height.
d. Peak flow monitoring is required of all asthmatic patients older than age 4.

23. All of the following choices are benefits of tracheostomy tube placement for mechanical ventilation EXCEPT

a. Reduction in aspiration risk
b. Ability to bypass upper airway obstructions
c. Less airway trauma with long-term ventilation
d. Patients can be mechanically ventilated at home

24. All of the following choices are benefits to oral airway placement EXCEPT

a. Patients are unable to bite down on an endotracheal tube.
b. Lower airway obstructions can be bypassed.
c. Suction catheters can be fed through the center channel.
d. Resuscitation masks fit over the oral airway.

25. A respiratory therapist is assigned a cystic fibrosis patient who is scheduled for the following therapies: chest physiotherapy (CPT) via vest for 20 minutes, 2.5 albuterol nebulizer Q4 h, 0.5 mg budesonide nebulizer BID. The patient is due for all three therapies. Which therapy should be provided LAST?

a. 2.5 albuterol nebulizer
b. 0.5 mg budesonide nebulizer
c. CPT via vest for 20 minutes
d. These therapies can be provided in any order.

26. Which of the following choices is NOT true regarding positive expiratory pressure (PEP) therapy?

a. Expiratory pressure is applied to the airway via oscillation.
b. PEP therapy is delivered via a handheld device known as a flutter valve.
c. The purpose of PEP therapy is to relieve bronchospasm and airway obstruction.
d. PEP therapy maneuvers should continue for up to 20 breaths per session.

27. All of the following conditions are contraindications for chest physiotherapy (CPT) EXCEPT

a. Chest tube placement
b. Eating a meal 10 minutes prior to therapy
c. History of flail chest
d. Rib fracture

28. The respiratory therapist is called to perform CPT on a patient with a history of syncope. The patient is admitted for pneumonia and shortness of breath. The physician's order asks for CPT with postural drainage of the lower lobes. In which position should the patient be placed to accomplish this request?

a. Supine
b. Prone
c. Head of bed elevated
d. Trendelenburg

29. The respiratory therapist is called to perform intrapulmonary percussive ventilation (IPV) therapy on a patient with pneumonia. The respiratory therapist prepares the equipment and starts the therapy. The IPV machine is not delivering any pressure or mist to the patient. All of the following troubleshooting steps would be helpful at this time EXCEPT

a. Ensuring an adequate power source
b. Ensuring an adequate gas source
c. Checking all connections
d. Sending the machine for repair

30. Which one of the following steps in a cough-assist maneuver is incorrect?

a. Place the palms of your hands on either side of the patient's navel.
b. Instruct the patient to exhale completely.
c. Push the patient's abdomen up and in during the cough attempt.
d. Sit the patient up or have them lie down.

31. The respiratory therapist is called to the bedside of a patient who has a tracheostomy tube in place. The nurse tells the respiratory therapist that the tube is dislodged and needs to be repositioned. What action should the respiratory therapist take FIRST?

a. Gather the necessary equipment.
b. Assess the patient for signs of respiratory distress.
c. Insert a new tracheostomy tube using clean technique.
d. Suction the patient.

32. The respiratory therapist is assisting the emergency room physician with the intubation of a patient who was the victim of a motor vehicle accident. The patient has several facial injuries as well as fractured ribs and contusions. The healthcare team attempted to intubate the patient three times with no success. Which one of the following choices is the best option for ventilating this patient?

a. Reattempt intubation with a Macintosh laryngoscope blade.
b. Attempt intubation with the laryngeal mask airway.
c. Place an oral airway.
d. Insert a tracheostomy tube.

33. All of the following choices are congenital defects of the upper airway EXCEPT

a. Choanal atresia
b. Pierre Robin sequence
c. Treacher Collins syndrome
d. Omphalocele

34. Which one of the following statements is true regarding heated high-flow nasal cannulas in the neonatal and pediatric populations?

a. A heated high-flow nasal cannula requires the use of an oxygen blender and humidifier.
b. A heated high-flow nasal cannula provides airway pressure similar to nasal continuous positive airway pressure (CPAP).
c. A heated high-flow nasal cannula provides benefits such as reduced nasal trauma and better bonding outcomes.
d. All of the above.

35. Which one of the following statements best describes an appropriately sized heated high-flow nasal cannula?

a. The patient's nares flare slightly when the prongs are inserted.
b. The prongs should fill the patient's nares with no gaps.
c. The prongs should fill one half of the nostril's diameter.
d. The prongs should fit loosely in the patient's nares.

36. Which one of the following statements is true regarding mesh nebulizers?

a. Mesh nebulizers hold high volumes and can be used as continuous nebulizers.
b. Mesh nebulizers use electricity to create vibrations that generate mist.
c. Mesh nebulizers use high flow rates from oxygen flow meters to generate mist.
d. Mesh nebulizers are small-volume pneumatic nebulizers.

37. The respiratory therapist is called to the emergency department for a patient who has an airway obstruction due to an enlarged tongue secondary to an allergic reaction. The healthcare team is attempting to ventilate the patient with a resuscitation bag and mask but is unsuccessful. The respiratory therapist places an oral airway, and resuscitation is reattempted. When the therapist squeezes the bag, the patient's chest rises only slightly and the bag is hard to squeeze. Which one of the following actions should the respiratory therapist perform FIRST?

a. Check the size of the oral airway and reposition it.
b. Attempt endotracheal intubation.
c. Suggest tracheostomy placement.
d. Order a stat chest X-ray.

38. Which one of the following choices best describes the process of determining the appropriate size of a nasal airway?

a. Measure the distance between the patient's nares and jaw in millimeters and convert to French.
b. The sizing is in French units and is standard based on the patient's weight.
c. Measure the distance from the patient's nares to ear in millimeters and convert to French.
d. Measure the diameter of the patient's nares and convert to French.

39. Which one of the following statements is true regarding the use of endotracheal tubes in the NICU?

a. Bronchial lavage should be performed after each suctioning attempt.
b. In-line suction catheters should be changed weekly to prevent infection.
c. Neonatal endotracheal tube cuffs have a low inflation volume.
d. Endotracheal tubes require either sterile suctioning technique or inline suction systems.

40. The respiratory therapist is called to the pediatric intensive care unit for a 9-year-old male patient who is mechanically ventilated. The nurse states that the patient's ventilator is alarming. The respiratory therapist enters the room and sees that the patient is agitated and the high-pressure alarm is alerting. All of the following actions are appropriate at this time EXCEPT

a. Remove the patient from the ventilator and manually ventilate him.
b. Attempt to suction the endotracheal tube.
c. Instruct the nurse to increase the patient's sedation.
d. Auscultate breath sounds bilaterally.

41. The respiratory therapist is called to a patient's bedside for suctioning. The patient has a tracheostomy tube with sterile suction catheter kits on the bedside table. The respiratory therapist introduces herself to the patient and describes the procedure. She opens the suction kit and attaches the wall suction tubing to the end of the catheter. She then puts the sterile glove on her dominant hand and advances the catheter into the endotracheal tube with her sterile-gloved hand. The catheter is advanced to a preset length, suction is applied with her nondominant hand, and the catheter is removed from the endotracheal tube with her dominant hand. What mistake did the respiratory therapist make during this procedure?

a. She used her nonsterile hand to apply suction to the catheter.
b. She should have put the sterile glove on first.
c. She used her nonsterile hand to advance the suction catheter.
d. She forgot to instill normal saline prior to suctioning.

42. Which one of the following statements is true regarding speaking valves on tracheostomy tubes?

a. They are a standard size and style.
b. They bypass the upper airway and send air to the vocal cords.
c. The tracheostomy tube cuff must be partially deflated when using a speaking valve.
d. The patient can receive supplemental oxygen and humidification while using a speaking valve.

43. The respiratory therapist is called to the emergency room to assist with an intubation. The physician has elected to use a laryngeal mask airway. The clinician places the patient in the sniffing position, coats the mask end of the airway in a facility-approved lubricant, and inserts the laryngeal mask airway into the mouth with the mask pointing up. The clinician then rotates the tube while feeding it through the oral cavity into the airway. The clinician feels resistance and stops advancing the tube. He then inflates the cuff. What mistake did the clinician make in this procedure?

a. There is no need to inflate a cuff because laryngeal mask airways are cuffless.
b. The clinician should insert the mask pointing down.
c. The clinician should have stopped inserting the tube prior to feeling resistance.
d. The clinician did not use sterile technique.

44. All of the following choices can provide inaccurate transcutaneous monitoring results EXCEPT

a. Cyanosis
b. Poor adhesion of sensor
c. Edema
d. High probe temperature

45. Which one of the following statements is true regarding transcutaneous monitoring systems?

a. The probe must be placed on the patient's arms to ensure an accurate reading.
b. Transcutaneous monitoring is as accurate as an arterial blood gas puncture.
c. Contact solution is required to allow for the measurement of oxygen and carbon dioxide.
d. No skin prep is required prior to placing the probes.

46. All of the following statements are true regarding insufflator-exsufflator therapy EXCEPT

a. Insufflator-exsufflator machines deliver positive pressure during inspiration and expiration.
b. Insufflator-exsufflator machines are commonly used on patients with insufficient respiratory muscle strength.
c. Adverse events are unlikely, but they can include pneumothorax and aggravation of gastroesophageal reflux disease (GERD).
d. The goal of insufflator-exsufflator therapy is to induce a cough.

47. Which one of the following statements is true regarding mechanical ventilation in the home environment?

a. Mechanical ventilation can only be used short term in the home environment.
b. Mechanical ventilation in the home can only be delivered noninvasively to ensure patient safety.
c. Prior to initiating mechanical ventilation in the home setting, the patient and caregivers must undergo a patient education session.
d. Mechanical ventilation must be delivered continuously in the home setting.

48. All of the following choices are examples of neonatal congenital myopathies EXCEPT

a. Neuromyotonia
b. Myelomeningocele
c. Scoliosis
d. Hirschsprung **disease**

49. A homecare respiratory therapist is called to the patient's home because the patient's CPAP machine is not delivering the set pressure. All of the following are appropriate actions to take at this time EXCEPT

a. Call the homecare company for a service call.
b. Check the circuitry for disconnections.
c. Look for kinks and obstructions in the tubing.
d. Disassemble and clean the machine.

50. A homecare respiratory therapist is called to the patient's home because the patient is not tolerating the CPAP machine well. The patient complains that the machine delivers too much pressure and it is causing sinus pain and a sore throat. All of the following are appropriate actions to take at this time EXCEPT

a. Adjust the ramp setting.
b. Reduce the pressure level.
c. Apply a humidifier.
d. Ask the patient how often the machine is cleaned.

51. The respiratory therapist is called to a patient's bedside in the NICU because of excessive rainout in the ventilator circuit. The patient is using a heated wire circuit with attached humidifier. All of the following actions are appropriate to take at this time EXCEPT

a. Titrate the heater temperature.
b. Titrate the level of humidity.
c. Adjust the isolette temperature.
d. Drain the condensation back into the humidifier.

52. Which one of the following neonatal patient populations can benefit from apnea monitors?

a. Patients with severe GERD
b. Patients who require supplemental oxygen at home
c. Patients who require mechanical ventilation in the home
d. All of the above

53. All of the following statements are true regarding home-based supplemental oxygen therapy EXCEPT

a. Oxygen is a drug and requires a physician's order.
b. Patients who use liquid oxygen need a backup system in case of power failure.
c. Oxygen tanks require special holders that must be used at all times.
d. The use of oxygen tubing extensions can result in reduced output.

54. All of the following are indications for bronchial lavage EXCEPT

a. Suspected lung cancer
b. Chronic refractory pneumonia
c. Cough of unknown origin
d. Severe refractory asthma

55. Which one of the following statements is true regarding obtaining a sample of lung tissue via bronchoscopy?

a. The collection of smaller cells requires the use of a brush tool.
b. Bronchial lavage is not a necessary intervention for obtaining a cellular sample.
c. Tissue samples are obtained to determine the presence of inflammation.
d. Brush tools are only used in conjunction with the scissor tool.

56. Which of the following pathogens are tested via nasal swab and nasal wash?

a. Influenza and pneumonia
b. Respiratory syncytial virus (RSV) and methicillin-resistant *Staphylococcus aureus* (MRSA)
c. Fungal infections
d. Fungal and bacterial infections

57. The respiratory therapist is called to the patient's bedside to obtain a sputum sample for pathogen testing. The respiratory therapist enters the room and sees that the patient is using a tracheostomy collar with aerosolized oxygen. The clinician opens a sterile suction kit, and using her nonsterile hand attaches a sputum trap with one end attached to wall suction and the other end attached to a sterile suction catheter. The respiratory therapist winds the suction catheter around her sterile hand and instills saline into the tracheostomy tube using her nonsterile hand. She then inserts the suction catheter into the tracheostomy tube with her sterile hand to a predetermined depth and quickly suctions the saline back out while holding the sputum trap horizontal to the patient's bed. Then the clinician labels and packages the specimen and transports it for testing. What mistake did the clinician make in this scenario?

a. She did not uphold sterile technique.
b. She should not have instilled saline because it dilutes the sample.
c. She should slowly suction the patient's tracheostomy tube after saline instillation.
d. She positioned the sputum trap incorrectly.

58. Which one of the following drug families is not commonly used during the process of intubating a patient?

a. Opioids
b. Hypnotics
c. Neuromuscular blocking agents
d. Analgesics

59. All of the following side effects are associated with the use of reversal agents EXCEPT

a. Stomach upset
b. Seizure
c. Headache
d. Irregular heartbeat

60. Vasoactive and inotropic agents improve the oxygen perfusion and cardiac output of all of the following diagnoses EXCEPT

a. Shock
b. Patent ductus arteriosus
c. Sepsis
d. Transposition of the great vessels

61. A respiratory therapist is covering the NICU when he gets called to the operating room. A patient is in preterm labor and is undergoing an emergency C-section. The patient was administered terbutaline in an attempt to slow labor. What effects on the fetus should the respiratory therapist expect from the terbutaline in the mother's system?

a. No adverse neonatal effects are common with terbutaline use in pregnant women.
b. Tremors and poor muscle tone
c. Tachycardia and blood sugar changes
d. Respiratory depression

62. Which one of the following choices is not common findings in neonates with renal failure?

a. Acidosis
b. Pulmonary edema
c. Hypoxia
d. Respiratory failure

63. All of the following statements are true regarding patients with neonatal hepatic failure EXCEPT

a. Complications of hepatic failure can include respiratory distress syndrome and renal failure.
b. Patients rarely require a liver transplant because hepatic failure can be adequately treated.
c. Supplemental oxygen and mechanical ventilation may be required in some cases of hepatic failure.
d. Patients may present with hypovolemia but can quickly experience fluid overload.

64. Which one of the following components is not routinely measured as part of hemoglobin (Hgb) electrophoresis and a complete blood count (CBC)?

a. Basophils and lymphocytes
b. Hemoglobin and platelets
c. Hematocrit and methemoglobin
d. Mean corpuscular volume

65. Which one of the following conditions puts a patient at risk for fluid overload?

a. Patent ductus arteriosus
b. Choanal atresia
c. Hyperbilirubinemia
d. Mitral valve regurgitation

66. Which one of the following neonatal conditions requires routine glucose testing?

a. Sepsis
b. Hepatic failure
c. Renal failure
d. Glucose testing is routine in all neonates.

67. Which one of the following conditions is diagnosed by sweat testing?

a. Cystic fibrosis
b. Bronchopulmonary dysplasia
c. Bronchiectasis
d. Transient tachypnea of the newborn

68. Which one of the following statements is true regarding Gram staining and sputum culture?

a. Staining the sputum sample allows for better inspection of viruses under the microscope.
b. A sputum culture evaluates the presence of bacteria and fungi.
c. Sputum samples for cultures can only be obtained from conscious patients.
d. Sputum samples cannot contain saline or saliva.

69. All of the following conditions are associated with drug overdoses EXCEPT

a. Depressed central nervous system
b. Seizure activity
c. Increased respiratory rate
d. Faint or weak pulse

70. Which one of the following conditions is commonly associated with neonatal abstinence syndrome?

a. Irritability and seizures
b. Increased respiratory rate
c. Hypoxia and hyperventilation
d. Excessive sleepiness

71. What does a large sail sign indicate on a chest X-ray?

a. Pneumothorax
b. Flail chest
c. Pneumomediastinum
d. Pleural effusion

72. All of the following conditions are commonly evaluated via lateral chest X-ray EXCEPT

a. Foreign body presence
b. Pneumothorax
c. Emphysema
d. Chest tube position

73. Which one of the following chest X-ray findings is consistent with tetralogy of Fallot?

a. Normal-shaped enlarged heart
b. Boot-shaped heart
c. "Egg-on-a-string" heart
d. Downturned cardiac apex

74. All of the following statements are true regarding tetralogy of Fallot EXCEPT

a. Tetralogy of Fallot requires immediate surgical correction.
b. The heart pumps unoxygenated blood throughout the body.
c. Heart murmur and cyanosis are common in this defect.
d. This defect includes an obstructed pulmonary valve and closed ventricular septum.

75. All of the following statements are true regarding transposition of the great vessels EXCEPT

a. Transposition of the great vessels requires immediate surgical correction.
b. Transposition of the great vessels results in hypoxia due to unoxygenated blood circulating through the body.
c. Patients may undergo cardiac catheterization and atrial enlargement.
d. In this condition, the pulmonary artery is attached to the right ventricle and the aorta is attached to the left ventricle.

76. Which one of the following diagnostic tests exposes the patient to radiation?

a. Computed tomography
b. Magnetic resonance imaging
c. Ultrasound
d. Echocardiogram

77. Which one of the following choices is not a risk associated with feeding intolerance of the newborn?

a. Abdominal distension and gastroesophageal reflux
b. Aspiration and infection
c. Apnea and bradycardia
d. Hyperglycemia

78. All of the following are challenges associated with the mechanical or manual ventilation of the morbidly obese patient EXCEPT

a. Some patients require extended-length tracheostomy tubes.
b. Some noninvasive ventilation masks don't maintain a tight seal.
c. Patients require higher tidal volumes during ventilation.
d. Patients often present with airway obstructions.

79. A 39-year-old male presents to the clinic complaining of sleepiness, headache, and general fatigue. The patient has a body mass index of 42, his heart rate is 80, and his respiratory rate is 20. Breath sounds are clear to slightly diminished. The patient states that he is constantly tired and takes a lot of naps. He also complains of headaches, mostly during the morning hours. He drinks several cups of coffee per day and drinks energy drinks to stay awake at work. What is the likely cause of this patient's fatigue?

a. GERD
b. Obstructive sleep apnea
c. Parasomnias
d. Narcolepsy

80. A respiratory therapist is called to the NICU to prepare for the delivery and possible resuscitation of a preterm neonate using a T-piece resuscitator. The physician's order indicates that she wants 5 cm of positive end-expiratory pressure (PEEP) in addition to a predetermined peak inspiratory pressure (PIP). The respiratory therapist plugs the unit into an adequate gas source. He then attaches the patient circuit and T-piece is to the machine, ensuring adequate gas flow through the T-piece. The oxygen flow meter is set at the predetermined liter flow, and PIP and PEEP settings are dialed in on the machine. The respiratory therapist attaches the T-piece to the patient mask and waits for the arrival of the patient. Which step in this setup procedure is incorrect?

a. The respiratory therapist failed to occlude the PEEP port during setup.
b. The clinician is using the wrong equipment because a T-piece resuscitator should not be used in the neonatal population.
c. The delivered PEEP is constant, and it does not require a physician's order.
d. PIP is based on flow and is not a setting on the machine.

81. All of the following statements are true regarding T-piece resuscitators EXCEPT

a. Patients require a tight-fitting mask to ensure an adequate seal and proper pressure delivery.
b. The manual breaths are provided by occluding the PEEP valve during inspiration.
c. T-piece resuscitators increase the risk of barotrauma by delivering a set pressure to the airway.
d. Alveolar recruitment is one benefit of T-piece resuscitator use.

82. What is the current Neonatal Resuscitation Program guideline for the ventilation rate during resuscitation?

a. 40–60 breaths per minute
b. 30–50 breaths per minute
c. 50–70 breaths per minute
d. 60–80 breaths per minute

83. Which one of the following hand positions is correct when performing chest compressions in accordance with Pediatric Advanced Life Support guidelines for resuscitation?

a. Heel of the hand on the chest with the opposite hand on top and fingers entwined
b. Two fingers in the center of the chest at the nipple line
c. Heel of one hand in the center of the chest at the nipple line
d. Compress to half the width of the chest from front to back

84. All of the following statements are true regarding a critical care patient evacuation EXCEPT

a. Oxygen tanks must be placed beneath patient beds for patients using oxygen or mechanical ventilation.
b. Resuscitation bags are required for each intubated patient, but masks are not necessary.
c. Portable cardiac and respiratory monitors need to be included in the patient's transport setup.
d. Patients may be evacuated from their rooms to the hallways during a severe weather event.

85. Which one of the following choices is not a goal of triage?

a. Ensure the highest rate of survival for victims.
b. Provide organization in times of crisis.
c. Treat the most critical patients first.
d. Reduce ER wait times for walk-ins.

86. The respiratory therapist is called to the emergency department to help with a mass-casualty event. An explosion took place at a nearby factory, and the fire spread to the school next door. The students are en route to the hospital. All of the following tools should be gathered at this time EXCEPT

a. Personal protective equipment and intubation kits
b. Oxygen tanks and nebulizers
c. Peak flow meters and valved holding chambers
d. Ventilators and resuscitation equipment

87. Which one of the following choices is not an example of interdisciplinary cooperation?

a. Cluster care in the NICU
b. Triage in the emergency room
c. In-room rounds
d. Report given in the respiratory department

88. All of the following options are parts of tracheostomy home care EXCEPT

a. Skin care
b. Oral care
c. Sterile suction technique
d. Clean technique for tube replacement

89. The respiratory therapist is preparing to suction a tracheostomy tube in the pediatric intensive care unit. The patient is a 7-year-old female with a tracheostomy tube and a closed suction system. First, the clinician ensures that the suction is attached to the catheter and the wall suction is set at an appropriate level. Then, he puts on gloves and grasps the suction catheter in preparation for suctioning. He advances the catheter into the tracheostomy to the preapproved depth and applies suction while slowly pulling the catheter out of the tracheostomy tube. The clinician then instills sterile saline into the catheter and suctions it back out to maintain a patent suction catheter. What mistake did the respiratory therapist make?

a. He didn't perform bronchial lavage during suctioning.
b. He didn't perform hand hygiene before suctioning.
c. He didn't uphold sterile technique.
d. He didn't preoxygenate the patient.

90. A respiratory therapist is called to the bedside of a 12-year-old tracheostomy patient who is dyspneic. The nurse reports that the patient has been coughing and agitated for several minutes. The patient is utilizing a tracheostomy collar at 30% FiO_2 with humidity. The respiratory therapist enters the room and assesses the patient. Breath sounds are coarse, the respiratory rate is 27, and accessory muscle use is noted. The patient is coughing and agitated. The patient's oxygen saturation is 96%, and the tracheostomy tube is in place. What action should be taken at this time?

a. Increase the FiO_2 to 40% for comfort.
b. Prepare to replace the tracheostomy tube.
c. Suction the tracheostomy tube.
d. Remove the humidifier.

91. All of the following are medical monitoring devices that can be used in the home setting EXCEPT

a. Transcutaneous monitor
b. Apnea monitor
c. Pulse oximeter
d. Peak flow meter

92. What is a car seat challenge?

a. The requirement that all neonates go home with a car seat
b. A test in which a preterm baby is placed in a car seat for at least 90 minutes to monitor their breathing
c. A test in which a preterm baby is placed in a car seat for 30 minutes to monitor their breathing
d. A test in which a term baby is placed in a car seat for home transport

93. Who is not responsible for educating a patient on home oxygen equipment?

a. The homecare company
b. The respiratory therapist
c. The nurse
d. The physician

94. The respiratory therapist is called to the emergency room to educate a patient on bronchodilators for home use. The patient is a 10-year-old female who had an asthma exacerbation during her school soccer game. The patient's breath sounds are clear, her respiratory rate is 18, and her oxygen saturation is 99%. The patient was administered one albuterol nebulizer treatment en route to the hospital in the ambulance, followed by an additional albuterol nebulizer treatment in the emergency room. The last treatment was given 30 minutes prior. Following their facility's respiratory protocol, the respiratory therapist has a choice of medication delivery systems to order for this patient. Which one of the following short-acting bronchodilator delivery devices is most effective for this patient?

a. Nebulizer
b. Metered-dose inhaler with spacer
c. Dry powder inhaler
d. Nebulizers and inhalers are equally effective.

95. Which one of the following statements is true regarding the testing of amniotic fluid?

a. Amniotic fluid is measured in four quadrants, and the median number is the index.
b. An index of less than 5 cm is potentially life-threatening.
c. A poor amniotic fluid index can be caused by trisomy disorders.
d. Measurements may be taken in areas with fetal structures present.

96. Which one of the following maternal medications is associated with low-birth-weight neonates?

a. Toradol
b. Fluticasone
c. Tramadol
d. Levalbuterol

97. All of the following are components of a fetus's biophysical profile EXCEPT

a. Measurement of amniotic fluid levels
b. Fetal movement
c. Amniocentesis
d. Fetal muscle tone

98. Who or what is the Apgar score named after?

a. Dr. Virginia Apgar
b. Appearance, pulse, grimace, activity, and respiration
c. Apnea, pulse, grimace, appearance, and respiration
d. Apgar General Hospital

99. How is fetal lung maturity determined?

a. Respiratory assessment after birth
b. Amniocentesis
c. Sweat test
d. Amniotic fluid index measurement

100. All of the following choices can be accessed via transillumination EXCEPT

a. Blood vessel location
b. Pneumomediastinum
c. Pleural effusion
d. Pneumothorax

101. The respiratory therapist is called to the NICU to perform an oxygen challenge test on a cyanotic neonate. The patient is a 37-week-gestation neonate who was born two days ago. The patient is on a 0.5-liter nasal cannula. The respiratory therapist obtains an arterial blood sample from the right radial artery. Then, the patient is placed on 100% oxygen for 10 minutes. The respiratory therapist draws a second blood gas. The two blood gas values are then compared. Which part of this process is incorrect?

a. The patient should have been on room air for the first blood draw.
b. The blood gas should have been drawn from the left radial artery.
c. The patient should have been placed on 50% oxygen for 10 minutes.
d. Oxygen challenge testing shouldn't be performed on preterm neonates.

102. What is the purpose of CO_2 verification after intubation?

a. To determine the patient's acid–base balance
b. To ensure adequate respiration
c. To confirm tube placement
d. To eliminate the need for imaging studies

103. All of the following choices are medical gases used to treat respiratory disorders EXCEPT

a. Heliox
b. Nitric oxide
c. Isoflurane
d. Medical air

104. How are tidal volumes calculated for term neonatal patients on volume-control mechanical ventilation?

a. 4–6 ml/kg
b. 5–10 ml/kg
c. 10–15 ml/kg
d. 15–20 ml/kg

105. The respiratory therapist is called to a neonatal patient's bedside to increase their inspiration:expiration (I:E) ratio from 1:2 to 1:1. Why would this change be necessary?

a. The patient's lung compliance has worsened.
b. The patient's airway resistance has decreased.
c. The patient's peak pressures have decreased.
d. The patient's MAP is decreasing.

106. All of the following statements are true regarding conventional mechanical ventilation modes EXCEPT

a. Pressure-controlled ventilation limits the pressures delivered to the airway while the volumes vary.
b. Volume ventilation prevents barotrauma in immature lungs.
c. In SIMV, patients are able to take additional spontaneous breaths delivered at varying tidal volumes.
d. To change a patient's minute ventilation in pressure-controlled ventilation, the clinician titrates the PIP.

107. All of the following statements are true regarding high-frequency jet ventilation and high-frequency oscillatory ventilation EXCEPT

a. Both modes use small tidal volumes and high rates.
b. These modes are indicated for critically ill patients such as those with respiratory distress syndrome.
c. High-frequency oscillation ventilation is used in tandem with traditional mechanical ventilators.
d. High-frequency jet ventilators deliver the tidal volume and the rate and initiates inspiration and expiration.

108. The respiratory therapist is called to the NICU to adjust a patient's ventilator settings. The patient is a 36-week-gestation neonate who has been on a high-frequency oscillatory ventilator for 24 hours. The patient's oxygen saturation is dropping. Chest X-rays show normal aeration with infiltrates. Which ventilator setting change should be made to improve the patient's oxygenation?

a. Titrate delta P.
b. Increase FiO_2.
c. Titrate the MAP.
d. Increase the hertz.

109. Which ventilator setting is not pre-set in volume-targeted mechanical ventilation?

a. Peak pressure
b. Tidal volume
c. FiO_2
d. Respiratory rate

110. Which one of the following statements is not true regarding airway pressure release ventilation (APRV) ventilation?

a. APRV offers a high- and a low-pressure setting.
b. APRV delivers inverse I:E ratios.
c. APRV delivers breaths with time cycling.
d. APRV is a widely used ventilator setting.

111. What is unique about neutrally adjusted ventilatory assist (NAVA) ventilation?

a. Diaphragmatic activity and respiratory drive are monitored via a probe.
b. NAVA prevents barotrauma by preventing overdistention of the lungs.
c. NAVA can be used with any traditional mechanical ventilator.
d. Neurological activity is monitored via scalp sensors.

112. How is the proper size and length of a NAVA catheter calculated?

a. Via the nose-ear-xiphoid (NEX) calculation
b. By measuring the distance between the nares and the jaw
c. By measuring the distance from the jaw to the xiphoid process
d. By measuring the distance from the nose to the cricoid cartilage

113. The respiratory therapist is called to set up a bubble continuous positive airway pressure (CPAP) unit for a 32-week-gestation neonate in the NICU. The therapist measures the patient's nares and determines the appropriate size nasal prongs. Next, the respiratory therapist gathers an oxygen flow meter, heated humidifier, oxygen analyzer, nasal prongs, pressure gauge, respiratory circuit, and water canister. She fills the water canister with sterile water and submerges the expiratory limb of the CPAP circuit. The flow meter is set according to physician's orders, and it is turned on. She then inserts the prongs into the patient's nares and secures them with Velcro straps included in the CPAP nasal prong kit. The respiratory therapist documents the FiO_2, flow rate, time of procedure, nasal prong size, and patient tolerance. What did the respiratory therapist forget?

a. She didn't record the depth of the expiratory limb submersion.
b. She should have submerged the inspiratory limb of the circuit.
c. She didn't secure the CPAP prongs correctly.
d. She should have used an unheated humidifier.

114. All of the following statements are true regarding lung recruitment EXCEPT

a. Prone positioning can help recruit alveoli in posterior lung lobes.
b. High peak pressures and increased PEEP for short periods of time can recruit alveoli.
c. Lung recruitment maneuvers can cause barotrauma and respiratory distress.
d. Lung recruitment maneuvers are not clinically proven to improve ventilatory status.

115. All of the following statements are true regarding extracorporeal membrane oxygenation (ECMO) EXCEPT

a. ECMO can be either veno-venous or arterial-arterial.
b. ECMO bypasses the lungs, allowing for external oxygenation and CO_2 removal.
c. Anticoagulation therapy is required during ECMO therapy.
d. Arterial blood gas testing is performed periodically during ECMO therapy.

116. Which one of the following choices indicates impaired gas exchange and shunting?

a. An elevated PaO_2:FiO_2 ratio
b. A reduced SaO_2:FiO_2 ratio
c. Elevated base excess
d. Increased PIP

117. A patient is being mechanically ventilated via the following settings: pressure control, PIP 20, rate 27, FiO_2 40%, 5 PEEP. The MAP is 22. An arterial blood gas was drawn, and the results are as follows: 7.23/17/88/–15/8. What is the patient's oxygen index?

a. 54.0
b. 7.1
c. 10.0
d. 48.4

118. Which one of the following equations calculates a patient's VD:VT ratio?

a. $FiO_2(PB - 47) - PaCO_2$
b. $\frac{PaCO_2 - PECO_2}{PaCO_2}$
c. $\frac{MAP \times FiO_2 \times 100}{PaO_2}$
d. $\frac{FiO_2 - PaCO_2}{R}$

119. A respiratory therapist is called to the ICU to perform a maximal inspiratory pressure (MIP) assessment on a spontaneously breathing patient. The respiratory therapist gathered a circuit with one-way valves and a pressure manometer. He then attaches the pressure manometer to the nipple adapter on the circuit. He instructs the patient to take a deep breath through the circuit and then occludes the one-way valve. The maneuver is repeated nine more times in 20 seconds. The respiratory therapist then records the highest (most-negative) reading on the manometer. The patient tolerates the testing well. What error did the respiratory therapist make in this vignette?

a. The respiratory therapist had the patient repeat the maneuver too many times.
b. The respiratory therapist had the patient repeat the maneuver for too long of a duration.
c. The respiratory therapist occluded the one-way valve too late.
d. The respiratory therapist should have recorded the lowest (least-negative) reading.

120. All of the following cardiac effects are associated with mechanical ventilation EXCEPT

a. Reduced cardiac output
b. Arrythmias
c. Fluid overload
d. Bronchospasm

121. All of the following statements are true regarding cerebral oximetry EXCEPT

a. Cerebral oximetry measures the oxygen level in the brain.
b. Cerebral oximetry is available in trend and absolute monitoring.
c. Sensor sizing is determined by the circumference of the patient's head.
d. Its use is supported by the Beer–Lambert law.

122. All of the following are ways to determine ventilator weaning readiness EXCEPT

a. Spontaneous breathing trials
b. Following respiratory protocols
c. NIF measurement
d. Reduced FiO_2

123. All of the following statements are true regarding permissive hypercapnia EXCEPT

a. Adequate oxygenation is more easily achieved in severe respiratory compromised patients.
b. Lungs are protected from overinflation due to high delivered volumes.
c. Lower airway pressures result in less barotrauma.
d. The benefits of hypercapnia often do not outweigh the risks.

124. Which one of the following statements is true regarding therapeutic hypothermia?

a. Its purpose is to preserve brain cells and brain function after critical illness or injury.
b. It is most effective in patients who regain consciousness after cardiac arrest.
c. Shivering is a common side effect of therapeutic hypothermia.
d. Upon completion of therapy, the patient is quickly rewarmed to normal body temperature.

125. Which one of the following statements is true regarding surfactant replacement therapy?

a. Surfactant replacement instillation can result in airway obstructions.
b. Procedures vary among facilities, but patients are often left supine during instillation.
c. Lung compliance often changes gradually after the administration of surfactant.
d. The patient's airway does not need to be suctioned prior to surfactant administration.

126. All of the following statements are true regarding airway instillations EXCEPT

a. Lidocaine is not routinely instilled for bronchoscopy procedures.
b. Instillation of epinephrine is most successful in adult patients with vascular access.
c. Epinephrine is instilled as an alternative to intracardiac injection.
d. Minimal side effects are associated with airway instillations.

127. At what level should the head of the patient's bed be elevated to minimize the risk of ventilator-associated pneumonia?

a. 90 degrees
b. 70 degrees
c. 50 degrees
d. 30 degrees

128. What is the difference between palliative care and hospice care?

a. Hospice care is for patients with one year or less to live.
b. Palliative care is for patients with chronic, progressive illnesses.
c. Palliative care is for patients with deadly diseases.
d. There is no difference; both treat patients at the end of their lifetime.

129. All of the following statements are true regarding brain death and withdrawal of support EXCEPT

a. Brain death refers to a patient's comatose state due to metabolic issues, electrolyte changes, or other disorders.
b. When the patient is undergoing brain death evaluation, he or she must be fully sedated.
c. EEG and O_2 challenge testing is used to determine brain death.
d. Withdrawal of support can be initiated based in part on advance directives and/or the patient's wishes.

Answer Key and Explanations

1. C: SPO_2 measurement, the evaluation of blood oxygen saturation, is a vital sign that is part of a comprehensive initial patient assessment; however, laboratory results are often not available during the patient's initial presentation to the ER. Laboratory testing is a secondary tool used to further evaluate a patient once the initial assessment has been made. Therefore, C is the correct answer.

2. D: There are numerous types of imaging studies that can be performed on neonatal and pediatric patients. Some imaging studies are interventional and therapeutic. This can include studies such as cardiac catheterization and angiography, both of which are used for diagnostic purposes as well as interventional and therapeutic reasons. Other imaging studies, such as chest X-rays and MRI scans, are used solely for diagnostic purposes, allowing healthcare providers to noninvasively measure, evaluate, and examine the internal structures of the body.

3. A: Accessory muscle use is a common sign of respiratory distress in adults and older pediatric patients. These patients often use secondary muscles in the neck and chest to help them breathe during episodes of respiratory distress. Infants in respiratory distress often present with several signs and symptoms including intercostal or subcostal retractions, grunting, and nasal flaring.

4. C: Sleep apnea can only be definitively diagnosed through sleep studies. These diagnostic interventions measure several criteria, such as heart rate, respiratory rate, occurrences of apnea, duration of apnea, oxygen saturation, and other measurements. Therefore, answer D is incorrect. Option A is incorrect because sleep studies are only performed during "regular" sleeping hours during the evening and nighttime. Option B is incorrect because pediatric patients may also undergo sleep study testing especially if sleep apnea is suspected.

5. B: A patient's neurological status is directly related to a patient's respiratory status. For example, if a patient has central nervous system insufficiency, he or she may suffer from respiratory failure due to decreased respiratory drive. Neurological disorders may also cause abnormal breathing patterns, which also can result in respiratory insufficiency or failure. Finally, neurological status can directly affect the successful intubation of a patient; when a patient is fully conscious and aware of their surroundings, they will fight intubation and ventilation. However, when neuromuscular blocking agents are administered to "change" their neurological status, the patient is easily intubated with no gag reflex or "fighting" of the procedure or mechanical ventilator.

6. D: Congenital heart defects affect the oxygen delivery to the tissues of the body. Hearts with congenital defects or abnormalities are often unable to effectively perfuse the body's organ systems. This causes symptoms such as desaturation (a low oxygen level in the blood), cyanosis (blue-tinged extremities, lips, or other appendages), and respiratory failure. Wheezing is not a symptom of a heart defect because wheezing is caused by bronchospasm and airway obstruction.

7. A: Croup is an acute viral illness of the upper airway characterized by constriction, swelling, respiratory distress, and a harsh, high-pitched "seal's bark" cough. Increased work of breathing and respiratory distress are often results of the underlying croup infection. Croup is diagnosed in part by auscultating the patient's neck because this is the location where the constriction occurs. If a patient has croup, the clinician will hear stridor and whistling at the neck during respiration.

8. D: Rhonchi, also known as coarse breath sounds, are not a common sign of an asthma exacerbation. Common breath sounds in asthmatic patients include diminished breath sounds, wheezing, and silent chest. Persistent cough is a common asthma symptom, and, in fact, it can be a patient's only symptom. It is important for clinicians to understand that many asthmatic patients never wheeze. Orthopnea, the inability to lie flat without shortness of breath, is a common asthma symptom, especially at night. Finally, many asthmatic patients experience throat clearing due to the excessive mucus production that is common in asthma exacerbations.

9. B: Bronchospasm is not a common symptom of blunt-force trauma to the chest. Bronchospasm is caused by airway obstruction, whereas chest trauma causes changes to the patient's compliance due to pulmonary contusions, pneumothorax, and other acute injuries to the chest wall. These serious injuries can result in respiratory failure and the need for ventilatory support including rescue breathing and mechanical ventilation.

10. C: Apnea is defined as the absence of breathing for at least 20 seconds.

11. B: Apnea of prematurity is not characterized by excessive fluid. Patients with bronchopulmonary dysplasia, pulmonary hypertension or congestive heart failure, and kidney failure all have problems regulating the fluid balance within the body. These patients often are fluid "overloaded," and this excessive fluid can contribute to respiratory failure and distress.

12. C: In diabetic ketoacidosis, high blood sugar causes the release of ketones, which results in an acid–base mismatch and impending respiratory failure. These patients' blood gases will show a rising pH and CO_2 and a falling PO_2. Diabetic ketoacidosis and its resulting acid–base mismatch have a direct effect on respiratory status, often causing impending respiratory failure that must be treated immediately. If diabetic ketoacidosis is not immediately treated, the patient's impending respiratory failure will quickly transition into full respiratory arrest.

13. A: Umbilical hernias are common disorders in the neonatal population. Although umbilical hernias can become complicated (strangulated) in some cases, generally speaking, it is considered safe to wait for the hernia to resolve spontaneously as the patient grows. Therefore, immediate surgery is not required. For more serious congenital defects of the digestive system, such as diaphragmatic hernia, esophageal atresia, and tracheoesophageal fistula, immediate surgery is required to resolve the defect and prevent complications.

14. D: Of the above options, D is the best choice. This patient is unable to adequately and safely feed. The current condition presents an aspiration pneumonia risk, which is especially dangerous for this preterm infant. Option A is incorrect because although supplemental oxygen during feeds may be helpful, it is never appropriate to automatically place a neonatal patient on 100% oxygen. Oxygen should be used in the lowest possible concentration to minimize retinopathy and other complications associated with oxygen use. Option B is incorrect because there is no indication that this patient has an allergic reaction or other adverse reaction in response to the type of formula given. Option C is incorrect because although smaller, more frequent feeds may be helpful in some cases, a longer duration of feeding is not helpful. This patient has respiratory symptoms during feedings, and prolonging the feeding may exacerbate those symptoms.

15. C: Jaundice is not a common symptom of necrotizing enterocolitis. Jaundice is a symptom of hyperbilirubinemia. Necrotizing enterocolitis is a bacterial infection of the bowels that can cause abdominal distension, bloody stools, respiratory distress, and gas buildup in the stomach and intestines.

16. A: When a spinal cord injury causes complete respiratory arrest and lack of respiratory drive, the injury is likely located above C5. In injuries that are located lower than C5 on the spinal cord, the resulting impairments often include pneumonia, reduced respiratory effort, and respiratory insufficiency.

17. D: Accurate end-tidal CO_2 monitoring is dependent upon several factors. The patient must be breathing adequately with no airway obstructions present. Apnea, hypoventilation, and hyperventilation all adversely affect the accurate measurement of end-tidal CO_2. Oxygen delivery, however, has no effect on end-tidal CO_2 measurement.

18. A: When obtaining a blood sample from an indwelling catheter for blood gas analysis, the clinician must first remove the cap from the three-way valve on the end of the patient's catheter and clean the port. He or she then inserts a nonheparinized 5 mL syringe and turns the tap to open the port. The clinician then obtains a sample of blood, removes the syringe, closes the port, and disposes of the sample. Next, the clinician repeats the procedure with a heparinized syringe and obtains a blood sample for blood gas analysis. The clinician closes the port and removes the syringe. A saline flush is attached, the port is opened, and saline is injected into the port to flush the system. The port is then closed, and the blood gas sample is placed on ice and sent to the lab for analysis. Answer A is incorrect because the syringe should not be heparinized.

19. B: Clinicians must never squeeze the heel when obtaining a capillary blood gas. When performed correctly, the blood will be free flowing and will not require squeezing. Squeezing of the foot produces inaccurate blood gas testing results. To properly obtain a capillary blood gas sample from a neonatal patient, the clinician warms the neonate's heel by applying a heel warmer for several minutes. The clinician then cleans the lateral side of the patient's heel, punctures the heel with a lancet, and allows the blood droplet to fall into the heparinized capillary tube without interference. The clinician must remove any air bubbles or blood clots in the sample. The clinician then places the sample on ice and transports it to the lab for analysis.

20. A: Although spirometry is commonly performed on patients who are 5 years of age and older, there is no contraindication for testing based solely on age. The maturity and ability of the patient to perform tasks is the most important factor in deciding whether spirometry can be performed on a patient. Therefore, the clinician should prepare the equipment, introduce him- or herself, and explain the procedure. In this scenario, the clinician should notify the physician that testing is not possible only after the test has been attempted.

21. C: Mean inspiratory testing requires the patient to inhale against a closed circuit. The patient's negative inspiratory force is measured by a manometer that is attached to the circuit during the procedure. This value indicates the strength of the patient's inspiratory muscles, and it is a common tool that is used to help determine a patient's readiness to be weaned from a mechanical ventilator.

22. C: Peak flow testing is helpful for some patients with asthma. The patient exhales hard and fast into a peak flow meter, and the meter gives the patient a numerical result. Patients can track these readings to determine when their asthma is exacerbated (the peak flows drop) or when their asthma is improving (the peak flows rise). Answer A is incorrect because peak flow monitoring zones should be based on the patient's personal best number, i.e., the highest peak flow value they have every achieved. This is the number to strive for. Option B is incorrect because most patients never achieve their predicted peak flow value because this number is based on their height and sex in a healthy, nonasthmatic individual. Option D is incorrect because peak flow monitoring is not required of any asthmatic patient; instead, it is a helpful tool for some patients, especially those who are poor perceivers of symptoms and severity.

23. A: The risks associated with tracheostomy tube usage in the mechanically ventilated patient include infection risk and risk of aspiration. The benefits associated with tracheostomy tube use includes less airway trauma with long-term mechanical ventilation, ability to bypass upper airway obstructions and abnormalities, and patients can be mechanically ventilated via tracheostomy in the home environment.

24. B: Oral airways, commonly known as bite blocks, are used for several purposes in the healthcare setting. Oral airways can be used to prevent a patient from biting down on an endotracheal tube or repositioning the patient's tongue to prevent it from falling back into the oropharynx. They can also be used to help bypass an upper airway obstruction or abnormality, and patients can be suctioned through the center channel on the airway. Resuscitation masks also fit over the airway, allowing the clinician to manually ventilate a patient with the bite block in place. Option B is the correct answer because oral airways alleviate upper airway obstructions, not lower airway obstructions.

25. B: Generally, CPT is performed after bronchodilation, but before the inhaled steroid to ensure maximum distribution of the steroid. The clinician should first administer albuterol because this is a bronchodilator, which will relax the airway. The patient would be more likely to expectorate mucus after the administration of a bronchodilator therapy when the airways are more relaxed. Next, CPT is performed to break up the mucus and clear the airway/lungs. The clinician would then administer budesonide, which is a localized inhaled steroid that reduces airway inflammation.

26. C: Positive expiratory pressure (PEP) therapy is an intervention in which a patient exhales into a PEP device (also known as a flutter valve). The PEP device oscillates during the patient's exhalation, delivering the oscillatory effect to the patient's airway. This helps to dislodge mucus within the lungs and allows the patient to expectorate it more easily. Option C is the correct answer because PEP therapy is used for the expectoration of airway secretions and has no effect on bronchospasm or other airway obstructions.

27. C: A history of lung injury or infection including flail chest is not necessarily a contraindication for chest physiotherapy (CPT). If the injury has healed and no further damage to the chest structures is present, then CPT can be administered. CPT is the therapeutic tapping or cupping on a patient's chest to help the patient expectorate mucus. This therapy is contraindicated in patients who have eaten within 30 minutes to an hour of therapy, patients with chest injuries such as rib fracture, and patients with chest tubes in place.

28. B: When draining the lower lobes, the patient should be placed in the prone position so that the affected area is facing up. The respiratory therapist can then perform percussion therapy on that area, allowing the lobes to drain while turning the patient side to side. Because Trendelenburg is a position in which the patient's head is down, and therefore the patient's lower lobes are up, the patient is inverted, which may cause lightheadedness and other complications. This is especially true in patients with a history of fainting (syncope).

29. D: Before sending the machine for repair, the clinician should troubleshoot the machine thoroughly. This can include checking that the power and gas sources are adequate; checking all circuit and nebulizer connections to ensure a tight fit; and looking for leaks, kinks, and obstructions in the circuitry. Only then should the respiratory therapist send the machine for repair.

30. B: A cough assist is performed by having the patient either lie down or sit up. The clinician places the palms of his or her hands on either side of the patient's navel, and the patient is instructed to inhale completely. The clinician then instructs the patient to attempt to cough while simultaneously pushing the patient's abdomen up and in. Option B is the correct answer because the patient does not exhale completely; instead, they inhale completely and then attempt to cough when instructed to do so.

31. B: Although all of the mentioned steps are required in the replacement of a tracheostomy tube, the respiratory therapist must first assess the patient for signs of respiratory distress and treat them accordingly. Displacement of a tracheostomy tube can result in respiratory distress or failure and is considered an emergency. Once the patient's safety and ventilatory status are assessed, then the respiratory therapist can begin the process of replacing the patient's tracheostomy tube.

32. B: Of the mentioned choices, B is the best answer. This patient is difficult to intubate, partly because of their facial injuries. Reattempting to intubate using a different laryngoscope is not helpful for this patient because the team has already attempted a traditional intubation multiple times. Placing an oral airway is not helpful because this patient needs full mechanical ventilation and ventilatory support. The patient does not require a bite block at this time. Option D is incorrect because prior to inserting a tracheostomy tube, which is a surgical intervention, the team should attempt intubation with a laryngeal mask airway. These airways are useful for the difficult-to-intubate patient because it is easier to move into place compared to the traditional endotracheal tube. This type of airway is especially useful for patients with facial injuries or abnormalities. In addition, fiber-optic scopes can be helpful visualization devices for patients with difficult intubations. Often, this specialized equipment is used by the anesthesia team, who can be called for assistance with difficult intubations.

33. D: Omphalocele is a congenital defect of the abdominal wall in which a newborn is born with their abdominal organs outside of their body. Congenital defects of the upper airway include but are not limited to choanal atresia, Pierre Robin sequence, and Treacher Collins syndrome.

34. D: Heated high-flow nasal cannulas are oxygen systems in which high-liter flows and heated and humidified gas are delivered to the patient's airway via nasal prongs. Like nasal CPAP, the high flow rate provides airway pressure that helps to decrease respiratory distress. Heated high-flow nasal cannulas require the use of an oxygen blender, flow meter, heater, and humidifier. The benefits associated with this therapy includes less nasal trauma compared to traditional nasal cannulas, better feeding and bonding outcomes, and better mobility.

35. C: Appropriately sized heated high-flow nasal cannula prongs are critical for the safety of the patient. Prongs that are too large can cause tissue breakdown, mucosal damage, fistulas, and other possibly permanent damage to the airway. To determine the correct prong size, clinicians should refer to the facility's policy and procedure and the manufacturer's guidelines. Generally speaking, the prongs should be approximately half of the diameter of the patient's nostrils to allow for exhalation and prevent excessive pressure on the mucosa of the nares. Prongs that fit too loosely will cause leaks and will become displaced or fall out of the patient's nares completely. The patient's nares should not flare out, and the prongs should not fill the entire nares.

36. B: Mesh nebulizers are small-volume nebulizers that use electricity to create vibrations that generate a medicated mist for the patient. In theory, mesh nebulizers could be used for continuous nebulizer treatments, but the clinician would have to refill the medication cup every few minutes. Therefore, option A is incorrect because these nebulizers do not hold high volumes of medication.

37. A: Before attempting any invasive procedures such as endotracheal intubation or tracheostomy placement, the respiratory therapist should first check the size and placement of the oral airway. If the airway is the wrong size or if it is displaced, it can cause an airway obstruction. This can happen due to the tongue falling back into the oral cavity if the oral airway is too small and is unable to displace the tongue properly, or the oral airway itself can act as an airway obstruction if it is too large. A stat chest X-ray is not helpful at this time because the patient is unable to be ventilated. This is a life-threatening situation, and oxygenation is the team's first priority.

38. A: To determine the appropriate size of a nasal airway, the clinician first measures the distance between the patient's nares and jaw in millimeters and then converts that measurement to French.

39. D: Patients who are ventilated via endotracheal tubes require either a sterile suction technique or a closed (in-line) suction system to prevent infection. Bronchial lavage (the instillation of saline into the airway and then suctioning it back out) is no longer recommended because this action can increase the patient's risk of pneumonia and other respiratory infections. In-line suction catheters should be changed only when soiled because this action helps prevent the introduction of microorganisms into the ventilator circuit and patient airway. Option C is incorrect because neonatal endotracheal tubes do not have cuffs.

40. C: The patient is agitated, and the high-pressure limit is alarming. This indicates an airway obstruction of some kind. The respiratory therapist's first priority is to relieve the obstruction and restore adequate ventilation. The respiratory therapist can remove the patient from the ventilator, manually ventilate him, and call for assistance. The respiratory therapist can also attempt to suction the endotracheal tube to assess the patient for an airway obstruction such as the tube being bitten or the presence of a mucus plug in the tube. The therapist should also assess the patient including auscultating breath sounds. Option C is incorrect because although sedation may be necessary if no obstruction is found, it is only appropriate to order it AFTER the patient has been properly assessed and treated for a possible airway obstruction.

41. B: The entire process outlined in this vignette is correct with the exception of the very first step. The respiratory therapist should have first opened the suction kit and then put the sterile glove on her dominant hand while touching only the folded cuff portion of the glove with her nonsterile hand. Failing to complete this step caused the entire suction kit to be contaminated and no longer usable.

42. D: A speaking valve is an adapter that is attached to a tracheostomy tube to allow the patient to speak. It works by providing one-way airflow with exhalation through the patient's upper airway. This allows the patient to speak. The tracheostomy tube cuff must be completely deflated for the duration of this procedure. Option A is incorrect because speaking valves' styles vary widely among different facilities and manufacturers. Option D is the correct answer because supplemental oxygen with or without humidification can be used while the speaking valve is in place.

43. B: The clinician should insert the tube into the mouth with the mask pointing down. This ensures that the mask is in place and ready to be placed over the larynx. There is no need to rotate a tube when it is placed mask-side down. Rotating a tube with the attached mask can result in airway trauma and other complications.

44. D: Although a high probe temperature is a danger to the patient due to the possibility of skin breakdown and burns, a high-temperature probe itself does not necessarily interfere with the ability of the probe to measure gas exchange. Conditions that can cause inaccurate transcutaneous monitoring results include, but are not limited to, cyanosis and poor perfusion, poor adhesion of the sensor, edema at the probe site, and skin lesions.

45. C: Prior to placing the probes on the patient's chest or abdomen, the skin must be prepped with an approved cleanser and then contact solution is applied to the probe to ensure adequate measurement of oxygen and carbon dioxide. Although the patient's arms and legs can be a site for probe attachment, they are rarely used and are not required. Accurate readings are generally more likely to occur when the probes are placed on the patient's abdomen or chest. Transcutaneous monitoring is fairly accurate, but an arterial blood gas is a more accurate gas measurement test.

46. A: Insufflator-exsufflator machines are used for the induction of a cough in patients with insufficient respiratory muscle strength such as patients with neuromuscular disorders. In this therapy, positive pressure is delivered to the airway on inhalation and negative pressure is delivered to the airway on exhalation. This change in pressures induces a cough. Adverse events are unlikely but include, and are not limited to, aggravation of acid reflux, pneumothorax, abdominal pain, stomach upset, and chest pain.

47. C: Prior to initiating mechanical ventilation in the home setting, the patient and caregivers must undergo a comprehensive patient education session. This allows the patient and family to be familiar with the equipment, understand its use, and understand how to treat possible adverse events. Mechanical ventilation is used in the home setting for patients who require long-term mechanical ventilation, such as those with congenital defects. Mechanical ventilation can be administered in the home setting either continuously or intermittently, depending on the patient's needs. Mechanical ventilation can also be invasive or noninvasive in the home setting. Invasive ventilation can include tracheostomy tubes, whereas noninvasive ventilation can be delivered via face mask.

48. D: Neonatal congenital myopathies are a collection of neuromuscular defects found in the neonatal population. These disorders include neuromyotonia, myelomeningocele, scoliosis, spina bifida, and other spinal defects. Hirschsprung disease is a gastrointestinal disorder.

49. A: Prior to calling the homecare company or manufacturer for an equipment service call, the clinician and patient should fully troubleshoot the machine. This includes checking for disconnections, leaks, kinks, and obstructions as well as disassembling and cleaning the machine as needed. Particle buildup can cause obstructions or clogs in the system. When the machine has been fully examined, the clinician can then ask for a service call or replacement.

50. B: This patient complains of sore throat and sinus pain, which can be caused either by dried-out mucosa or infection. The clinician should apply a humidifier to the machine with either sterile water or saline depending on the manufacturer's guidelines. The clinician should also ask how often the patient cleans the machine because dirty machines are associated with an increased risk of infection. The patient also says that the machine delivers too much pressure. Rather than lowering the pressure setting, which should only be done with a doctor's order, the clinician should set the ramp setting. This setting "ramps up" the pressure from a low level to full pressure over a set period of time. This allows the patient to relax and get used to the lower level pressure before it ramps up to the set pressure level. The ramp setting helps to ensure patient comfort and is associated with better patient compliance.

51. C: Adjusting the isolette temperature is not appropriate because the ambient temperature within the isolette is optimized for that patient's needs. When rainout is discovered in a ventilator circuit, the clinician can either titrate the level of humidity or the heater temperature to minimize rainout. The clinician can also drain the condensation back into the humidifier, taking care not to allow condensation near the endotracheal tube opening because this can lead to aspiration and subsequent infection.

52. D: Apnea monitors continuously measure a patient's heart rate and respiratory rate, alarming when the patient stops breathing for a set period of time. This alarm is commonly used in neonates younger than 1 year of age who suffer from severe refractory GERD, patients who require supplemental oxygen, patients who are mechanically ventilated in the home, and patients with respiratory disorders that result in periods of apnea.

53. B: Patients who use liquid oxygen can potentially run out of oxygen if they aren't informed as to how long their supply will last. However, power failure is not a concern with this oxygen system. Instead, oxygen concentrators, which pull oxygen from ambient air, are powered by electricity. These concentrators require an adequate power source including a battery backup system or emergency oxygen tanks on standby. Oxygen is a drug according to the FDA and requires a physician's written order. Oxygen tanks must be secured using a special tank holder in order to ensure patient safety. Dropping or knocking over an oxygen tank can cause the tank to explode, resulting in bodily injury or death. Oxygen tubing, such as that used with nasal cannulas, can be attached to extension tubing to help a patient move about their homes. However, excessive use of oxygen extension tubing can result in reduced oxygen flow to the patient.

54. D: Bronchial lavage is a diagnostic intervention in which saline is instilled into the patient's lungs via bronchoscope and then suctioned back into a specimen cup. This bronchial "wash" allows the physician to test the cells of the airways and determine the presence of lung cancer, pneumonia, fungal infections, and other disorders. Severe refractory bronchospasm is not an indication for bronchial lavage because no infection is suspected. If the patient was described to have a high fever or other signs of infection with refractory bronchospasm, then bronchial lavage may be indicated.

55. A: When obtaining a biopsy of lung tissue via bronchoscopy, various tools are used depending on the type of sample needed. For smaller cellular samples, a brush tool is required. Bronchial lavage is also commonly used during cellular sampling because the saline acts as a rinsing agent that helps to collect the smaller cells after the brush tool is used. Tissue samples for biopsy are not examined for the presence of inflammation but are instead tested for malignancy and infection.

56. B: Nasal swabs and nasal washes are used to obtain mucus samples for testing. Nasal washes test for pathogens such as RSV, whereas nasal swabs test for pathogens such as influenza and MRSA. Pneumonia is not a pathogen; therefore, it is not tested via nasal swabs or washes. Fungal infections are also not commonly tested via nasal swabs or washes.

57. D: The clinician in this vignette positioned the sputum trap incorrectly. She held the trap horizontal to the patient's bed, which means that it was tipped sideways. When this happens, the sputum does not fall into the trap. Instead, the sample moves straight out the opposite end of the trap and lands in the wall suction receptacle.

58. D: When intubating a patient, the healthcare team must sedate and paralyze the patient. Hypnotics and neuromuscular blocking agents are used to paralyze the patient and help them "forget" that the procedure took place. In addition, opioids can be used for blockage of the patient's vagal response resulting in an easier intubation.

59. C: Side effects associated with the use of reversal agents such as naloxone and neostigmine include allergic reaction, stomach upset, seizure, anxiety, pain, sleepiness, dizziness, rash, and irregular heartbeat.

60. D: Transposition of the great vessels requires the administration of prostaglandin to keep the patient's ductus arteriosus open. This allows for pulmonary blood flow and oxygenation until the patient can undergo a surgical repair. Vasoactive and inotropic agents are medications used for the improvement of oxygenation and cardiac output in patients with cardiogenic shock, patent ductus arteriosus, and sepsis.

61. C: The use of terbutaline in pregnant women is associated with neonatal tachycardia and blood sugar changes. Respiratory depression and poor muscle tone are common side effects associated with other smooth-muscle relaxants such as magnesium sulfate, but these effects are not common with the use of terbutaline. Tremors and shakiness are possible side effects for mothers on terbutaline, but not for the neonate.

62. D: Neonates with kidney failure are unable to regulate their fluid status, resulting in electrolyte, serum creatinine, and serum nitrogen imbalances. These patients often have reduced urine output and fluid overload. Due to the patient's excessive fluid levels, patients may suffer from pulmonary edema and subsequent hypoxia. Patients may also present with an acidosis or other blood gas changes due to the insufficient acid–base balance associated with renal failure.

63. B: Hepatic failure is a life-threatening condition associated with respiratory failure, respiratory distress syndrome, and renal failure. Patients often require a liver transplant. Patients may present with hypovolemia at first, but without careful fluid management, they can quickly experience fluid overload due to potential renal failure secondary to the hepatic failure. Respiratory failure associated with hepatic failure may require supplemental oxygen and mechanical ventilation.

64. C: Although hematocrit is a common component measured by CBC testing, methemoglobin is not. Methemoglobin is measured in a separate test. CBC and Hgb electrophoresis measure hemoglobin, basophils, lymphocytes, monocytes, leukocytes, platelets, hematocrit, and mean corpuscular volume.

65. A: Patients with patent ductus arteriosus and bronchopulmonary dysplasia are at an increased risk for fluid overload and subsequent respiratory distress or failure. Electrolyte imbalances can affect a patient's respiratory status by altering their blood gas values due to changes in potassium, sodium, and calcium. Hyperbilirubinemia is not associated with fluid overload. Patients with hyperbilirubinemia have excess levels of bilirubin in their blood and require phototherapy and/or albumin administration for treatment of the condition.

66. A: Patients with a diabetic mother, sepsis, endocrine system deficiencies, congenital heart defects, and increased work of breathing all require routine glucose testing. This ensures that the patient's energy expenditure needs are met and the patient is not hypoglycemic. Hypoglycemia can be life-threatening and requires immediate treatment.

67. A: Cystic fibrosis, a genetic disorder characterized by enzyme deficiencies and excess mucus production in the lungs, is diagnosed in part by sweat testing. Sweat testing measures the chloride levels in a patient's sweat by first provoking the sweating response and then collecting and analyzing the sweat sample. Patient with cystic fibrosis excrete excessive amounts of chloride through their sweat glands.

68. B: A sputum culture is a test in which a sputum sample is tested for the presence of pathogens including bacteria and fungi. Staining the sample, as in Gram staining, allows for better inspection of bacteria, not viruses. Sputum cultures can be obtained by conscious or unconscious patients. Unconscious patients, such as those on mechanical ventilation, can have their airway suctioned by a clinician in order to obtain a sputum sample for culture.

69. C: Common signs of a drug overdose can include depressed central nervous system, depressed respiratory drive, seizure activity (in some cases), and faint or weak pulses. An increased respiratory rate is not a common symptom of drug overdose because these patients often present with respiratory depression, respiratory failure, or complete respiratory arrest.

70. A: Irritability, seizures, crying, digestive upset, and respiratory distress or arrest are all associated with neonatal abstinence syndrome. Neonatal abstinence syndrome is a collection of neonatal symptoms that are associated with maternal drug use. These newborns are undergoing withdrawal from the drugs in the mother's system.

71. C: The sail sign is the triangular-shaped thymus gland that is visible on chest X-rays. An abnormally large sail sign indicates the presence of air in the chest cavity, displacing the thymus gland. This condition is known as pneumomediastinum. Immediate treatment of pneumomediastinum is required by first treating the underlying cause. Pneumomediastinum can be caused by injury to the chest, meconium aspiration, infection, and barotrauma.

72. C: Chest X-rays are commonly taken in an anterior and a posterior (front and back) view. On occasion, a lateral (side) view might be necessary for further evaluation of specific conditions and disorders. The conditions that commonly require a lateral chest X-ray include suspected pneumothorax, foreign body, mass in the lungs, chest tube placement, drain placement, and umbilical artery and vein catheter placement. Although emphysema can be evaluated by lateral chest X-ray in some cases, it is commonly evaluated by anterior and posterior chest X-rays.

73. B: Tetralogy of Fallot, a combination of four separate heart defects, will present as a boot-shaped heart outline on a chest X-ray with an upturned cardiac apex. An "egg-on-a-string" heart outline on a chest X-ray is associated with transposition of the great vessels, a cardiac defect in which the blood vessels of the heart are reversed.

74. D: Tetralogy of Fallot is a life-threatening cardiac defect that requires immediate emergency surgical correction. In this defect, an obstructed pulmonary valve and open ventricular septum need to be surgically repaired, and the pulmonary valve may need to be replaced in some cases. Unoxygenated blood is pumped throughout the body causing cyanosis and hypoxia. Heart murmurs are also common findings in this defect.

75. D: Transposition of the great vessels is a cardiac defect in which the pulmonary artery is attached to the left ventricle and the aorta is attached to the right ventricle. This reversal of blood vessels results in unoxygenated blood circulating throughout the body, causing hypoxia, cyanosis, and respiratory distress. Transposition of the great vessels requires surgical intervention but can be delayed in some cases until the patient is in a more stable condition. Some patients may undergo a cardiac catheterization procedure in which the atria are enlarged to allow for blood flow and oxygenation.

76. A: Computed tomography scans, use radiation to give cross-sectional views of the patient's body and internal structures. MRI uses magnets to give cross-sectional views of the patient's anatomy. Ultrasound uses sound waves to provide the healthcare team with views of the organs and structures of the body. Some ultrasounds, such as echocardiograms, can also show blood or urine flow.

77. D: Feeding intolerance in the neonate is associated with risks such as abdominal distension, aspiration, infection, gastroesophageal reflux, apnea, and bradycardia. If left untreated, the patient will fail to thrive and may require mechanical ventilation and other invasive interventions. Nasogastric feeding tube placement may be required in this patient population, but care must be taken to not disturb or displace the feeding tube because this action is associated with increased aspiration pneumonia risks.

78. C: Patients with morbid obesity often carry excess weight in their neck and chest, making airway obstructions common in this patient population. The use of oral airways may be helpful in treating these airway obstructions. Patients who use noninvasive mechanical ventilation often have poorly fitting masks that don't seal properly because these masks are designed for average-weight patients. Patients with morbid obesity often benefit from extended-length tracheostomy tubes, which allow for adequate ventilation when a patient has a larger neck. Lastly, despite extra weight in the chest area, these patients do not require higher tidal volumes to deliver adequate ventilation. Excessive tidal volumes can result in barotrauma, and patients' tidal volumes should be set according to their ideal body weight, not their current weight.

79. B: With a body mass index of 42, this patient is considered morbidly obese. This condition is associated with sleep apnea and gastroesophageal reflux; however, reflux is often not disrupting a patient's sleep enough to cause extreme daytime fatigue. Obstructive sleep apnea, a condition in which a patient wakes up many times throughout the night due to an obstructed airway, can cause daytime fatigue, headache, and sleepiness. Parasomnias, a collection of sleep disorders including sleepwalking and sleep talking, is not consistent with the patient's symptoms. Narcolepsy, a condition in which a patient falls asleep unexpectedly during normal activity, is also not consistent with this patient's symptoms and underlying disease process.

80. A: When setting up a T-piece resuscitator, the clinician must occlude the PEEP port to ensure that the desired pressure is delivered to the T-piece. Obstructing the PEEP valve is a necessary step in setting the inspiratory pressure because the obstruction allows the clinician to determine the pressure that is being delivered to the patient during a breath.

81. B: T-piece resuscitators are associated with a reduced risk of barotrauma when compared to flow inflating or self-inflating resuscitation bags because T-piece resuscitators deliver a set pressure to the airway on inhalation and exhalation, reducing the risk of overinflating or underinflating the lungs. The clinician delivers a breath by occluding the PEEP valve during inspiration and removing his or her thumb from the port during exhalation. The patient's mask must have a tight fit to ensure an adequate seal and proper gas delivery.

82. A: The current Neonatal Resuscitation Program guidelines state that ventilation should be delivered at a rate of 40–60 breaths per minute via mask and bag ventilation.

83. C: When performing chest compressions in accordance with Pediatric Advanced Life Support guidelines, the clinician should place the heel of their hand on the chest at the nipple line and compress to a depth of one third of the width of the chest measuring from front to back.

84. B: When preparing for an evacuation, the healthcare team must obtain oxygen sources, such as oxygen tanks and be assigned to each patient using mechanical ventilation or supplemental oxygen. Additional portable monitors are required for each patient in a critical care area. Resuscitation bags and masks are required of all patients, including those who are intubated and mechanically ventilated. Masks must be included because if the patient loses their airway, or if the patient accidentally extubates, the clinician will only be able to ventilate the patient via a mask. Finally, some emergency situations may not require a full evacuation, such as a severe weather event. In these cases, moving the patients away from the windows and into interior corridors may be adequate.

85. D: The term triage refers to the act of assessing patients for severity and then treating the most critical patients first. This happens daily in the emergency department, but it is also an important part of disaster preparedness. Triage allows the healthcare team to ensure the highest survival rate for victims and provides organization and direction in times of crisis.

86. C: During a mass-casualty event, the healthcare team must be prepared for patients in various stages of injury and distress. In this vignette, an explosion has taken place, resulting in a fire that has injured students. Respiratory therapists should be ready to treat smoke inhalation, bronchospasm, respiratory arrest, carbon monoxide poisoning, and other respiratory disorders and injuries. Although peak flow meters and valved holding chambers are useful for patients with bronchospasm, they are not essential tools for the treatment of critically injured patients. The other choices, including personal protective equipment, intubation kits, oxygen tanks, nebulizers, ventilators, and resuscitation equipment, are essential pieces of equipment for mass-casualty events.

87. D: Interdisciplinary cooperation, or the working together of members of different healthcare departments, is an important part of comprehensive care in the hospital setting. Clinicians, including physicians, nurses, respiratory therapists, and other health professionals, must work in collaboration to provide the best patient care. Some examples of interdisciplinary cooperation include cluster care in the NICU, triage in the emergency room, and in-room patient rounds. Although giving report to another therapist is an example of clinician cooperation, it is not interdisciplinary.

88. C: When suctioning a tracheostomy in the home setting, sterile technique is not required. Clean technique, including minimizing contamination of the tube, is used in the home setting. Skin care and oral care are also important parts of tracheostomy care at home. All of these actions help to prevent subsequent infection.

89. B: Prior to performing any task in the healthcare setting, hand washing is required. Option A is incorrect because bronchial lavage is not required when suctioning; in fact, some studies indicate that bronchial lavage can increase the patient's risk of nosocomial infection. Option C is incorrect because the patient has a closed suction system, and no sterile technique is needed. Option D is incorrect because although preoxygenating the patient would be helpful if the patient was on a ventilator, there is no indication in the vignette that the patient is being mechanically ventilated.

90. C: This patient is coughing and experiencing shortness of breath, likely due to an airway obstruction or increased secretions. The patient's breath sounds are coarse, which indicates a buildup of secretions in the airway. Suctioning the patient should be the therapist's first action because this can indicate whether there is an obstruction in the tube or simply a buildup of secretions that requires clearing. Increasing the FiO_2 is not necessary because this patient has a near-normal oxygen saturation. Replacing the tracheostomy tube is not indicated because there is no mention of the tube being displaced. In the vignette, the tube is stated to be "in place." The tube may need to be replaced if an obstruction is found, but that can only be assessed via suctioning attempt.

91. A: Transcutaneous monitors require specialized medical equipment that is not commonly used in the home environment. Transcutaneous monitors are more often used in critical care areas of the hospital. Apnea monitors, which monitor the patient for lapses in respiration, are often used at home. Pulse oximeters, monitors that measure oxygen saturation, are often used in the home for patients with immature lungs or other respiratory disorders. Finally, peak flow meters are the most common home monitoring devices on this list because they are used to measure asthma severity when patients are not in the clinic. Peak flow meters may also be used in the clinical setting, but they are also frequently used in the home environment.

92. B: A car seat challenge is a test in which a preterm infant, often 37 weeks in gestation or fewer, is placed in a car seat for at least 90 minutes to monitor their breathing. Any change in oxygenation, respiratory rate, or heart rate is recorded, and if the patient is demonstrating signs of distress, then he or she has failed the test. The healthcare team then reattempts the test at a later date. The patient may not go home until they have passed a car seat challenge.

93. D: Although oxygen equipment is traditionally the respiratory therapist's responsibility, there is a shared responsibility for patient education among members of the healthcare team. The homecare company, respiratory therapist, and nurse must all work together to educate patients on their home medical equipment. Although the depth and duration of the education varies among the different healthcare providers, education is required from all of the clinicians. The physician orders the therapy but is often not able to educate the patient in the time allotted for an office visit. The physician will refer the patient to an education session with other clinicians. For example, the nurse may educate the patient on their need for oxygen and then refer them to the respiratory therapist for more in-depth education. Then the homecare company can educate the patient on their exact make and model of oxygen concentrator or other oxygen delivery device. Simply discharging the patient and assuming that the homecare company will conduct education is irresponsible and potentially dangerous.

94. D: All of the aforementioned delivery devices are equally effective when used correctly. Nebulizers are more effective than metered-dose inhalers only when the patient is experiencing severe bronchospasm that doesn't allow him or her to take a big breath. This patient is resting comfortably with normal vital signs and adequate air flow in the lungs. Option C may be surprising to some students because dry powder inhalers are often corticosteroids or long-acting bronchodilators; however, new short-acting bronchodilators are now in the marketplace including breath-actuated dry powder inhalers such as RespiClick.

95. B: The amniotic fluid index is the level of amniotic fluid found in the four quadrants of the uterus. The measurement is taken in each of the four quadrants in areas in which there are no structures present (including the fetal body and/or the umbilical cord). The test adds the readings of each quadrant together, and the resulting number is the mother's amniotic fluid index. If the amniotic fluid index is less than 5 cm, there is insufficient amniotic fluid to support the fetus. This is a potentially life-threatening condition for the fetus. A low amniotic fluid index can be caused by early rupture of the membranes, fetal abnormalities such as trisomy disorders, and other defects or disorders.

96. C: Tramadol is an opioid. This classification of drugs is not recommended for use in pregnancy because their use is associated with low birth weight, congenital defects, respiratory distress, and other pregnancy complications. Fluticasone and levalbuterol are safe medications for use in pregnancy because their benefits for the mother outweigh the risks for the fetus. Fluticasone and levalbuterol are used for the treatment of asthma, chronic obstructive pulmonary disease, and other respiratory diseases. The mother needs optimal respiration in order to provide oxygen to the fetus; therefore, most respiratory medications are acceptable for use during pregnancy and are not associated with serious adverse effects on the fetus. Option A, Toradol, is a nonsteroidal anti-inflammatory drug (NSAID) pain reliever that should not be taken during pregnancy because NSAIDs are associated with the premature closure of the ductus arteriosus. This medication class is not, however, associated with low-birth-weight neonates.

97. C: Amniocentesis is not a component of a fetus's biophysical profile. The term "biophysical profile" refers to the noninvasive testing of a fetus's overall health. The tests measure the amniotic fluid levels, fetal movement, and fetal muscle tone. The test is scored on a scale of 1 to 10, where scores of 8 or higher indicate a healthy fetus.

98. A: The Apgar score was named after Dr. Virginia Apgar. Dr. Apgar devised a system in which a patient was assessed for signs of respiratory distress and overall health. The Apgar score includes assessments of appearance, pulse, grimace, activity, and respiration in neonates. Each criterion is given a score of 0 to 2, and the sum of the different components is the Apgar score. The Apgar score is taken twice, one immediately after birth and one within 5 minutes of birth. If the score is less than 7, the test is repeated every 5 minutes for up to 20 minutes.

99. B: Fetal lung maturity indices are criteria that are measured to determine the relative maturity of a fetus's lungs. Amniocentesis, a procedure in which amniotic fluid is extracted through a needle inserted into the mother's abdomen, can measure the levels of surfactant in the fetus's lungs. Surfactant is a collection of phospholipids that reduce the surface tension of the alveoli. Preterm infants have insufficient levels of surfactant, resulting in the need for respiratory support such as supplemental oxygen, mechanical ventilation, and surfactant replacement therapy.

100. C: Transillumination is the process of placing a light source against a patient's chest in an effort to assess for air in the pleural space or for the determination of blood vessel location. In the event of air leakage in the chest, the light will appear in a diffuse pattern around the light source, whereas in a healthy chest, the light has a small circumference around the source. Transillumination can also be used to determine the location of blood vessels for catheterization or blood sampling.

101. A: When performing an oxygen challenge test, no supplemental oxygen can be used during that measurement. The patient should be on room air for approximately 20 minutes to counteract the effect of the previously delivered supplemental oxygen. In oxygen challenge testing, the clinicians are attempting to determine if the cause of the patient's cyanosis is respiratory or cardiac in nature. Normally, the patient will have a PaO_2 reading of between 40 and 25 mmHg while not using any supplemental oxygen. The patient will also have a PaO_2 reading of greater than 80 mmHg while breathing 100% oxygen if they do not have a cardiac defect. If the patient's PaO_2 does not rise dramatically after inspiring 100% oxygen, then the clinician can deduce that the cause of the patient's hypoxia and cyanosis is cardiac in nature.

102. C: CO_2 verification is the process of measuring exhaled carbon dioxide after intubation. This can be achieved by using a CO_2 detector that attaches to an endotracheal tube. When CO_2 passes through the detector via the patient's exhalation, the litmus paper inside the detector changes color. This provides a visual clue to the clinician that the endotracheal tube is in the correct position because exhaled CO_2 is present in the system. Although these tools are very helpful for tube placement confirmation in critical clinical situations, their use does not replace the need for a physical assessment of the patient or imaging studies.

103. C: Isoflurane is an anesthetic gas that can cause bronchospasm, respiratory depression, and other adverse effects. Isoflurane is not used to treat respiratory disorders. Heliox, a combination of helium and oxygen, is used to help oxygenate patients who have airway obstructions such as patients with severe asthma and refractory bronchospasm. The laminar flow of heliox passes through the constricted airways, improving oxygenation. Nitric oxide is a medical gas used to treat pulmonary hypertension in patients with congenital defects, pulmonary hypertension of the newborn, and other respiratory disorders. Nitric oxide dilates the pulmonary vasculature, allowing for better oxygenation. Finally, medical air is a medical gas used to treat respiratory disorders such as hyperoxia in patients with hypoplastic left heart syndrome. These patients require a lower FiO_2 than ambient air; therefore, air is delivered at subambient levels to treat these patients.

104. B: The normal tidal volume calculation for a term neonate on volume-control ventilation is 5–10 ml/kg. The normal tidal volume calculation for a preterm neonate is 4–6 ml/kg.

105. A: When a patient's lung compliance worsens (decreases), the lungs become stiffer. In these instances, an inspiration:expiration (I:E) ratio of 1:1 allows for better aeration and more alveolar recruitment. The exhalation time is lower when the I:E ratio is 1:1, which prevents the alveoli from collapsing on exhalation.

106. B: Immature lungs require careful monitoring of airway pressures to prevent barotrauma. Pressure-controlled ventilation limits airway pressure while delivering varying tidal volumes. To change a patient's minute volume in pressure-control mode, the clinician must titrate the PIP. In SIMV mode, which is commonly used in older pediatric patients, a set tidal volume and respiratory rate is set on the ventilator, and the patient is able to initiate additional spontaneous breathing delivered at varying tidal volumes.

107. C: High-frequency oscillation ventilation is delivered by a freestanding ventilator and is not used in tandem with traditional mechanical ventilators. Conversely, jet ventilators are used in conjunction with traditional mechanical ventilators and the two machines are connected via an endotracheal tube. The traditional mechanical ventilator delivers PEEP, and the jet ventilator delivers the tidal volume and rate. High-frequency jet ventilators initiate inspiration and expiration; neither is passive. Both modes of ventilation use very small tidal volumes and high rates to ventilate critically ill patients such as those with respiratory distress syndrome.

108. C: When a patient's lung compliance changes, the MAP can be titrated to support the patient's oxygenation needs. Although increasing the FiO_2 is a quick way to improve a patient's oxygenation, it is not the first change that should take place when a patient is on an oscillator. Low FiO_2 levels are preferred on high frequency oscillatory ventilation; therefore, option C is the best answer. Titrating delta P is helpful when a patient's CO_2 is changing; however, there is no indication in the above vignette that the patient has a change in carbon dioxide levels. Increasing the hertz changes the patient's frequency (rate), which may not be helpful in improving the oxygenation. MAP titration has a definite effect on oxygenation.

109. A: In volume-targeted mechanical ventilation, a pre-set and consistent tidal volume and respiratory rate are delivered. FiO_2 is also set based on the patient's oxygenation status. Pressure then varies in order to meet the tidal volume need. This mode of mechanical ventilation offers lung protection from barotrauma by limiting airway pressures but still delivering a set tidal volume.

110. D: Airway pressure release ventilation (APRV) is a mode of mechanical ventilation that delivers inverse I:E ratios. Airway pressures are set, whereas the delivered tidal volumes vary. Patients breathe "between" two set pressures (also known as BiVent), including a high- and a low-pressure setting, with time cycling. This mode of ventilation is not widely available, but it is becoming more popular in the marketplace.

111. A: Neutrally adjusted ventilatory assist (NAVA) is a mode of mechanical ventilation in which the patient's diaphragmatic activity is monitored via the mechanical ventilator, assessing the patient's respiratory muscle strength and respiratory effort and allowing for better synchrony with the ventilator. In this mode, ventilation depends upon the electrical activity in the patient's diaphragm. When there is more activity in the diaphragm, the ventilator delivers less ventilatory support. This mode of ventilation can help to prevent overdistention of the lungs and subsequent barotrauma. This mode is not common and may not be available in all facilities or on all ventilators.

112. A: A NAVA catheter is sized by first measuring the patient's height and weight. Then the respiratory therapist adds the sum of the measurements from the nares to the ear and the ear to the xiphoid process. This sum is known as the nose-ear-xiphoid (NEX) calculation. The NEX value is then compared to a chart provided by the manufacturer to calculate the insertion depth. The catheter is inserted into the patient's nares or mouth with no lubricant. It is inserted to the predetermined depth and secured. The catheter must be secured and in place; otherwise, the waveforms will show deflections or interruptions in the signal, and the catheter will need to be repositioned.

113. D: When using bubble continuous positive airway pressure (CPAP), the pressure gauge will read the level of CPAP delivered by measuring the back pressure created by submerging the expiratory limb into the water canister. Alternatively, the submersion level on the water canister is the level of CPAP delivered to the patient. Therefore, both A and B are correct because they are two different ways to measure the same pressure. In regards to securing CPAP prongs, this process varies by facility and manufacturer. Clinicians should refer to their manufacturer's instructions and facility's preferences for CPAP prong securement.

114. D: The term lung recruitment maneuver refers to the therapeutic increase of peak pressures and PEEP for short periods of time to "pop open" consolidated alveoli in compromised patients. Lung recruitment maneuvers' benefits often outweigh the risks, which include barotrauma and subsequent respiratory distress. Prone positioning is another form of lung recruitment in which the patient is positioned lying on their abdomen, with their back facing up. This position removes some of the body weight from the chest wall, recruiting the posterior lower lobe alveoli. Option D is the correct answer because although lung recruitment efficacy is still being studied in neonates, it is widely used in older patient populations due to its positive effects on critically ill patients with respiratory compromise and atelectatic lung tissue.

115. A: Extracorporeal membrane oxygenation (ECMO), also known as heart-lung bypass, is a therapeutic intervention in which the patient's blood is circulated through the ECMO machine, which oxygenates the blood and removes CO_2. In veno-venous ECMO, the patient's blood is circulated into and out of the machine via a catheter in the right atrium. Only patients without cardiovascular compromise can use this version of ECMO. Conversely, in veno-arterial ECMO, the patient's blood is circulated into the machine via a catheter in the right jugular artery. This catheter removes blood from the patient's right atrium and returns it to the body through a catheter in the right carotid artery. Lab tests such as arterial blood gas monitoring are required during this therapy to ensure acid–base balance, adequate oxygenation, adequate CO_2 removal, and hemodynamic stability. Anticoagulation therapy is also required because coagulation can interfere with the flow of the blood through the machine and reduce the therapy's efficacy.

116. B: The SaO_2:FiO_2 ratio compares the patient's oxygen saturation to the amount of oxygen being delivered to the patient. A reduced SaO_2:FiO_2 ratio indicates gas exchange impairment and shunting such as in cases of sepsis, lung injury, respiratory distress syndrome, and other respiratory conditions. The PaO_2:FiO_2 ratio shows the relationship between the partial pressure of arterial oxygen content to the amount of oxygen delivered to the patient. A normal PaO_2:FiO_2 ratio is 300–500. A reduced PaO_2:FiO_2 ratio is consistent with gas exchange impairment and shunting.

117. C: A patient's oxygen index (OI) can be calculated using the following equation:

$$OI = \frac{MAP \times FiO_2 \times 100}{PaO_2}$$

This equation calculates the ventilatory support required for adequate oxygenation of this patient. The higher the ratio, the higher the level of ventilatory support needed. An oxygen index of 40 or higher can indicate a need for ECMO intervention. This patient's OI is 10.0.

118. B: A VD:VT ratio is the comparison of dead space to tidal volume. A normal VD:VT ratio is between 0.28 and 0.33, or 150 ml of dead space to 500 ml of tidal volume. The patient's VD:VT ratio can be determined by the following equation:

$$\frac{PaCO_2 - PECO_2}{PaCO_2} = \frac{V_D}{V_T}$$

An increased VD:VT ratio indicates decreased ventilation and is associated with poor patient outcomes.

119. C: When performing a maximal inspiratory pressure (MIP) or negative inspiratory force (NIF) assessment, the respiratory therapist must occlude the one-way valve before instructing the patient to inhale. This allows for an accurate measurement of the patient's respiratory muscle strength. The maneuver can be repeated 10 times for up to 20 minutes' total duration, and the clinician records the highest (most negative) number. A normal MIP is between –80 and –100 mmHg.

120. D: In mechanical or positive-pressure ventilation, the pressure changes within the chest wall to facilitate respiration. These changing pressures can result in cardiac effects such as reduced venous return, positive intrathoracic pressure, and reduced cardiac output due to reduced right atrial filling. Vagal stimulation due to mechanical ventilation's effects on the cardiac system can result in fluctuations of the heart rate as well as cardiac arrhythmias. Some patients, such as those with pulmonary edema and pulmonary hypertension, may present with fluid overload due to changing pressures within the chest. Option D, bronchospasm, is not an adverse effect commonly associated with mechanical ventilation.

121. C: Cerebral oximetry is the measurement of oxygen within the patient's brain tissue using near-infrared spectroscopy. Light probes are sized according to the patient's weight and are attached to the patient's head. The light passes through the cranium into the patient's brain, and the light is reabsorbed by the probe on its way back out of the brain. The saturation of oxygen within the brain is determined by the amount of light that is sent into the brain and the returned light that is received by the probe on the patient's forehead. The difference in these two numbers determines the patient's percentage of cerebral oxygen saturation. This phenomenon is supported by the Beer–Lambert law, which states that the brightness of light decreases as it passes through higher concentrations of matter. This type of oxygen monitoring can be achieved in either absolute or trending monitoring. In absolute monitoring, the clinician bases clinical decisions on the exact percentage of cerebral oxygen saturation at any given time. In trend monitoring, the clinician bases clinical decisions on the saturation trends such as decreases or increases over time.

122. D: Ventilator weaning readiness can be determined in several ways. Some facilities have respiratory protocols that outline the criteria needed to be met in order to begin the weaning process. Other facilities use spontaneous breathing trials such as CPAP, pressure support, or T-piece trials. In these trials, patients are breathing spontaneously either with the assistance of added airway pressure (pressure support and CPAP) or without extra support (T-piece). NIF (MIP) measurement is another way to determine ventilator weaning readiness. This measurement determines the strength of a patient's respiratory muscles and is an indicator of a patient's ability to breathe spontaneously. FiO_2 reduction is not an accurate measure of a patient's ventilatory status because the patient may not need supplemental oxygen, but will still require ventilatory support.

123. D: Permissive hypercapnia, maintaining intentionally high levels of carbon dioxide in the blood, is often associated with very severe respiratory diseases that require high levels of mechanical ventilation. In these cases, the patient's ventilator settings are at a maximum level in order to maintain oxygenation but are still not able to successfully remove carbon dioxide from the patient's blood. Permissive hypercapnia allows the patient's lungs to be protected from overinflation and barotrauma due to excessive ventilator-delivered pressures and volumes. The benefits of permissive hypercapnia often outweigh its risks.

124. A: Therapeutic hypothermia is an intervention in which patient's body or head is cooled to below the body temperature in an effort to preserve brain cells and brain function after a critical injury or illness. This can include illnesses and injuries such as cardiac surgery and traumatic brain injury. Patients who regain consciousness after cardiac arrest are not good candidates for therapeutic hypothermia. Shivering during therapy should be minimized because this increases the patient's metabolic rate and negates the efficacy of therapeutic hypothermia. Once the therapy is completed, the patient is gradually warmed back up to body temperature over several hours. Quick rewarming can be dangerous.

125. A: Surfactant, a lipid-based substance found in mature lungs, reduces the surface tension in the lungs and keeps alveoli open for gas exchange. Premature infants have a deficit of surfactant and often need replacement therapy. This is achieved by instilling surfactant through the patient's endotracheal tube and then turning the patient side to side or placing the patient in various positions to help the surfactant travel to all of the lung lobes. Lung compliance often dramatically improves after instillation of surfactant, and clinicians must be ready for quick ventilator setting changes to prevent barotrauma. Prior to surfactant administration, the patient's airway should be suctioned to allow for maximum absorption of the surfactant. Finally, surfactant administration can result in airway obstructions such as clogs in the endotracheal tube due to the thick, slippery nature of the surfactant.

126. C: Airway instillation is the process of administering a drug through the endotracheal tube. This is most often successful in neonatal and pediatric patients who do not have vascular access. Their blood vessels are small and are sometimes hard to access. Lidocaine, a local anesthetic, is routinely instilled for bronchoscopy procedures because it numbs the airway and minimizes coughing and gagging during the procedure. Epinephrine is often instilled as an alternative to intracardiac injection because this is an invasive and somewhat dangerous procedure. Finally, some serious side effects are associated with airway instillations, such as bronchospasm and respiratory distress, and patients should be carefully and constantly monitored during the procedure.

127. D: The head of a patient's bed should be elevated between 30 and 45 degrees to minimize the risk of ventilator-associated pneumonia. This positioning prevents oral secretions and endotracheal tube condensation from traveling through the tube into the patient's airway, causing potentially serious infections.

128. B: The best answer to this question is option B. Palliative care and hospice care are often used interchangeably, but there are differences between these care plans. Hospice care is traditionally for patients who have 6 months to live or less. It is end-of-life care, with the goal of care being the comfort of the patient. Palliative care, conversely, is treatment of patients who have chronic, progressive illnesses. Patients in palliative care may live for decades or just a few months; there is no stipulation regarding their suspected lifetime. The goal of palliative care is to manage the symptoms of the disease so that the patient can perform the activities of daily life. It is not necessarily end-of-life care.

129. D: Withdrawal of support, either for brain death or other reasons, can be initiated based on clinical findings, physician advice, patient wishes, and/or advance directives. Determining brain death is a complicated process in which the patient must not be sedated, must not be able to gag or make other reflexive movements, and the patient's vital signs must be stable. Then, neurological testing can be performed such as EEG tests and CO_2 challenge testing. Brain death cannot be determined as a result of treatable disorders such as metabolic changes, electrolyte imbalances, or other reversible conditions.

How to Overcome Test Anxiety

Just the thought of taking a test is enough to make most people a little nervous. A test is an important event that can have a long-term impact on your future, so it's important to take it seriously and it's natural to feel anxious about performing well. But just because anxiety is normal, that doesn't mean that it's helpful in test taking, or that you should simply accept it as part of your life. Anxiety can have a variety of effects. These effects can be mild, like making you feel slightly nervous, or severe, like blocking your ability to focus or remember even a simple detail.

If you experience test anxiety—whether severe or mild—it's important to know how to beat it. To discover this, first you need to understand what causes test anxiety.

Causes of Test Anxiety

While we often think of anxiety as an uncontrollable emotional state, it can actually be caused by simple, practical things. One of the most common causes of test anxiety is that a person does not feel adequately prepared for their test. This feeling can be the result of many different issues such as poor study habits or lack of organization, but the most common culprit is time management. Starting to study too late, failing to organize your study time to cover all of the material, or being distracted while you study will mean that you're not well prepared for the test. This may lead to cramming the night before, which will cause you to be physically and mentally exhausted for the test. Poor time management also contributes to feelings of stress, fear, and hopelessness as you realize you are not well prepared but don't know what to do about it.

Other times, test anxiety is not related to your preparation for the test but comes from unresolved fear. This may be a past failure on a test, or poor performance on tests in general. It may come from comparing yourself to others who seem to be performing better or from the stress of living up to expectations. Anxiety may be driven by fears of the future—how failure on this test would affect your educational and career goals. These fears are often completely irrational, but they can still negatively impact your test performance.

Elements of Test Anxiety

As mentioned earlier, test anxiety is considered to be an emotional state, but it has physical and mental components as well. Sometimes you may not even realize that you are suffering from test anxiety until you notice the physical symptoms. These can include trembling hands, rapid heartbeat, sweating, nausea, and tense muscles. Extreme anxiety may lead to fainting or vomiting. Obviously, any of these symptoms can have a negative impact on testing. It is important to recognize them as soon as they begin to occur so that you can address the problem before it damages your performance.

The mental components of test anxiety include trouble focusing and inability to remember learned information. During a test, your mind is on high alert, which can help you recall information and stay focused for an extended period of time. However, anxiety interferes with your mind's natural processes, causing you to blank out, even on the questions you know well. The strain of testing during anxiety makes it difficult to stay focused, especially on a test that may take several hours. Extreme anxiety can take a huge mental toll, making it difficult not only to recall test information but even to understand the test questions or pull your thoughts together.

Effects of Test Anxiety

Test anxiety is like a disease—if left untreated, it will get progressively worse. Anxiety leads to poor performance, and this reinforces the feelings of fear and failure, which in turn lead to poor performances on subsequent tests. It can grow from a mild nervousness to a crippling condition. If allowed to progress, test anxiety can have a big impact on your schooling, and consequently on your future.

Test anxiety can spread to other parts of your life. Anxiety on tests can become anxiety in any stressful situation, and blanking on a test can turn into panicking in a job situation. But fortunately, you don't have to let anxiety rule your testing and determine your grades. There are a number of relatively simple steps you can take to move past anxiety and function normally on a test and in the rest of life.

Physical Steps for Beating Test Anxiety

While test anxiety is a serious problem, the good news is that it can be overcome. It doesn't have to control your ability to think and remember information. While it may take time, you can begin taking steps today to beat anxiety.

Just as your first hint that you may be struggling with anxiety comes from the physical symptoms, the first step to treating it is also physical. Rest is crucial for having a clear, strong mind. If you are tired, it is much easier to give in to anxiety. But if you establish good sleep habits, your body and mind will be ready to perform optimally, without the strain of exhaustion. Additionally, sleeping well helps you to retain information better, so you're more likely to recall the answers when you see the test questions.

Getting good sleep means more than going to bed on time. It's important to allow your brain time to relax. Take study breaks from time to time so it doesn't get overworked, and don't study right before bed. Take time to rest your mind before trying to rest your body, or you may find it difficult to fall asleep.

Along with sleep, other aspects of physical health are important in preparing for a test. Good nutrition is vital for good brain function. Sugary foods and drinks may give a burst of energy but this burst is followed by a crash, both physically and emotionally. Instead, fuel your body with protein and vitamin-rich foods.

Also, drink plenty of water. Dehydration can lead to headaches and exhaustion, especially if your brain is already under stress from the rigors of the test. Particularly if your test is a long one, drink water during the breaks. And if possible, take an energy-boosting snack to eat between sections.

Along with sleep and diet, a third important part of physical health is exercise. Maintaining a steady workout schedule is helpful, but even taking 5-minute study breaks to walk can help get your blood pumping faster and clear your head. Exercise also releases endorphins, which contribute to a positive feeling and can help combat test anxiety.

When you nurture your physical health, you are also contributing to your mental health. If your body is healthy, your mind is much more likely to be healthy as well. So take time to rest, nourish your body with healthy food and water, and get moving as much as possible. Taking these physical steps will make you stronger and more able to take the mental steps necessary to overcome test anxiety.

Mental Steps for Beating Test Anxiety

Working on the mental side of test anxiety can be more challenging, but as with the physical side, there are clear steps you can take to overcome it. As mentioned earlier, test anxiety often stems from lack of preparation, so the obvious solution is to prepare for the test. Effective studying may be the most important weapon you have for beating test anxiety, but you can and should employ several other mental tools to combat fear.

First, boost your confidence by reminding yourself of past success—tests or projects that you aced. If you're putting as much effort into preparing for this test as you did for those, there's no reason you should expect to fail here. Work hard to prepare; then trust your preparation.

Second, surround yourself with encouraging people. It can be helpful to find a study group, but be sure that the people you're around will encourage a positive attitude. If you spend time with others who are anxious or cynical, this will only contribute to your own anxiety. Look for others who are motivated to study hard from a desire to succeed, not from a fear of failure.

Third, reward yourself. A test is physically and mentally tiring, even without anxiety, and it can be helpful to have something to look forward to. Plan an activity following the test, regardless of the outcome, such as going to a movie or getting ice cream.

When you are taking the test, if you find yourself beginning to feel anxious, remind yourself that you know the material. Visualize successfully completing the test. Then take a few deep, relaxing breaths and return to it. Work through the questions carefully but with confidence, knowing that you are capable of succeeding.

Developing a healthy mental approach to test taking will also aid in other areas of life. Test anxiety affects more than just the actual test—it can be damaging to your mental health and even contribute to depression. It's important to beat test anxiety before it becomes a problem for more than testing.

Study Strategy

Being prepared for the test is necessary to combat anxiety, but what does being prepared look like? You may study for hours on end and still not feel prepared. What you need is a strategy for test prep. The next few pages outline our recommended steps to help you plan out and conquer the challenge of preparation.

Step 1: Scope Out the Test

Learn everything you can about the format (multiple choice, essay, etc.) and what will be on the test. Gather any study materials, course outlines, or sample exams that may be available. Not only will this help you to prepare, but knowing what to expect can help to alleviate test anxiety.

Step 2: Map Out the Material

Look through the textbook or study guide and make note of how many chapters or sections it has. Then divide these over the time you have. For example, if a book has 15 chapters and you have five days to study, you need to cover three chapters each day. Even better, if you have the time, leave an extra day at the end for overall review after you have gone through the material in depth.

If time is limited, you may need to prioritize the material. Look through it and make note of which sections you think you already have a good grasp on, and which need review. While you are studying, skim quickly through the familiar sections and take more time on the challenging parts.

Write out your plan so you don't get lost as you go. Having a written plan also helps you feel more in control of the study, so anxiety is less likely to arise from feeling overwhelmed at the amount to cover.

Step 3: Gather Your Tools

Decide what study method works best for you. Do you prefer to highlight in the book as you study and then go back over the highlighted portions? Or do you type out notes of the important information? Or is it helpful to make flashcards that you can carry with you? Assemble the pens, index cards, highlighters, post-it notes, and any other materials you may need so you won't be distracted by getting up to find things while you study.

If you're having a hard time retaining the information or organizing your notes, experiment with different methods. For example, try color-coding by subject with colored pens, highlighters, or post-it notes. If you learn better by hearing, try recording yourself reading your notes so you can listen while in the car, working out, or simply sitting at your desk. Ask a friend to quiz you from your flashcards, or try teaching someone the material to solidify it in your mind.

Step 4: Create Your Environment

It's important to avoid distractions while you study. This includes both the obvious distractions like visitors and the subtle distractions like an uncomfortable chair (or a too-comfortable couch that makes you want to fall asleep). Set up the best study environment possible: good lighting and a comfortable work area. If background music helps you focus, you may want to turn it on, but otherwise keep the room quiet. If you are using a computer to take notes, be sure you don't have any other windows open, especially applications like social media, games, or anything else that could distract you. Silence your phone and turn off notifications. Be sure to keep water close by so you stay hydrated while you study (but avoid unhealthy drinks and snacks).

Also, take into account the best time of day to study. Are you freshest first thing in the morning? Try to set aside some time then to work through the material. Is your mind clearer in the afternoon or evening? Schedule your study session then. Another method is to study at the same time of day that you will take the test, so that your brain gets used to working on the material at that time and will be ready to focus at test time.

Step 5: Study!

Once you have done all the study preparation, it's time to settle into the actual studying. Sit down, take a few moments to settle your mind so you can focus, and begin to follow your study plan. Don't give in to distractions or let yourself procrastinate. This is your time to prepare so you'll be ready to fearlessly approach the test. Make the most of the time and stay focused.

Of course, you don't want to burn out. If you study too long you may find that you're not retaining the information very well. Take regular study breaks. For example, taking five minutes out of every hour to walk briskly, breathing deeply and swinging your arms, can help your mind stay fresh.

As you get to the end of each chapter or section, it's a good idea to do a quick review. Remind yourself of what you learned and work on any difficult parts. When you feel that you've mastered the material, move on to the next part. At the end of your study session, briefly skim through your notes again.

But while review is helpful, cramming last minute is NOT. If at all possible, work ahead so that you won't need to fit all your study into the last day. Cramming overloads your brain with more information than it can process and retain, and your tired mind may struggle to recall even previously learned information when it is overwhelmed with last-minute study. Also, the urgent nature of cramming and the stress placed on your brain contribute to anxiety. You'll be more likely to go to the test feeling unprepared and having trouble thinking clearly.

So don't cram, and don't stay up late before the test, even just to review your notes at a leisurely pace. Your brain needs rest more than it needs to go over the information again. In fact, plan to finish your studies by noon or early afternoon the day before the test. Give your brain the rest of the day to relax or focus on other things, and get a good night's sleep. Then you will be fresh for the test and better able to recall what you've studied.

Step 6: Take a Practice Test

Many courses offer sample tests, either online or in the study materials. This is an excellent resource to check whether you have mastered the material, as well as to prepare for the test format and environment.

Check the test format ahead of time: the number of questions, the type (multiple choice, free response, etc.), and the time limit. Then create a plan for working through them. For example, if you have 30 minutes to take a 60-question test, your limit is 30 seconds per question. Spend less time on the questions you know well so that you can take more time on the difficult ones.

If you have time to take several practice tests, take the first one open book, with no time limit. Work through the questions at your own pace and make sure you fully understand them. Gradually work up to taking a test under test conditions: sit at a desk with all study materials put away and set a timer. Pace yourself to make sure you finish the test with time to spare and go back to check your answers if you have time.

After each test, check your answers. On the questions you missed, be sure you understand why you missed them. Did you misread the question (tests can use tricky wording)? Did you forget the information? Or was it something you hadn't learned? Go back and study any shaky areas that the practice tests reveal.

Taking these tests not only helps with your grade, but also aids in combating test anxiety. If you're already used to the test conditions, you're less likely to worry about it, and working through tests until you're scoring well gives you a confidence boost. Go through the practice tests until you feel comfortable, and then you can go into the test knowing that you're ready for it.

Test Tips

On test day, you should be confident, knowing that you've prepared well and are ready to answer the questions. But aside from preparation, there are several test day strategies you can employ to maximize your performance.

First, as stated before, get a good night's sleep the night before the test (and for several nights before that, if possible). Go into the test with a fresh, alert mind rather than staying up late to study.

Try not to change too much about your normal routine on the day of the test. It's important to eat a nutritious breakfast, but if you normally don't eat breakfast at all, consider eating just a protein bar. If you're a coffee drinker, go ahead and have your normal coffee. Just make sure you time it so that the caffeine doesn't wear off right in the middle of your test. Avoid sugary beverages, and drink enough water to stay hydrated but not so much that you need a restroom break 10 minutes into the test. If your test isn't first thing in the morning, consider going for a walk or doing a light workout before the test to get your blood flowing.

Allow yourself enough time to get ready, and leave for the test with plenty of time to spare so you won't have the anxiety of scrambling to arrive in time. Another reason to be early is to select a good seat. It's helpful to sit away from doors and windows, which can be distracting. Find a good seat, get out your supplies, and settle your mind before the test begins.

When the test begins, start by going over the instructions carefully, even if you already know what to expect. Make sure you avoid any careless mistakes by following the directions.

Then begin working through the questions, pacing yourself as you've practiced. If you're not sure on an answer, don't spend too much time on it, and don't let it shake your confidence. Either skip it and come back later, or eliminate as many wrong answers as possible and guess among the remaining ones. Don't dwell on these questions as you continue—put them out of your mind and focus on what lies ahead.

Be sure to read all of the answer choices, even if you're sure the first one is the right answer. Sometimes you'll find a better one if you keep reading. But don't second-guess yourself if you do immediately know the answer. Your gut instinct is usually right. Don't let test anxiety rob you of the information you know.

If you have time at the end of the test (and if the test format allows), go back and review your answers. Be cautious about changing any, since your first instinct tends to be correct, but make sure you didn't misread any of the questions or accidentally mark the wrong answer choice. Look over any you skipped and make an educated guess.

At the end, leave the test feeling confident. You've done your best, so don't waste time worrying about your performance or wishing you could change anything. Instead, celebrate the successful completion of this test. And finally, use this test to learn how to deal with anxiety even better next time.

Review Video: Test Anxiety
Visit mometrix.com/academy and enter code: 100340

Important Qualification

Not all anxiety is created equal. If your test anxiety is causing major issues in your life beyond the classroom or testing center, or if you are experiencing troubling physical symptoms related to your anxiety, it may be a sign of a serious physiological or psychological condition. If this sounds like your situation, we strongly encourage you to seek professional help.

Online Resources

Due to our efforts to try to keep this book to a manageable length, we've created a link that will give you access to all of your online resources:

mometrix.com/resources719/nps

It's Your Moment, Let's Celebrate It!

Share your story @mometrixtestpreparation